D1616633

A GUIDE TO THE SOLO SONGS
OF JOHANNES BRAHMS

Joh. Brahms.

A GUIDE TO THE
SOLO SONGS
OF JOHANNES BRAHMS

LUCIEN STARK

INDIANA UNIVERSITY PRESS

Bloomington and Indianapolis

Frontispiece: Drawing of Brahms at the Piano (c. 1895) by Willy von Beckerath. Reproduced by permission of Hans Christians Druckerei und Verlag, Hamburg.

The paper used in this publication meets the minimum requirements of American National Standard for Information Sciences—Permanence of Paper for Printed Library Materials, ANSI Z39.48-1984.

Manufactured in the United States of America

Library of Congress Cataloging-in-Publication Data

Stark, Lucien, date
    A guide to the solo songs of Johannes Brahms / Lucien Stark.
      p. cm.
    Includes the German texts with idiomatic English prose translations.
    Includes bibliographical references and index.
    ISBN 0-253-32891-8
    1. Brahms, Johannes, 1833–1897. Songs. 2. Songs—19th century—Analysis, appreciation. I. Brahms, Johannes, 1833–1897. Songs. Texts. English & German.
MT115.B73S73   1995
782.42168'092—dc20   94-45737

1 2 3 4 5 00 99 98 97 96 95   MN

To Paul, Vida, Justin, and Elena

CONTENTS

PREFACE

Brahms has been my favorite composer since my first student encounter with an intermezzo. In due course, I learned all of his piano music and both concertos, and the performance of his chamber music with piano has been a frequent and reliable source of pleasure throughout my life. It therefore struck me as curious that despite countless collaborative performances with singers, I had not been called upon to play—in fact, had seldom heard—more than the same double handful of Brahms's songs, and, further, that singers in general seemed reluctant to venture outside a basic core group of the tried and true. So, when a sabbatical leave provided me with a gift of time, I determined to begin to acquaint myself with the solo songs of Johannes Brahms.

I first read everything relevant that I could find, then plunged into the songs themselves. It soon became clear that the relative neglect of so many was not because of their inferiority—the well known include some of the greatest, but most of the remainder would enrich any recital program, and all would repay study—but at the same time, that to undertake the exploration of so large a body of unfamiliar literature is a daunting task indeed. The primary aim of this study is to ease that task for those performers who wish to expand their Brahms repertoire beyond the previously known, by providing background information and pointing out features that might facilitate their selection and study of new songs.

Works that contributed substantially to the content of this guide are listed in the selective bibliography; I am deeply indebted to those sources, whose identifying of the songs' distinctive characteristics often suggested the course for my own investigation. Citations in the text are usually abbreviated.

During the process of writing, I continually consulted three other resources:

Brahms's correspondence, primarily the two volumes in English of *Letters of Clara Schumann and Johannes Brahms 1853–1896*, edited by Berthold Litzmann (New York: Vienna House, 1973, a reprint of the London 1927 publication) and *The Herzogenberg Correspondence*, edited by Max Kalbeck, translated by Hannah Bryant (New York: Vienna House, 1971).

Max Kalbeck's four-volume biography, *Johannes Brahms* (Berlin: Deutsche Brahms-Gesellschaft, 1904–14; reprinted in 1974 by Schneider in Tutzing).

Margit L. and Donald M. McCorkle's remarkable catalog of Brahms's works, *Johannes Brahms Thematisches-Bibliographisches Werkverzeichnis* (Munich: G. Henle Verlag, 1984).

The song texts in German are from Gustav Ophüls's *Brahms-Texte, vollständige Sammlung der von Brahms komponierten Dichtungen*

(Berlin: Brahms-Gesellschaft, 1898), and in most cases they reflect any changes Brahms made to the originals. I have modernized the spelling. A new edition of *Brahms-Texte* by Kristian Wachinger was published in 1983 by Langewiesche-Brandt, Ebenhausen bei München.

With the exception of a very few single words where a different rendering has seemed preferable, the English translations of the songs are those prepared by Stanley Appelbaum for the 1979–80 Dover reprint of the Breitkopf & Härtel complete works edition and are used by permission of Dover Publications, Inc. The English versions of the *Vier ernste Gesänge*, Op. 121, are from the King James Bible.

Presuming that this volume is more likely to be consulted than read, I have tried to make each song's discussion self-contained; thus some redundancy has been unavoidable.

References to specific pitches and keys are to those of the original publication (reprinted by Dover) and to the low-key C. F. Peters complete edition, both of which are widely available.

Among the many individuals who have given me assistance and encouragement, I am particularly grateful to Prof. Phyllis Jenness (now emeritus) of the University of Kentucky voice faculty, who volunteered without hesitation to sing through all of the songs with me, some of them many, many times; her suggestions, insights into the music, and enthusiasm for the project have been invaluable.

A GUIDE TO THE SOLO SONGS
OF JOHANNES BRAHMS

BRAHMS AS SONG COMPOSER

Brahms published 196 art songs for solo voice with piano. They appeared in thirty-two sets, most of which contained from four to nine songs, though Op. 91 has only two and Op. 33 has fifteen. The two of Op. 91 add an obbligato viola, and the five of Op. 84 may be sung as duets. In addition, there are two individual songs without opus number and the solo version of eight of the *Zigeunerlieder* quartets, Op. 103—a total of 206 songs.*

"Heimkehr," Op. 7/6, is the earliest, dating from May 1851, and is the work of a boy barely eighteen; the latest, the *Vier ernste Gesänge*, Op. 121, were completed about the time of Brahms's last birthday, forty-five years later. Song composition was therefore a lifelong, if intermittent, activity. Sporadic groups of up to as many as ten songs sometimes appeared as the result of interest in a specific poet or text source; many—the exact number is unknown—were suppressed and have been lost. The youthful songs exhibit a certain romantic excess but are already clearly the work of a master; maturity brought not so much a change of approach as a continuing process of refinement and concentration.

Approximately one-fourth of the total are simple strophic settings, where the same music is repeated for each stanza, sometimes with slight variation. The strophic design was particularly associated with folk song texts. Brahms used it for many of the early songs and returned to it occasionally until 1886, when it made its last appearance in "Das Mädchen spricht," Op. 107/3. Obviously, strophic form is appropriate only for texts where the mood, or succession of moods, is similar in each verse. About another quarter of the songs are through-composed, reflecting Brahms's interest, particularly in the late 1850s and 1860s, in setting longer texts of greater emotional complexity and diversity.

Roughly half of the songs, therefore, are in a form which seemed to evolve almost inevitably from his general compositional technique of developing variation and which Brahms made uniquely his own—the varied strophic

---

*The five *Ophelia–Lieder* WoO Posth. 22, first published in 1935, were commissioned for a Prague production of *Hamlet*. They were intended for unaccompanied performance; Brahms provided the skeletal piano parts only as a learning aid.

form. In its most typical configuration, the opening material is varied or developed to provide contrast before it reappears more recognizably to round out the design. Of course, such constructions outwardly resemble the traditional repetition-after-contrast forms (three-part song form, rondo, etc.); the distinction lies in the derivation of the contrasting material from that of the opening strophe. The kinship may be readily apparent, but at times it may be revealed only in such small details as a rhythm, a melodic contour, or a pattern of phrase lengths. It was an ideal formal plan for Brahms because it allowed him to reconcile his fondness for strophic song with his desires for minutely detailed dramatic underlining and for organically evolved musical structure.

In broad outline then, the three forms are defined by the role played in them by repetition: strophic forms repeat exclusively; through-composed, minimally, if at all; and varied strophic, after related contrast. In actuality, several of the songs defy precise formal labeling. The structure or dramatic implications of certain texts prompted hybrid designs or freer variation, which, though unfailingly apt, tended to blur the formal distinctions.

Aside from some *Romanzen* and a few *Gedichte*, all of the songs are called *Lieder* or *Gesänge*. The former term was usually reserved for simple, often strophic, constructions, while the latter implied a more elaborate treatment.

The strongest influences on Brahms's song composition were folk song, or what he believed to be folk song, and the songs of Schubert. The preoccupation with folk song of nineteenth-century German musicians, Brahms among them, was an outgrowth of the Romantic movement's reverence for nature and all things natural. Two collections of folk poetry, Herder's *Volkslieder* (1778–79), retitled *Stimmen der Völker in Liedern* in 1807, and the Arnim-Brentano *Des Knaben Wunderhorn* (1805–08), were, and remain, highly respected. They in turn stimulated collections of folk melodies, among them scholarly work by Hagen and Büsching (1807), Silcher (1826), Ditforth (1855), and especially Ludwig Erk (*Deutscher Liederhort*, 1856) and Franz Böhme (*Altdeutsches Liederbuch*, 1877). After Erk's death in 1883, Böhme took up the editing of his papers, and the resulting *Deutscher Liederhort*, a huge collection of more than 2,000 songs, was published in three volumes by Breitkopf & Härtel in 1893–94.

But in 1777–78, a certain Friedrich Nicolai, disapproving of what he considered the intellectually dangerous excessive concern with folk song already becoming apparent, published in protest a collection under the obviously satirical title *Eyn feyner kleyner Almanach vol schönerr echterr Liblicherr Volsklieder*. All the tunes in it were parodies, composed by himself or by his friend Johann Friedrich Reichart. Sixty years later, the editors Andreas Kretzschmer and August Wilhelm von Zuccalmaglio included at least thirty of these counterfeits in their highly influential *Deutsche Volkslieder mit ihren Original-Weisen* (1838–40), assigning them fictitious places of origin. Zuccalmaglio added many of his own imitation folk songs, also with false identifications, mixing them among less-dubious items in order to aid their acceptance.

Brahms was attracted to folk song throughout his life. His interest was encouraged by the Hamburg teacher of his youth, Eduard Marxsen, and volumes he found in the Schumanns' library allowed him to further it. Among his solo songs there are some thirty-five original settings of folk song texts besides the *Zigeunerlieder*; many others are reminiscent of folk song in their poetry, their music, or both. He also made well over 200 arrangements of pre-existing folk song melodies. Many of these were not published, having been intended for the Hamburg Ladies' Choir, the Detmold choir, or the Singakademie. There were, however, two significant published collections. The earlier group, dating from 1856–57, comprises forty-six folk songs arranged for voice and piano and dedicated to the Schumann children. Fourteen were published anonymously and without opus number in 1858 as *Volks-Kinderlieder*; the remaining thirty-two, four of them for mixed chorus, were left in less-finished form and were published posthumously in 1926 as *Neue Volkslieder*. But Brahms's culminating achievement in the genre is the monumental *Deutsche Volkslieder* for voice and piano, published in 1894 in seven books of seven songs each, the last set adding antiphonal four-part chorus, the piano part optional. At the time of its publication, Brahms intended it to be his last work, and it is one of the few of his own works of which he spoke with pride.

Yet despite his enduring involvement with folk song, Brahms's true relation to it is ambiguous and somewhat puzzling. His favorite collections were those tainted ones of Nicolai and Kretzschmer-Zuccalmaglio, and he remained loyal to them even after irrefutable evidence proved them bogus. When forced to accept that at least one of the songs he had selected for his *Deutsche Volkslieder*—No. 13, "Wach auf, mein Hort"—was in fact a fabrication, Brahms wrote blithely to Philipp Spitta on 6 April 1894, "Not really folk music? Well, then we have one more good composer." He let no opportunity pass to find fault with the more reliable collectors on aesthetic grounds, while the authentic folk songs in his own 1894 collection can be counted on the fingers of two hands.[1] In the early folk song arrangements, the accompaniments are simple, even naive, but later they assume more importance and independence, until the settings are in fact indistinguishable from art songs. Brahms claimed repeatedly that when he wanted to invent a melody he recalled German folk song; yet the qualities he admired in supposed folk song were exactly those which coincided with the conservative mainstream of art music, and therefore with his own style and with his own deep convictions concerning the relation of music and text.

What Brahms loved in this music, real or imitation, was its perceived innocence and its directness of expression; and his devotion to it sprang to some extent from an inherent streak of sentimentality and even more from his intense patriotism. He doubtless also felt a connection between folk song and the music of earlier centuries, about which he was perhaps more knowledgeable than any other major composer.

With Schubert, Brahms shared not only this preference for melodic simplicity but also the love of strophic design, an unfailing sense of the emotive implications of harmonic relationships, and a continual striving for conciseness. He attributed his very sparing use of marks of expression, particularly for the singer, to his emulation of Schubert's practice. Schubert had changed forever the relationship between the voice and the piano in the *Lied*, showing how the piano could enhance and participate in the drama. Brahms elevated the role of the piano to that of equal but independent partner, not only supporting the vocal line but complementing, continuing, commenting upon it, even communicating meaning not explicit in the text.

Though Brahms did not eschew obvious word-painting entirely, he did not often indulge in it. His inclination was to portray the general mood of a poem rather than individual details, and to devise purely musical metaphors for specific phenomena or psychological states. Slowly rising left-hand arpeggios, for example, he associated with dreaming. Falling rain is usually suggested by staccato eighth notes, the idea of death by descending melodic thirds, often in bare octaves. The repeated rhythm of half note-quarter note in triple meter evokes coldness or isolation. Pain may be depicted melodically by the tritone, harmonically by the augmented triad. Certain harmonies were used in similar contexts with sufficient consistency to make it apparent, for example, that Brahms attributed gentleness to the subdominant, poignancy to the Neapolitan, and an aura of unreality to the submediant from the minor mode.

A particular feature of Brahms's songs is the sturdiness and freshness of their bass lines. (There are numerous reports too of the unusual firmness with which Brahms played bass lines when he accompanied singers.) George Henschel writes that Brahms advised him, "In writing songs you must endeavor to invent, simultaneously with the melody, a healthy, powerful bass."[2] Max Graf relates that, when he took some of his early songs to Brahms,

> at once he plunged two fingers between the first and third staffs of the score. I was somewhat surprised to see him cover up my middle voices of which I was inordinately proud. . . . Seeing my astonishment he growled, "When I look over a new song I always cover the middle voices. I only want to see the melody and the bass. If these two are right everything is right.[3]

Brahms has often been criticized for his seeming lack of sensitivity to the literary quality of the texts he chose to set. No more than a quarter of his songs are based on the work of poets of the first rank, and he did not always choose their best works; about a third are on poems by eight minor figures whose names would hardly be remembered otherwise—Daumer, Groth,

Wenzig, Lemcke, Candidus, Halm, Kapper, and Schenkendorf. Yet we know that, though Brahms was to a large degree self-educated, he was exceptionally well-read, and the *Schatzkästlein* into which he copied favorite passages represents the greatest names in world literature.

It seems evident that his choice of song texts was affected also by criteria other than quality. Presumably the primary consideration for Brahms, as for any song composer, would be that the poem arouse in him a lyrical response; if the text appealed to his musical imagination, and the wording and construction were of sufficient competence not to inhibit the creation of a song, the relative quality of the poem itself apparently became unimportant. Furthermore, Brahms seems to have believed that truly great poetry was complete in itself, incapable of improvement by musical setting. In 1876 he commented to George Henschel:

> Schubert's *Suleika* songs are to me the only instances where the power and beauty of Goethe's words have been enhanced by the music. All other of Goethe's poems seem to me so perfect in themselves that no music can improve them.[4]

Brahms expressed a related idea in a letter in 1877, writing that although the poem "takes possession of one's mind," one must "in a certain sense free himself of it."[5] The poem, in other words, is the stimulus to creation, but at some time it must yield to the flow of musical idea; a great poem may fail to become a song simply because it remains a poem in the composer's mind.

Brahms believed that a song's melody should somehow reflect the number of metrical feet in the poem. Richard Heuberger reports that, when he took some of his songs for criticism, Brahms

> immediately singled out a passage . . . and showed me that the music did not correctly imitate the rhythms of the poem in its material. . . . Then he took an empty sheet of music paper and began writing down the text, which I had set to music, in the empty measures designated only by the barlines, so that every word stood there rhythmically correctly. He thought this was a very good system for the beginner.[6]

In his own work, Brahms often achieved the desired result by the same simple means of placing the stressed syllables of the poem on the stressed beats of the measure. However, he also freely varied this potentially monotonous procedure in order to change mood, to heighten tension, to place particular stress, etc. If a sensible reading of the poem might slight certain syllables which should be stressed according to the poetic meter, Brahms adjusted the melody accordingly; if this caused a shortened phrase, he might restore it to its expected length by text repetition, or by a compensating insertion of piano melody. The trademark broadening of final phrases—

so characteristic as almost to constitute a mannerism—also commonly involved text repetition, a purely musical consideration, to the detriment of
the poem's formal structure (though often at the same time greatly enhanc-
ing its dramatic impact).

Despite his usual care, the logic of musical development sometimes took
precedence, and Brahms let awkwardnesses in declamation stand, presumably counting on the singer's skill to smooth them out. From time to time, he
even went so far as to change words or alter the arrangement of lines if that
better suited his purpose. He sometimes added syllables to, or removed
them from, a line of poetry if the rhythm of his melody required it. Clearly,
for him the essence of a song lay in its music. He was not so much interested
in setting a poem to music as in creating its musical equivalent.

Several of Brahms's comments about the creative process have been preserved. They reveal a great deal about his attitudes toward composition and
about his own method of working. To Fritz Simrock, he remarked:

> Invention is like a grain of seed which lies in the earth: either it comes up or
> it does not. . . . If it comes up, and a melody occurs to me—now I make a note
> of it, but do not look at it again until it comes to me once again by itself. If it
> does not come, then it was not worth anything and I throw it away.[7]

Along the same line of thought, Henschel records that Brahms told him,
during a trip together from Coblenz to Wiesbaden on 26 February 1876:

> There is no real creating without hard work. That which you would call in-
> vention, that is to say, a thought, an idea, is simply an inspiration from above,
> for which I am not responsible, which is no merit of mine. Yea, it is a present,
> a gift, which I ought even to despise until I have made it my own by right of
> hard work. And there need be no hurry about that, either. It is as with the
> seed corn; it germinates unconsciously and in spite of ourselves. When I, for
> instance, have found the first phrase of a song, . . . I might shut the book then
> and there, go for a walk, do some other work, and perhaps not think of it again
> for months. Nothing, however, is lost. If afterward I approach the subject
> again, it is sure to have taken shape; I can now begin to really work at it. But
> there are composers who sit at the piano with a poem before them, putting
> music to it from A to Z until it is done. They write themselves into a state of
> enthusiasm which makes them see something finished, something important,
> in every bar.[8]

And perhaps most revealing of all, a few months later, concerning one of
Henschel's manuscript songs, Brahms suggested:

> Let it rest, let it rest and keep going back to it and working at it over and over
> again, until it is completed as a finished work of art, until there is not a note
> too much or too little, not a bar you could improve upon. Whether it is *beau-
> tiful* also is an entirely different matter, but perfect it *must* be. You see, I am

rather lazy, but I never cool down over a work, once begun, until it is perfected, unassailable.[9]

To those who involve themselves with the songs of Brahms, it is a constant source of wonder that they are at the same time "perfected" and ravishingly beautiful, yet seemingly utterly spontaneous, as though they had sprung fully formed from the composer's imagination in a single flash. Among them are some of the greatest treasures of the art song repertoire. Many are familiar and deservedly famous, many more should be lifted from the relative obscurity in which they incomprehensibly remain. Performers need not be reluctant to browse among the unfamiliar—one can hardly go astray!

NOTES

1. Concerning the provenance of the melodies included in *Deutsche Volkslieder*, see Max Harrison, *The Lieder of Brahms* (London: Cassell, and New York: Praeger Publishers, 1972), 91–92.

2. George Henschel, *Personal Recollections of Johannes Brahms* (Boston: Richard G. Badger, The Gorham Press, 1907; reprinted, New York: AMS Press, 1978), 44.

3. Max Graf, *Legend of a Musical City* (New York: Philosophical Library, 1945), 107–108.

4. Henschel, 45.

5. Quoted in Helmuth Osthoff, *Johannes Brahms und seine Sendung* (Bonn: Bonner-Universitäts-Buchdruckerei, 1942), 10–11.

6. Richard Heuberger, *Erinnerungen an Johannes Brahms. Tagebuchnotizen aus den Jahren 1875 bis 1897*, ed. Kurt Hofmann (Tutzing: Hans Schneider, 1971), 14.

7. Reported in Max Kalbeck, *Johannes Brahms*, 4 vols. (Berlin: Deutsche Brahms-Gesellschaft, 1904–14), II$_1$, 179n.

8. Henschel, 22–23.

9. Ibid., 39.

SIX GESÄNGE
FOR TENOR OR SOPRANO,
OP. 3

Sechs Gesänge für eine Tenor- oder Sopranstimme mit Pianofortebe-gleitung componirt und Bettina von Arnim gewidmet von Johannes Brahms (Six Songs for Solo Tenor or Soprano Voice with Piano Accompaniment, Composed and Dedicated to Bettina von Arnim by Johannes Brahms), Op. 3. Published in December 1853 by Breitkopf & Härtel in Leipzig; publication number 8835.

A second edition appeared in the collection *Lieder und Gesänge für eine Singstimme mit Begleitung des Pianoforte von Johannes Brahms* (Songs for Solo Voice with Piano Accompaniment by Johannes Brahms), published [1888] by N. Simrock in Berlin; publication numbers, 8982 high key, 8983 low key.

The first edition has German text only; the second, German and English. In the first, the vocal part has a large number of tempo and dynamic indications, which are duplicated in the piano part; in the second, Brahms had most of them deleted.

Brahms met Elizabeth (Bettina) Brentano von Arnim (1785–1854) at the Schumanns' in Düsseldorf, having already come into contact with the Arnim family through Joachim. She had always stood at the center of the Romantic movement; she was on intimate terms with both Goethe and Beethoven, and her husband, Achim (1781–1831), together with her brother, Clemens Brentano (1778–1842), had published the large and important compilation of German folk song texts *Des Knaben Wunder-horn*. Brahms's dedication of his songs to her was thus symbolic of his devotion to Romantic art.

The ordering of the songs reveals preferences for grouping according to poet and for a compatible sequence of (somewhat unusual) keys: the two Hoffman von Fallersleben songs (both in B major) and the two Eichendorff songs (in F♯ minor/major and A major) are placed together; both of the remaining songs are in E♭ minor.

Liebestreu, Op. 3/1 (Fidelity in Love)

Text by Robert Reinick (1805–1852)

"O versenk', o versenk' dein Leid, mein Kind,
In die See, in die tiefe See!"
Ein Stein wohl bleibt auf des Meeres Grund,
Mein Leid kommt stets in die Höh'.

"Und die Lieb', die du im Herzen trägst,
Brich sie ab, brich sie ab, mein Kind!"
Ob die Blum' auch stirbt wenn man sie bricht,
Treue Lieb' nicht so geschwind.

"Und die Treu', und die Treu', 's war nur ein Wort,
In den Wind damit hinaus."
O Mutter, und splittert der Fels auch im Wind,
Meine Treue, die hält ihn aus.

"Oh, sink, oh sink your sorrow, my child, in the sea, in the deep sea!" "A stone may rest on the ocean bottom; my sorrow always rises to the surface."
"And the love that you bear in your heart, break it off, break it off, my child!" "Even if the flower dies when it is broken off, faithful love does not die so quickly."
"And your faith, and your faith, it was just a word, out into the wind with it!" "Oh, Mother, even if the cliff face splinters in the wind, my faith endures it."

Composed in Hamburg in January 1853.

Though there are records of earlier private performances, in 1853 and 1856, the first public performance was given on 18 February 1857 at the Saal von Mengershausen in Göttingen, at a concert of Julius Otto Grimm with Clara Schumann and Joseph Joachim.

Strophic, the last half of the final strophe varied and extended as coda.

The text is from Reinick's *Lieder* (Berlin, 1844). In the second, enlarged edition, which appeared eight years later, the poet changed "im Wind" in the third stanza to "im Sturm."

The format of dialogue between mother and daughter is common in German folk poetry; Reinick's use of it is presumably deliberately evocative of folklore. Here the mother advises her daughter to put aside her lovesick grief—to sink it in the sea like a stone, to break it off like a flower, to discard it for the wind to carry away. The daughter replies that the advice is useless: the sorrow would rise to the surface of the sea, the love would refuse to fade like a broken blossom, and her faith would withstand the wind's destructive force, though rock might be worn away.

The song's structure derives from, but enhances, that of the poem. Brahms causes the mother's exhortations to grow in vehemence by increasing the tempo for each, and finally the loudness as well. The daughter answers twice in dreamy distraction, but, driven by mounting agitation, her climactic third response blazes forth strongly and passionately. The change to the major mode allows the vocal line to rise to its highest pitches on "Fels" in m. 27 and "Treue" in m. 28 before trailing off, as the minor returns, inevitably but by almost imperceptible stages.

The piano's opening melodic motive generates both a bass line that seems to symbolize the depth of the girl's grief and, by a process that begins as free canonic imitation, the mother's eloquent vocal line. (The expanding augmentation of the same motive in the postlude is an early example of what was to become one of Brahms's most characteristic stylistic features—the written-out ritard.) The repeated accompanying chords vibrate in triplets that conflict uneasily with the plain eighths of the melody and bass line; this chordal figure rises again and again to the top of the texture, like the girl's sorrow, which will not remain submerged.

One observes with some surprise that strophes only ten measures long contain drama of such intensity. The song is a masterpiece in every way, standing out among its coeval works and pointing far into the future. Its place in Brahms's *oeuvre* is like that of "Gretchen am Spinnrade" in Schubert's— astonishing, from so youthful a composer, in its power and originality, and already displaying all the traits of mature mastery. Brahms was right to place it at the head of his published songs; one can easily understand the excitement of Joachim and the Schumanns upon hearing it for the first time.

Liebe und Frühling I, Op. 3/2 (Love and Spring I)

Text by August Heinrich Hoffmann von Fallersleben (1798–1874)

> Wie sich Rebenranken schwingen
> In der linden Lüfte Hauch,
> Wie sich weiße Winden schlingen
> Luftig um den Rosenstrauch:
>
> Also schmiegen sich und ranken
> Frühlingsselig, still und mild,
> Meine Tag- und Nachtgedanken
> Um ein trautes, liebes Bild.

As vine tendrils tremble in the breath of the mild breezes, as white bind-weeds curl airily about the rosebush—that is how my thoughts by day and night, joyful with springtime, calmly and gently embrace and twine around a beloved and dear image.

Composed in Göttingen in July 1853; revised 1882.
First performed by Alice Barbi in Vienna on 27 November 1891.
Through-composed, actually a miniature set of variations.

The texts for this song and for "Liebe und Frühling II," which follows, were written by Hoffmann von Fallersleben during the summer of 1833 and printed in his *Gedichte* (Leipzig, 1834 and 1843).

Here the poet likens the persistent intrusion of the beloved's image into his every springtime thought to the encroaching intertwining of bindweeds with roses. Musically, the image becomes two themes inching their stepwise way, like the vine tendrils of the text, one upward, the other downward, entwining in canon, in contrary motion, or in contrasting note values.

The opening vocal melody is doubled by the piano in unison octaves; beginning in m. 5, it is treated canonically, as the text describes the curling of the bindweed about the rosebush. The second stanza introduces a new melody in counterpoint. At first it seems to be the earlier theme in contrary motion, but it takes on a resemblance to Zerlina's aria "Batti, batti" from Act 1, Scene 4, of Mozart's *Don Giovanni*. (In m. 16 the resemblance is even stronger.) Kalbeck assures us (I$_1$, 152) that the allusion is deliberate—Brahms had been charmed by a soprano who sang the role. The musical simile then is the joining of the memory of Zerlina in the treble with the entwisting vine shoots in the bass.

As coda, the vocal line repeats the last half of the stanza to the original melody in daydreaming augmentation, while the image of Zerlina lingers in the piano's high register. A melting dissonance on "liebes" in m. 27 resolves to bring the vocal melody to a close. The piano postlude extends the image of creeping tendrils in the slow chromatic descent of thirds in half notes, as the vine motive, now reduced to six quarter notes, is sounded twice in the bass, then varied sinuously and extended to three measures to end the song.

The few changes in the 1882 reworking remedy the textural problems that arise when a female voice causes the vocal line to sound an octave higher. In fact, only female singers should sing the second version; men should sing the first. In mm. 5–8 and 12–13 of the revision, the vocal line is made to double the right hand of the piano part rather than the left, in order that neither line sounds in octaves. The piano's lovely 9–8 suspension in m. 27 is removed in the second version because it sounds in implied parallel fifths with the female voice.

The song is filled with imagination and is rich in imagery; one wishes that it unfolded with more naturalness, that its contrapuntal ingenuities were a bit less self-conscious.

Liebe und Frühling II, Op. 3/3 (Love and Spring II)

Text by August Heinrich Hoffmann von Fallersleben (1798–1874)

> Ich muß hinaus, ich muß zu dir,
> Ich muß es selbst dir sagen:

Du bist mein Frühling, du nur mir
In diesen lichten Tagen.

    Ich will die Rosen nicht mehr sehn,
Nicht mehr die grünen Matten;
Ich will nicht mehr zu Walde gehn,
Nach Duft und Klang und Schatten.

    Ich will nicht mehr der Lüfte Zug,
Nicht mehr der Wellen Rauschen,
Ich will nicht mehr der Vögel Flug
Und ihrem Liede lauschen.

    Ich will hinaus, ich will zu dir,
Ich will es selbst dir sagen:
Du bist mein Frühling, du nur mir
In diesen lichten Tagen.

I must leave my house, I must go to you, I must tell you this myself: you are my springtime, only you, in these bright days.

I don't want to see the roses any more, nor the green meadows; I no longer want to go to the forest for fragrance and nature's sounds and the shade.

I no longer want the coolness of the breezes, nor the murmur of the waves; I no longer want to see the birds fly nor hear them sing.

I want to leave my house, I want to go to you, I want to tell you this myself: you are my springtime, only you, in these bright days.

Composed in Göttingen in July 1853.

First performed by a Fräulein A. von Baumgarten on a concert of the pianist Gisela Gulyas in Vienna on 6 November 1885.

A B B' A'; the B material is derived from that of A.

The text, found in the poet's *Gedichte* of 1834 and 1843, in effect extends that of the preceding song. (The relationship is reinforced by retaining the same key and by the references to the "Zerlina" melody in mm. 17–20 and again beginning in m. 27.) In an impulsive declaration of love, the poet longs to tell his beloved that she, rather than the reawakening of nature, is springtime for him.

The poem's artful simplicity hides a meticulously detailed web of parallels and contrasts: stanzas 1 and 4 are parallel, but contrast with stanzas 2 and 3, which are themselves parallel; stanzas 1 and 4 contrast "ich/dir" with "du/mir," while stanzas 2 and 3 parallel successive statements of "nicht mehr." The contrast of "muß" in stanza 1 with "will" in the otherwise identical stanza 4 represents the poet's emotional progress—his intervening recognition of the nature of love transforms an *impulse* to declare his love into the *desire* to do so.

The construction of Brahms's setting conceals comparable complexity. The impetuous rising scale with which the vocal line begins (reminiscent of the second half of the previous song's opening phrase) is mirrored inexactly by a descending scale in the piano, which gradually wends its way down in the inner voices to the bass-clef octave in m. 9; a precise mirroring, interval for interval, begins in the alto voice of mm. 13–14 and continues down the tenor of mm. 17–18, and another, a half step lower, begins in the tenor of mm. 21–22 and continues in mm. 27–28. The voice's upward-resolving dissonances in mm. 3 and 7 are mirrored by the piano's resolutions downward in mm. 4 and 8, each of which the voice echoes to begin its next phrase. The piano's opening three descending half steps are answered palindromically by the bass movement from the middle of m. 7 through m. 9; another palindrome occurs mid-stanza with the tenor half notes in mm. 4–5 and the first three pitches of the voice in m. 6. The vocal line's fall in mm. 9–10 from G♯ to B (E to G in the lower key) is echoed by the tenor in m. 10 and by the bass in mm. 11–12.

Though it begins by imitating the rhythm of the beginning, the music of the middle strophes is less ardent, tenderer. A new motive, featuring a rising sixth and a falling appoggiatura, first appears in m. 14. Its augmentation in the vocal line, while the piano twice imitates its contour in spiraling eighth notes, contributes to the expansion of the more introspective third strophe.

The opening music returns for strophe 4. Heightened emotion is represented by the substitution of *tremolando* for the earlier sixteenths and by the prolongation of the vocal line's final cadence.

In a *Tristan*-like symbol of unfulfilled love, the tonality is unstable through much of the song, even ambiguous at times. It is made amply clear, however, by the last vocal phrase, with its long dominant pedal and its threefold repetition of diminished seventh to dominant seventh; and it is firmly anchored by the postlude's references to the subdominant side of the key.

Lied, Op. 3/4 (Song)

from the poem *Ivan* by
Friedrich Martin von Bodenstedt (1819–1892)

Weit über das Feld durch die Lüfte hoch
Nach Beute ein mächtiger Geier flog.

Am Stromesrande im frischen Gras
Eine junge weißflüglige Taube saß;

O verstecke dich, Täubchen, im grünen Wald!
Sonst verschlingt dich der lüsterne Geier bald!

Eine Möwe hoch über der Wolga fliegt,
Und Beute spähend im Kreise sich wiegt.

O, halte dich, Fischlein, im Wasser versteckt,
Daß dich nicht die spähende Möwe entdeckt!

Und steigst du hinauf, so steigt sie herab,
Und macht dich zur Beute und führt dich zum Grab.

Ach, du grünende feuchte Erde du!
Tu' dich auf, leg' mein stürmisches Herz zur Ruh'!
Blaues Himmelstuch mit der Sternlein Zier,
O trockne vom Auge die Träne mir!
Hilf, Himmel, der armen, der duldenden Maid!
Es bricht mir das Herz vor Weh und Leid!

Far over the fields, high through the sky, a mighty vulture flew after prey.
By the river bank in the fresh grass sat a young white-winged dove;
Oh, hide, little dove, in the green forest, or else the greedy vulture will soon gobble you up!
A seagull flies high above the Volga and, spying prey, circles with a rocking motion.
Oh, keep hidden in the water, little fish, so the spying gull doesn't discover you!
If you ascend, it will descend and make you its prey and bring you to the grave.
Ah, you moist green earth! Open wide and set my stormy heart at rest! Blue cloth of heaven, adorned with the little stars, oh, dry the tears from my eyes! Heaven, assist the poor, patiently waiting girl! My heart is breaking from pain and sorrow!

Composed in Göttingen in July 1853.
First performed by Helene Marschall in Vienna on 20 April 1885.
Strophic with coda.
The poem was first published in *Ivan, der Sohn des Starost, Poetische Farbenskizze aus Rußland* in 1842, then in the poet's *Gedichte* (1853). A girl, watching a hunting vulture over the steppe and a watchful seagull high above the Volga, compares their unwary prey to her own broken heart and calls upon earth and heaven to end her pain and sorrow. Brahms varied the rhythm slightly from verse to verse to allow for subtle differences in the declamation. In line 11, he changed the poet's "herauf" to "hinauf," perhaps finding it easier to sing.

The fiery rise of the opening phrase is splendid, and the gentler fall of the second phrase creates an air of expectancy for what is to follow. Furtive afterbeats in the accompaniment, beginning in mm. 5 and 21, portray the hidden dove and fish; the gradually rising pitch and the *sempre crescendo* characterize the girl's mounting excitement. Her attempt at warning is underlined by the change to the major mode, but the minor returns, like her grief, for the concluding vocal cadence and the piano interlude. The poem's dramatic last line brings an expansion both intervallically and rhythmically to the song's highest pitches and longest notes for the impassioned *fortissimo* outcry "vor Weh und Leid!" in mm. 45–46. The repetition of the same words to a similar rhythm, but *piano*, falling in pitch, and harmonized by an augmented triad and two chords without thirds, effectively depicts the depth of the girl's despair to end the song.

Yet, despite its originality and its many felicitous details, the song fails to ring quite true. Its dramatic range seems too large for its small dimensions, too extreme for the repetitions dictated by its strophic format. It can easily sound overwrought and theatrical.

In der Fremde, Op. 3/5 (Far from Home)

Text by Joseph von Eichendorff (1788–1857)

Aus der Heimat hinter den Blitzen rot,
Da kommen die Wolken her.
Aber Vater und Mutter sind lange tot,
Es kennt mich dort keiner mehr.

Wie bald, ach wie bald kommt die stille Zeit,
Da ruhe ich auch, und über mir
Rauscht die schöne Waldeinsamkeit,
Und keiner kennt mich mehr hier.

Behind the red lightning-flashes, the clouds are coming from the direction of my home. But Father and Mother are long dead, no one there knows me any more.

How soon, ah, how soon that peaceful time will come when I, too, shall rest and the beautiful lonely forest will rustle over my head, and no one here will know me any more.

Composed in November 1852 in Hamburg.

The first performance is not documented.

Two similar strophes, slightly but tellingly different.

The poem first appeared in the 1833 novella *Viel Lärmen um nichts*; it was later published in the *Totenopfer* section of Eichendorff's collected *Gedichte* (Berlin, 1837). Schumann chose it to open his 1840 cycle *Liederkreis*, Op. 39, but he made several alterations in the last four lines, which originally read:

Wie bald, wie bald kommt die stille Zeit,
Dann ruhe auch ich, und über mir
Rauschet die schöne Waldeinsamkeit,
Und keiner mehr kennt mich auch hier.

Brahms apparently did not consult Eichendorff's original, taking over Schumann's altered version (together with his key of F♯ minor).

The young Brahms's pensive setting is in no way inferior to Schumann's deservedly famous earlier version. In fact, it captures subtleties in the poem's form and content that are slighted by Schumann's more general focus.

The eight lines of the poem fall into two groups of four, which contrast the familiar with the foreign, companionship with loneliness, past death with future death, awareness with oblivion. Brahms's strophic form recognizes and heightens this parallelism, while Schumann's through-composition masks it.

Brahms handles the enjambment between lines 6 and 7 with particular sophistication; the piano's phrase extension in m. 8 is replaced in mm. 20–21 by a metaphorical high-note prolongation of the word "über," bridging the expected separation of vocal phrases.

The ends of the two strophes represent early explorations of the potential of harmonic relationships for conveying psychological states. At the first strophe's "Es kennt mich dort keiner mehr," the tonality veers from tonic minor to submediant major, its tenderness elicited by memories of father and mother, while repetitions of the melodic motive G, E, F♯ (E♭, C, D in the low key) gradually diminish (like remembrance of the poet) in the piano. The second strophe's analagous "Und keiner kennt mich mehr hier" is introduced by a painful dissonance in the piano in mm. 23–24, which, however, leads to the tonic major, where the rest of the song remains. The poet's acceptance and anticipation of his own approaching death are symbolized by gentle subdominant and supertonic harmonies over a tonic pedal, while the reiterated melodic motive this time falls in pitch with each appearance, gradually slowing and softening as it approaches its final peaceful resolution.

Lied, Op. 3/6 (Song)

Text by Joseph von Eichendorff (1788–1857)

Lindes Rauschen in den Wipfeln,
Vöglein, die ihr fernab fliegt,
Bronnen von den stillen Gipfeln,
Sagt, wo meine Heimat liegt?

Heut' im Traum sah ich sie wieder,
Und von allen Bergen ging
Solches Grüßen zu mir nieder,
Daß ich an zu weinen fing.

Ach! hier auf den fremden Gipfeln:
Menschen, Quellen, Fels und Baum—
[Wirres Rauschen in den Wipfeln]
Alles ist mir wie ein Traum!

Muntre Vögel in den Wipfeln,
Ihr Gesellen dort im Tal,

> Grüßt mir von den fremden Gipfeln
> Meine Heimat tausendmal!

You soft rustling in the treetops, you little birds who are flying far away, you streams that come from the silent peaks, tell me where my home is.

Today in a dream I saw it again, and from every mountain such a warm greeting came down to meet me that I began to weep.

Ah, here on the unfamiliar mountaintops, people, streams, cliffs and trees are all like a dream to me!

You cheerful birds in the treetops, you young men there in the valley, bring a thousand greetings from me in these strange mountaintops to my home!

Composed in Hamburg in December 1852.

First performed by Anna Schmidtler in Vienna on 10 April 1866 as part of a concert by the pianist Julius Epstein.

Varied strophic; A A B A'.

The poem, like the text of the preceding song, is from the 1833 novella *Viel Lärmen um nichts*. The prince's hunting party hears the first three stanzas sung in the woods before the singer, a hunter named Florentin (actually the Countess Aurora in disguise), becomes visible. After some dialogue, the party disbands and Florentin again disappears, leaving the prince alone watching his friends as they recede into the distance. But after a while, Florentin reappears high up on the cliffs, waves his hat, and sings the fourth stanza after the departing hunters.

In this context, the poem of course has no title. In the collected *Gedichte* of 1837, it appears in the *Wanderlieder* section under the title "Erinnerung" (Remembrance), and the fourth stanza has been deleted, presumably because its call to "you young men there in the valley" connects it too closely with the novella from which it was extracted. The deletion, however, allows the poem to end in dreamlike confusion, its character completely changed.

The title "Lied" seems to have been Brahms's invention. His four-stanza version of the text is obviously taken from the novella rather than from the collected poems; indeed, his setting goes beyond the content of the poem itself to draw upon certain aspects of the dramatic situation in which it appears.

Brahms's rhythmic rendering of the text here is less meticulous than usual, and the singer must try to compensate for some awkwardnesses in declamation.

The three main stanzas share an accompanying figure in constant alternating sixteenth notes, representing the "soft rustling in the treetops." Breathless short phrases on tonic and dominant yield to an affecting *sostenuto* turn to the Neapolitan at "meine Heimat" in m. 8 and "zu weinen" in m. 18. This harmony prepares the enharmonic change of A♯ to B♭ (F♯ to G♭ in the low key) in m. 21 to introduce the lowered submediant F (D♭), with its dream-world associations, for the contrasting third stanza.

Contrast here is provided not only by the change of key but also by the sudden replacement of sixteenth-note motion by gently undulating eighths. The relationship of the vocal part to that preceding is not readily apparent, but it shares stepwise chromatic motion with the opening phrases, and its rhythmic structure resembles that of the phrase that ends each of the earlier strophes.

With astonishment, one becomes aware that Brahms has omitted an entire rhyming line, "Wirres Rauschen in den Wipfeln." That the omission was mere oversight is almost inconceivable; it is more likely (though scarcely less strange) that he felt that additional musical portrayal of "rustling in the treetops" would weaken the contrast he sought. The piano interlude he substituted interrupts with an imitation of hunting horns—an element not even hinted at by the poem itself and sensible only to one who is familiar with the scene in the novella. Two additional repetitions of the hunting-horn motive underlie the last line of the stanza and descend (somewhat lamely) to the dominant of the principal key to prepare its return. Without question or close rival, these few measures constitute the most peculiar passage in all of the Brahms songs!

The closing stanza begins to the same music as the opening, but at a higher dynamic level and with the rustling accompaniment raised an octave, perhaps representing Florentin's repositioning on the cliffs above. The music builds quickly to a climactic lengthened closing phrase, with the song's highest pitches on the words "meine Heimat." Immediately both voice and piano drop to a lower register for a reflective repetition of the word "tausendmal," *piano, ritardando e diminuendo*, a presumed evocation of the departing hunters' disappearing from view or of the song's echoing through the valley below. (Much of the preceding is adapted from Ludwig Finscher's informative and insightful "Brahms's Early Songs: Poetry versus Music" in *Brahms Studies*. See Bibliography.)

Each of the vocal options for the final "tausendmal" has its advantages: the large notes imitate the immediately preceding melodic shape; the small notes recall "wie ein Traum!" from the end of stanza 3.

SIX GESÄNGE FOR SOPRANO
OR TENOR, OP. 6

Sechs Gesänge für eine Sopran- oder Tenor-Stimme mit Begleitung des Pianoforte componirt und den Fraülein Luise und Minna Japha zugeeignet von Johannes Brahms (Six Songs for Solo Soprano or Tenor Voice with Piano Accompaniment, Composed and Dedicated to the Misses Luise and Minna Japha by Johannes Brahms), Op. 6. Published in December 1853 by Bartolf Senff in Leipzig; publication numbers 95–100.

Luise Japha (1826–1889) was a Hamburg-born pianist who was studying with Clara Schumann in Düsseldorf when Brahms traveled there in 1853 to visit the Schumanns; her sister Minna was also in Düsseldorf, studying painting. Luise became particularly known for her performances of Schumann's piano music. A lifelong friend of Brahms, she was the pianist for the French première of his Piano Quintet, Op. 34, in Paris in 1868.

Schumann gave a copy of the songs to the Misses Japha without waiting for Brahms's dedication copy to arrive. He wrote on it: "Den Fräulein Japha, zum Andenken an das Weihnachtsfest, 1853, als Vorbote des eigentlichen Gebers" (". . . as a souvenir of Christmas 1853, in anticipation of the real donor").

The ordering of songs within the opus reveals the grouping together of contemporaneous songs and a certain symmetry in the progression of keys. Four songs composed in April 1852 (in A minor/major, E major, A♭ major, and E♭ major) are followed by two Hoffmann von Fallersleben songs from July 1853 (one in B major, the other in A♭ major with a middle section in E major).

Spanisches Lied, Op. 6/1 (Spanish Song)

German text by Paul von Heyse (1830–1914)

> In dem Schatten meiner Locken
> Schlief mir mein Geliebter ein;
> Weck' ich nun auf?—Ach nein!
>
> Sorglich strählt' ich meine krausen
> Locken täglich in der Frühe,

> Doch umsonst ist meine Mühe,
> Weil die Winde sie zerzausen;
> Lockenschatten, Windessausen
> Schläferten den Liebsten ein;
> Weck' ich ihn nun auf?—Ach nein!
>
> Hören muß ich, wie ihn gräme
> Daß er schmachtet schon so lange,
> Daß ihm Leben gäb' und nähme
> Diese meine braune Wange.
> Und er nennt mich seine Schlange
> Und doch schlief er bei mir ein;
> Weck' ich ihn nun auf?—Ach nein!

In the shadow of my tresses my lover has fallen asleep; shall I awaken him now? Oh, no!

Every day early in the morning I have carefully combed my curly hair, but my efforts go for nothing because the wind dishevels it; shadow of tresses and humming of wind have lulled my lover to sleep; shall I awaken him now? Oh, no!

I must put up with his telling me how grieved he is at yearning for so long now, how this brown cheek of mine gives him life and takes it away. And he calls me his serpent, and yet he fell asleep beside me; shall I awaken him now? Oh, no!

Composed in Hamburg in April 1852, just after the publication of the text.

First performed (as "Spanische Serenade") by Joseph Deynhart on 16 February 1883 in Vienna as part of a concert by Lotte von Eisl.

Varied strophic; A B A' B' A.

The text appears in the Geibel-Heyse *Spanisches Liederbuch* (Berlin, 1852), where the fifth line from the end has "geb' und nehme" rather than "gäb' und nähme."

Brahms divides the poem into five stanzas of alternately three and four lines. Stanzas 1, 3, and 5 are set to the same music in A minor (F♯ minor in the lower key), while stanzas 2 and 4 are given a shorter, stronger treatment in the key of the dominant; the rhythm of the second section is derived from that of the first. In stanzas 3, 4, and 5, the opening pair of phrases is slightly varied rhythmically and melodically.

The song is distinctively atmospheric and somewhat unsettling. Characteristically, Brahms chooses merely to hint at the Spanish color—the strumming of guitars and the rhythms of a staid bolero are suggested rather than imitated. The girl's indecision and mood changes are reflected in the vacillation between minor and major, the alternately quiet and bold character, the abrupt dynamic contrasts, and particularly the many harmonic movements by third in the music of the opening section. Over all, seemingly happy thoughts of love are colored by subtle shadows of perplexity and frustration—the chromatically altered harmonies in mm. 12, 23, and 24 are unexpectedly pungent. One senses almost subconsciously that the affair has reached a turning point.

Brahms associated the sound of horn fifths not only with the hunt but with the outdoors generally. Their appearance in the music for stanzas 2 and 4 may have been prompted by the notion of the wind's tossing the girl's hair.

It should be noted that Brahms, in his own copy of the first edition, later changed the falling third in the vocal line in mm. 20, 22, 42, and 44 to a falling sixth, E to G♯ (D♭ to F), in order to avoid parallel octaves with the bass; these changes have been incorporated into the complete Breitkopf & Härtel edition (and the Dover reprint), but do not appear in many other commonly available editions, Friedländer's for C. F. Peters, for example.

Der Frühling, Op. 6/2 (Springtime)

Text by Johann Baptist Rousseau (1802–1867)

Es lockt und säuselt um den Baum:
Wach' auf aus deinem Schlaf und Traum,
Der Winter ist zerronnen.
Da schlägt er frisch den Blick empor,
Die Augen sehen hell hervor
An's goldne Licht der Sonnen.

Es zieht ein Wehen sanft und lau,
Geschaukelt in dem Wolkenbau
Wie Himmelsduft hernieder.
Da werden alle Blumen wach,
Da tönt der Vögel schmelzend Ach,
Da kehrt der Frühling wieder.

Es weht der Wind den Blütenstaub
Von Kelch zu Kelch, von Laub zu Laub,
Durch Tage und durch Nächte.
Flieg' auch, mein Herz, und flatt're fort,
Such' hier ein Herz und such' es dort,
Du triffst vielleicht das Rechte.

The breezes murmur temptingly around the tree: awaken from your sleep and your dream; the winter has thawed. Now it looks up vigorously, its eyes gaze brightly upon the sun's golden light.

A gentle, tepid stirring, rocked in the mass of clouds, descends like a heavenly fragrance. Now all the flowers awaken, now the melting sigh of the birds resounds, now springtime is returning.

The wind wafts the pollen from calyx to calyx, from leaf to leaf, all through the days and nights. You, too, my heart, take wing and fly away, seek out a heart in this place and that; perhaps you'll find the right one.

Composed in April 1852 in Hamburg.

First performed (together with "Nachwirkung," Op. 6/3) by Wilhelmina Gips on 2 February 1881 in The Hague.

Simple strophic, with postlude.

The text first appeared in 1826 in Rousseau's *Spiele der lyrischen und dramatischen Muse*, then in 1832 in his collected *Gedichte*.

The poem is a joyous celebration of the coming of spring. It welcomes the awakening of various phenomena of nature, turning only at the end toward the human heart and the tentative hope that love may be found. In this form, the text finds perfect realization in Brahms's rapturous strophic setting, with its climactic and dreamily expressive postlude; Brahms, however, chose to set only stanzas 1, 2, and 4 of the poem, omitting stanza 3:

> Es zuckt und bebt im Blute was,
> Die Wimpern werden tränennaß,
> Es pochet leis im Herzen.
> O Mensch, du fühlest Frühlingslust,
> Und Liebe hebet deinen Ernst,
> Und wecket süße Schmerzen!

Something in the blood quivers and trembles, the lashes become moist with tears, the heart throbs gently. O Man, you feel the joy of spring, and love leavens your gravity, and awakens sweet sorrows! [My translation.]

Finscher ("Brahms's Early Songs," *Brahms Studies*, 337) suggests that, while the young composer might have found the strong emotional content of this stanza appealing, its inclusion would have necessitated a different musical treatment because it anticipates and overemphasizes the human element that Brahms's version treats so subtly. There is no doubt that, for the composer's purpose, the revision improves the poem even while damaging its integrity. "Der Frühling" is an early example—he was not yet nineteen— of Brahms's keenness of judgment concerning poetry's potential for musical realization.

The eight-measure introduction, with its impassioned pulsating appoggiaturas and its Wagnerian evasion of tonic, sets the song's exuberant tone. Breathlessly, the voice enters in suppressed excitement over an accompaniment that alternately dances and recalls the introduction's appoggiatura motive, all over a rising bass. The second phrase is extended to five measures by a falling dominant arpeggio in the piano.

The shorter third line of text is set twice, the second time a third higher in sequential repetition. The first of this pair of phrases leads from the dominant minor to its relative major; the second leads from *its* minor to the Neapolitan.

Line 4 is set to a two-measure phrase in which both melody and harmony unwind chromatically over a bass pedal on the Neapolitan's dominant. Its repetition in *crescendo* for line 5 ends with the vocal line's sudden leap up a tritone, and the bass finally resolves downward to the dominant proper, *forte*. Another measure of dominant arpeggio in the piano, this time ascending, again extends the segment, now to six measures.

The first four measures of the introduction are then jubilantly recalled, somewhat more richly harmonized. The first two accommodate the sixth line of text; the third and fourth lead to a culminating repetition of the line, less active rhythmically but expanded to five measures to end the strophe.

An adaptation of this closing structure serves also as the postlude. Here, repetitions of a one-measure condensation of the introduction's appoggiatura figure rise quickly to the song's highest melodic pitch. The ensuing downward stepwise motion of the line soon yields to upward stepwise movement (echoing the closing vocal phrase) as the general pitch continues to fall, the activity lessens, the dynamic level drops, and the whole structure broadens to allow the song to end in quiet contemplation.

Nachwirkung, Op. 6/3 (Aftereffect)

Text by Alfred von Meissner (1822–1885)

Sie ist gegangen, die Wonnen versanken,
Nun glühen die Wangen, nun rinnen die Tränen,
Es schwanken die kranken,
Die heißen Gedanken,
Es pocht das Herz in Wünschen und Sehnen.

Und hab' ich den Tag mit Andacht begonnen,
Tagüber gelebt in stillem Entzücken,
So leb' ich jetzt träumend,
Die Arbeit versäumend
Von dem, was sie schenkte in Worten und Blicken.

So hängen noch lang nach dem Scheiden des Tages
In säuselnder Nachtluft, beim säuselnden Winde
Die Bienen, wie trunken
Und wonneversunken
An zitternden Blüten der duftenden Linde.

She has gone away, all bliss has vanished; now my cheeks are hot, now my tears pour down; my sick, feverish mind is reeling, my heart pounds with wishing and longing.

If formerly I began my day with thankful prayer and lived through each day in calm delight, now I neglect my work and only dream of the words and glances she used to bestow on me.

Thus do the bees, long after the day has departed, in the whistling night air, through the whistling wind, still cling, as if intoxicated and sunk in rapture, to trembling blossoms of the fragrant linden tree.

Composed in Hamburg in April 1852.

First performed (together with "Der Frühling," Op. 6/2) by Wilhelmina Gips on 2 February 1881 in The Hague.

Simple strophic.

The text is from Meissner's *Gedichte* (2d ed., Leipzig, 1846). In the third verse, Brahms changed "in schweigender Nachtluft" to "in säuselnder Nachtluft" for no obvious reason. The resulting two appearances of the adjective "säuselnd" are set to the same melodic motive, but in the other two stanzas no recurrence of text is associated with that motive's repetition. The altered version is so inferior to the original that careless oversight seems the only reasonable explanation. Brahms also changed "Bienlein" to "Bienen" in the line that follows, presumably believing it easier to sing, or perhaps finding the diminutive form overly precious.

The first line of text is set to a vigorous two-measure phrase, diatonic and sequentially constructed, which is anticipated by the brief introduction and is repeated, in mm. 9–11, for the first statement of line 5. In both cases, quieter, mostly stepwise melodic material follows, its harmonies expressively colored by chromaticism. The tripled note values of the characteristically expanded closing phrase cause the repetition of line 5 to occupy one more measure than the earlier settings of lines 2, 3, and 4 combined.

To set a poem in which all the rhymes are feminine constitutes a particular problem for a composer, and here, almost inevitably, weak syllables fall on strong beats at each principal cadence, in mm. 9 and 17. In both cases, however, Brahms has taken pains to temper the potential awkwardness: in m. 9, the resolution in the piano of the bass and the harmony is withheld until the second beat; in m. 17, the downbeat arrives at the end of the *diminuendo* that extends through the progressive resolution of the sharp dissonance in m. 15.

Particularly in the first stanza, the song's alternating vehemence and poignancy, agitation and reflection, are effective, but stanzas 2 and 3 seem ill-suited to such dramatic extremes, and care must be taken to avoid monotony as the performance proceeds.

Juchhe, Op. 6/4 (Hurrah!)

Text by Robert Reinick (1805–1852)

Wie ist doch die Erde so schön, so schön!
Das wissen die Vögelein;
Sie heben ihr leicht Gefieder,
Und singen so fröhliche Lieder
In den blauen Himmel hinein.

Wie ist doch die Erde so schön, so schön!
Das wissen die Flüß' und See'n;

Sie malen im klaren Spiegel
Die Gärten und Städt' und Hügel,
Und die Wolken, die d'rüber geh'n!

Und Sänger und Maler wissen es,
Und es wissen's viel and're Leut',
Und wer's nicht malt, der singt es,
Und wer's nicht singt, dem klingt es
Im Herzen vor lauter Freud'!

How beautiful the earth actually is, how beautiful! The little birds know it;
they lift their light plumage, and sing such happy songs to the blue heavens.

How beautiful the earth actually is, how beautiful! The rivers and lakes
know it; in their clear mirror they paint the gardens and towns and hills, and
the clouds that pass overhead!

And poets and painters know it, and many other people know it! And whoever doesn't paint it, sings it; and whoever doesn't sing it, hears music in his
heart from pure joy!

Composed in Hamburg in April 1852.

First performed on 6 January 1863 in Vienna by Marie Wilt with Brahms
at the piano.

Strophic, A A A'.

The text is found in Reinick's *Lieder* (Berlin, 1844). There, the third
stanza has "andere Leut'" and "in dem Herzen."

The song overflows with charm and youthful exuberance, and it recalls
"Der Frühling," Op. 6/2, in mood and subject matter. Among its many felicitous touches are the horn calls of the introduction, which return in the
postlude in ecstatic contradiction of the voice's quiet ending; the accompaniment's lightly repeated chords, vibrating in exhilaration; the little interludes
that echo in diminution the vocal phrases immediately preceding; in the long
interlude between strophes, the virtuosic rocket bursts of the rising scales,
yielding to a falling figure in single staccato eighths as the excitement gradually subsides to prepare the next verse; and, finally, in the third strophe, the
expanded climax over the rising bass, reached through a different modulation
via the tonic minor, the voice then gradually falling back as though overcome
by the "pure joy" of which it sings.

But the poem rests somewhat uneasily in its strophic mold. The lilting joyousness of Reinick's lines results at least in part from their seemingly random
alternation of iambic and anapestic feet. The beginnings of the lines, however,
are all iambic except for the fifth in each stanza (in the original), plus the
second line of the last stanza, where anapests produce a sense of climax at
the end of each verse, with a little additional quickening in stanza 3.

Brahms's prevailing single eighth-note upbeats accommodate the poem's
initial iambs nicely, and in the first two strophes, the culminating effect of
the repeated last line's anapestic beginning is effectively highlighted by the
two-eighth upbeats in mm. 24 and 28. But curiously, at the parallel point in

stanza 3 (m. 55), Brahms reverts to the single eighth-note upbeat, actually removing a syllable from the line of text to avoid the anapestic anacrusis. Since the variant third strophe departs from the others at the midpoint, one assumes that the change resulted from some not readily apparent musical consideration. Perhaps Brahms felt that his choice of a quieter repetition of the last line rendered this rhythmic climax inappropriate, or perhaps he regarded the arrival on the tonic $^6_4$ as sufficiently climactic in itself.

In the basic strophe, Brahms repeated the short second line in a phrase that duplicates the rhythm of the first statement but reverses the order of tonic and dominant harmony, suggesting the effect of a sequence. (The retention of this pair of phrases in the third strophe probably prompted his removal of a syllable from "andere Leut'" to preserve their rhythmic integrity.) This prepared the way for his masterful exploitation, through repetition and sequence, of the parallelism of lines 3 and 4 in the first stanza. The music rises in pitch and increases in excitement until the vocal line's breathless iteration of "und singen" and the piano's tightening rhythm lead directly to the climactic last line. But in the second stanza, the poet replaced the two parallel lines with a single continuous sentence, presenting a problem that Brahms simply sidestepped without solving, settling for the less than satisfactory modified repetition:

> Sie malen im klaren Spiegel
> Die Gärten und Städt' und Hügel,
> Sie malen im klaren Spiegel
> Die Gärten und Hügel.

What in the first strophe had been the affecting excited repetition of "und singen" here sounds particularly lame, as the vocal line merely omits the middle noun from a series of three.

There is no denying the rapturous effectiveness and freshness of the setting, but at the same time, it is evident that Brahms was not yet quite able to surmount the poem's inherent obstacles to strophic composition. (See Finscher, "Brahms's Early Songs," *Brahms Studies*, 334–337.)

Wie die Wolke nach der Sonne, Op. 6/5
(As the Cloud for the Sun)

Text by August Heinrich Hoffmann von Fallersleben (1798–1874)

> Wie die Wolke nach der Sonne
> Voll Verlangen irrt und bangt,
> Und durchglüht von Himmelswonne
> Sterbend ihr am Busen hangt.

> Wie die Sonnenblume richtet
> Auf die Sonn' ihr Angesicht

Und nicht eh'r auf sie verzichtet
Bis ihr eig'nes Auge bricht.

Wie der Aar auf Wolkenpfade
Sehnend steigt ins Himmelszelt
Und berauscht vom Sonnenbade
Blind zur Erde niederfällt:

So auch muß ich schmachten, bangen,
Späh'n und trachten, dich zu sehn,
Will an deinen Blicken hangen
Und an ihrem Glanz vergehn.

As the cloud wanders and yearns for the sun, full of longing, and, warmed through with heavenly rapture, clings dying to its breast:
As the sunflower turns its face to the sun and does not relinquish it until its own eye is clouded in death:
As the eagle, on its path of cloud, yearningly ascends to the vault of heaven and, dazzled by its immersion in sunlight, falls back to earth blinded:
Thus must I, too, long, yearn, gaze and think about seeing you, thus do I want to stare into your eyes and perish from their brightness.

Composed in July 1853 in Göttingen.
First performed on 17 December 1891 by Eduard Gärtner in Vienna.
Varied strophic, A A B A'.
The text is from Hoffman von Fallersleben's *Gedichte* (Leipzig, 1843). There the poet subtly links the beginnings of stanzas 1 and 2 by repeating "nach der Sonn'" in line 2 of the second stanza; Brahms's change to "auf die Sonn'" weakens the connection.
The song begins with a diatonic melody reminiscent of folk song. The suggestion of distant horns in the accompaniment evokes the outdoor setting of all of the poem's images; the right hand gently doubles the melody in afterbeats.
The dramatic shift of the second half of the stanza is announced by a turn to the subdominant, as the piano takes over the previous melody and the voice is given a new phrase with an expressive suspension in m. 6. The stanza's crux, in line 4, is strikingly set off by a lovely move through A major (low key, G♭ major) and the extension of the vocal phrase to three measures as it slows and softens to close inconclusively on the leading tone. The piano interlude reiterates the opening motive with decreasing assurance, hovering noncommittally on the dominant ninth.
After the second strophe, the interlude proceeds through the minor ninth and an unadorned seventh to introduce the tonic minor for stanza 3. Brahms's musical description of the eagle's flight and fall is almost visual in effect and is stunning in its simplicity. To a new accompaniment figure with upper pedals and incomplete triplets, the melody begins as before, though *forte*, but quickly soars to the song's highest pitch, to which it returns again

and again. At the climax, the bird's dazzlement is evoked by Neapolitan harmony, its blinded plunge from the heavens by a tritone-spanning descent in the voice, which broadens and diminishes as it falls and is doubled in the piano's inner voices.

The fourth strophe is nearly identical to the first two, but it retains the accompaniment figure from the third, unifying the last half of the song and heightening the poet's self-comparison with the eagle.

The song has neither prelude nor postlude—a rare occurrence among Brahms's songs—but the function of postlude is eloquently supplanted by a beautiful extended repetition of the last line of the poem, in which the voice floats wistfully over the piano's recalling of motives from earlier in the song harmonized (mostly) with the dominant ninth or the subdominant.

Nachtigallen schwingen, Op. 6/6 (Nightingales Beat)

Text by August Heinrich Hoffmann von Fallersleben (1798–1874)

> Nachtigallen schwingen
> Lustig ihr Gefieder,
> Nachtigallen singen
> Ihre alten Lieder.
> Und die Blumen alle,
> Sie erwachen wieder
> Bei dem Klang und Schalle
> Aller dieser Lieder.
>
> Und meine Sehnsucht wird zur Nachtigall
> Und fliegt in die blühende Welt hinein,
> Und fragt bei den Blumen überall,
> Wo mag doch mein, mein Blümchen sein?
>
> Und die Nachtigallen
> Schwingen ihren Reigen
> Unter Laubeshallen
> Zwischen Blütenzweigen,
> Von den Blumen allen
> Aber ich muß schweigen.
> Unter ihnen steh' ich
> Traurig sinnend still:
> Eine Blume seh' ich,
> Die nicht blühen will.

Nightingales beat their feathery wings merrily, nightingales sing their old songs. And all the flowers awaken once more to the tuneful sound of all these songs.

And my longing becomes a nightingale and flies off into the blossoming world, and asks everywhere of the flowers, where my, my little flower can be.

And the nightingales perform their round dance in leafy bowers amid blossoming branches, but I must be silent about all the flowers. I stand among them silently with my sad thoughts: I see one flower that refuses to bloom.

Composed in July 1853 in Göttingen.

First performed on 9 November 1862 by Frau Walter-Fastlinger at the Casino in Basel.

A B A'.

The text is found in the poet's *Gedichte* (Leipzig, 1843); in the next-to-last line, Brahms changed Hoffmann's "eine Knospe" (one bud) to "eine Blume" (one flower).

The impassioned setting begins with a joyous, broadly arching melody over the piano's jubilation of twittering birdsong. A sudden *piano* marks the flowers' awakening, and some chromatically altered harmonies prepare the way for an enharmonic modulation to the submediant from the minor, in which key the longing lover laments his loneliness.

To the eye, the rhythms of this middle section appear to present some thorny ensemble problems, but in practice, they prove to be minimal; the feeling of *alla breve*, which the harmonic rhythm creates despite the meter signature of common time, merely continues. The lessened activity in the piano part and the prevalence of quarter-note triplets in the vocal line, aided by the minor inflections and hesitant delivery toward the end of the stanza, successfully express the poet's internal sorrow, in contrast to the brightness of his surroundings.

But the exuberance of birds and blossoms soon intrudes upon his reverie. The third stanza begins like the first, but with telling differences as the poet finds himself silenced by grief at the image of himself as the only flower in all of creation that will not bloom. One phrase earlier than before, the dynamic drops to *piano* in m. 40, and the accompaniment's left hand unexpectedly abandons its doubling of the right to embark alone upon an expressive quarter-note countermelody in the viola register, a moving metaphor for the poet's isolation.

The poem's third verse has two more lines than the first, and its setting is accordingly expanded by three measures, allowing for a sequential rise to the song's highest pitch on the word "traurig" in m. 45. In mm. 41 and 47, darker minor harmonies replace the corresponding major triads and seventh chords. The vocal melody ends pensively on the third, and the postlude commiserates softly.

The song is very beautiful. Performers should be aware that its effect depends on the clarity of the contrast between its opposing emotions.

SIX GESÄNGE, OP. 7

Sechs Gesänge für Singstimme mit Begleitung des Pianoforte componirt und Albert Dietrich gewidmet von Johannes Brahms (Six Songs for Solo Voice with Piano Accompaniment, Composed and Dedicated to Albert Dietrich by Johannes Brahms), Op. 7. Published in November 1854 by Breitkopf & Härtel in Leipzig; publication number 8946.

The second edition was published by Simrock after that firm acquired the rights to Brahms's Breitkopf & Härtel publications in 1888. As in Op. 3, many of the dynamic indications in the vocal part were deleted in the second edition; publication numbers, high key 8990, low key 8991.

Brahms met Schumann's pupil Albert Dietrich (1829–1908) during his 1853 visit to the Schumanns in Düsseldorf. They maintained an intimate lifelong friendship. Dietrich composed and served as Kapellmeister at Oldenburg.

The ordering of the songs within the opus places two poems by Eichendorff together (though they were composed at separate times) and reveals a sequence of related keys—F♯ minor, E minor/major, A minor/major, E Phrygian, A Aeolian, B minor/major. But the primary consideration seems to have been the texts, which form a progression of sorts—the stories of a collection of lonely maidens are followed by that of a boy joyously returning home. This rather naive narrative arrangement is Brahms's apparent motivation for placing the dramatic *scena* "Heimkehr," his earliest extant song, at the end of Op. 7 rather than at the beginning of Op. 3.

Treue Liebe, Op. 7/1 (True Love)

Text by Eduard Ferrand (pseudonym for Eduard Schulz; 1813–1842)

Ein Mägdlein saß am Meeresstrand
Und blickte voll Sehnsucht in's Weite:
"Wo bleibst du, mein Liebster, wo weilst du so lang?
Nicht ruhen läßt mich des Herzens Drang.
Ach, kämst du, mein Liebster, doch heute!"

Der Abend nahte, die Sonne sank
Am Saum des Himmels darnieder.

"So trägt dich die Welle mir nimmer zurück?
Vergebens späht in die Ferne mein Blick.
Wo find' ich, mein Liebster, dich wieder?"

Die Wasser umspielten ihr schmeichelnd den Fuß,
Wie Träume von seligen Stunden,
Es zog sie zur Tiefe mit stiller Gewalt;
Nie stand mehr am Ufer die holde Gestalt,
Sie hat den Geliebten gefunden!

A girl sat by the seashore and looked into the distance longingly: "Where are you, my beloved, where do you tarry so long? The pressure of my heart gives me no rest. Ah, if you would only come today, my beloved!"

Evening approached, the sun sank at the edge of the sky. "So then, the waves will never bring you back to me? It is in vain that my eyes peer into the distance. Where will I find you again, my beloved?"

The water flatteringly played about her feet like dreams of happy hours; she was drawn into the deep by some silent force. The lovely figure never stood upon the shore again; she found her loved one!

Composed in Hamburg in November 1852.

First performed (together with "Parole," Op. 7/2) on 6 January 1863 in Vienna by Marie Wilt and Brahms.

Varied strophic; two verses set to the same music, plus a reshaped and elaborated final strophe.

The text is found in the poet's *Gedichte* of 1834. There, the second verse has "am Saume"; Brahms's dropping of a syllable from "Saume" is puzzling since it requires a change in rhythm from the first verse—it can hardly have been an oversight.

A lonely girl sits on the seashore yearning for her absent beloved; finally she is drawn by some irresistible force into the deep to join him. The poem is melodramatic, but it contains all of the elements necessary to inspire Brahms to compose a fine song—it evokes musical imagery, and its single dramatic situation moves straightforwardly to its climax. The result is a moving and powerful little *scena* of desolation, longing, and love faithful even unto death.

Verses 1 and 2 are ideally suited to strophic composition because of their parallel construction. Over an accompaniment figure that suggests the breaking of waves on a deserted beach, the wistful melody begins softly and simply. References to "the distance" in stanza 1 and "the edge of the sky" in stanza 2 elicit a yearning digression to the submediant in mm. 4–5. The earlier melody returns for line 3, *pianissimo* and suspended over the piano's dominant pedal. The growing excitement of lines 4 and 5 is reflected in their sequentially rising melody and diminished-seventh harmony. The last line is repeated in a climactic closing phrase that blazes forth *forte*, its crux a painful rising tritone. As though exhausted by the outburst, the voice immediately falls back to an inconclusive dominant, and the piano's vehemence yields to the resumption of its earlier surflike motion.

The structure of the poem's third verse differs from that of the others, and Brahms alters the musical design accordingly. The increased rhythmic activity of the opening line—all iambs in stanza 1, now all anapests after the initial iamb—reflects a higher level of agitation, which in turn is matched by the escalation of the accompaniment figure to triplets, plus its newly acquired appoggiatura. The dramatic climax of the verse (indeed, of the entire poem) arrives in line 3, leaving the two closing lines to function as a kind of epilogue. Stormily, and with increasingly numerous appoggiaturas, the music rises quickly to its own climax—a prolonged lingering on the otherworldly submediant, already prepared by earlier references but now minor, and made even more poignant by its own augmented mediant in m. 20, its Neapolitan in m. 21, and a shower of chromatic lower neighbors as the arpeggio figure subsides in mm. 22–24.

The tonic key returns, and the piano's arpeggios cease for the moment. The vocal line laments heartbrokenly, underlined by affectingly expressive harmonies (including one more reference, in m. 26, to the submediant); it culminates, like the closing phrases of the earlier strophes, in a rising tritone, but this time its upper pitch is pushed yet a half step higher to become an anguished 9–8 suspension. The undulating arpeggios, having resumed quietly in the piano's upper register, gradually sink lower and lower as they become softer and softer, and the song ends with three almost inaudible reiterations of a bleak bass octave, like final heartbeats.

Parole, Op. 7/2 (Watchword)

Text by Joseph von Eichendorff (1788–1857)

> Sie stand wohl am Fensterbogen
> Und flocht sich traurig das Haar,
> Der Jäger war fortgezogen,
> Der Jäger ihr Liebster war.

> Und als der Frühling gekommen,
> Die Welt war von Blüten verschneit,
> Da hat sie ein Herz sich genommen
> Und ging in die grüne Heid.

> Sie legt das Ohr an den Rasen,
> Hört ferner Hufe Klang—
> Das sind die Rehe, die grasen
> Am schattigen Bergeshang.

> Und Abends die Wälder rauschen,
> Von fern nur fällt noch ein Schuß,
> Da steht sie stille zu lauschen:
> "Das war meines Liebsten Gruß!"

Da sprangen vom Fels die Quellen,
Da flogen die Vöglein in's Tal.
"Und wo ihr ihn trefft, ihr Gesellen,
O, grüßt mir ihn tausendmal!"

She stood at her arched window and sadly braided her hair; the huntsman had gone away, the huntsman was her sweetheart.

And when the springtime came and the world was snowy with blossom, she took courage and went out to the green moorland.

She puts her ear to the turf, she hears the sound of far-off hoofbeats; that is the deer grazing on the shady mountain slope.

And in the evening the forests rustle, only a shot is still heard from afar off; then she stands still to listen: "That was my sweetheart's greeting!"

Then the streams broke forth from the rocky cliffs, then the birds flew swiftly into the valley! "You companions, wherever you chance to meet him, oh, bring him a thousand greetings from me!"

Composed in November 1852 in Hamburg.

First performed (together with "Treue Liebe," Op. 7/1) on 6 January 1863 in Vienna by Marie Wilt, with Brahms at the piano.

Varied strophic; A A B B A'.

The text first appeared, untitled, in the 1834 novel *Dichter und ihre Gesellen*. The title "Parole" (originally "Die Parole") is found in the first two editions of Eichendorff's collected poems (Berlin, 1837 and 1843); after the poet's death, his eldest son prepared a new edition in which the same poem is called "Die Verlassene" (The Forsaken Girl).

The title "Parole" makes it evident that Brahms took the poem from the earlier collected *Gedichte* (he owned a copy of the 1843 edition), but several compositional details that would otherwise be enigmatic stem from his familiarity with its context in the novel, where it is introduced as follows:

Apart from the merry little crowd, however, there stood leaning against the mast in the middle of the ship a most beautiful youth in graceful hunter's dress [actually, of course, a girl in disguise]; in his arm he carried a zither which he had found in the cabin. . . . [He] looked brightly from under his traveler's hat into the distance, and sang: [Here appear the five stanzas which constitute the poem in the collected edition and in Brahms's setting.]

In the novel, two additional stanzas are part of the narrative that follows the singing of the song—actually rhymed dialogue—while the five original stanzas are a complete and independent poem, which Eichendorff could publish without alteration.

Brahms changed "ihr Haar" to "das Haar" in the first verse, and added the exclamation "O" before the last line. The first change is insignificant; the other is understandable, since the entire song is based on the rhythm of the iambic beginning of all the other lines of the poem. But the addition of an initial syllable transfers the climax from the poet's "grüßt" without anacrusis to Brahms's "tausendmal" as joyous codetta.

Bozarth points out ("'Poetic' Andantes," *Brahms Studies*, 353) that, although other songs from the period show Brahms's concern with the correlation between key and psychological state, this is the earliest in which the large-scale tonal design underlines the elements of the text's central dramatic conflict, namely the separation of the girl from her sweetheart and her resulting anxiety. Brahms places the singer in the tonic minor but allows her thoughts of the distant beloved to appear in the Neapolitan (later, the subdominant). Modulations are frequent, and root-position tonic harmony is postponed or avoided—the tonic of the principal key appears in root position only after the change to major in the last stanza—effectively mirroring in musical terms the instability of the situation described and the yearning associated with it.

The song begins with an accumulation of hunting-horn calls, apparently in the key of C major (low key, A♭), although the principal tonality is E (C) and the absent lover's Neapolitan is F (D♭). This temporary false tonic is a seeming equivalent of the parenthetical role of the song in the novel, just as the use of introductory horn calls is surely an acknowledgment of the singer's costume, since the idea of the actual hunt does not enter the text until stanza 3. The choice of this opening sonority is in fact a masterly touch; the augmented-sixth chord that results from Brahms's poignant addition of A♯ (F♯) to lead to the actual tonic key is also heard enharmonically as the dominant seventh of the secondary tonality, so the one harmonic structure relates to both keys, and the same music can serve as both introduction and interlude.

The vocal line for strophes 1 and 2 opens with a simple descending phrase reminiscent of folk song; the piano then takes up the same melody while the voice continues in duet a third below. The third and fourth phrases are constructed from rising interlocked tritones, evoking the painful absence of the hunter-sweetheart (and hinting at his key). The accompaniment figure may be intended to suggest the zither from the scene in the novel (though Brahms often associated descending arpeggios with separation), and the rocking barcarolle-like rhythm may pay homage to the shipboard locale.

Horn calls abound as the emphasis shifts to the hunter's milieu in stanzas 3 and 4. Against hopeful-sounding pedal points in the treble, the left hand of the piano part doubles a melody in rising sequence, which derives its rhythm from that of the preceding strophe.

The fifth stanza begins like the first, but soon starts its shift to the tonic major for the jubilant concluding repetitions of "tausendmal!" In the postlude, the horn calls from the introduction seem propelled by the singer's exuberance to a yet higher melodic climax, but wistfulness returns to end the song.

Anklänge, Op. 7/3 (Reminiscences)

Text by Joseph von Eichendorff (1788–1857)

Hoch über stillen Höhen
Stand in dem Wald ein Haus;
So einsam war's zu sehen,
Dort über'n Wald hinaus.

Ein Mädchen saß darinnen
Bei stiller Abendzeit,
Tät seid'ne Fäden spinnen
Zu ihrem Hochzeitskleid.

High above the silent heights a house stood in the forest; it was such a lonely sight out there over the woods.
In it there sat a girl in the silent evening hour, spinning silken threads for her wedding dress.

Composed in Hamburg in March 1853.
First performed on 12 November 1855 in Göttingen by Julius Otto Grimm.
Through-composed, with a return of opening material.
The text appears in the first collected edition of Eichendorff's *Gedichte* (Berlin, 1837) as the second of three poems which, under the title "Anklänge," open the section "Frühling und Liebe." But in the same collection there is a long ballad—twenty-four four-line verses—first printed in the novel *Ahnung und Gegenwart* (1815), that has a very similar beginning:

Hoch über den stillen Höhen
Stand in dem Wald ein Haus,
Dort war's so einsam zu sehen
Weit über'n Wald hinaus.

D'rin saß ein Mädchen am Rocken
Den ganzen Abend lang,
Der wurden die Augen nicht trocken
Sie spann und sann und sang.

In *Ahnung und Gegenwart*, the poem has no title, but is referred to as "eine alte Romanze." In the 1837 collection, it is found in the section *Romanzen* as "Der Reitersmann," a title retained in the later editions by the poet's son. These editions print the long poem in its entirety but omit the two-verse variant which is the basis of the song.
Brahms's setting is a haunting portrayal of a lonely girl spinning the threads for a wedding dress that the music tells us she will never wear. The song is in fact filled with foreboding, though the poem itself gives little indication of approaching tragedy. In the long poem of 1815, however, the

heroine becomes infatuated with a hunter and is unfaithful to her beloved knight, who returns as a ghost and slays her. It seem evident that Brahms, while choosing the short version as text, has actually composed the content of the long version, even referring to the hunter in a series of horn fifths in mm. 19–26.

The serious tone is already apparent in the brief introduction, which establishes the afterbeats that are to underlie the entire song, and the upper pedal on the dominant, which is to toll, knell-like, throughout the first half. The vocal line is restricted in range, has mostly small intervals, and is limited almost throughout to the half note–quarter note rhythm that Brahms so often associated with isolation. The entire song is in four-measure phrases until the concluding extension, but the vocal line has alternately four and three measures, leaving the fourth to the piano.

The opening melody arches slowly upward—down a step, up a third—but descends stepwise only. Much of the song's distinctive sound results from the peculiar doubling of the melody, both in the bass register of the piano and, constantly retarded by a half beat, within the right hand's afterbeat octaves. Contrasting melodic material outlines triads in mm. 19–25, first major, then minor. As the emotional intensity increases in mm. 26–33, octave-spanning melodic segments descend, then rise to the vocal line's highest pitch. The song is extended by a climactic repetition of the last two lines of text to the melody from the opening, beginning *forte*; the bass doubling now includes a third above the melody, the afterbeat octaves have become a tonic pedal, and a fateful tonic drumbeat is added as a new element. The last phrase is sung in *diminuendo*. The activity gradually lessens, but even a final turn to the major cannot dispel the overwhelming sense of desolation and unspecified tragedy.

Volkslied, Op. 7/4 (Folk Song)

> Die Schwälble ziehet fort, ziehet fort,
> Weit an en andre[, andre] Ort;
> Und i sitz do in Traurigkeit,
> Es isch a böse, schwere Zeit.
>
> Könnt i no fort durch d' Welt, fort durch d' Welt,
> Weil mir's hie gar net, gar net g'fällt!
> O Schwälble komm, i bitt, i bitt!
> Zeig mir de Weg und nimm mi mit!

The little swallow flies away, flies away, far off to some other, other place; and I sit here in sadness; it's an evil, hard time.

I wish I could go out into the world, out into the world, because I don't like it here at all, not at all! Oh, come, little swallow, I beg you, I beg you! Show me the way and take me along!

Composed in August 1852 in Hamburg.

First performed on 30 December 1871 by Helene Magnus in Vienna.

Strophic.

The text is from Georg Scherer's collection *Deutsche Volkslieder* (Leipzig, 1851).

Written when he was only nineteen, this is the earliest of Brahms's settings of folk song texts. His strong identification with the genre is evident, and all of the elements of the mastery which was to become so consummate are already present—the artful simplicity, the economy of means, the compressed emotional intensity.

In the poem, a lonely girl laments her empty life and envies the swallow's freedom. The setting is in Aeolian mode and avoids the raised leading tone almost completely. Another archaism is the use of a Picardy third in the interior cadence in mm. 14–16.

The accompaniment, in eighth notes throughout, doubles the diatonic melody discreetly. The piano introduction's broken tonic triad rises slowly, like the girl's hope, but the vocal melody that joins it cannot break free of its dominant tether; the little two-measure echo only underscores its static quality. The succeeding phrase, symbolic of the swallow's flight, quickly spirals to the song's dramatic high point, the relative major representing the "other place" longed for so ardently. The piano interlude imitates "andre Ort" and lingers pensively on the tonic major. The concluding vocal melody begins like a return of the opening material, but this time it manages to climb to the upper tonic before descending a full octave scalewise. The piano again imitates, continuing to sink, like the wretched girl's unfulfilled aspirations, back to the same pitches with which the song began.

Die Trauernde, Op. 7/5 (The Unhappy Girl)

German Folk Song

Mei Mueter mag mi net,
Und kein Schatz han i net,
Ei warum sterb' i net,
    Was tu i do?

Gestern isch Kirchweih g'wä,
Mi hot mer g'wis net g'seh,
Denn mir isch's gar so weh,
    I tanz ja net.

Laßt die drei Rose stehn,
Die an dem Kreuzle blühn:
Hent ihr das Mädle kennt,
    Die drunter liegt?

My mother doesn't love me, and I have no sweetheart; oh, why don't I die? What am I doing here?

Yesterday there was a parish fair, but I'm sure nobody looked at me, because I'm so unhappy that I don't dance.

Leave alone the three roses that bloom by the little cross: did you know the girl who lies beneath it?

Composed in Hamburg in August 1852.

The first public performance was given by Marie Wilt on 12 November 1870 at a *Künstlerabend* of the Gesellschaft der Musikfreunde in Vienna.

A A B (or A A A').

The text is from Georg Scherer's *Deutsche Volkslieder* (Leipzig, 1851). The earliest printed version is in the collection *Kriegs- und Volkslieder* (Stuttgart, 1824). Originally there were five verses; the present first verse "Mei Mueter mag mi net" came third, "Gestern ist Kirchweih g'wä" was second, and "Laßt die drei Rose stehn" last. The first verse of the longer version is:

> Wenn I zum Brünnle geh,
> Seh andre Mädel steh,
> Alle stehn bei ihrem Schatz,
> Wer ständ bei mir?

When I go to the well, seeing the other girls there, all stand close to their sweethearts. Who would stand close to me?

and the next-to-last:

> Wenn i nu gstorbe bin,
> Tragt mi zum Kirchhof hin,
> Legt mi ins Grab hinei:
> Wer weint um mi?

When I then am dead, carry me over to the churchyard, lay me into the grave: who will weep for me? [My translations.]

The Swabian poet Wilhelm Hauff, who edited the 1824 collection anonymously, shortened and rearranged the poem. It is to his artistic taste and judgment that we owe its present taut and masterly form—a lament of haunting desolation.

Brahms matches the conciseness of the text with a setting of supreme simplicity. The drooping melody, falling repeatedly to the lower dominant, reflects the hopelessness of the girl's lonely, loveless life. At the beginning of the third stanza, it attempts in vain to rise, only to fall back as though exhausted by the effort.

The austere accompaniment is allotted only a repeated cadence bar beyond its chordal support of the voice. Its harmonies are modal, avoiding the dominant harmony except at cadences. The avoidance of the raised leading tone sounds both archaic and otherworldly, suggesting the agelessness of the girl's plight and her longing to escape into death from the harshness of reality. The impassioned outcries at the beginning of verse 3, with their yearning vacillation between minor and major, are achingly poignant.

The song exerts far greater power than its miniature proportions might lead one to expect. Long after the music has ended, its mood continues to resonate in the memory.

Heimkehr, Op. 7/6 (Homecoming)

Text by Ludwig Uhland (1787–1862)

O brich nicht, Steg, du zitterst sehr,
O stürz' nicht, Fels, du dräuest schwer;
Welt, geh nicht unter, Himmel, fall nicht ein,
Bis ich mag bei der Liebsten sein!

O footbridge, don't break—you are trembling so! O cliff, don't crumble—you are threatening so! World, do not perish; sky, don't fall down, until I'm with the girl I love!

Composed in May 1851 in Hamburg.
First performed on 26 November 1886 by Hermine Spies.
Through-composed.
The poem, according to the poet's diary, was written on 19 November 1811; it is found in the collected *Gedichte* (Stuttgart and Tübingen, 1815). The poet proclaims that no obstacle will prevent his returning home to his sweetheart. Brahms changed "eh' ich mag" to "bis ich mag" in the last line, perhaps considering it easier to sing.

In this earliest of his published songs, Brahms created a brief scene of almost operatic dramatic intensity, resembling an accompanied recitative and arioso. The triplet accompaniment provides strength and agitation. The jagged upward-leaping motive of the introduction generates both the opening of the vocal line and its answering bass, and returns (in augmentation) in the piano's concluding gesture at the end of the song; with the threefold repetition of "bis ich mag bei der Liebsten sein," the melodic leaps turn downward instead, imitated by the bass. The final *fortissimo* climax in the major is splendid.

But despite its passion and its craft, the song does not quite succeed. It seems too grandiose for its brevity, and more significantly, too melodramatic for its rather unassuming text.

Choose a tempo on the moderate side of *Allegro*, while protecting the agitated character.

LIEDER AND ROMANZEN, OP. 14

Lieder und Romanzen für eine Singstimme mit Begleitung des Pianoforte von Johannes Brahms (Songs and Romances for Solo Voice with Piano Accompaniment by Johannes Brahms), Op. 14. Published in December 1860 or January 1861 by J. Rieter-Biedermann in Winterthur; publication number 169.

Though the eight melodies are original with Brahms, all but one of the texts are folk songs from collections by Karl Simrock, Johann Gottfried Herder, and Kretzschmer and Zuccalmaglio. The one exception, "Ein Sonett," No. 4, is a medieval French sonnet, translated by Herder and included in his collection of folk songs. Many of the texts have overtones of medieval romance, and the idea of separation, either by parting or by death, colors them all. All eight were composed in 1858.

Vor dem Fenster, Op. 14/1 (Outside the Window)

Folk Song

Soll sich der Mond nicht heller scheinen,
Soll sich die Sonn' nicht früh' aufgeh'n,
So will ich diese Nacht geh'n freien,
Wie ich zuvor auch hab' getan.

Als er wohl auf die Gasse trat,
Da fing er an ein Lied und sang,
Er sang aus schöner, aus heller Stimme,
Daß sein fein's Lieb zum Bett aussprang.

Steh' still, steh' still, mein feines Lieb,
Steh' still, steh' still und rühr' dich nicht,
Sonst weckst du Vater, sonst weckst du Mutter,
Das ist uns Beiden nicht wohl getan.

Was frag' ich nach Vater, was frag' ich nach Mutter,
Vor deinem Schlaffenster muß ich steh'n,
Ich will mein schönes Lieb anschauen,
Um das ich muß so ferne geh'n.

40

Da standen die zwei wohl bei einander
Mit ihren zarten Mündelein,
Der Wächter blies wohl in sein Hörnelein,
Ade, es muß geschieden sein.

Ach Scheiden, Scheiden über Scheiden,
Scheiden tut meinem jungen Herzen weh',
Daß ich mein schön Herzlieb muß meiden,
Das vergeß' ich nimmermehr.

"If the moon doesn't shine too brightly, if the sun doesn't rise too early, I will go out serenading tonight as I've done in the past."

When he stepped out into the street, he began a song and sang, he sang with a beautiful, clear voice, so that his sweetheart jumped out of bed.

"Be quiet, be quiet, my sweetheart, be quiet, be quiet and don't move, or you'll wake up Father, or you'll wake up Mother, and that would be bad for both of us."

"What do I care about your father, what do I care about your mother? I must stand outside your bedroom window, I want to look at my beautiful sweetheart, for whose sake I have to go so far away."

Then the two stood side by side joining their tender lips; the watchman blew his horn. "Farewell, we must part."

"Oh, parting, one parting after another, parting hurts my young heart; I'll never forget that I have to be separated from my beautiful darling."

Composed in Göttingen in September 1858.

First performed (together with Op. 14/4, "Ein Sonett") by Julius Stockhausen in Hamburg on 4 April 1862.

Varied strophic; verses 1–3 and 5 are set to the same music in minor, verses 4 and 6 to the same related music in the tonic major.

The text is found in Karl Simrock's collection *Die deutschen Volkslieder* (Frankfurt am Main, 1851) and in Franz Ludwig Mittler's *Deutsche Volkslieder* (Marburg and Leipzig, 1855). Brahms made several insignificant alterations. Thirty-three years later, he wrote a piano accompaniment for the folk song melody and included it as No. 35 in his forty-nine *Deutsche Volkslieder*.

The poem describes the parting of two lovers outside the girl's window. The setting breaks the poem's regularity by inserting occasional little piano interruptions. The arrangement of phrases and interludes is as follows, in the minor:

4 mm. [2 mm.] 4 mm., 4 mm. [2 mm.] 5 mm. [overlaps 5 mm.]

and, in the major:

4 mm., 4mm. [2mm.] 4 mm., 4mm. [2 mm.].

The song begins with a two-measure introduction and ends with a postlude of six measures.

The seemingly random breaking-off of phrases, as though the speakers were breathless with emotion, and the frequent feminine phrase endings help to evoke the pain of the farewell. It is particularly affecting when, in the strophe in the major, the voice cries out in its higher register above the principal melodic figure from the minor strophe in the piano, the whole *più forte*, *crescendo*, and *forte*.

The long *diminuendo* and the repetitions in the ending and postlude of the song suggest the lover's slipping away reluctantly into the night, and a gentle turn to the subdominant reflects his tender feelings.

Vom verwundeten Knaben, Op. 14/2 (About the Wounded Boy)

Folk Song

Es wollt' ein Mädchen früh aufsteh'n
Und in den grünen Wald spazieren geh'n.

Und als sie nun in den grünen Wald kam,
Da fand sie einen verwund'ten Knab'n.

Der Knab, der war von Blut so rot,
Und als sie sich verwandt, war er schon tot.

Wo krieg ich nun zwei Leidfräulein,
Die mein fein's Lieb zu Grabe wein'n?

Wo krieg ich nun sechs Reuterknab'n,
Die mein fein's Lieb zu Grabe trag'n?

Wie lang soll ich denn trauern geh'n?
Bis alle Wasser zusammengeh'n?

Ja, alle Wasser geh'n nicht zusamm'n,
So wird mein Trauern kein Ende han.

A girl decided to get up early and take a walk in the green forest.
And as she now entered the green forest, she found a wounded boy.
The boy was all red with blood, and when she turned aside he was already dead.
"Where can I now find two women mourners who will sing funeral chants for my beloved?
"Where can I now find six youthful knights who will bear my beloved to his grave?
"How long, then, shall I continue mourning? Until all waters flow together?
"Yes, all waters will never flow together, so my mourning will have no end."

Composed in January 1858 in Hamburg.
The first performance is not documented.

Varied strophic; verses 1–3 and 7 are set to the same music in A (low key, G) minor, but 4 shifts to the dominant of the relative major, 5 is in the key of the submediant, and 6 modulates from the subdominant back to the original key. Stanzas 1–3, 6, and 7, all of which deal with the girl and her mortally wounded lover only, share the same melodic material, featuring skips upward *piano*. (The melody is given briefly to the piano at the beginning of stanza 6.) Stanzas 4 and 5, in which she calls for outsiders—mourners and pallbearers— also share melodic material, but featuring skips downward *più forte*.

The text is found in Gottfried Herder's *Volkslieder* (Tübingen, 1778/79) and *Stimmen der Völker in Liedern* (1807), and in expanded form in Georg Scherer's *Deutsche Volkslieder* (Leipzig, 1851). Herder has, in verse 2, "verwundeten"; in verses 4 and 5, "feines Lieb"; and in verse 7, "trauren" instead of "trauern."

Brahms set this mournful ballad in a simple chordal style, mostly in the middle register of both voice and piano. Its archaic sound derives from the quasi-modal harmonic progressions, the sparing use of seventh chords, and especially from the distinctive and often-repeated cadence that rises melodically from the third to the fifth of the key, harmonized with tonic when it appears in the voice but with mediant and dominant when the piano echoes. The song is a moving evocation of loss and grief.

Murrays Ermordung, Op. 14/3 (The Assassination of Murray)

Translated from the Scottish by
Johann Gottfried von Herder (1744–1803)

O Hochland und o Südland!
Was ist auf euch gescheh'n!
Erschlagen der edle Murray,
Werd' nie ihn wiederseh'n.

O Weh dir! Weh dir, Huntley!
So untreu, falsch und kühn,
Sollst ihn zurück uns bringen,
Ermordet hast du ihn.

Ein schöner Ritter war er,
In Wett- und Ringelauf;
Allzeit war uns'res Murray
Die Krone oben d'rauf.

Ein schöner Ritter war er
Bei Waffenspiel und Ball;
Es war der edle Murray
Die Blume überall.

> Ein schöner Ritter war er
> In Tanz und Saitenspiel;
> Ach, daß der edle Murray
> Der Königin gefiel.
>
> O, Königin, wirst lange
> Seh'n über Schlosses Wall,
> Eh' du den schönen Murray
> Siehst reiten in dem Tal.

O highlands, and O southern land! What has happened upon you? Slain is the noble Murray, I shall never see him again.

O woe to you, woe to you, Huntley! So faithless, false and bold; you must bring him back to us; you have killed him.

He was a handsome knight in races and tourneys; our Murray was at all times the crowning champion.

He was a handsome knight in war games and ball games; noble Murray was the choicest flower everywhere.

He was a handsome knight in dancing and playing the lute; how unfortunate that noble Murray was pleasing to the Queen!

O, Queen, you will long gaze over the castle wall before you see the handsome Murray riding in the valley.

Composed in Hamburg in January 1858.

The first performance is not documented.

A B A. Verses 1, 2, and 6 are all to the same music; verses 3, 4, and 5 share the same contrasting music, but the ending of verse 5 is varied slightly in order to return to the original key.

Herder's translation of the old Scots ballad *The Bonny Earl of Murray* appears in his *Volkslieder* (Tübingen, 1778–79) and *Stimmen der Völker in Liedern* (1807).

While the traditional melody is elegiac, focusing on the mourning of those who loved Murray, Brahms's setting is martial and dramatic, energized by anger at the wrong inflicted by the false Huntley.

The principal strophe features dotted rhythms, relieved by a brief passage with canonic triplets. The elision of phrases at all cadences allows considerable emotional tension to accumulate through sheer rhythmic vigor.

The three contrasting stanzas, which dwell on the memory of the handsome Murray ("Ein schöner Ritter war er . . ."), are quieter in mood and begin *piano*, though each succeeding stanza is marked *più forte*. The vocal line is smoothed out to even eighths and quarters; the accompaniment is reduced to sonorous supporting chords, their quasi-modal progressions creating an aura of archaism.

The original music returns for the last strophe, and with it, its dramatic energy, which mounts until the piano's final cadence reverberates like a vehement cry for vengeance.

Ein Sonett, Op. 14/4 (A Sonnet)

Thirteenth century; German text by Herder, after
Thibau[l]t IV (French, 1201–1253)

Ach, könnt' ich, könnte vergessen sie,
    Ihr schönes, liebes, liebliches Wesen,
Den Blick, die freundliche Lippe die!
    Vielleicht ich möchte genesen!
Doch ach, mein Herz, mein Herz kann es nie!
Und doch ist's Wahnsinn, zu hoffen sie!
    Und um sie schweben,
    Gibt Mut und Leben,
    Zu weichen nie.
Und denn, wie kann ich vergessen sie,
    Ihr schönes, liebes, liebliches Wesen,
Den Blick, die freundliche Lippe die?
    Viel lieber nimmer genesen!

Oh, if I could only, only forget her, her beautiful, lovely, loving nature, her glance, her friendly mouth! Perhaps I could then grow well!

But ah, my heart, my heart can never do so! And yet it is madness to hope for her! And to hover about her gives courage and life, never to draw away.

And then, how can I forget her, her beautiful, lovely, loving nature, her glance, her friendly mouth? Much better never to grow well!

Composed in Göttingen in September 1858.

First performed (together with "Vor dem Fenster," Op. 14/1) on 4 April 1862 by Julius Stockhausen in Hamburg.

Varied strophic; A B A'. Except for the customary lengthening of the last phrase, each of the three stanzas comprises three four-measure vocal phrases and one of three measures, all united, despite separations and interludes, by the continuous flow of the accompaniment.

The poem is by Thibau[l]t IV, Count of Champagne, King of Navarre; with an ornate melody it appears as the opening selection in the anthology *Chansons choisies* (Paris, 1765); this version is reproduced by Friedländer (*Brahms's Lieder*, 20).

The text is a medieval troubadour song masquerading among folk songs, and Brahms eschews the direct strophic repetition found in the other songs of the set to compose a deeply felt love song. It is like a folk song only in its unpretentiousness, and suggests instead a dignified slow dance in triple time.

As the warmly elegant melody with its feminine cadences yearns "only to forget her," the piano doubles unobtrusively and depicts the poet's despairing lovesickness by means of a long line that descends, step by inevitable step, from the tonic in the alto in m. 1 to a dominant nearly two and a half octaves lower, in the bass in m. 7. A shorter descent in parallel thirds accompanies as the voice resumes its opening material to complete the strophe. But "the heart cannot forget," and loving memory returns in rapturous chromatic harmonies and a line which first rises in thirds, then in sixths, and finally erupts into a climactic shower of triads which "hover" in stately dance over a long dominant pedal. The sighing prolongation of "nie" in mm. 34–35 is particularly affecting.

The opening material returns but yields to an impassioned, sad ending, its reiterated flatted seventh and plagal cadence expressive of unfulfilled longing that is emphasized by the characteristic broadening in the last two bars.

Trennung, Op. 14/5 (Separation)

Folk Song

> Wach' auf, wach' auf, du junger Gesell',
> Du hast so lang geschlafen.
> Da draußen singen die Vögel hell,
> Der Fuhrmann lärmt auf der Straßen!
>
> Wach' auf, wach' auf, mit heller Stimm'
> Hub an der Wächter zu rufen,
> Wo zwei Herzlieben beisammen sind,
> Da müssen sie sein gar kluge.
>
> Der Knabe war verschlafen gar,
> Er schlief so lang', so süße,
> Die Jungfrau aber weise war,
> Weckt ihn durch ihre Küsse!
>
> Das Scheiden, Scheiden tuet not,
> Wie Tod ist es so harte,
> Der scheid't auch manches Mündlein rot
> Und manche Buhlen zarte.
>
> Der Knabe auf sein Rößlein sprang
> Und trabte schnell von dannen,
> Die Jungfrau sah ihm lange nach,
> Groß Leid tat sie umfangen!

"Awake, awake, you young lad, you have slept so long; outside, the birds are brightly singing, the carter clatters on the road!

"Awake, awake, in a clear voice the watchman has begun to call; when two sweethearts are together, it behooves them to be prudent."

The boy was really drowsy, he slept so long, so sweetly; but the girl was wise and aroused him with her kisses!

Parting, parting is needful; it's as cruel as death, which parts many a pair of red lips and many tender lovers.

The boy leapt onto his steed and departed at a swift trot; for a long time the girl gazed after him; deep sorrow enveloped her!

Composed in November 1858 in Detmold.

First performed on 6 March 1895 by Louise von Ehrenstein at a "popular" concert of the Männergesangverein in Vienna.

Varied strophic; stanzas 1–3 and 5 are set to the same music; stanza 4 differs, though it is related.

The text is found in the Kretzschmer-Zuccalmaglio *Deutsche Volkslieder* (Berlin, 1838–40) under the heading "Westphalia."

Like "Vor dem Fenster," Op. 14/1, "Trennung" is about the parting of lovers, but in contrast to the earlier song's chaste yearning at the window, the girl here awakens to find her lover still sleeping beside her as morning approaches. She rouses him with kisses and he rides swiftly away, leaving her reluctantly alone.

Brahms's setting, marked *Sehr schnell*, is light-hearted and rollicking, gently humorous rather than threatening. Except for the stepwise third phrase harmonized by a circle of fifths from the subdominant side, melody and accompaniment adhere to the bright principal triads of the key. The piano's sixteenth-note afterbeats lend a sense of breathless urgency and ensure a light approach if the tempo indication is to be observed literally.

The poem's fourth stanza interrupts the narrative to comment on the cruelty of separation, and Brahms accordingly departs from strict strophic design. A *piano* in the accompaniment replaces the *poco forte* of the other verses, added stepwise movement softens the vocal line, and the pianist's left hand is given a line made up of legato eighths. A tiny double descending chromatic scale illustrates "It's as cruel as death" in mm. 14–15, and the end of the verse turns thoughtfully to the major submediant.

The original music returns unchanged for the final stanza. The "deep sorrow" of the text is illustrated only by the piano's postlude, which slows and softens as its register falls like the pensively downcast eyes of the now forlorn maiden.

Gang zur Liebsten, Op. 14/6 (Visiting His Sweetheart)

Folk Song

Des Abends kann ich nicht schlafen geh'n,
Zu meiner Herzliebsten muß ich geh'n,
Zu meiner Herzliebsten muß ich geh'n,

Und sollt' ich an der Tür bleiben steh'n,
Ganz heimelig!

Wer ist denn da? Wer klopfet an,
Der mich so leis' aufwecken kann?
Das ist der Herzallerliebste dein,
Steh' auf, mein Schatz, und laß mich ein,
Ganz heimelig!

Wenn alle Sterne Schreiber gut,
Und alle Wolken Papier dazu,
So sollten sie schreiben der Lieben mein,
Sie brächten die Lieb in den Brief nicht ein,
Ganz heimelig!

Ach, hätt' ich Federn wie ein Hahn
Und könnt' ich schwimmen wie ein Schwan,
So wollt' ich schwimmen wohl über den Rhein,
Hin zu der Herzallerliebsten mein,
Ganz heimelig!

"In the evening I can't go to sleep; I must go to my loved one, I must go to my loved one, even if I stop short outside her door—quite secretly!"

"Who's there? Who's knocking that can awaken me so softly?" "It's your lover; wake up, darling, and let me in—quite secretly!"

"If all the stars were scribes and all the clouds were paper, and they wrote to my darling, they couldn't get all my love into the letter—quite secretly!"

"Oh, if I had feathers like a rooster and could swim like a swan, I'd swim across the Rhine to see my sweetheart—quite secretly!"

Composed in Detmold in December 1858.

The first performance is not documented.

Strophic; the four stanzas are all set to the same music, which comprises five two-measure phrases, plus an additional two-measure ending for the piano.

The poem is found in the second volume of the Kretzschmer-Zuccalmaglio collection *Deutsche Volkslieder* (Berlin, 1838–40) under the heading "From the Lower Rhine."

The setting is quietly expressive in intimate folk song style. The key is ambiguous. Phrase 1 hints at minor, but seems to establish the relative major; phrase 2 begins in major but veers back to a minor dominant of the original minor; phrase 3 is harmonized in major, while the nearly identical phrase 4 is harmonized in minor. When the raised leading tone is finally allowed to sound in the last phrase, it has acquired great expressive significance by its absence. This final vocal phrase is remarkable also in that the voice is for the first time allowed to soar, not only above the limited range of the rest of the song but also free of the doubling by the pianist's right hand. The strong first syllable of "heimelig" is made so emphatic that its last syllable seems unaccented despite its placement on a downbeat, an impression that is aided by its deceptive-cadence harmonization.

The piano concludes with codetta-like imitations of the final vocal phrase, first in the middle register, then (varied and extended) in the bass.

Ständchen, Op. 14/7 (Serenade)

Folk Song

Gut' Nacht, gut' Nacht, mein liebster Schatz,
Gut' Nacht, schlaf' wohl, mein Kind!
Daß dich die Engel hüten all',
Die in dem Himmel sind!
Gut' Nacht, gut' Nacht, mein lieber Schatz,
Schlaf' du, von nachten lind!

Schlaf' wohl, schlaf' wohl und träume von mir,
Träum' von mir heute Nacht!
Daß, wenn ich auch da schlafen tu',
Mein Herz um dich doch wacht;
Daß es in lauter Liebesglut
An dich der Zeit gedacht.

Es singt im Busch die Nachtigall
Im klaren Mondenschein,
Der Mond scheint in das Fenster dir,
Guckt in dein Kämmerlein;
Der Mond schaut dich im Schlummer da,
Doch ich muß zieh'n allein!

Good night, good night, my darling, good night, sleep well, my dear! May all the angels that are in Heaven protect you! Good night, good night, my darling, sleep peacefully through the night!

Sleep well, sleep well and dream of me, dream of me tonight! So that, when I'm asleep, too, my heart will still keep a vigil for you; so that, in a full blaze of love, it may think about you during that time.

The nightingale is singing in the bushes in the bright moonlight; the moon shines into your window, peeps into your bedroom; the moon sees you sleeping there, but I must depart alone!

Composed in September 1858 in Göttingen.

First performed by Ben Davies on 18 January 1889, the place undocumented.

Strophic.

The text is found in the second volume of the Kretzschmer-Zuccalmaglio *Deutsche Volkslieder* (Berlin, 1838–40) under the heading "From the Lower Rhine." Brahms made a few inconsequential alterations, particularly in stanza 1, apparently in order to bring the three stanzas into rhythmic correspondence.

Among serenades, this one is unusual in that the singer makes no request for his sweetheart to join him, but merely wishes that her sleep may be peaceful, with dreams only of him, so that he may continue his vigil even though he is separated from her.

The vocal melody is peculiarly uningratiating, but, combined with the gracefully strumming accompaniment and its colorful modulations, the setting overall is full of charm.

The repetitive rhythm is hypnotic. Because of its length, the song's success is particularly dependent on the choice of an appropriate tempo; a quality of unhurried gentleness should prevail.

Sehnsucht, Op. 14/8 (Longing)

Folk Song

> Mein Schatz ist nicht da,
> Ist weit über'm See,
> Und so oft ich dran denk',
> Tut mir's Herze so weh!
>
> Schön blau ist der See
> Und mein Herz tut mir weh,
> Und mein Herz wird nicht g'sund,
> Bis mein Schatz wiederkommt.

My lover isn't here, he's far over the sea, and every time I think of him my heart hurts so badly!

The sea is beautifully blue and my heart hurts, and my heart won't get well until my lover returns!

Composed in Detmold in November 1858.

The first performance was sung by Marie Wilt on 12 November 1870 at the Gesellschaft der Musikfreunde in Vienna.

· Through-composed; the setting of the second verse is repeated in slightly varied, somewhat more dramatic form.

The text is found under the heading "From Tyrol" in the second volume of the Kretzschmer-Zuccalmaglio *Deutsche Volkslieder* (Berlin, 1838–40), where the first verse reads:

> Mein Schatz ist nit da,
> Ist weit über dem See,
> Und so oft ich dran denk'
> Herzel tut mir weh!

The second verse uses "mei" rather than "mein" throughout.

The song is a touching lament for a long-absent lover. The melody acquires plaintiveness from its consistent avoidance of the raised leading tone
and from its preponderance of falling shapes.

By its ambivalence between tonic minor and relative major, the harmony
supports the lowered seventh, but it supplies the raised leading tone at
cadences. Though the piano is assigned minimal importance, it has two strikingly expressive moments—the long-held tonic triad which serves as introduction and the stressed second beat of the common-time third-to-last
measure, which is like a sobbing intake of breath.

Brahms made several alterations in his own copy of the first edition: in
mm. 12 and 14, he changed the first of the pair of eighth notes from A to G
(low key, G to F) so that the vocal melody duplicates the piano melody in a
different rhythm; similarly, in m. 22, he changed the first eighth note to A
(G); in m. 20, he revised the rhythm to conform with that in m. 22—quarter
note, quarter rest, two eighth notes. The Breitkopf & Härtel complete edition and the Dover reprint incorporate these emendations.

FIVE GEDICHTE, OP. 19

Fünf Gedichte für eine Singstimme mit Begleitung des Pianoforte componirt von Johannes Brahms (Five Lyrics for Solo Voice with Piano Accompaniment, Composed by Johannes Brahms), Op. 19. Published in March 1862 by N. Simrock in Berlin; publication number 6205.

Brahms's immersion in folk materials during much of the period 1856–58 resulted in the *Volks-Kinderlieder*, the posthumously published *Neue Volkslieder*, and the *Lieder und Romanzen*, Op. 14; the five songs of the present set represent to varying degrees the influence of folk song on Brahms's own musical thinking—only No. 5, "An eine Äolsharfe," seems relatively free of folk-inspired stylization.

Another influence at the time was his infatuation with Agathe von Siebold, whom Brahms met during the summer of 1858 while staying in Göttingen with his friends the Grimms. The dark-haired Agathe (who had, according to Joachim, a singing voice "like an Amati violin") was the attractive daughter of a university professor. Their friendship developed to the point of their secretly exchanging rings the following year, but when the time came for an irrevocable commitment, Brahms characteristically asked to be released from the engagement.

Der Kuß, Op. 19/1 (The Kiss)

Text by Ludwig Hölty (1748–1776)

> Unter Blüten des Mai's spielt' ich mit ihrer Hand,
> Kos'te liebend mit ihr, schaute mein schwebendes
> Bild im Auge des Mädchens,
> Raubt' ihr bebend den ersten Kuß.

> Zuckend fliegt nun der Kuß, wie ein versengend Feu'r
> Mir durch Mark und Gebein. Du, die Unsterblichkeit
> Durch die Lippen mir sprühte,
> Wehe, wehe mir Kühlung zu!

Beneath blossoms of May I toyed with her hand, caressed her lovingly, gazed at my floating image in the girl's eyes, tremblingly stole the first kiss from her.

That kiss now races palpitatingly through my inmost being like a searing fire. Now that you have shot flames of immortality through my lips, give me, give me cooling comfort!

Composed in Göttingen in September 1858.
There is no record of the first performance.
Through-composed.

The poem was written in 1776 and first published only after Hölty's death in a form shortened and altered by Johann Heinrich Voss, first in Voss's *Musenalmanach für das Jahr 1778*, then in the collected *Gedichte von Ludwig Heinrich Christoph Hölty* (1804). Hölty's original four-stanza version, which Brahms did not know, reads as follows:

> Ward Unsterblichkeit mir? Stieg ein Olympier
> Mit der Schale herab? Bebte sein goldner Kelch,
> Voll der Trauben des Himmels,
> Um die Lippe des Taumelnden?
>
> Wehe Kühlung mir zu, wann du mir wiederum
> Reichst den glühenden Kelch, daß mir die Seele nicht
> Ganz im Feuer zerfließe;
> Wehe, wehe mir Kühlung zu!
>
> Unter Blüten des Mais spielt ich mit ihrer Hand;
> Koste liebelnd mit ihr, schaute mein schwebendes
> Bild im Auge des Mädchens;
> Raubt ihr bebend den ersten Kuß!
>
> Ewig strahlt die Gestalt mir in der Seel' herauf;
> Ewig flieget der Kuß, wie ein versengend Feu'r,
> Mir durch Mark und Gebeine;
> Ewig zittert mein Herz nach ihr!

Had I become immortal? Did an Olympian ascend with the chalice? Did his golden goblet, full of the grape of heaven, tremble at the lip of the intoxicated?

Give me cooling comfort when you extend the glowing goblet to me anew, that my soul not completely melt in the fire; give me, give me cooling comfort!

Beneath blossoms of May I toyed with her hand, caressed her lovingly, gazed at my floating image in the girl's eyes, tremblingly stole the first kiss from her!

The scene is forever radiant in my soul; forever that kiss races, like a searing fire, through my entire being; my heart quivers forever at the thought of her! [My translation.]

The poem's meter, like that of the text of "Die Mainacht," Op. 43/2, Brahms's most famous Hölty setting (which see), is that of an asclepiadic ode. Though the $\frac{3}{8}$ meter of Brahms's setting does little to reveal the rhythm of the poem, the almost exclusive use of five- and three-measure phrases effectively portrays its sense of wonder.

As prelude, a gently undulating dominant-tonic alternation begins in the bass, the rhythm of which, ostinato-like, underlies the entire song. Each of the two opening five-measure phrases ends with a tentative turn to the subdominant; the piano doubles the melody in sixths or thirds in its warm middle register, evoking the couple's tranquil accord. The higher pitch of the second phrase suggests intensifying passion, which becomes overt in the third phrase with its expressive dissonances and chromatic alterations, its *crescendo*, and the growing independence of the piano. Quiet returns for the fourth phrase, which suggests the time-stopping miracle of the first kiss by the simple means of suspending the dominant over, and alternating it with, its own dominant. The piano again doubles and continues the pattern beyond the vocal line's end to round out the expected five measures.

The memory of that kiss erupts suddenly in three fervent three-measure phrases that modulate quickly to the supertonic, submediant, and mediant; the piano's ardent chain of thirds and octaves supports, connects, and finally goes its own way as the voice rises alone to the song's highest pitch in m. 29. A one-measure interlude reintroduces the dominant, and the music of the last half of the preceding stanza returns. This time, the accompaniment is further enriched by full-chord doublings and some additional chromaticism.

The repetition of "Kühlung zu" as codetta seems to express almost unbearable longing. The vocal line concludes by rising yearningly from third to fifth, the piano melody responds uncertainly from fifth to third, and the bass ostinato continues, as though forever.

Scheiden und Meiden, Op. 19/2 (Parting and Separation)

Text by Ludwig Uhland (1787–1862)

So soll ich dich nun meiden,
Du meines Lebens Lust!
Du küssest mich zum Scheiden,
Ich drücke dich an die Brust!

Ach, Liebchen, heißt das meiden
Wenn man sich herzt und küßt?
Ach, Liebchen, heißt das scheiden,
Wenn man sich fest umschließt?

So I am now to stay away from you, joy of my life! You kiss me as we part, I press you to my breast!

Oh, darling, is it separation when two people hug and kiss? Oh, darling, is it parting when two people are in close embrace?

Composed in Detmold in October 1858.

The first performance is undocumented.

Simple strophic.

The poem was written on 18 August 1811 and appears as the second in a group called "Wanderlieder" in Uhland's collected *Gedichte* (Stuttgart and Tübingen, 1815). There it begins "So soll ich nun dich meiden."

The text recalls folklore in its rhythms and motifs, and Brahms's straightforward strophic setting captures its suppressed passion perfectly. The mournful melody and sighing piano slurs unfold touchingly over an accompaniment of rising arpeggios, the emotional import revealed all the more eloquently through the restraint of its presentation.

Though "Scheiden und Meiden" is complete in itself and can be sung independently, it is actually a companion song to "In der Ferne," Op. 19/3, with which it shares material.

Of "Scheiden und Meiden," Clara Schumann wrote on 20 December 1858, "I could not help thinking it must be a folk song—I mean, a popular melody."

In der Ferne, Op. 19/3 (Far Away)

Text by Ludwig Uhland (1787–1862)

> Will ruhen unter den Bäumen hier,
> Die Vöglein hör' ich so gerne.
> Wie singet ihr so zum Herzen mir?
> Von unsrer Liebe was wisset ihr
> In dieser weiten Ferne?
>
> Will ruhen hier an des Baches Rand,
> Wo duftige Blümlein sprießen.
> Wer hat euch Blümlein hierher gesandt?
> Seid ihr ein herzliches Liebespfand
> Aus der Ferne von meiner Süßen?

I want to rest under the trees here, I so enjoy hearing the little birds. How is it that your song goes so directly to my heart? What do you know about our love in this far-off place?

I want to rest here on the edge of the brook, where fragrant flowers are sprouting. Who sent you flowers here? Are you a heartfelt love token from my darling far away?

Composed in Detmold in October 1858.

The first performance is undocumented.

Strophic, with some variation; it begins in minor before changing, in m. 13, to major for the remainder of the song. The second strophe has a different interlude and a new accompaniment figuration.

The text appears in Uhland's *Gedichte* (Stuttgart and Tübingen, 1815) immediately following that of the preceding song, though it was written five years earlier, on 2 June 1806.

Emphasizing the relatedness of their subject matter, the setting of "In der Ferne" begins as though it were another strophe of "Scheiden und Meiden," in the same tempo and with similar music. But some alteration is necessary because the poems differ metrically, and the song soon goes its own way.

The second phrase veers toward the relative major via its dominant. The interlude, extended, leads to the tonic major instead; its melodic thirds, which in the preceding song drooped downward, now reach upward. A new vocal melody, bearing some relation to the closing phrase of the earlier song, spirals quickly upward to the song's highest (and longest) pitch before its scalar descent. The repeated last line of the stanza is set to melodic materials which clearly recall the second phrase of "Scheiden und Meiden."

With only slight variation, the second strophe has the same vocal melody as the first, but all in major.

The accompaniment evokes the outdoor setting, suggesting the swaying of rustling trees in the first strophe's *legato* afterbeats, the babbling brook in the shimmering triplets of the second strophe, and the drone of folk instruments in the music that concludes each strophe.

Though self-contained, the song is in effect a gentler transformation of the preceding song's lyric simplicity. Here the undercurrent of sadness is lightened to a mere hint of wistfulness.

Der Schmied, Op. 19/4 (The Blacksmith)

Text by Ludwig Uhland (1787–1862)

Ich hör' meinen Schatz,
Den Hammer er schwinget,
Das rauschet, das klinget,
Das dringt in die Weite
Wie Glockengeläute
Durch Gassen und Platz.

Am schwarzen Kamin
Da sitzet mein Lieber,
Doch geh' ich vorüber,
Die Bälge dann sausen,
Die Flammen aufbrausen,
Und lodern um ihn.

I hear my lover, he swings the hammer; the noise and sound penetrate the distance like the ringing of bells through streets and squares.

By the blackened hearth my darling sits, but when I pass by, the bellows wheeze, the flames shoot up and flicker around him.

Composed in May 1859, probably in Hamburg.

The first performance was given on 15 December 1878 by Auguste Hohenschild at the Allgemeine Musik-Gesellschaft in Basel.

Strophic.

The poem, written on 21 July 1809, is found in Uhland's *Gedichte* (Stuttgart and Tübingen, 1815).

"Der Schmied" is one of Brahms's most often performed and best-loved songs. The swinging vocal line, which evokes so well both the girl's loving pride in her blacksmith lover and his wielding of the heavy hammer, is made up entirely of two-measure units except for the last, with its inspired tension-increasing extension to three bars. The characteristic avoidance of the tonic pitch in the arpeggiated figure of the opening several measures contributes to the aura of rustic naiveté.

In the accompaniment one can almost picture the sturdy figure of the ruddy-faced smithy as well as the strong blows of the hammer on the anvil and their lighter resultant rebounds.

Take the *allegro* marking literally with regard to spirit, but temper it toward *moderato* as an indication of speed—the song's character demands a certain weightiness, which is lost if the tempo is too quick.

An eine Äolsharfe, Op. 19/5 (To an Aeolian Harp)

Text by Eduard Mörike (1804–1875)

Angelehnt an die Efeuwand
Dieser alten Terrasse,
Du, einer luftgebor'nen Muse
Geheimnisvolles Saitenspiel,
Fang' an,
Fange wieder an
Deine melodische Klage!

Ihr kommet, Winde, fern herüber,
Ach, von des Knaben,
Der mir so lieb war,
Frisch grünendem Hügel.
Und Frühlingsblüten unterweges streifend,
Übersättigt mit Wohlgerüchen,
Wie süß bedrängt ihr dies Herz!
Und säuselt her in die Saiten,
Angezogen von wohllautender Wehmut,
Wachsend im Zug meiner Sehnsucht
Und hinsterbend wieder.

Aber auf einmal,
Wie der Wind heftiger herstößt,
Ein holder Schrei der Harfe

Wiederholt, mir zu süßem Erschrecken,
Meiner Seele plötzliche Regung;
Und hier—die volle Rose streut, geschüttelt,
All' ihre Blätter vor meine Füße!

Propped up against the ivy-clad wall of this old terrace, you, the mysterious lute of some air-born muse—begin, once more begin your melodious lament.

You come here, winds, from far off, ah, from the fresh green hill—home of the boy I loved so well. And brushing spring blossoms on your way, saturated with fragrances, how sweetly you oppress my heart! And you rustle this way, through the strings, attracted by euphonious melancholy, growing in the course of my longing and dying away again.

But all at once, as the wind blows this way more violently, a lovely cry of the harp repeats, to my pleasant alarm, my soul's sudden stirring, and here the full-blown rose, shaken, strews all its petals at my feet.

Composed in Göttingen in September 1858.

First performed by Minna Tiedemann in Strasbourg on 14 December 1881.

Through-composed.

The text first appeared in Mörike's *Gedichtsammlung* for 1838. This great and famous poem, prompted by the death of the poet's younger brother, represented an important advance toward the work of the Symbolists, whose intent was evocative rather than descriptive. An aeolian harp stands foremost among the poetic images, but its importance is secondary to other, subtler strands of association, such as death, nature, and rebirth.

Similarly forward-looking and suggestive, Brahms's setting is perhaps the crowning masterpiece of his songs to date. It is unlike any song written earlier by any composer, and it anticipates his more exploratory works of the decade to follow. It assigns a new spontaneity to the vocal line, which freely combines recitative with emotionally charged arioso. The atmospheric accompaniment, with its mysterious harmonies and its exquisite modulations and textures, helps to reveal psychological implication and binds the whole into a tone poem of haunting beauty.

The song begins with a quiet recitative in the minor mode; poignant appoggiaturas figure prominently in the vocal line, as indeed they do throughout the song, symbolizing the poet's grief. The appeal to the silent strings to begin their melodious lament is underlined by a gradual change to the major mode and by striking mediant (mm. 10–11) and submediant (mm. 21–22) harmonies. The piano has almost imperceptibly begun a faint chordal strumming in its upper register, the harmonies brightening inevitably as the major mode asserts itself, while the conflict of its quarter-note triplets with the even quarter-note pairs of the vocal line establishes the pervading metric ambivalence that is a prominent feature of the song.

The arioso proper begins with a harp-evocative combination in the piano of high-register chords and a rhythmic ostinato consisting of a rising quarter-note triplet and a falling quarter-note pair. The opening sentence already combines the principal themes of nature, death, and rebirth in the images of wind and the freshly greening grass on the dead boy's grave.

Brahms's setting abounds in symbolic brightenings after darkenings: the bass that gradually descends to the low dominant in m. 32 before ascending to the dominant an octave higher in m. 37; the bass F♭ (low key, C♭) in m. 31 contrasting with the treble F♮ (C♮) two measures later; the bright juxtaposition of D♮ (A♮) in mm. 35–36 with the prominent D♭ (A♭) preceding; and the falling fourth to the word "Knabe" in m. 32 of the vocal line, anticipating the pitch an octave higher to which "frisch" is set three measures later.

There is further exploitation of the rise and fall of pitch for expressive purposes. A falling melodic line depicts the grave (mm. 35–37). The stunningly lyrical image of the wind's becoming saturated with the fragrance of spring blossoms is embodied in a rising line (mm. 43–46), continued by the piano as the voice breaks off to murmur "wie süß," first in the enchanted key of the Neapolitan, then, as though returning to reality, a half step lower, in the tonic key. The setting of "bedrängt ihr dies Herz" is particularly arresting, with its minor inflection, its unexpectedly prolonged diminished-seventh harmony, and its descent concluding in another falling fourth, to the vocal line's lowest pitch. (See Platt, *Text-Music*, 114–122.)

The "euphonious melancholy" of the passage that follows is portrayed in a sensuous harmonic drifting, which luxuriates enharmonically in the major submediant from the minor mode and, later, the major mediant, harmonically relating "wohllautender Wehmut" here with the opening recitative's "geheimnisvolles Saitenspiel" and "melodische Klage." The growing intensity of longing is symbolized by long appoggiaturas in five successive measures, beginning at "Wehmut" in m. 61 and climaxing at "Sehnsucht" in m. 65; its waning is marked by a return to the dominant and the falling register of the piano melody.

All of the poem's elusive themes are united in its rich final image—a sudden gust of wind causes the harp to cry out, and emotion is reborn in the poet's soul as the full-blown rose is shattered. This shorter last stanza is set apart by an initial soft diminished-seventh chord in the piano and a brief vocal recitative, begun unaccompanied. The rose petals' falling is associated with gently increased rhythmic activity in the piano (though in a slower tempo), both in the right hand and in the left-hand ostinato, and with tender harmonies from the subdominant side of the key.

The preponderance of subdominant harmony in the closing measures can make the final cadence sound inconclusive; its finality can be enhanced by discreet emphasis on the dominant harmony in m. 96.

LIEDER AND GESÄNGE
TO TEXTS BY
PLATEN AND DAUMER,
OP. 32

Lieder u. Gesänge von Aug. v. Platen und G. F. Daumer in Musik ge-
setzt für eine Singstimme mit Begleitung des Pianoforte von Johannes
Brahms (Songs to Texts by Aug[ust] v[on] Platen and G[eorg] F[riedrich]
Daumer, Set to Music for Solo Voice with Piano Accompaniment by Johannes
Brahms), Op. 32. *Heft 1. Heft 2* (Volumes I and II). Published in January
1865 by M. Rieter-Biedermann, Leipzig and Winterthur; publication number
400ab.

Although this collection is not a cycle in the customary sense, the contents share a certain consistency of mood and style. Brahms's growing
mastery reveals itself in generally increased conciseness; greater emotional
intensity results from the paring away of excess. Piano and voice are ever
more tightly integrated, and the harmonic coloring and rhythmic suppleness
continue to grow in subtlety.

All of the songs were written in Baden-Baden in September 1864. Most of
the texts deal with various aspects of an emotional rift between lovers—
pain, frustration, depression, despair—though their ordering suggests that
the love, however beleaguered, may endure.

When offering these songs, together with the first six of the Magelone romances, to Breitkopf & Härtel, Brahms wrote on 5 October 1864:

> The first collection contains nine songs, but this will not create, I think, too
> big a volume. Should you wish to divide them, please leave the first four and
> the remaining five together. But, since they will also appear separately, I
> believe it would be better to keep them all together.

Breitkopf in fact refused the set because of the difficulty of the piano parts;
Rieter-Biedermann published it in two volumes, divided as Brahms had suggested.

"Wie rafft ich mich auf in der Nacht," Op. 32/1
(How I roused myself in the night)

Text by August von Platen (1796–1835)

Wie rafft ich mich auf in der Nacht, in der Nacht,
Und fühlte mich fürder gezogen,
Die Gassen verließ ich vom Wächter bewacht,
Durchwandelte sacht
In der Nacht, in der Nacht,
Das Tor mit dem gotischen Bogen.

Der Mühlbach rauschte durch felsigen Schacht,
Ich lehnte mich über die Brücke,
Tief unter mir nahm ich der Wogen in Acht,
Die wallten so sacht
In der Nacht, in der Nacht,
Doch wallte nicht eine zurücke.

Es drehte sich oben, unzählig entfacht
Melodischer Wandel der Sterne,
Mit ihnen der Mond in beruhigter Pracht,
Sie funkelten sacht
In der Nacht, in der Nacht,
Durch täuschend entlegene Ferne.

Ich blickte hinauf in der Nacht, in der Nacht,
Und blickte hinunter auf's Neue:
O wehe, wie hast du die Tage verbracht,
Nun stille du sacht
In der Nacht, in der Nacht,
Im pochenden Herzen die Reue!

How I roused myself in the night, in the night, and felt myself drawn onward. I left the lanes guarded by the watchman, and softly in the night, in the night, walked through the gate with the Gothic arch.

The millstream murmured through the rocky gorge; I leaned over the bridge; far below me I observed the waves that were rolling so softly in the night, in the night, but not one of them rolled back.

Above, kindled in infinite number, the stars were turning melodiously in their courses, and with them the moon in pacified splendor; they twinkled softly in the night, in the night, through deceptively remote distances.

I looked up in the night, in the night, and looked down again: alas, how you have spent your days; now softly in the night, in the night, silence the regret in your pounding heart!

Composed in Baden-Baden in September 1864.
The first performance is not documented.

Through-composed; stanzas 2 and 3 have the same melody and harmony but different accompaniment textures; and stanza 4, though sharing its melodic rhythm and phrase structure with stanza 1, differs substantially from it.

The poem, written on 14 December 1820, may be found among the *Romanzen und Jugendlieder* of Platen's *Gesammelte Werke* (Stuttgart, 1870).

Brahms's setting is taut and somber, and it perfectly captures the poet's endless, tortured night-wandering. The entire song seems to grow out of the sinister, striding bass octaves of the opening, which initiate the distinctive tonal ambivalence between F minor and Db major (Eb minor and Cb major in the low key). The half-measure rhythmic pulsation that the octaves establish continues relentlessly, binding into a powerful whole all of the subtleties of composition that seem to catch and illuminate every nuance of Platen's lines.

The words "in der Nacht" occur twelve times in the poem; their reiteration contributes to a sense of feverish agitation, as does the frequently conflicting rhythm between voice and piano. Brahms chooses also to repeat other key phrases in each verse, to dramatic effect.

At the beginning, the poet rouses himself to symbolically intensifying rhythmic activity, thickening texture, and rising pitch. The melodic shape to which the first line of text is set becomes a unifying factor, reappearing in the piano's bass to announce stanza 2 and in its high register to begin stanza 3, and again in the vocal line, a fifth higher, in stanza 4. The second line's compulsion onward is realized metaphorically in the piano's now constant dotted rhythms and the pitch's inching upward before its quicker descent. In the remainder of the stanza, the poet's despairing unrest is evoked by the piano's many triplets against the voice's duplets and by the stark, brooding octaves of mm. 11–13. A degree of anguish overflows into the interlude, with its rise and fall of tenor melody and its alternation of tonic and Neapolitan harmonies.

Continuous triplets portray the murmuring millstream of stanza 2 and, leading the ear into the piano's upper register, the twinkling stars of stanza 3; the opening motive's return is a reminder of the poet's unceasing quest. The new vocal line begins more quietly, but increasing agitation leads to an impassioned climax at each stanza's last line and its repetition.

The last stanza resembles the first, but with its rhythmic complexity, texture, and vocal register intensified, like the poet's mounting distress. The song culminates in the repeated desolate outcry "O wehe, wie hast du die Tage verbracht," which Brahms clothes in tonally unstable chromatic harmony over a bass that rises by half steps to a throbbing pedal on Db (B♮). The harmony settles tentatively in the tragic key of the minor Neapolitan, anticipating the Neapolitan's important role in both the final vocal cadence and the postlude. The latter augments and intensifies the music of the earlier interlude, transferring its melody, now sonorously doubled, into the treble register.

"Nicht mehr zu dir zu gehen," Op. 32/2
(Not to go to you any more)

Translated from the Moldavian by
Georg Friedrich Daumer (1800–1875)

Nicht mehr zu dir zu gehen
Beschloß ich und beschwor ich,
Und gehe jeden Abend,
Denn jede Kraft und jeden Halt verlor ich.

Ich möchte nicht mehr leben,
Möcht' Augenblicks verderben,
Und möchte doch auch leben
Für dich, mit dir, und nimmer, nimmer sterben.

Ach, rede, sprich ein Wort nur,
Ein einziges, ein klares;
Gib Leben oder Tod mir,
Nur dein Gefühl enthülle mir, dein wahres!

I decided not to go to you any more, and I swore it, and I go every evening, because I have lost all my strength and all my steadfastness.

I would like to stop living, I would like to perish instantly, and yet I would like to live for you, with you, and never, never die.

Oh, speak, say just a word, a single word, a clear word; give me life or death, but please reveal your feelings to me, your true feelings!

Composed in Baden-Baden in September 1864.

First performed, together with Op. 32/3, by Rosa Girzick in Vienna on 11 March 1872.

Varied strophic; A B A.

The poem introduces the section "From Moldavia" in Daumer's *Hafis* (Hamburg, 1846), a collection of translations of Persian poems with additional poetry from various regions and peoples.

This song is Brahms's first setting of a text from the works of Daumer, which were to provide him with nearly sixty—more than those of any other poet. It is a remarkable song, which breaks new dramatic ground and is striking in its originality, economy, and stark power.

The suffering poet cannot continue with or without his hurtful lover. He vows to stop seeing her but is compelled to return to her each evening; he invokes death but yearns to share life with her; finally, he begs only for some revelation of her feelings toward him. Brahms enhances the poem's tone of desperation with a vocal line that imitates the fragmented speech of one overpowered by emotion. Hovering between song and recitative, it gasps out its text in painful bits and pieces. It is full of anguished appoggiaturas, as is the similarly breathless piano melody that bridges its rests. The sighing three-note motive with which the right hand enters in m. 2 is assigned particular prominence; it appears often in the accompaniment and occasionally in the vocal line.

From its bleak opening octaves, the principal strophe struggles to gather strength until the third line of text, from which it trails off again helplessly. The ensuing interlude broods on the opening phrase. The melody of the middle strophe begins with an approximate inversion of this motive and proceeds with more coherence than before, but its rhythmic conflict with the piano's triplets and not quite synchronous melodic doubling lends a feeling of anxiety and restlessness. The interlude in mm. 20–22 ponders and extends the closing motive, to which the words "nimmer sterben" were set, gradually preparing the despairing return of the earlier material, *pianissimo*.

The piano's postlude, like the earlier interlude, dwells on the upward-striving principal motive, but suddenly, overlapping statements of the short sighing idea climb quickly to a *forte* and the song's dramatic climax. The right hand's augmentation in full chords recalls the "sterben" motive, which gradually recedes, while the melody of the left-hand octaves continues its long cheerless descent into the extreme low register of the keyboard.

"Ich schleich' umher betrübt und stumm," Op. 32/3
(I drag myself along, worried and mute)

Text by August von Platen (1796–1835)

> Ich schleich' umher
> Betrübt und stumm,
> Du fragst, o frage
> Mich nicht, warum?
> Das Herz erschüttert
> So manche Pein!
> Und könnt' ich je
> Zu düster sein?

> Der Baum verdorrt,
> Der Duft vergeht,
> Die Blätter liegen
> So gelb im Beet,
> Es stürmt ein Schauer
> Mit Macht herein,
> Und könnt' ich je
> Zu düster sein?

I drag myself along, worried and mute; you ask—oh, don't ask me why! My heart is shaken by so many sorrows! Is it possible for me to be too gloomy?

The tree withers, the fragrance evaporates, the leaves lie so yellow in the flowerbed; a shower pours in violently. Is it possible for me to be too gloomy?

Composed in Baden-Baden in September 1864.

First performed, together with the preceding song, by Rosa Girzick in Vienna on 11 March 1872.

Strophic.

The poem was written on 30 June 1820; Platen later included it in his *Romanzen und Jugendlieder*, where it may be found in the *Gesammelte Werke* (Stuttgart, 1870).

The poet describes the disabling melancholy that can sometimes, for no discernible reason, overwhelm one's heart and mind. Brahms's deeply felt setting derives much of its conviction from a melodic line which is a series of metaphors: the nearly static small intervals of the opening phrase are a literal interpretation of the text; the chromatic descent on "o frage mich nicht" underlines the anguish it expresses, and the upward turn to m. 8 realizes the question "warum?"; growing passion motivates the rising figures of the third phrase, which culminates affectingly in the chromatic darkening of the word "Pein"; the gradual descent of the last two phrases and the foreshortening of the last convey a sense of powerlessness; the partial repetition of the closing line (which recurs like a refrain) seems to imply a degree of acceptance by means of its final downturn.

The absence of a piano introduction increases the song's immediacy. The right hand of the accompaniment loosely doubles the vocal line, but it independently echoes the end of the second phrase and starts the last phrase. The downward-creeping eighth notes of the left hand reinforce the sense of the opening text, but a change to wide-spaced triplets in m. 10 marks the intensifying emotion. Toward the end, the left hand's rhythmic activity decreases as its pitch descends: in the first ending, it resumes even eighth notes to effect the return for the second strophe; in the second ending, eighths and quarters broaden to the final chord, suggesting a deepening of the gloom to which the text refers.

"Der Strom, der neben mir verrauschte," Op. 32/4
(The stream that rushed past me)

Text by August von Platen (1796–1835)

Der Strom, der neben mir verrauschte, wo ist er nun?
Der Vogel, dessen Lied ich lauschte, wo ist er nun?
Wo ist die Rose, die die Freundin am Herzen trug,
Und jener Kuß, der mich berauschte, wo ist er nun?

Und jener Mensch, der ich gewesen und den ich längst
Mit einem andern Ich vertauschte, wo ist er nun?

The stream that rushed past me, where is it now? The bird to whose song I
listened, where is it now?
Where is the rose my loved one wore on her heart, and that kiss which intoxicated me, where is it now?
And that man I used to be, for whom I have long since substituted a different self, where is he now?

Composed in Baden-Baden in September 1864.
The first performance is not documented.
Through-composed; an apparent return is short-lived.

Dating from January 1821, the text may be found in the *Ghazal* section of
Platen's *Gesammelte Werke* (Stuttgart, 1870). A ghasel is a poetic form of
Arabic origin, in which a rhyme appears in lines 1 and 2, and in every second
line thereafter. The rhyming words (here, "verrauschte," "lauschte," "berauschte," and "vertauschte") may appear anywhere in the line, but must be
followed in each case by the same words (here, "wo ist er nun?").

With each repetition the anxious question acquires increased urgency, a
characteristic that Brahms adopts as the prominent feature of his setting.
"Wo ist er nun?" is always set to a rising melodic sweep, a whole or half step
higher with each new appearance. At each occurrence, the piano sustains
the emotional tension with successive imitations of the rising motive, while
a $\frac{3}{2}$ bar is inserted after the question, punctuating the structure without
interrupting the momentum. At the end of the song, the voice also enters
into the imitative interplay with a heartbroken repetition of the question in
an augmented variant. The piano takes up this version too, and its statement
over its own inversion in the bass provides the material for the postlude,
before its murmuring *diminuendo* and *ritardando*.

The setting of text seems, for Brahms, unusually direct—the urgent an-
ticipatory "wo ist"s in lines 4 and 6 are the only other repetitions—and the
enjambment between lines 5 and 6 is masterfully handled, driving the song
headlong toward its climactic conclusion.

As Brahms's direction suggests, the song's success depends less on speed
than on a quality of agitation, to which its rhythmic structure contributes
greatly; large patterns of fluctuating rhythmic energy accumulate and recede
like ocean waves. From the opening dominant trumpet call, the bass entrance propels the voice into the first of a pair of rhythmic designs that begin
with dotted quarters and eighths but intensify through successions of eighth
notes to the sustained last note. The piano, meanwhile, has triplets on alternate beats, then every beat; it finally adds a cross-rhythm of even eighths
before calming to stable undulating triplets only, poised to repeat the
pattern. The middle section offers tonal contrast but exhibits a similar
process of rhythmic tightening. The final section, *Più agitato*, begins like

the first but is driven to an even higher level of excitement by the paired triplet eighths in m. 23 and the offbeat *sforzandi* in mm. 23–24.

The song is intensely dramatic, enhanced by an elaborate, restless accompaniment. Even the unpredictable harmonic progressions contribute to the sense of unease; the sound of the minor subdominant in a temporarily major context in mm. 15 and 22–25 is particularly anxiety-evocative.

"Wehe, so willst du mich wieder," Op. 32/5
(Alas, you want to hold me fast again)

Text by August von Platen (1796–1835)

> Wehe, so willst du mich wieder,
> Hemmende Fessel, umfangen?
> Auf, und hinaus in die Luft!
> Ströme der Seele Verlangen,
> Ström' es in brausende Lieder,
> Saugend ätherischen Duft!
>
> Strebe dem Wind nur entgegen
> Daß er die Wange dir kühle,
> Grüße den Himmel mit Lust!
> Werden sich bange Gefühle
> Im Unermeßlichen regen?
> Atme den Feind aus der Brust!

Alas, you want to hold me fast again, you impeding fetters? Up and out into the air! Let my soul's desiring flow forth, let it flow forth in thundering songs, inhaling ethereal fragrance!

Struggle against the wind so it cools your face, greet the sky with joy! Will feelings of fright stir in the immeasurable expanse? Exhale the enemy from your breast!

Composed in Baden-Baden in September 1864.

First performed by Therese Treml on 21 December 1867 at a concert of the Vienna Singakademie.

Strophic.

The poem was written on 14 July 1820 and is found among *Romanzen und Jugendlieder* in Platen's *Gesammelte Werke* (Stuttgart, 1870).

The poet implores the forces of nature to help him break his emotional shackles and surmount his grief. The verses express exhilaration, defiance, and a degree of rapture, all of which Brahms's setting captures admirably.

Marked *Allegro*, it is the only fast song of the set. The two-measure introduction establishes the restless rhythms over incessant triplets, the unstable harmonies, and the mounting excitement that are characteristic of this song. Its melody gives rise to the opening vocal line, bass imitations of which bridge the first two vocal phrases and underlie the interlude in mm. 6–8, which recalls the introduction's tortured harmonies. The third and fourth phrases reflect the increasing fervor of their text in a seeming contraction from $\frac{9}{8}$ to $\frac{6}{8}$ meter, as the melody rises sequentially through the tonic major to an ardent cadence on the dominant, marked by duplet eighths as the feeling of $\frac{9}{8}$ is restored.

The piano's bass line joins in the duplet eighths and retains them through much of the song's remainder as an agitation-increasing cross-rhythm. In the last half of the song, the harmony digresses boldly into what seems to the eye a sea of accidentals, but which the ear perceives as related keys—both minor and major forms of the submediant from the major, and the dominant's dominant—all spelled (in the original key of B minor) enharmonically in flats. The voice, meanwhile, inches its freely sequential way upward toward another soaring cadence, a more-extended, elaborate variant of its earlier counterpart, recalling its duplet rhythms and duplicating its important pitches.

The postlude begins, *forte*, as though to introduce another strophe but is led instead through a long process of dying away, involving (in addition to the marked *diminuendo* and *ritenuto*) a two-measure hemiola figure, the repetition of a normal three-beat measure, and a change from triplets to duplets in the next-to-last measure.

"Du sprichst, daß ich mich täuschte," Op. 32/6
(You say I was in error)

Text by August von Platen (1796–1835)

Du sprichst, daß ich mich täuschte,
Beschworst es hoch und hehr,
Ich weiß ja doch, du liebtest,
Allein du liebst nicht mehr!

Dein schönes Auge brannte,
Die Küsse brannten sehr,
Du liebtest mich, bekenn' es,
Allein du liebst nicht mehr!

Ich zähle nicht auf neue,
Getreue Wiederkehr:
Gesteh' nur, daß du liebtest,
Und liebe mich nicht mehr!

You say I was in error; you swore it solemnly; I know that you were in love, but you are no longer in love!

Your beautiful eyes burned, your kisses burned intensely; you loved me, confess it, but you are no longer in love!

I do not count on a new, faithful return: just admit that you were in love, and after that, love me no longer!

Composed in Baden-Baden in September 1864.

The first performance was given in Leipzig in early February 1874 by Robert Wiedemann with pianist Theodor Loetsch.

The form is a hybrid and resists labeling; except for the characteristically expanded final phrase, the three stanzas are set to vocal melodies that share the same rhythm and phrase structure, though the intervals and harmonies differ with the implications of the text.

The poem dates from 24 August 1819 and may be found in the poet's *Gesammelte Werke* (Stuttgart, 1870).

The four-measure introduction is among Brahms's most poignant. Its expressive descending melody, harmonized in thirds and sixths over a grieving offbeat bass ostinato, effectively depicts the rejected lover's heartache. The rhythmic figure in the alto voice in mm. 3 and 4 (even eighths with triplets on the third beats) assumes an important role as the song progresses.

The vocal line begins somberly in the tonic minor, its first two phrases developing the piano's opening melody, while the ostinato rhythm continues, darkly harmonized, over a bass that descends chromatically from tonic to dominant. The growing vehemence of the stanza's last half is reflected dynamically, but also in the tightening rhythm and rising pitch: in the left hand, long chains of continuous eighths now place a bass note on every afterbeat; the voice's simpler scalewise-descending melody begins higher with each entrance, as do the piano's imitations of it at contracted metric intervals. Both voice and piano attain their highest pitches in m. 12, where the piano's melodic eighth notes give the effect of additional entrances in diminution. As the vocal line broadens to half notes in m. 13 to prepare the cadence, a rising triplet arpeggio in the left hand thrusts the accompaniment into an aching dominant minor ninth, which quickly dissolves into a return of the music of the introduction.

In the second stanza, the poet's remembrance of his former lover elicits a more benign turn, which is reflected in the music's modulation to the relative major; and, to temper the sorrowing ostinato rhythm, the longing eighths-plus-triplet figure from the end of the interlude is retained. But in the last half, intensifying emotion brings exactly the same melody as before to the vocal line; the piano attempts to continue in the major, even while repeating its earlier rhythmic quickening, but is soon dissuaded, and the stanza culminates in the same lacerating minor ninth as did the first.

The beginning of the third stanza is generally quieter; half-note harmonies from the subdominant side of the key support the voice over a tonic pedal, while the longing motive works its way gradually downward from the alto in mm. 29–30 to the bass-register tonic in m. 34. Despite the many pedal points, the prevailing subdominant harmonies, and a final turn to the major mode, the closing line's change to the imperative tense elicits a surprisingly vehement *crescendo*, as the longing motive is reiterated more and more accusingly in the piano's tenor register, and the ostinato rhythm's throbbing resumes in the bass.

"Bitteres zu sagen denkst du," Op. 32/7
(You think you are saying bitter things)

Translated by Georg Friedrich Daumer (1800–1875)
from Mohammad Shams od-Dīn Hafiz (Persian; c.1326–c.1390)

> Bitteres zu sagen denkst du;
> Aber nun und nimmer kränkst du,
> Ob du noch so böse bist.
> Deine herben Redetaten
> Scheitern an korall'ner Klippe,
> Werden all' zu reinen Gnaden,
> Denn sie müssen, um zu schaden,
> Schiffen über eine Lippe,
> Die die Süße selber ist.

You think you are saying bitter things, but you can never give pain, as angry as you are. Your attempts at harsh speeches are wrecked on a coral reef; they all become pure acts of grace, because in order to do harm, they must sail past lips that are sweetness itself.

Composed in Baden-Baden in September 1864.

The first performance was given in Vienna by the contralto Hermine Spies on 22 March 1887.

The form lies somewhere between strophic and through-composed, with characteristics of both; like the preceding song, it is a formal experiment that resembles strophic design but departs from exact repetition as the text demands.

The poem appears in Daumer's *Hafis. Eine Sammlung persischer Gedichte nebst poetischen Zugaben aus verschiedenen Völkern und Ländern* (Hamburg, 1846).

Brahms's setting is a love song of tender beauty, characterized by gracefully arching melodic phrases and a gently flowing accompaniment whose pervading eighth notes are often replaced by rests on strong beats.

The piano anticipates the opening vocal melody with an introduction and, with few exceptions, doubles the voice throughout the song. The references to pain and anger in lines 2 and 3 prompt some chromatic inflections, borrowed from the minor mode. The piano's sequential repetition in m. 6 is its first brief attempt at independence from the voice. Lines 4 and 5 are set to a two-measure rising sequence, which, together with accumulating chromaticism, momentarily obscures the tonality. To end the section, line 5 is repeated in free augmentation on a third level in the sequence, slightly altered intervallically in order to confirm the original key. The piano doubles the vocal line's pitches but largely ignores its augmentation, retaining the prevailing rhythmic patterns instead; thus it completes its statement a bar earlier than the voice and is assigned a bar of new material leading into a new, increasingly tranquil two-bar interlude.

The voice reenters as though to repeat the earlier music, but many differences soon become evident, some of them resulting from the fact that only four of the poem's nine lines remain to be set. Too, since the text here contrasts "sweetness" with the earlier "bitterness," the chromaticism derives more often from the subdominant side of the key than from the minor mode. The first digression occurs in m. 23, as the voice joins the piano in its sequence. In m. 25, rather than cadencing as in m. 8, the melody embarks upon another rising sequence, its one-measure contour derived from the two-measure shape of mm. 10–11 and 12–13 by the simple means of omitting the high note. In m. 27, the piano, shadowed by the voice, condenses into one measure its cadential melody from mm. 16–17. As before, the section ends with a repetition of the closing line in longer note values, this time to a free augmentation of the melody of the piano interlude in mm. 18–19. Again it leads to a recurrence of the opening melody, this time for the piano's postlude, which quotes two measures exactly, then restates its second measure in augmentation as it broadens to a close.

The first section of the song, with its five lines of text, occupies seventeen measures, while the remaining four lines fill only fourteen; Brahms's addition of the rather long postlude brings the two unequal sections into perfect balance.

"So steh'n wir, ich und meine Weide," Op. 32/8
(These are the terms my darling and I are on)

Translated by Georg Friedrich Daumer (1800–1875)
from Mohammad Shams od-Dīn Hafiz (Persian; c. 1326–c.1390)

So steh'n wir, ich und meine Weide,
So leider mit einander Beide.

Nie kann ich ihr was tun zu Liebe,
Nie kann sie mir was tun zu Leide.

Sie kränket es, wenn ich die Stirn ihr
Mit einem Diadem bekleide;

Ich danke selbst, wie für ein Lächeln
Der Huld, für ihre Zornbescheide.

Unfortunately, these are the terms my darling and I are on. I can never do
anything she likes, she can never do anything to give me pain.
It irritates her when I adorn her brow with a diadem; I am thankful even for
her wrathful answers, as if they were gracious smiles.

Composed in Baden-Baden in September 1864.

First performed publicly by Fanny Freistädt on 2 January 1893 for the
Tonkünstlerverein in Vienna.

Through-composed with a partial return, for which purpose Brahms restated the first two lines of the poem.

The text is found in Daumer's *Hafis* (Hamburg, 1846). In the last two
verses, the poet underlined the initial words "Sie" and "Ich."

Brahms's setting largely ignores the poem's irony in favor of ardent plaintiveness. The use throughout of quarter notes in simultaneous duplets and
triplets creates a sense of urgency, which is enhanced by the free-ranging
modulations and the melody's many expressive dissonances.

At the beginning, the thin texture and the accompaniment figure's silent
strong beats suggest a certain tentativeness, which yields to growing assurance as the song unfolds. The falling-third motive in half notes that sets the
opening words "So steh'n wir" is immediately imitated twice in the bass, beginning a measure later, obscuring the already ambiguous tonality and
symbolizing the absence of common ground between the two lovers; it reappears later in the song and underlies the whole of the closing section.

The central portion of the song (mm. 8–32) comprises a series of dissimilar phrases that are related by the scalewise ascending fourth with which
they all begin. Each imaginatively portrays some central word or concept of
its text. A touching 4-3 suspension in the major mode illustrates "Liebe" in
m. 10 while a turn to the minor and double appoggiaturas mark the prolonged contrasting "Leide" in mm. 13–15; the piano echoes at the fourth
below and shifts the key. A hard-won high note on the last syllable of
"Diadem" in m. 21 crowns the next phrase; the piano again echoes, at the
third below. The words "für ihre Zornbescheide" in mm. 28–30 elicit minor
inflections amid the prevailing major (and bass reminiscences of the "gulf
between us" motive); the interlude elaborates and extends the same melodic
contour before trailing off into the tonal and rhythmic indecision that is to
characterize the remainder of the song.

The return of the opening text calls forth the opening measures of music,
but any semblance of tonal stability is soon dissolved. The three-note motive
occurs in the bass at four different pitch levels, none of them that of the
voice's statement. Finally it settles into an uneasy alternation of C minor with
Ab major (B minor and G major in the low key) under a melody that is also
tonally vague. The piano postlude repeats the same melody over the same
bass and harmony but prolongs the penultimate note an additional measure,

so that fewer vestiges of the minor harmony linger in the ear as the music settles in the major. There is no real cadence, only the cessation of motion and the dying away of sonority. What course of action remains, the music seems to ask, when differences seem irreconcilable?

"Wie bist du, meine Königin," Op. 32/9
(My queen, how rapturous you are)

Translated by Georg Friedrich Daumer (1800–1875)
from Mohammad Shams od-Dīn Hafiz (Persian; c.1326–c.1390)

Wie bist du, meine Königin,
    Durch sanfte Güte wonnewoll!
Du lächle nur—Lenzdüfte weh'n
    Durch mein Gemüte wonnevoll!

Frisch aufgeblühter Rosen Glanz,
    Vergleich' ich ihn dem deinigen?
Ach, über alles was da blüht
    Ist deine Blüte, wonnevoll!

Durch tote Wüsten wandle hin—
    Und grüne Schatten breiten sich,
Ob fürchterliche Schwüle dort
    Ohn' Ende brüte, wonnevoll.

Laß mich vergeh'n in deinem Arm!
    Es ist in ihm ja selbst der Tod,
Ob auch die herbste Todesqual
    Die Brust durchwüte, wonnevoll!

My queen, how rapturous you are when you are gentle and kind! Just smile, and spring fragrances waft through my spirit rapturously!

The brightness of newly opened roses—shall I compare it to your brightness? Ah, your bloom is beyond all else that blooms, rapturous!

Walk through lifeless deserts, and green shadows will spread—even if fearful sultriness reigns there without end—rapturously.

Let me perish in your arms! There death itself, even if the sharpest mortal pains rage through my breast, is rapturous!

Composed in Baden-Baden in September 1864.

The first public performance was given by Louise Dustmann on 22 December 1869 in Vienna, at a Clara Schumann concert.

Varied strophic; stanzas 1, 2, and (with slight deviation) 4 are set to the same music, stanza 3 to a development thereof.

The poem is from Daumer's *Hafis* (Hamburg, 1846). Each stanza ends with the word "wonnevoll"; through Brahms's repetitions, it assumes the significance of a refrain and becomes one of the setting's most striking features.

Deservedly, this beautiful work has won a place among the best-loved of all the songs of Brahms—indeed, of the entire art-song repertoire. At the same time, many have noted the flaws in the opening pair of phrases in accentuation and syntax. It seems plausible that this inverted arch of melody may have been inspired by the beginning of stanza 4, which it fits to perfection, rather than by the first lines of the poem, where it rests less easily; singers must simply rejoice in so elegant a line and muster their skill and taste to ameliorate any awkwardness.

The song's distinctive character is evident from the first few notes of the introduction, as two tender melodies unfold together over dreamworld-evocative rising arpeggios. Throughout the principal strophe, the piano's melodies and countermelodies double, complement, and bridge the elements of the vocal line. In the last phrase, the piano even becomes the leader, the voice the imitator. The absence of rigidity in the phrase structure contributes to the pervasive aura of caressing gentleness; the five-measure introduction yields to four vocal phrases, two of three measures and two of four, the last of which is begun by the piano and overlapped by the return of the introductory material as interlude.

Little chromaticism appears in strophes 1 and 2; a couple of secondary dominants only strengthen the effect of diatonicism. The third strophe, however, with its reference to "lifeless deserts," begins in the tonic minor and soon winds itself into the key of the Neapolitan, notated enharmonically in sharps. (In the low key edition the key signature is changed to sharps for the entire strophe.) "Fearful sultriness" is depicted in a jarringly dissonant figure in the painful key of the Neapolitan minor, "reigns without end" is portrayed symbolically by the reiteration of that figure over a span of six measures, its ferocity gradually abating as the pitch drops in stepwise stages. The voice now takes the lead in the altered "wonnevoll" refrain, surrounded by the piano's converging two-hand arpeggios. A sense of awe, which is part of the connotation of "wonnevoll" in German, is movingly conveyed by the near-magical restoration of the tonic major (by way of the submediant, made German sixth).

The serene earlier music returns, like a smile after tears, for the fourth stanza. In mm. 73–74, the flatted second, sixth, and seventh steps of the key underscore the darker tone implied in "mortal pains," tinting with the color of the Neapolitan what previously was subdominant and permitting a little sob of minor inflection at "durchwüte." With newly acquired confidence, the voice again initiates the "wonnevoll" refrain, leaving the piano first to imitate it, then to recall from strophes 1 and 2 its usual amiable cadential countermelody, and finally to bring the song to a richly sonorous conclusion.

ROMANZEN FROM TIECK'S "MAGELONE," OP. 33

Julius Stockhausen gewidmet. Romanzen aus L. Tieck's Magelone für eine Singstimme mit Pianoforte componirt von Johannes Brahms (Dedicated to Julius Stockhausen. Romances from L[udwig] Tieck's "Magelone" Composed for Solo Voice with Piano by Johannes Brahms), Op. 33. Published in five parts of three songs each, parts 1 and 2 in September 1865 and the remainder in December 1869, by J. Rieter-Biedermann, Leipzig and Winterthur; publication numbers 401a–e.

Brahms had met the *Meistersänger* Julius Stockhausen (1826–1906) in 1856 at the Rhine Music Festival in Düsseldorf. A close friendship developed between them, and they later often concertized together. Stockhausen became one of the most highly regarded interpreters of Brahms's songs, many of which were written for him.

Not all of the dates and places of composition of the "Magelone" Romances are known. Numbers 1–4 were written in July 1861, presumably in Hamburg; numbers 5, 6, 13, and probably 12 were composed in May 1862, probably also in Hamburg; numbers 14 and 15 date from May 1869 in Karlsruhe or Baden-Baden; the remainder, numbers 7–11, are presumed to have been composed at some time during the period between May 1862 and May 1869.

The *Wundersame Liebesgeschichte der schönen Magelone und des Grafen Peter aus der Provence* (The Wondrous Love Story of the Beautiful Magelone and Count Peter of Provence) appeared first in the second volume of *Volksmärchen von Peter Leberecht* (a pseudonym for Ludwig Tieck [1773–1853]) in 1797, then in the collection *Phantasus* (Berlin, 1812). Brahms used Tieck's second, revised version.

It is a short novel whose romantic prose is interspersed with poems—lyric reflections on the situation, scene, or mood. The twelfth-century Provençal folk tale that it retells has been absorbed into the literature of many European countries through translation and adaptation. Brahms certainly was familiar with it; during his summer holidays in Winsen, he and his childhood friend Lieschen Giesemann had read and loved the story. It is likely that he came across Tieck's reworking of it in the Schumanns' library.

The work contains seventeen poems (in addition to an introductory, non-dramatic one), of which Brahms set fifteen. (The title "Romanzen" was invented by Brahms, not Tieck.) The opus stands apart from his other songs of the time, and from the process of increasing refinement and concentration that they display. Most of the "Magelone" songs are lengthy, sectional, and a bit operatic; the cycle as a whole seems, for Brahms, extravagant and unwieldy. On the other hand, it is a work which its composer obviously regarded as important, since he devoted so much time to its completion. It is richly inventive, full of youthful exuberance appropriate to its subject matter, and maintains a distinct identity.

Except for the downward-arpeggiated tonic triad of the vocal line's opening and concluding phrases, which figure appears only occasionally and almost coincidentally elsewhere in the work, there is no apparent attempt at thematic unity. The work does acquire a certain coherence, however, from the relatedness of its keys (not scrupulously observed in the low-key edition), and from its consistently mythic aura.

When the entire set is performed nowadays, all fifteen songs are customarily sung by one male voice, usually a baritone, but actually they are associated with four different characters: a minstrel sings the first; number 11 belongs to Magelone; number 13, to the sultan's daughter, Sulima; and the others are assigned to Count Peter, though the final song is supposedly a unison duet for the reunited Peter and Magelone. Actually, it is not at all certain that Brahms even regarded the fifteen songs as constituting a cycle in the usual sense. He was, after all, content at first with the publication of only six, and in a March 1870 letter to the music critic Adolf Schübring, he wrote:

> In the case of the Magelone Romances one does not need many at one go, and should not pay any attention to narrative at all. It was only a touch of German thoroughness which led me to compose them through to the last number.

Yet it is evident throughout that Brahms had in mind the narrative in which the texts occur and that he expected his audience to know the plot too, since the poems are not fully comprehensible out of context:

At the ancestral castle in Provence, young Peter is distracted and unhappy, but distinguishes himself at a great tournament given by his father. Among the admiring spectators is an itinerant minstrel, who persuades Peter to travel in order to broaden his mind. (No. 1, "Keinen hat es noch gereut.")

The minstrel's counsel strikes a responsive chord with Count Peter, and he goes immediately to his parents to seek their consent to set out in search of adventure. His father grants his blessing, and his mother gives him three gold rings. In high spirits, Peter sets out on his noble steed, boldly singing an old song that is running through his mind. (No. 2, "Traun! Bogen und Pfeil sind gut für den Feind.")

After several days' journey, he arrives in Naples, having heard on the way much talk of the king's beautiful daughter, Magelone, and a tournament to be given shortly, which Peter decides to enter. He has two silver keys placed on his helmet in honor of his patron, St. Peter, and when the day arrives, wins not only the tournament but also the interest of the fair Magelone. He admires her from afar and, smitten with love for her, returns to his quarters and sings a love song. (No. 3, "Sind es Schmerzen, sind es Freuden.")

Magelone wants to know more about the mysterious Peter. She enlists the aid of her duenna, Gertrude, who finds him at prayer in the cathedral the next day. When she makes her errand known, he admits his love for Magelone but withholds his name. He entrusts Gertrude with two gifts for her mistress—one of the gold rings and a small parchment on which he has inscribed a love poem. (No. 4, "Liebe kam aus fernen Landen.")

Magelone hangs Peter's ring on a strand of pearls around her neck and dreams that he sends her another ring. When Peter meets the duenna again in church the next day, she tells him that he has indeed found favor with the princess. Joyfully he sends a second ring and another parchment with a confession of his love. (No. 5, "So willst du des Armen dich gnädig erbarmen.")

At their third encounter, the duenna makes Peter swear his honorable intent as a condition of her arranging a rendezvous for him with Magelone for the following evening. Filled with delight at the prospect, Peter returns home, where he takes up his lute and sings to calm himself. (No. 6, "Wie soll ich die Freude, die Wonne denn tragen.")

When at last they meet, Peter gives his beloved the third ring and kisses her hand. Deeply moved, she puts a heavy gold chain around his neck. They swear eternal love and exchange kisses. Back in his room, Peter, overcome with happiness, again takes up the lute in ardent song. (No. 7, "War es dir, dem diese Lippen bebten.")

The king wants his daughter to marry Sir Henry of Carpone, so Magelone suggests to Peter that they secretly leave Naples together. Overjoyed at this further sign of her affection, Peter bids farewell to his room, to the town, and to his faithful lute. (No. 8, "Wie müssen uns trennen, geliebtes Saitenspiel.")

The next day, the lovers travel for miles through forests along the coast. When Magelone becomes tired, Peter lays her down in the shade of a leafy tree and sings a tender lullaby. (No. 9, "Ruhe, Süßliebchen.")

As she sleeps, Peter becomes curious about a little red purse attached to her necklace. He removes it and discovers that it contains the three rings he has given her. As he is lost in loving contemplation, a raven suddenly sweeps down and carries it away. He pursues the bird to the seashore, but it drops the bag on a rock far out in the water and flies away. At last Peter finds a boat, but he is swept past the rock and, despairing, far out to sea. (No. 10, "Verzweiflung: So tönet denn, schäumende Wellen.")

Magelone awakens and, after wandering many days through the forest in search of Peter, is taken in by an old shepherd and his wife. She tells them nothing of her story but willingly undertakes whatever services she can perform. When the old people go out, she minds the cottage, and she often sits alone at the door with her spinning wheel, singing. (No. 11, "Wie schnell verschwindet so Licht als Glanz.")

Peter, meanwhile, has been picked up by Moorish pirates and taken to the sultan's court as a slave. Assigned the duty of caring for the sultan's gardens, he often wanders lonely among the flowers, thinking of his beloved Magelone. (No. 12, "Muß es eine Trennung geben.")

But the sultan has a beautiful daughter, Sulima. She falls in love with Peter, who has come to believe that Magelone is dead, and arranges to flee with him. The signal is to be a song that she often sings and of which Peter is fond. But Peter has a dream of Magelone and realizes that he can belong only to her. He steps into a little boat, and as he takes the oars and bravely rows out to sea, he hears Sulima's song from the garden. (No. 13, "Sulima: Geliebter, wo zaudert dein irrender Fuß.")

As the sound of the song dies away in the distance, Peter regains courage and sings of his relief at being free and of his hope of reunion with his beloved Magelone. (No. 14, "Wie froh und frisch mein Sinn sich hebt.")

Peter's parents, having received no word from their son, fear that they will never see him again. But as a large fish is being prepared for a feast, the three gold rings are found in its stomach, and this is taken as a sign that Peter will indeed return home.

Soon, in fact, Peter is rescued by a Christian ship bound for France. After much wandering and many more adventures, he at last finds his beloved in the shepherd's cottage. They embrace, weeping, rejoicing in their happiness. Eventually, they return to Peter's home in Provence, where they are married amid great joy—even the king of Naples is well pleased.

On the spot where they had been reunited, Peter builds a magnificent summer palace and leaves it in the care of the shepherd, who has been handsomely rewarded. In front, the young couple plant a tree as a symbol of their undying love, which they return to celebrate in song each spring. (No. 15, "Treue Liebe dauert lange.")

"Keinen hat es noch gereut," Op. 33/1
(No one has ever regretted)

> Keinen hat es noch gereut,
> Der das Roß bestiegen,
> Um in frischer Jugendzeit
> Durch die Welt zu fliegen.
>
> Berge und Auen,
> Einsamer Wald,
> Mädchen und Frauen
> Prächtig im Kleide,

Golden Geschmeide,
Alles erfreut ihn mit schöner Gestalt.

Wunderlich fliehen
Gestalten dahin,
Schwärmerisch glühen
Wünsche in jugendlich trunkenem Sinn.

Ruhm streut ihm Rosen
Schnell in die Bahn.
Lieben und Kosen,
Lorbeer und Rosen
Führen ihn höher und höher hinan.

Rund um ihn Freuden,
Feinde beneiden,
Erliegend, den Held.—
Dann wählt er bescheiden
Das Fräulein, das ihm nur vor allen gefällt.

Und Berge und Felder
Und einsame Wälder
Mißt er zurück.
Die Eltern in Tränen,
Ach, alle ihr Sehnen—
Sie alle vereinigt das lieblichste Glück.

Sind Jahre verschwunden,
Erzählt er dem Sohn
In traulichen Stunden,
Und zeigt seine Wunden,
Der Tapferkeit Lohn.
So bleibt das Alter selbst noch jung,
Ein Lichtstrahl in der Dämmerung.

No one has ever regretted mounting his steed to dash through the world in his lively youthful days.

Mountains and meadows, lonely forest, maidens and ladies splendid in dress, golden jewelry—everything delights him with its beautiful form.

Forms flee miraculously by, desires glow dreamily in his dazzled young mind.

Fame swiftly strews roses on his path. Love and caresses, laurel and roses lead him higher and higher upward.

Round about him, joys; succumbing, his enemies envy the hero; then modestly he chooses the young woman who alone pleases him above all others.

And he wends his way back over mountains and fields and through lonely forest. His parents in tears, ah, all their longing—they are all united in charming happiness.

After years have slipped by, he relates his adventures to his son in confidential moments, and shows him his wounds, the reward of bravery.

Thus even his old age remains young, a beam of light in the dusk.

Composed in July 1861, probably in Hamburg.

First performed from manuscript by Julius Stockhausen and Brahms on 4 April 1862 at a concert of the Hamburg Philharmonic.

The form is a large rondo-like design, with a long introduction (mm. 1–40) and a postlude (mm. 242–257).

	A	B	A	C	D	A'	A''
mm.	41–59	60–81	82–100	101–119	120–151	152–189	190–241

In the 1821 and 1841 collections of his poetry, Tieck gathered all but the second of the Magelone poems under the collective title *Des Jünglings Liebe*. In these later editions, this first poem is entitled "Ermunterung" (Encouragement).

The song begins with a flourish of horns, suggesting youth, chivalry, and the open air, as well as establishing the contrary motion that is a feature of this opening section. The piano's upward sweep is answered by a downward tonic arpeggio in the voice—a "heroic" motive that recurs occasionally as the cycle proceeds. After two recitative-like vocal phrases, the piano in m. 14 introduces the galloping rhythm that is to underlie much of the song. When the voice reenters in m. 18, this rhythm is transferred to the left hand, and the left-hand contrary-motion melodies from the interlude reappear in the voice and the piano treble. A turn to the minor mode and recurring diminished-seventh harmonies suggest a momentary doubt about the unknown world that awaits, but the galloping rhythm proves irresistible. A catalog of enticing sights and incidents ensues.

The music that functions as a rondo theme (mm. 41–55) is constructed mainly from rising sequences. A melodic figure introduced in m. 43, with a characteristic falling fourth, plays an important unifying role; it might be termed the "adventure" motive. It dominates the piano interlude (mm. 56–59), and hints of it permeate the accompaniment of the next section. The hushed, sustained vocal line, whose gradual stepwise descent balances the earlier ascending sequences, combines with the active accompaniment to portray the dreaming youth's dazzlement by the flurry of passing images as he gallops on in imagination.

The music of mm. 82–100 exactly repeats that of mm. 41–59. After the interlude, the accompaniment continues in the same style in the key of the dominant, but there is a new vocal line. The reference to envious enemies is accompanied by a modulation to the relative minor; the idea of choosing the desired young woman elicits a shift to the major mode, together with warmer harmonies, richer textures, and gentler rhythms; the text's repetition brings a return to the tonic (and the song's highest pitch for the voice at the second syllable of "Fräulein").

The "adventure" motive and galloping rhythm return for the piano interlude in mm. 147–152, but yield to a simple flowing accompaniment figure. Each of the poem's last two stanzas is set to music that begins by recalling the melody of the rondo theme but proceeds with variation and development. In each case, the second vocal phrase abandons the former sequential construction, though the bass line's motivic repetition fulfills a similar function. Broader variants of the falling-fourth motive are prominent throughout, treated in sequence or in imitation, the fourth as a leap or scalar. "Einsame Wälder" in mm. 157–160 is marked by a chromatic darkening; in the phrases that follow, the parents' tears and longing are evoked by rising sequences in which the falling fourth is often diminished and supported by augmented harmonies. The interlude briefly continues the effect of rising sequence before subsiding for the closing stanza.

The poignant thought of sharing these adventures with a son prompts expressive dissonances in mm. 199–205. The word "Tapferkeit" (bravery) in mm. 207–208 is reverentially harmonized with the major submediant from the minor and is set to the "heroic" motive in the vocal line, supported by its inversion in the bass. The tender sequential imitation of mm. 169–177 is recalled in mm. 211–221 with the roles of the piano and voice reversed. As the song nears its end, reflection on the affecting image of a beam of light in the dusk is accommodated by decreasing rhythmic motion, the repetition of text to greatly extended vocal phrases, and mystical harmonies, including the Neapolitan and its dominant.

The galloping rhythm returns for the long postlude; it gradually recedes into the distance under remembrances of the "adventure" motive and the inverted "heroic" motto.

"Traun! Bogen und Pfeil sind gut für den Feind," Op. 33/2 (Surely! Bow and arrow are useful against the enemy)

> Traun! Bogen und Pfeil
> Sind gut für den Feind,
> Hülflos alleweil
> Der Elende weint;
> Dem Edlen blüht Heil,
> Wo Sonne nur scheint,
> Die Felsen sind steil,
> Doch Glück ist sein Freund.

Surely! Bow and arrow are useful against the enemy; the weak-natured man weeps all the time in his helplessness.

Health and happiness bloom for the noble man wherever the sun shines; the cliffs are steep but good fortune befriends him.

Composed in July 1861, presumably in Hamburg.

First performed by Julius Stockhausen on 6 June 1865 during the Rhine Music Festival in Cologne.

Rondo; a refrain with two similar, but different, contrasting sections.

$$\begin{array}{ccccc} \text{A} & \text{B} & \text{A} & \text{B'} & \text{A'} \\ \end{array}$$

mm.   1–15   16–27   28–43   44–55   56–72

The text appears in the 1797 *Wundersame Liebesgeschichte* . . . and the
1812 revision, *Phantasus*. Of *Magelone*'s seventeen dramatically integrated
poems, only this one is omitted from Tieck's later individually titled compilation, *Des Jünglings Liebe*.

The absence of an introduction symbolizes Count Peter's eagerness to set
out in search of adventure. The refrain comprises three four-measure
phrases; the first two are vigorous and straightforward; the third, which repeats the second line of text, introduces appoggiaturas and afterbeats in
acknowledgment of its less bellicose subject.

The Dorian raised sixth and lowered seventh lend an archaic aura to the
first phrase. The second phrase is parallel in construction but gains brightness from its higher range and its modulation to the relative major. The
section ends somewhat expectantly in the dominant, but at the end of the
song the voice soars into its higher register to lead the way confidently into
the tonic. (Intelligible accentuation of "hülflos" will require some help from
the singer.) In each case, the piano confirms the key as it develops a motive
suggestive of weeping.

The two contrasting sections share the same text and a structure of two
similar repeated two-measure phrases plus a three-measure phrase. Appropriate to the text's images of nobility and nature, the music of both sections
exploits the first song's "heroic" motto and the sound of horn fifths. The
earlier section begins in the relative major, moves sequentially to the Neapolitan, and thence to the dominant; the latter starts in the tonic major,
moves to the subtonic (the piano maintains the sequential relationship
though the voice does not), and to the dominant, postponed by an arresting
appoggiatura borrowed from the returning tonic minor.

In the refrain's final appearance, the entire accompaniment takes on the
rhythm usually assigned only to the third phrase, which should result in increased excitement; prudent pianists will guard against clattering. The
concluding harmony's raised third is another archaism.

"Sind es Schmerzen, sind es Freuden," Op. 33/3
(Are these pains, are these joys)

> Sind es Schmerzen, sind es Freuden,
> Die durch meinen Busen ziehn?
> Alle alten Wünsche scheiden,
> Tausend neue Blumen blühn.
>
> Durch die Dämmerung der Tränen
> Seh' ich ferne Sonnen stehn—

Welches Schmachten! welches Sehnen!
Wag' ich's? soll ich näher gehn?

Ach, und fällt die Träne nieder,
Ist es dunkel um mich her;
Dennoch kömmt kein Wunsch mir wieder,
Zukunft ist von Hoffnung leer.

So schlage denn, strebendes Herz,
So fließet denn, Tränen, herab.
Ach, Lust ist nur tieferer Schmerz,
Leben ist dunkles Grab.
Ohne Verschulden
Soll ich erdulden?
Wie ist's, daß mir im Traum
Alle Gedanken
Auf und nieder schwanken!
Ich kenne mich noch kaum.

O, hört mich, ihr gütigen Sterne,
O, höre mich, grünende Flur,
Du, Liebe, den heiligen Schwur:
Bleib' ich ihr ferne,
Sterb' ich gerne.
Ach, nur im Licht von ihrem Blick
Wohnt Leben und Hoffnung und Glück!

Are these pains, are these joys that are shooting through my heart? All the old desires depart, a thousand new flowers bloom.

Through the twilight of my tears I see distant suns stand; what a yearning! what a longing! Do I dare? Shall I go closer?

Ah, and when the teardrop falls, it is dark all around me; and yet no desire comes back to me, the future is devoid of hope.

So beat, then, my ambitious heart; so flow down then, my tears. Ah, pleasure is only a deeper pain, life is a dark grave.

Shall I endure this through no fault of my own? How is it that in my dreams my thoughts waver in every direction? I scarcely recognize myself.

Oh, hear me, you kindly stars, oh, hear me, green meadow; you, O Love, hear my sacred oath; if I remain far from her, I'll gladly die. Ah! only in the light of her eyes dwell life and hope and happiness!

Composed in July 1861, presumably in Hamburg.
First performed by Josef Hauser on 2 November 1864 in Karlsruhe.
A large bipartite form with introduction and postlude:

		A			B					
Intro.	a	b	b'	c	c'	d	c''	c'''	Post
mm. 1–9 ‖: 10–19 :‖ 20–32	33–44	45–56	67–70	71–85	86–96	97–108	109–115

In later editions of his poetry, Tieck collected the *Magelone* poems, individually titled, as *Des Jünglings Liebe*; there, this text is called "Zweifel" (Doubt). It deals with the beginnings of love, from the early dazed confusion of joy with pain to the succeeding rapturous necessity of being near the beloved one.

The setting begins with a long introductory serenade, its melody tenderly doubled in thirds or sixths and accompanied by lutelike strummings. A preponderance of dominant-seventh harmonies combines with the avoidance of resolution to create an atmosphere of yearning. The entrance of the voice duplicates the questioning twice-stated two-measure melody of the introduction; what sounds at first like sequential repetition becomes a balancing longer phrase, extended to five measures by prolongation of key words. The harmonic irresolution intensifies as dominant seventh follows secondary dominant seventh—even the tonic, when it appears in root position in mm. 14–15, has temporarily become a dominant.

The poem's third stanza brings resolution at last, but in the tonic minor, as Peter laments the seeming hopelessness of his situation in a new melody that sobs and sighs. Reminiscences of the opening melody lead through melting minor-subdominant and Neapolitan harmonies to the cadence, still in the tonic minor. The fourth stanza is set to a slightly varied repetition of the same music, with the piano part even more affectingly elaborated in the last phrase.

Suddenly the tempo quickens, as Peter is filled with knightly resolve. The declamation becomes quasi-operatic, and horn fifths appear with their hint of the "heroic" motto, but the tonic-avoiding harmony reminds us that his longing remains unfulfilled. The text is repeated to a variant of the same music, the half-cadence on the dominant being replaced by a long-awaited full close in the tonic.

The common-time section that follows has been the subject of considerable textual confusion. Originally the vocal line began on beat 4 and rose stepwise in imitation of the bass. However, Brahms penciled another beginning into his copy of the first edition—a descending dominant-seventh arpeggio beginning on beat 2—and on 6 February 1894 requested that his publisher replace the original version with this revision. Max Friedländer's edition for C. F. Peters prints the original, with the revision in small type as a variant; Mandyczewski, assuming it to be Brahms's final word on the matter, adopted the revision in his edition for Breitkopf & Härtel (reprinted by Dover), relegating the original version to his editorial comment. But in a subsequent letter, dated 9 April 1895, to Edmund Astor, head of the Rieter-Biedermann publishing firm, Brahms asked that the original version be restored, referring to his revision as "eine große Dummheit." Evidently it is the scalewise-ascending version that is in fact the composer's last word.

Rising lines and sequences with agitated afterbeats evoke Peter's mounting passion and commitment, culminating in his vows of love in mm. 82–85, delivered *ad libitum* over solemn white-note piano chords.

A variant of the entire earlier $\frac{6}{8}$ *Vivace* section sets the poem's closing couplet and its repetition. The spirited postlude concludes the song with satisfying finality.

"Liebe kam aus fernen Landen," Op. 33/4
(Love came from distant lands)

Liebe kam aus fernen Landen
Und kein Wesen folgte ihr,
Und die Göttin winkte mir,
Schlang mich ein mit süßen Banden.

Da begann ich Schmerz zu fühlen,
Tränen dämmerten den Blick:
Ach! was ist der Liebe Glück,
Klagt' ich, wozu dieses Spielen?

Keinen hab' ich weit gefunden,
Sagte lieblich die Gestalt,
Fühle du nun die Gewalt,
Die die Herzen sonst gebunden.

Alle meine Wünsche flogen
In der Lüfte blauen Raum,
Ruhm schien mir ein Morgentraum,
Nur ein Klang der Meereswogen.

Ach! wer löst nun meine Ketten?
Denn gefesselt ist der Arm,
Mich umfleugt der Sorgen Schwarm;
Keiner, keiner will mich retten?

Darf ich in den Spiegel schauen,
Den die Hoffnung vor mir hält?
Ach, wie trügend ist die Welt!
Nein, ich kann ihr nicht vertrauen.

O, und dennoch laß nicht wanken,
Was dir nur noch Stärke gibt,
Wenn die Einz'ge dich nicht liebt,
Bleibt nur bitt'rer Tod dem Kranken.

Love came from distant lands and no being followed her; and the goddess beckoned me, encircled me with delightful bonds.

Then I began to feel pain; tears veiled my sight. "Alas, what is love's happiness?" I lamented, "to what purpose is this game?"

"I have found no one far and wide," the figure said sweetly; "now you must feel the power that used to bind people's hearts."

All my desires flew into the blue space of the sky; fame seemed like an idle dream to me, merely a roar of the ocean waves.

> Alas! who will now unloose my chains? For my arm is fettered; a swarm of
> cares flies about me; will no one, no one save me?
>   May I look into the mirror that hope holds up to me? Ah, how deceptive the
> world is! No, I cannot trust it.
>   Oh, but in spite of all, do not allow your only source of strength to falter; if
> the woman of your choice doesn't love you, only bitter death is left for the sick
> man.

Composed in July 1861, presumably in Hamburg.

First performed on 7 December 1867 in the Leipzig Gewandhaussaal by Julius Stockhausen and Clara Schumann.

A truncated tripartite form:

A			B			A'	
a	b	a'	c	d	c'	a'' + postlude	
	mm. 1–37			38–71		72–86	

In *Des Jünglings Liebe*, this poem is entitled "Hoffnung" (Hope).

The opening music, which recurs as a refrain, is ingratiatingly unassuming, filled with warm, tender harmonies. Eighth-note afterbeats and a caressing little motive in paired eighth notes are pervasive. The piano's tenor register doubles the voice at the outset and leads a point of imitation in m. 4. The afterbeats imply counterpoint. Rhythmically, and because of their chromaticism, mm. 7 and 8 stand apart from their context; they depict, with seemingly equal appropriateness, "Banden" here and in mm. 31–32, and "bitt'rer Tod" in mm. 78–79.

The piano interlude, mm. 11–12, uses the caressing eighth-note motive both to balance the voice's odd two-measure phrase that precedes it and to predict the shape of the melody that is to follow.

Consideration of "Schmerz" and "Tränen" prompts a turn to the relative minor for stanza 2. The replacement of afterbeat chords by bare octaves at "klagt' ich" in m. 19 is a particularly effective stroke; it also serves to justify the single-line sound of the interlude in mm. 23–24, which, like its earlier counterpart, both completes its segment and prepares the next.

Stanza 3 repeats the opening melody exactly, with the same harmonies; only the textures of the piano part are different, with less emphasis than before on the afterbeats and more on the higher register.

The piano interlude is extended to three measures to accommodate a modulation to the mediant major, D♭ to F (C to E in the low key), for the highly contrasting music that follows. The new section is marked by increased, and increasing, animation. A new accompaniment figure in triplets is made up of the descending arpeggios that Brahms so often associated with loneliness or separation. Frequent changes of harmony undermine the tonality. The melody, related to the refrain by its many falling fourths, is at first shared by voice and piano, but the piano gains independence and importance until it finally concludes alone, with an echo of the vocal line's cadence.

But with the shift to the minor mode in m. 48, the voice assumes primary responsibility for a new melody, related to the preceding one by its opening rhythm. The piano is assigned an accompaniment pattern of striking originality, which both lightly doubles the vocal line and contributes to the mounting agitation; an ascending half-step figure sounds in the rhythm of normal eighth to quarter as the low voice of the right-hand chords, then is echoed immediately and dissonantly in triplet eighths by the left hand, each appearance preceded by a gasp of rest. At the words "mich umfleugt der Sorgen Schwarm" in mm. 51–53, the restless harmonies settle briefly in A (A♭) major—a further major-mediant relationship—before wending their way gradually back to the tonic of this large secondary section.

Stanza 6 of the poem is set to a somewhat varied version of the music for stanza 4. The piano masks the join by retaining the rhythmic figure of stanza 5 until the middle of m. 60, where it yields to the triplet arpeggios from before.

The transition to the refrain's final appearance reverses the rhythmic process as caressing eighths replace triplets, and the minor mode leads to the dominant of the home key. The refrain's vocal line is again repeated exactly, as the accompaniment explores fresh new figurations. The piano's conclusion, now in triplet guise, is extended to become a gradually declining postlude.

"So willst du des Armen dich gnädig erbarmen?" Op. 33/5
(And so you are willing to show gracious mercy to
the unfortunate man?)

So willst du des Armen
Dich gnädig erbarmen?
    So ist es kein Traum?
Wie rieseln die Quellen,
Wie tönen die Wellen,
    Wie rauschet der Baum!

Tief lag ich in bangen
Gemäuern gefangen,
    Nun grüßt mich das Licht;
Wie spielen die Strahlen!
Sie blenden und malen
    Mein schüchtern Gesicht.

Und soll ich es glauben?
Wird keiner mir rauben
    Den köstlichen Wahn?
Doch Träume entschweben,
Nur lieben heißt leben:
    Willkommene Bahn!

> Wie frei und wie heiter!
> Nicht eile nun weiter,
>> Den Pilgerstab fort!
> Du hast überwunden,
> Du hast ihn gefunden,
>> Den seligsten Ort!

And so you are willing to show gracious mercy to the unfortunate man? And so it isn't a dream? How the fountains purl, how the waves murmur, how the trees rustle!

I lay a prisoner deep in frightful castle walls; now the light greets me; how the beams play! They dazzle and illumine my timid face.

And shall I believe it? Will no one rob me of this precious delusion? But dreams fade away, only loving is living: a welcome path!

How free and how cheerful! Don't hasten any farther, away with your pilgrim's staff! You have overcome, you have found it, the most blessed spot!

Composed in May 1862, presumably in Hamburg.

First performed on 7 March 1868 in Berlin by Julius Stockhausen and Brahms.

A hybrid form; bipartite, but tripartite in effect because of its components' recurrence in reverse order:

	A	B	B'	A'
mm.	1–21	22–44	45–68	69–89

As one of the group assembled under the collective title *Des Jünglings Liebe* in the later editions of Tieck's poetry, this poem is called "Glück" (Happiness). Brahms added the initial word "So"; the resulting upbeat enhances the song's lilting joyousness.

The piano introduces the principal melodic motive, a descending chord outline in eighth notes, over a quarter-note bass in contrary motion. The voice begins by continuing the descending-chord pattern, while the piano continues its bass in contrary motion and adds energizing triplets above. Instigated by the piano bass's lengthened statement of the eighth-note motive, a cadence on the mediant arrives at "So ist es kein Traum?" Step by step, evoking happily growing acceptance of the reality of good fortune, imitative interplay with the piano lifts the voice from the submediant back to the tonic key to conclude the section.

The piano interlude overlaps the vocal cadence; it repeats the music of the introduction plus the first two measures of what was the opening vocal phrase.

The melody of the succeeding section also alludes to the descending-arpeggio motive, but the piano no longer shares in the melodic interest. Many unisons, modulations, and stepwise transpositions of whole or partial phrases make the tonality highly unstable, symbolizing the delusional irresolution suggested by the text. At "nun grüßt mich das Licht" in mm. 27–30 and at the analogous "den köstlichen Wahn" in mm. 50–53, the music hangs suspended on an ambiguous subtonic. In the former instance, chromatic drifting soon resumes; but in the latter, the text is repeated to a dominant-seventh inflection, and suddenly, eight measures earlier than expected, the tonic key, the piano's left-hand octaves with right-hand triplets, and the joyous exuberance of the opening reappear—a musical metaphor for the dawning of reality. The climactic highest pitch of the vocal line arrives in the cadential repetition of "willkommene Bahn!" The same piano interlude as before again overlaps the vocal cadence.

The music of the first stanza returns for the fourth with only insignificant rhythmic adjustments. The postlude extends the song's cheerful high spirits.

"Wie soll ich die Freude," Op. 33/6
(How am I then to bear the joy)

Wie soll ich die Freude,
Die Wonne denn tragen?
Daß unter dem Schlagen
Des Herzens die Seele nicht scheide?

Und wenn nun die Stunden
Der Liebe verschwunden,
Wozu das Gelüste,
In trauriger Wüste
Noch weiter ein lustleeres Leben zu Ziehn,
Wenn nirgend dem Ufer mehr Blumen erblühn?

Wie geht mit bleibehang'nen Füßen
Die Zeit bedächtig Schritt vor Schritt!
Und wenn ich werde scheiden müssen,
Wie federleicht fliegt dann ihr Tritt!

Schlage, sehnsüchtige Gewalt,
In tiefer, treuer Brust!
Wie Lautenton vorüber hallt,
Entflieht des Lebens schönste Lust.
        Ach, wie bald
Bin ich der Wonne mir kaum noch bewußt.

Rausche, rausche weiter fort,
Tiefer Strom der Zeit,
Wandelst bald aus Morgen Heut,
Gehst von Ort zu Ort;
Hast du mich bisher getragen,

Lustig bald, dann still,
Will es nun auch weiter wagen,
Wie es werden will.

Darf mich doch nicht elend achten,
Da die Einz'ge winkt,
Liebe läßt mich nicht verschmachten,
Bis dies Leben sinkt!
Nein, der Strom wird immer breiter,
Himmel bleibt mir immer heiter,
Fröhlichen Ruderschlags fahr' ich hinab,
Bring' Liebe und Leben zugleich an das Grab.

How am I then to bear the joy, the rapture, and keep my soul from departing as my heart pounds?

And now, if the hours of love vanish, to what purpose is the desire to drag on a pleasureless life in a melancholy desert, if flowers blossom nowhere along the shore?

How time passes with lead-weighted feet circumspectly step by step! And when I shall have to depart, how its foot will fly with feathery lightness!

Beat, force of my longing, deep in my faithful heart! Just as the note of a lute dies away, life's most beautiful pleasure flies off.

Ah, how soon I will scarcely be conscious of the bliss.

Rush, rush on, deep current of time, you soon change tomorrow to today; you go from place to place. If you have borne me up to now, sometimes merrily, sometimes quietly, I'll have the courage to continue—however it may turn out.

Nevertheless, I shouldn't consider myself unfortunate, for the woman of my choice is beckoning to me; love won't let me perish of longing until my life comes to an end!

No, the stream becomes broader and broader, Heaven remains always cheerful to me; with a happy stroke of the oar I continue downstream, bringing life together with love, until the grave.

Composed in May 1862, presumably in Hamburg.

First performed on 18 January 1877 at the Gewandhaussaal in Leipzig by George Henschel and Brahms.

Through-composed:

A			B		C	D	
a	a'	b	c	c'	develops a	d	d'
mm. 1–10	11–22	23–43	35–65	66–97	98–108	109–142	143–187

In *Des Jünglings Liebe*, the poem is called "Erwartung" (Anticipation); in the poet's version, the last word of verse 2 is "entblühn."

The lengthy text is set to a sonatina-like succession of connected contrasting movements: the opening *Allegro* comprises stanzas 1–3; the more introspective stanzas 4 and 5 become an expressive slow movement in the key of the submediant; the first half of stanza 6 is the basis of a modulating transition; the last four lines (with extensive repetition) generate a rapturous finale, which rounds out the form satisfyingly by introducing, near the end, a variant of the first movement's theme.

The piano introduction establishes the sequential construction and the melodic duplets against accompanying triplets that are characteristic of the opening section. Its scalar ascents to upward-resolving dissonances in mm. 1 and 2 are mirrored by the voice's scalar descents to downward-resolving dissonances in mm. 5 and 6; its sequential rise and arching fall, mm. 3–4, are elaborated and extended by the voice, mm. 7–10. The piano's distinctive melodic trills, first heard in the bass in m. 5, become an important unifying factor as they recur later in the song.

The music of the introduction is repeated as interlude, and the second stanza begins like the first, but at the prospect of love's vanishing, modulates to the relative minor. After the sequences of mm. 19–20, the texture changes suddenly at "wenn nirgend dem Ufer mehr Blumen erblühn"; anticipating the "leaden feet" of the coming text, the bass introduces a passacaglia-like scalar descent with cadence, which is stated four times in succession to underlie the last line of this stanza, the first two lines of the next, and the intervening interlude. Sparsely accompanied, the vocal line doubles for a few notes, but yields to a formulaic cadence figure to end stanza 2 and recitative-like declamation to begin stanza 3. But the earlier texture returns with the change of mood at the verse's midpoint, and a varied equivalent of the first stanza's music provides the setting for the last two lines (and the repetition of the last line). The harmony considers a change to the major mode, but not yet fully committed, settles temporarily for a cadence on the dominant.

Changes of tempo and meter, and melting chromatically inflected chords lead the ear into a submediant-major dreamworld for Peter's musings on the vagaries of time and the transitory nature of happiness. Two hauntingly beautiful musical materials are the bases of this central section: the first takes up the melting-chord idea, extending and developing it into phrases of six and seven measures; the second introduces triplets into the accompaniment, most notably in a swaying melodic figure in sixths or thirds, under a vocal melody that begins with a memorable falling sixth at the repeated "Ach, wie bald" and continues with nearly continuous quarter notes throughout its two six-measure phrases. Stanza 4 ends on the dominant, which the interlude sustains; stanza 5 repeats the same material, slightly elaborated and varied to fit the text, but ending on the tonic. The piano continues dreamily, but suggestions of the minor mode and a shift by the right hand to eighth notes hint that change is near.

Suddenly the opening stanza's texture, rhythm, bass melody with trill, and sequential construction return (along with its approximate tempo) as Peter is roused from his reverie by thoughts of the love that awaits him. Excitement increases with the rising sequence but falls off again with the repetition of "bis dies Leben sinkt." An ambiguous odd measure of transition resolves, Phrygian style, to the dominant of the home key to begin the song's concluding section.

A faster tempo, breathless sixteenth-note figures, and eight measures of rising melodic and harmonic patterns over a dominant pedal depict Peter's growing ardor. The vocal melody evokes earlier material without, at first, actually quoting it: the falling sixths at "Nein, der Strom" recall the falling sixths at "Ach, wie bald," though their accentuation is reversed; the subsequent rising sequence exemplifies yet again a basic element of the song's construction; the chord outlines of "fröhlichen Ruderschlags" and "fahr ich hinab" call to mind the cycle's "heroic" motto; the contours of the settings of "Liebe und Leben" in mm. 132–136 resemble those of "die Seele nicht scheide" in mm. 9–10. Finally, in mm. 159–170 the music of stanza 1 is repeated in its entirety, beginning in a variant form but including a literal quotation of its last phrase. Emotional intensity mounts as emphasis on the subdominant in mm. 171–174 gives way, in mm. 175–178, to harmonic embellishment of the dominant. The last vocal phrase undertakes an extended scalewise ascent, but again the line fails to rise above the sixth scale step, its upper limit throughout the song; the piano postlude's attempt achieves the upper tonic, with cathartic effect.

"War es dir, dem diese Lippen bebten," Op. 33/7 (Was it you whose lips trembled)

War es dir, dem diese Lippen bebten,
Dir der dargebotne süße Kuß?
Gibt ein irdisch Leben so Genuß?
Ha! wie Licht und Glanz vor meinen Augen schwebten,
Alle Sinne nach den Lippen strebten!

In den klaren Augen blinkte
Sehnsucht, die mir zärtlich winkte,
Alles klang im Herzen wieder,
Meine Blicke sanken nieder,
Und die Lüfte tönten Liebeslieder!

Wie ein Sternenpaar
Glänzten die Augen, die Wangen
Wiegten das goldene Haar,
Blick und Lächeln schwangen
Flügel, und die süßen Worte gar
Weckten das tiefste Verlangen:
O Kuß, wie war dein Mund so brennend rot!
Da starb ich, fand ein Leben erst im schönsten Tod.

Was it you whose lips trembled, proffered for a sweet kiss? Does earthly life give such pleasure? Ha, how light and splendor gleamed before my eyes, and all my senses strove toward those lips!

In your clear eyes, longing flashed, beckoning to me tenderly; everything reverberated in my heart; I cast my eyes down, and the breezes played songs of love.

Your eyes shone like a pair of stars, your golden hair cradled your face, your glance and smile took wing, and your sweet words roused my deepest longing.

Oh, the kiss—how burning red your lips were! I died, found life for the first time in that most beautiful death.

Composed, presumably, sometime between May 1862 and March 1864; the exact date is uncertain.

The first performance is undocumented.

An abbreviated tripartite form:

	A			B			A'
a	b	a'	c	d	d'		a''
mm. 1–33	34–46	47–74	75–82	83–98	99–111		112–138

In *Des Jünglings Liebe*, this poem is called "Erinnerung" (Recollection).

The song's ardent principal section is notable for its irregular phrase lengths and its downbeat dissonances. The absence of a true introduction lends an air of impetuousness, which is abetted by the activated bass pedal in eighth notes, with its neighboring tones and its gasping rests. The harmonies of the setting of lines 3 and 4, which contrast earthly life with light and splendor, are particularly striking; with graphic symbolism, the music darkens to the tonic minor for "irdisch Leben," eases into its gentler relative major for "so Genuß," and at "Licht und Glanz" reemerges into the brightness of the home major to end the section. An almost literal repetition of the same music sets the remainder of verse 2 after the relatively static opening pair of lines.

Like these two tranquil phrases, the less urgent setting of the third stanza's beginning seems to have been prompted by the memory of the beloved's eyes. Almost like a folk song in its simplicity, this music provides contrast through the regularity of its four-measure phrases and its reluctance to modulate—only a few altered harmonies appear, in the second part. The absence of a tempo indication for the succeeding section suggests that the *Animato* relates to mood, not pace.

Under Peter's musing "O Kuß," the principal music returns for the poem's closing lines. The upbeat in m. 115 and the repeated "O Kuß" in Breitkopf & Härtel (and Dover) reflect a postpublication revision by Brahms.

The song's prevailing restlessness gradually abates in the piano postlude, which recalls the more serene music associated with the eyes of the beautiful Magelone.

"Wir müssen uns trennen," Op. 33/8
(We must be separated)

Wir müssen uns trennen,
Geliebtes Saitenspiel,
Zeit ist es, zu rennen
Nach dem fernen, erwünschten Ziel.

Ich ziehe zum Streite,
Zum Raube hinaus,
Und hab' ich die Beute,
Dann flieg' ich nach Haus.

Im rötlichen Glanze
Entflieh' ich mit ihr,
Es schützt uns die Lanze
Der Stahlharnisch hier.

Kommt, liebe Waffenstücke,
Zum Scherz oft angetan,
Beschirmet jetzt mein Glücke
Auf dieser neuen Bahn!

Ich werfe mich rasch in die Wogen,
Ich grüße den herrlichen Lauf,
Schon mancher ward niedergezogen,
Der tapfere Schwimmer bleibt oben auf.

Ha! Lust zu vergeuden
Das edele Blut!
Zu schützen die Freude,
Mein köstliches Gut!
Nicht Hohn zu erleiden,
Wem fehlt es an Mut?

Senke die Zügel,
Glückliche Nacht!
Spanne die Flügel,
Daß über ferne Hügel
Uns schon der Morgen lacht!

We must be separated, beloved lute; it is time to race toward the far-off goal of my desire.

I am departing for the fray, for plunder, and after I obtain my booty I shall speed homeward.

In the reddish glow I shall escape with her; my lance will protect us, my steel armor here.

Come, my dear weapons and armor, often worn for sport, now guard my happiness on this new path!

I cast myself swiftly into the billows, I hail the splendid course; many a man before now was pulled in by the current, but the brave swimmer will keep his head above water.

Ha! what pleasure to waste one's precious blood! To protect my joy, my priceless possession! When it comes to avoiding scorn, who lacks courage?

Drop your reins, happy night! Open wide your wings, so that over the distant hills morning will soon smile upon us!

Probably composed after May 1862 but before September 1865; the exact date is uncertain.

The first performance is undocumented.

A truncated tripartite form:

	A			B				A'
	a	b	a'	c	d	c'	d'	a''
mm.	1–8	9–13	14–19	20–31	32–48	49–60	61–71	72–84

In *Des Jünglings Liebe*, this poem is called "Entschluss" (Resolution).

The setting's strong contrasts reflect the complexities of Peter's emotional state—sad at the prospect of leaving but happy in his new-found love, anxious about the unknown but eager for adventure.

The introduction's sighing, solemn chords, with their lagging left-hand rhythm, set a tone of seriousness tinged with unease. The plaintive vocal melody is surprisingly wide-ranged. In the accompaniment the detached right-hand sixteenth notes evoke the lute, while the left-hand afterbeats continue the sense of unrest. At "dem fernen, erwünschten Ziel" in mm. 6–8, there is a metaphorical modulation to the "distant" dominant of the mediant.

At "Ich ziehe zum Streite," the accompaniment recalls the introduction's sighing chords in the key of the mediant minor, and adds a rhythmic figure that suggests the muffled drums of a dead march. The vocal line's dotted rhythms also take on solemn martial overtones. An inexact sequence repeats the two-measure phrase in the home key's dominant, and a one-measure extension in the piano prepares the return of the home tonic.

The earlier melody is then repeated with little change, but a new accompaniment figuration, less anxious but more somber, retains the drumbeat rhythm as Peter invokes the protection of his armor and lance.

The modulation at the end leads this time to a sharply contrasting section, *Allegro* and *alla breve*, in the key of the mediant major. Peter considers the alluring prospect of valorous deeds of chivalry to music whose straightforward diatonicism and cheerful enthusiasm recall the style of the first two songs in the cycle. The metaphor of the brave swimmer prompts a flow of countermelody in the piano, amid a buoyant surf of quarter-note triplets with ties. After the fermata at "bleibt oben auf," the piano's triplets continue as the previous diatonic music returns.

The question "Nicht Hohn zu erleiden, wem fehlt es an Mut?" in mm. 60–64 is set to a variant of mm. 31–35. In the earlier case, the succeeding phrase was a sequential whole step higher; here, the repetition rises only a half step, and, aided by the chromatic inflections in mm. 59 and 62–63, it reestablishes the home tonic key (enharmonically in Brahms's original publication, unaltered in the low-key edition).

The piano transition gradually restores calm, and the sad opening melody reappears. Its simpler accompaniment seems to replace the earlier disquiet with a benign impatience for the adventure to begin. The repetition of the last line of text elicits a tender digression into the key of the Neapolitan before the quietly expectant closing measures.

"Ruhe, Süßliebchen," Op. 33/9
(Rest, my darling)

Ruhe, Süßliebchen, im Schatten
    Der grünen, dämmernden Nacht;
Es säuselt das Gras auf den Matten,
Es fächelt und kühlt dich der Schatten,
    Und treue Liebe wacht.
        Schlafe, schlaf' ein,
    Leiser rauscht der Hain,
    Ewig bin ich dein.

Schweigt, ihr versteckten Gesänge,
    Und stört nicht die süßeste Ruh!
Es lauscht der Vögel Gedränge,
Es ruhen die lauten Gesänge,
    Schließ', Liebchen, dein Auge zu.
        Schlafe, schlaf' ein,
    Im dämmernden Schein,
    Ich will dein Wächter sein.

Murmelt fort, ihr Melodien,
    Rausche nur, du stiller Bach.
Schöne Liebesphantasien
Sprechen in den Melodien,
    Zarte Träume schwimmen nach.
        Durch den flüsternden Hain
    Schwärmen goldene Bienelein
    Und summen zum Schlummer dich ein.

Rest, my darling, in the shade of the dusky green night; the grass in the meadows is whispering, the breeze fans and cools you, and true love stands guard. Sleep, fall asleep, the grove is rustling more softly; I am eternally yours.

Be still, you hidden songsters, and do not disturb her sweet slumbers! The crowd of birds listens, their loud songs cease; close your eyes, beloved. Sleep, fall asleep, in the glow of twilight; I will guard you.

Murmur on, you melodies; rush on, you quiet brook. Beautiful love fantasies speak in the melodies, gentle dreams float after them. Through the whispering grove, golden bees swarm and hum you to sleep.

The date of composition is uncertain—probably between May 1862 and mid-July 1868.

First performed by Heinrich Vogl in Frankfurt on 5 December 1871.

A large varied strophic form; the three closing lines of each stanza are set to the same melody, their five opening lines to different developments of related materials:

	A		A'		A''	
	a	b	a'	b	a''	b
mm.	1–23	23–48	49–67	67–92	93–111	111–138

In *Des Jünglings Liebe*, the poem is entitled "Schlaflied" (Lullaby).

The setting begins as though from a nocturnal hush, with a *pianissimo* melody in dreamily rising thirds, which later, associated with the words "Schlafe, schlaf' ein," announces the refrain. The accompanying syncopations that elsewhere often suggest agitation here evoke warmth and tenderness. They sometimes anticipate and sometimes trail the right-hand harmonies, and together with the stable rhythms, the prolonged postponement of tonic, and the many merely oscillating melodic and harmonic progressions, create a sense of blissfully suspended time.

The vocal line is economically constructed. "Ruhe, Süßliebchen" and "Schatten der grünen" are set to the same melody, as are "es säuselt das Gras auf den Matten" and "es fächelt und kühlt dich der Schatten"; both patterns lie within a perfect fifth, feature a falling fourth, and end with a stepwise descent. The ascending triad and half step of "Schlafe, schlaf' ein" are mirrored by the descending triad and half step of "leiser rauscht der Hain." The word "grünen" in m. 8 begins a (slightly embellished) scalewise descent of a fifth to end that passage; scalewise fifths downward also set "treue Liebe wacht" to finish the section and both statements of "ewig bin ich dein" to conclude the entire strophe. The long-drawn piano melody intertwines with the voice, often anticipating its entrances.

Although the first section modulates to the key of the mediant from the minor mode, and the refrain to the subdominant, the tonic itself is not definitely established until the strophe's final cadence. The piano interlude that follows, a quiet pastoral tune over a bass tonic pedal, abandons the syncopations and serves to anchor the key further.

In the second strophe, Peter implores the birds to be silent lest they wake his beloved, and the accompaniment evokes the forest's soft rustling. Variants of the first strophe's melodic shapes pass through the relative minor, its Neapolitan, the relative minor again, and the dominant minor before easing at last into the home dominant to prepare the recurrence of the refrain.

The more animated third strophe adopts a flowing accompaniment style suggestive of the text's quiet brook. The direction of the opening melodic fourth leap is reversed in order to facilitate proper accentuation of the words. The abstract subject matter—melodies, fantasies, dreams— is reflected in an immediate turn to the Neapolitan and related harmonies over a pedal on its dominant. The words "schöne Liebesphantasien" prompt yet another modulation, to the mediant major. At "Melodien," after the change of key signature, the piano introduces the song's only independent countermelody; gradually the home dominant is revealed, and the refrain returns.

The rhythmic activity decreases in successive stages as the song approaches its end. The right hand's sixteenths are relinquished at the refrain's reappearance, the left hand's for the final vocal phrase. The gentle syncopations from the opening are recalled with the return of the interlude music as postlude. Stretched from eight measures to ten, and subject to a long *diminuendo* and *ritardando*, it is gradually reduced to a static pulsation, and finally, a complete stop.

Verzweiflung (Despair), Op. 33/10

So tönet denn, schäumende Wellen,
Und windet euch rund um mich her!
Mag Unglück doch laut um mich bellen,
Erbost sein das grausame Meer!

Ich lache den stürmenden Wettern,
Verachte den Zorngrimm der Flut;
O, mögen mich Felsen zerschmettern!
Denn nimmer wird es gut.

Nicht klag' ich, und mag ich non scheitern,
In wäßrigen Tiefen vergehn!
Mein Blick wird sich nie mehr erheitern,
Den Stern meiner Liebe zu sehn.

So wälzt euch bergab mit Gewittern,
Und raset, ihr Stürme, mich an,
Daß Felsen an Felsen zersplittern!
Ich bin ein verlorener Mann.

So resound, then, foaming waves, and curl yourselves about me! Let misfortune howl loudly around me; let the cruel sea be angry!

I laugh at the raging storms, contemn the fury of the waters; oh, may I be smashed against the rocks!—for things will never again be good.

I do not complain, even if I am now to be wrecked and to perish in the watery deep! My glance will never again be cheered at seeing the star of love.

So dash downward, [waves,] in the storms, and assail me, tempests, in your frenzy, so rocks crack against rocks! I am a lost man.

The date of composition is uncertain, presumably between May 1862 and December 1866.

There is no record of the first performance.

Expanded tripartite; a condensed variant of the opening section precedes the appearance of contrasting material:

	A	A'	B	A
mm.	1–23	23–42	43–57	58–84

The title "Verzweiflung" is Tieck's. According to Fox Strangways (*Music and Letters*, 1940, 215), only this poem and "Sulima" (No. 13) were titled in the edition that Brahms used. Friedländer reports (*Brahms's Lieder*, 53–54) that Brahms wrote to Rieter-Biedermann on 17 June 1869, "In *Sulima* and *Verzweiflung* I wish the titles to be kept."

The piano's swirling sixteenths and anxious syncopations depict a violent storm at sea; the vocal line's initial rocketing ascent suggests the intensity of Peter's emotional turmoil as he musters defiance in the face of despair. At the stanza's midpoint, the accompaniment adopts a turbulent new figure in triplets, tossed from hand to hand. It rapidly mounts in excitement and buoys the voice to a climactic high pitch on "grausame" in m. 20. The final words of text are repeated as the line descends and broadens into the cadence. The entire stanza is marked by irregular phrase lengths and unpredictable, quick harmonic movement, from which much of its impassioned character derives.

As interlude, the piano repeats its introduction in somewhat more restrained form, and the second stanza's setting follows its lead with regular two-measure phrases of sequential construction and nonmodulating harmony that emphasizes the subdominant. The triplet figure reappears midway; a shorter and less vehement passage than before leads nonetheless to the same closing phrases and cadence.

The second interlude interchanges the materials of the two hands; decreasing activity and a modulation to the submediant minor symbolize Peter's withdrawal from awareness of the storm's raging in order to examine his own feelings. An undercurrent of wavelike motion continues in the accompaniment's left-hand triplets with their neighboring-tone embellishment. The thought of the beloved Magelone elicits a shift to the major; the fear of never seeing her again is expressed in a long impassioned line that soars to a touching prolonged flatted seventh. At the climax of the phrase, the piano adds, over a bass pedal, a fervent doubling at the third above and climbing eighths in the tenor register.

Ardor yields to poignant reflection, but suddenly the storm, its fury undiminished, intrudes. A biting dominant minor ninth slowly resolves into a return of the music of the first stanza, almost unaltered, to set the fourth. The storm's violence overruns the final vocal cadence, suffusing the postlude; the piano concludes with a tempestuous arpeggiated figure that spans nearly the entire keyboard and culminates in a massive tonic-chord sonority.

"Wie schnell verschwindet so Licht als Glanz," Op. 33/11
(How soon light and splendor vanish)

Wie schnell verschwindet
So Licht als Glanz,
Der Morgen findet
Verwelkt den Kranz,

Der gestern glühte
In aller Pracht,
Denn er verblühte
In dunkler Nacht.

Es schwimmt die Welle
Des Lebens hin,
Und färbt sich helle,
Hat's nicht Gewinn;

Die Sonne neiget,
Die Röte flieht,
Der Schatten steiget
Und Dunkel zieht:

So schwimmt die Liebe
Zu Wüsten ab,
Ach, daß sie bliebe
Bis an das Grab!

Doch wir erwachen
Zu tiefer Qual:
Es bricht der Nachen,
Es löscht der Strahl;

Vom schönen Lande
Weit weggebracht
Zum öden Strande,
Wo um uns Nacht.

How soon light and splendor vanish; morning finds the wreath withered that gleamed in full glory yesterday, for it lost its bloom in the dark night.

The wave of life floats by; even if it takes on bright colors, there is no profit. The sun declines, the red glow flees; shadows lengthen and darkness spreads.

Thus love floats away to desert lands; ah, if it could only last until the grave! But we awaken to deep sorrow; the boat breaks, the beam is extinguished;

We are carried far off from the beautiful land to a barren shore where night surrounds us.

The date of composition is uncertain, presumably sometime between May 1862 and May 1869.

There is no record of the first performance.

Varied strophic; contrast is achieved through development.

	A		B	A'	
	a	a'		a''	a'
mm.	1–24	25–42	43–58	59–75	76–93

The poem has the title "Trauer" (Grief) in *Des Jünglings Liebe*.

Brahms's setting combines the simplicity of folk song with a wealth of expressive variant detail, reminiscent of Schubert in its richness and subtlety. The piano introduction sets the tone with its melodic variation in m. 3, its chromatic alteration in m. 5, and its brief turn to the relative major in m. 6.

The vocal melody imitates that of the introduction, but without the variant. Its formula—two similar two-measure phrases balanced by a four-measure phrase—is standard for the song. In its second eight measures (the poem's second stanza), the voice cedes its sixteenth-note rhythmic pattern to the piano; the two-measure phrases rise sequentially through the subdominant to the submediant, where the strophe ends.

The submediant pedal that underlies the last phrase of strophe 1 is replaced by another on the dominant, a half step lower, for the short interlude and the opening of strophe 2. Since the second strophe sets only one stanza of text rather than two, its construction is somewhat contracted. The second of the opening pair of two-measure vocal phrases adopts the introduction's variant, but the balancing four-measure phrase is missing. Instead, continuing like the introduction, another two-measure phrase moves to the relative major; it is imitated sequentially a step lower, arriving at the Neapolitan. The pair this time is balanced by the expected four-measure phrase, itself derived from the formula in miniature—sequential repetition of a one-measure fragment over a dominant pedal, balanced by a two-measure group with a cadence on the tonic. The piano alone repeats the closing four measures, now functionally harmonized, effectively extending this strophe to sixteen measures to balance the first.

A change to the major mode, *pianissimo*, implies a contrasting setting for stanza 4, but the melody develops from that of the cadence just heard, and a quasi-sequential rise to the submediant recalls the first strophe's harmonic shape. Each of the two phrases has a two-measure extension in the piano; the second has a further extension of four measures, which sinks a half step to reestablish the tonic minor and, somewhat naively, evoke the text's lengthening shadows and spreading darkness.

The melody of the strophe that follows begins like that of the second but adheres to the structure of the first; again, it sets two stanzas of text. A new, more active accompaniment figure derives from the rhythmic pattern of three sixteenths; apparently suggested by the word "schwimmt," its passage from hand to hand is prepared in eighth notes at the end of the interlude. The song's strongest emotional outburst occurs in the second half of the strophe; the melody that belonged exclusively to the piano at the analogous point in strophe 1 is now intensified into octaves (some of them harmonized) and doubled by the voice a third below, while the left hand continues to provide a complementary rhythm based on the three sixteenths.

Fervor gradually subsides and yields to a quiet repetition of the music of strophe 2 for the final stanza. The piano's echoing of the last phrase concludes the song in the same simple style and melancholy mood in which it began.

"Muß es eine Trennung geben," Op. 33/12
(Must there be a separation)

Muß es eine Trennung geben,
Die das treue Herz zerbricht?
Nein, dies nenne ich nicht leben,
Sterben ist so bitter nicht.

Hör' ich eines Schäfers Flöte,
Härme ich mich inniglich,
Seh' ich in die Abendröte,
Denk' ich brünstiglich an dich.

Gibt es denn kein wahres Lieben?
Muß denn Schmerz und Trennung sein?
Wär' ich ungeliebt geblieben,
Hätt' ich doch noch Hoffnungsschein.

Aber so muß ich nun klagen:
Wo ist Hoffnung, als das Grab?
Fern muß ich mein Elend tragen,
Heimlich bricht das Herz mir ab.

Must there be a separation that breaks the faithful heart? No, I don't call this living, even dying isn't this bitter.

When I hear the shepherd's flute I suffer inward torment; when I gaze into the sunset, I think ardently of you.

Does no true love exist, then? Must there, then, be pain and separation? If I had remained unloved, I would at least still have a ray of hope.

But, as it is, I must now lament; where is hope except in the grave? I must take my misery far away; my heart is secretly breaking.

Probably composed in early 1862 in Hamburg.

First performed by Magdalene Murjahn on 2 February 1871 in the Leipzig Gewandhaussaal.

Varied strophic; A A B A.

In the 1821 and 1841 editions of Tieck's poetry, these verses appear under the title "Trennung" (Parting). There, the second line of stanza 3 reads "Muß denn Schmerz und Trauer sein" and the last line of the poem is "Heimlich stirbt das Herz mir ab."

The sorrowful melody unfolds affectingly in three-measure phrases over an accompaniment of descending arpeggios, symbolizing separation. The first phrase gently opens to the dominant, where the second phrase begins and ends. Chromatically altered to minor, the dominant functions as a pivot chord to permit a modulation to the supertonic, where the third phrase imitates the first a step higher. Another minor inflection on the last syllable of "leben" sets in motion the return to the tonic, now major. The piano interlude touchingly echoes the closing pitches of the vocal line in augmentation, *pianissimo*; the Aeolian-mode harmonies subtly suggest the exotic locale.

The contrasting third strophe quite obviously derives its melodic material—first for the voice, later for the piano—from that of the principal strophe. The unstable harmonies hint at the submediant, but it is displaced by an augmented-sixth chord that leads instead to the dominant (m. 36). Strikingly, the prevailing sixteenth-note motion stops for six measures as the piano recalls the main melody, in the dominant for the voice's *forte* "Wär ich ungeliebt geblieben" and in the subdominant for the *piano* "hätt' ich doch noch Hoffnungsschein."

The earlier melody returns to the vocal line for the fourth strophe, though its beginning is disguised by the subdominant retained in the piano. The harmonies are now poignantly enriched through chromaticism, symbolizing the increased pain and heartbreak that this closing stanza expresses.

During the extended postlude, the voice reenters, overlapping the piano's augmentation with another of its own, with particularly moving effect. The harmonies waver indecisively between minor and major; the eventual choice of major seems to evoke resignation rather than cheer.

Sulima, Op. 33/13

Geliebter, wo zaudert
Dein irrender Fuß?

Die Nachtigall plaudert
Von Sehnsucht und Kuß.

Es flüstern die Bäume
Im goldenen Schein,
Es schlüpfen mir Träume
Zum Fenster herein

Ach! kennst du das Schmachten
Der klopfenden Brust?
Dies Sinnen und Trachten
Voll Qual und voll Lust?

Beflügle die Eile
Und rette mich dir,
Bei nächtlicher Weile
Entfliehn wir von hier.

Die Segel, sie schwellen,
Die Furcht ist nur Tand:
Dort, jenseit den Wellen
Ist väterlich Land.

Die Heimat entfliehet,
So fahre sie hin!
Die Liebe, sie ziehet
Gewaltig den Sinn.

Horch! wollüstig klingen
Die Wellen im Meer,
Sie hüpfen und springen
Mutwillig einher,

Und sollten sie klagen?
Sie rufen nach dir!
Sie wissen, sie tragen
Die Liebe von hier.

Beloved man, where do your wandering feet now tarry? The nightingale babbles of longing and kisses.

The trees are whispering in the golden glow, dreams are slipping into my window.

Ah! do you know how my yearning heart is beating, how all my thoughts are full of sorrow and pleasure?

Add wings to your haste and rescue me for your sake; under cover of night we will escape from here.

The sails are billowing, fear [the correct German word is *Furcht*, not *Frucht*] is only a bauble: there, beyond the waves, is your father's country.

My homeland is vanishing—well, let it go! Love is drawing my mind on powerfully.

Listen! the waves in the sea have a sensual sound; they are hopping and leaping wantonly around us,

And should they complain? They are calling to you! They know they are carrying love away from here.

Composed in May 1862 in Hamburg.

The first performance took place on 18 or 19 September 1871 at the Concertsaal der Harmonie in Magdeburg; the performers' names are not recorded.

Strophic; each of the two long sections has the form a a b.

The title "Sulima" is in Tieck's original text; in the later collection *Des Jünglings Liebe*, the poem is retitled "Lockung" (Allurement), presumably to sever its connection to the *Magelone* story.

Within the opus, the song is as remarkable for its reluctance to modulate as for the relentless repetitiveness of its rhythm. Rising phrases and rising sequences are prominent; the overall effect is that of passionate impatience.

Seemingly unrelated to textual considerations, the occasional borrowings from the minor mode, particularly the use of the minor subdominant in cadences that are otherwise major, lend a tinge of orientalism.

The two strophes are virtually identical except for a revision of both melody and harmony at "sie hüpfen und springen mutwillig einher," three lines from the end of the second strophe, and the repositioning of the accidental sign in the accompaniment of the vocal line's next-to-last full measure.

A sense of restless waiting persists through the postlude, and beyond.

"Wie froh und frisch mein Sinn sich hebt," Op. 33/14
(How gaily and vigorously my spirits rise)

Wie froh und frisch mein Sinn sich hebt,
Zurück bleibt alles Bangen,
Die Brust mit neuem Mute strebt,
Erwacht ein neu Verlangen.

Die Sterne spiegeln sich im Meer,
Und golden glänzt die Flut.
Ich rannte taumelnd hin und her,
Und war nicht schlimm, nicht gut.

Doch niedergezogen
Sind Zweifel und wankender Sinn;
O tragt mich, ihr schaukelnden Wogen,
Zur längst ersehnten Heimat hin.

In lieber, dämmernder Ferne,
Dort rufen heimische Lieder,
Aus jeglichem Sterne
Blickt sie mit sanftem Auge nieder.

Ebne dich, du treue Welle,
Führe mich auf fernen Wegen

Zu der vielgeliebten Schwelle,
Endlich meinem Glück entgegen!

How gaily and vigorously my spirits rise; all fears are left behind. My heart is ambitious with new-found courage; a new desire awakes.

The stars are mirrored in the sea, and the waters have a golden glow. I dashed dizzily here and there and was neither bad nor good.

But my doubts and the wavering of my thoughts are now dispelled; oh, carry me, you rocking waves, off to my long wished-for homeland.

In the familiar, twilit distance—there songs of home are calling; from every star She looks down with gentle eyes.

Become smooth, you faithful waves, lead me on distant paths to the dearly beloved threshold, finally to meet my happiness!

Composed in May 1869, probably in Karlsruhe or Baden-Baden.

First performed on 17 January 1874 in Leipzig by Sophie Löwe (a student of Stockhausen) and pianist Isidor Seiss.

Rondo form; A B A C A.

In *Des Jünglings Liebe*, the poem is called "Neuer Sinn" (Fresh Thoughts); the second line of the fourth stanza reads "dort rufen einheimische Lieder."

In the original key of G major, the emphatic introduction's beginning on the submediant helps to smooth the transition from the E major of the preceding song, a nicety rendered meaningless by the low-key edition's inconsistent choice of transposed keys (C major for No. 13 to E major for No. 14).

The vocal line rings out joyously, borne on the splendid sweep of the brilliant accompaniment. Two two-measure phrases are answered by two of three measures, striving upward toward the high pitch finally attained in the section's penultimate measure. Expressive harmonies underscore "hebt" in m. 4, "Bangen" in m. 6, and "erwacht ein neu (Verlangen)" in m. 10. The piano's transition climbs yet a third higher melodically before modulating to the key of the dominant for the next verse.

Quietly moving quarter-note harmonies and stable accompanying triplets in eighths create a far less tumultuous background for Peter's admiration of the beauties of nature. The sense of a pause for contemplation is enhanced by the repetition in augmentation of "golden glänzt die Flut" over a slowed harmonic rhythm. The stanza's last two lines are accompanied by a return to quarter-note motion and a shift to the tonic minor. The second of the two similar phrases broadens to end in quarter notes rather than the eighths of the first; their suggestion of balancing the earlier augmentation is reinforced by the piano's prolongation of the newly arrived dominant harmony, and its metric expansion—two measures of triplets in hemiola and two measures of dotted half notes over which melodic quarters descend to initiate the return of the music from the opening.

Only a few rhythmic alterations are required to accommodate the music of stanza 1 to the text of stanza 3; the most notable differences are at the cadence, since the first verse ends with a weak syllable and the third with a stressed one. The colorful harmonies now, with equal aptness, mark "niedergezogen," "wankender," and "Längst ersehnten."

Over a tonic pedal in the bass, the interlude grows calmer and modulates to the benign subdominant as Peter's thoughts turn to home and the beloved Magelone. Tender doublings and countermelodies in the piano complement the vocal line. The phrase "Sie mit sanftem Auge" is given particular significance by rhythmic broadening, both at its first appearance, where the musical phrase that includes it is extended to five measures, and at its repetition, where it is accompanied by kaleidoscopic harmonic shifting and the piano's reminiscence of the eighth-note melody with which the section began.

The spirited opening music returns once more for the final stanza, again with some minor rhythmic adjustment to the text. Both voice and piano join in an ecstatic codetta which seems to push toward the happy ending to come.

"Treue Liebe dauert lange," Op. 33/15
(True love is long-lasting)

Treue Liebe dauert lange,
Überlebet manche Stund',
Und kein Zweifel macht sie bange,
Immer bleibt ihr Mut gesund.

Dräuen gleich in dichten Scharen,
Fordern gleich zum Wankelmut
Sturm und Tod, setzt den Gefahren
Lieb' entgegen, treues Blut.

Und wie Nebel stürzt zurücke,
Was den Sinn gefangen hält,
Und dem heitern Frühlingsblicke
Öffnet sich die weite Welt.

Errungen,
Bezwungen
Von Lieb' ist das Glück,
Verschwunden
Die Stunden,
Sie fliehen zurück;
Und selige Lust,
Sie stillet,
Erfüllet

> Die trunkene, wonneklopfende Brust;
> Sie scheide
> Von Leide
> Auf immer,
> Und nimmer
> Entschwinde die liebliche, selige, himmlische Lust!

True love is long-lasting; it survives many an hour, and no despair frightens it; its courage is always staunch.

Even if storm and death threaten it with numerous armies, even if they strive to weaken its resolve, love counters the dangers with fidelity.

And all that held the mind captive, is blown away like mist, and the wide world opens up to the happy springtime gaze.

Happiness is won, conquered by love; vanished the hours—they fly away—and blessed joy calms and fills the reeling, rapturously beating heart; let it be parted from pain forever, and never may lovely, blessed, heavenly joy disappear!

Composed in May 1869, probably in Karlsruhe or Baden-Baden.
The first performance is not documented.
Rondo form:

	A	B	A'	C	A''
mm.	1–21	22–35	36–53	54–104	105–116

In *Des Jünglings Liebe*, the poem is called "Treue" (Fidelity).

Returning to the key of the cycle's first song, the setting constitutes an epilogue of affecting simplicity. After an almost hymnlike opening, increased rhythmic activity enlivens the second phrase. A change to $\frac{3}{4}$ meter coincides with both the establishment of a background of constant triplets and the first of the song's several allusions to the cycle's initial "heroic" motto, here in the bass and imitated by the voice.

In the second stanza, a series of minor harmonies a third apart depicts the threatening of storm and death, and an enharmonic shift to a glowing major on the submediant from the minor portrays the contrasting faithful love.

The music of the principal strophe is recalled for the third stanza, its beginning, in triple meter, less solemn than before.

At the *Lebhaft*, the piano extends the rising vocal line's outburst of joy, as quarter-note twos against threes reflect growing excitement. Constant eighths after the fermata underscore the breathlessness of the vocal line's short phrases. Minor inflections evoke pain at "sie scheide von Leide auf immer"; "und nimmer, und nimmer" prompts a symbolic absence of event. But fervor mounts, evidenced by the piano's syncopations and quickened harmonic rhythm, and culminating in the voice's long sweep upward to a whole note on the song's (indeed the cycle's) highest pitch for the word "Lust" in m. 103.

The hymnlike opening music returns softly to end the song. Brahms recalls the poem's initial line but breaks off to reiterate the recently heard
closing lines; the composite text effectively summarizes the underlying
theme of the entire cycle. The waning closing measures also round it out
musically with the reappearance of the "heroic" motto from the opening in
two different rhythms in melody and bass.

FOUR GESÄNGE, OP. 43

Vier Gesänge für eine Singstimme mit Begleitung des Pianoforte componirt von Johannes Brahms (Four Songs for Solo Voice with Piano Accompaniment Composed by Johannes Brahms), Op. 43. Published in December 1868 by J. Rieter-Biedermann, Leipzig and Winterthur; publication numbers 599a–d.

The peculiar diversity of this opus came about as a result of Rieter-Biedermann's desire to publish "Von ewiger Liebe" and "Die Mainacht," which he had heard Stockhausen sing in Zurich. At first Brahms tried to dissuade him, writing on 26 June 1868, "I have long promised the young Simrock something, and if I take two out of the middle, I can only order the remaining songs badly." But by 5 July, Brahms had given in: "I am busy with ordering a small group of songs and, since I am happy to give you the two you want, I fear I am forced to throw the poets into complete confusion." Finally, on 9 August he sent Rieter-Biedermann a set of four songs, to be published as Op. 43. Besides the two coveted, it contained "a long *vom Herrn von Falkenstein*" and a solo version of the first of the Op. 41 partsongs for male voices, "Ich schell' mein Horn," which Brahms felt should be "shown to the public in this way."

At the same time, the four sets of songs to be published as Opp. 46–49 were sent off to Simrock. It is clear from the correspondence that "Von ewiger Liebe" and "Die Mainacht" were originally included among them, probably grouped with the other settings of folk song texts and Hölty poems.

Von ewiger Liebe, Op. 43/1 (Of Everlasting Love)

Text by August Heinrich Hoffmann von Fallersleben (1798–1874)

Dunkel, wie dunkel in Wald und in Feld!
Abend schon ist es, nun schweiget die Welt.
Nirgend noch Licht und nirgend noch Rauch,
Ja, und die Lerche sie schweiget nun auch.
Kommt aus dem Dorfe der Bursche heraus,
Gibt das Geleit der Geliebten nach Haus,

Führt sie am Weidengebüsche vorbei,
Redet so viel und so mancherlei:

"Leidest du Schmach und betrübest du dich,
Leidest du Schmach von Andern um mich,
Werde die Liebe getrennt so geschwind,
Schnell wie wir früher vereiniget sind.
Scheide mit Regen und scheide mit Wind,
Schnell wie wir früher vereiniget sind."

Spricht das Mägdelein, Mägdelein spricht:
"Unsere Liebe, sie trennet sich nicht!
Fest ist der Stahl und das Eisen gar sehr,
Unsere Liebe ist fester noch mehr.
Eisen und Stahl, man schmiedet sie um,
Unsere Liebe, wer wandelt sie um?
Eisen und Stahl, sie können zergehn,
Unsere Liebe muß ewig bestehn!"

Dark, how dark in forest and field! It is already evening; now the world is silent. Nowhere any more light and nowhere any more smoke, yes, and the lark is now silent, too.

The lad comes out of the village, escorts his sweetheart home, leads her past the willow grove, speaks of so many and such varied things:

"If you are suffering disgrace and you are grieving, if you are suffering disgrace before other people on my account, let our love be sundered as swiftly, as quickly as we were formerly united. Depart in rain and depart in wind as quickly as we were formerly united."

The girl says, the girl says: "Our love cannot be sundered! Steel is firm and iron very much so; our love is even firmer. Iron and steel can be reforged; who can transform our love? Iron and steel can disintegrate; our love must endure eternally!"

Composed in 1864 in Vienna.

First performed from manuscript (together with the next song, "Die Mainacht") on 11 March 1868 in Hamburg by Julius Stockhausen and Brahms.

Through-composed; three parts, each with its own characteristic musical material.

The text appears in Hoffmann von Fallersleben's *Gedichte* of 1837 and is a free transcription of a translation from the Wendish by Leopold Haupt. Brahms's attribution of the poem to Joseph Wenzig is an error that has been perpetuated by all editions.

The form derives from the form of the text, which comprises three stanzas: the first sets the scene of a couple at dusk on the way to the girl's home outside the village; in the second, the boy voices his fear that their relationship has in some unspecified way become a source of trouble for her, but he becomes upset at the thought of separating; the narrator reappears at the third stanza to introduce the girl, who reassures the boy that their love is indestructible.

The dark B-minor bass melody with its accompaniment of walking eighth notes not only is a musical image of the scene and situation but also introduces several of the song's principal thematic motives, among them the broken descent of a sixth (from the D in m. 2 to the F♯ in m. 4) and the double neighboring-tone figures around tonic and dominant that decorate that descent.

The voice enters with an imitation of the same melody, now developed into a full double period. The piano increases in fullness, reverses the roles of the two hands, and leads the way temporarily into D minor to begin the second period. A repetition of the whole section completes the first stanza.

The music of the introduction is repeated as interlude, now *mf* and *crescendo*, signalling the boy's growing agitation, which is characterized by incessant triplets and a new pervasive rhythm featuring a dotted quarter plus eighth note. The many cadences without third represent his insecurity; the stepwise ascent with which all melodic fragments end reflects his need for reassurance (Platt, *Text-Music*, 215).

The piano transition bridging the second and third stanzas would alone mark the song as a masterpiece. It overruns the boy's final words, revealing even more powerfully than they the extent of the torment lurking in his imagination; yet, as the passion wanes, the stage is readied as if by magic for the entrance of the girl.

The music slows, softens, and changes to $\frac{6}{8}$ meter and the major mode to begin its confirmation of eternal love. Warming to the task, it illustrates the immutable nature of that vow by repeating the same rhythms and figurations over and over. The girl's reassurance is at first quietly comforting, but it grows in intensity as her confidence and resolve increase, rising in two stages to a climactic high F♯ in m. 113. The climax is clearly marked by a *crescendo* to *forte*, an apparent broadening to $\frac{3}{4}$ meter in the piano, and a shift to five-measure phrase structure—the voice's final five-measure phrase overlaps a five-bar postlude in the piano. The stretching of the final "ewig" is a subtle bit of word-painting.

The song constitutes an entire dramatic *scena*, spacious in design and unfailingly effective in performance.

Die Mainacht, Op. 43/2 (The May Night)

Text by Ludwig Hölty (1748–1776)

Wann der silberne Mond durch die Gesträuche blinkt,
Und sein schlummerndes Licht über den Rasen streut,
Und die Nachtigall flötet,
Wand'l ich traurig von Busch zu Busch.

> Selig preis' ich dich dann, flötende Nachtigall,
> Weil dein Weibchen mit dir wohnet in einem Nest,
> Ihrem singenden Gatten
> Tausend trauliche Küsse gibt.

Überhüllet vom Laub girret ein Taubenpaar
Sein Entzücken mir vor; aber ich wende mich,
Suche dunklere Schatten,
Und die einsame Träne rinnt.

Wann, o lächelndes Bild, welches wie Morgenrot
Durch die Seele mir strahlt, find' ich auf Erden dich?
Und die einsame Träne
Bebt mir heißer die Wang' herab.

When the silvery moon gleams through the shrubbery and spreads its drowsy light over the lawn, and the nightingale sings, I walk sadly from bush to bush.

Roofed over with foliage, a pair of doves coo their rapture in my hearing; but I turn around, seek out deeper shadows, and the lone tear flows.

When, O smiling image that beams through my soul like dawn, will I find you on earth? And the lone tear trembles more hotly down my cheek.

Composed in April 1866 in Karlsruhe.

First performed, together with "Von ewiger Liebe," Op. 43/1, from manuscript on 11 March 1868 in Hamburg by Julius Stockhausen and Brahms.

Varied strophic; A B A'.

Hölty's poem was written in May 1774 and first published in the Göttingen *Musenalmanach* in 1775. Typically, it was considerably altered by Johann Heinrich Voss, whose 1804 edition Brahms used. The poem is an asclepiadic ode, the metrical structure of which is:

$$(1) \quad \textbf{x x} - \smile \smile - - \smile \smile - \smile -$$
$$(2) \quad \textbf{x x} - \smile \smile - - \smile \smile - \smile -$$
$$(3) \quad \textbf{x x} - \smile \smile - \smile$$
$$(4) \quad \textbf{x x} - \smile \smile - \smile -$$

Brahms set the first stanza with remarkable fidelity to its meter, but later the musical development takes precedence.

The song is a prime example of the varied strophic approach to ternary form that Brahms came to favor in his middle years. The guiding principle is that the middle section provides contrast through variation and development of the opening strophe, which is then recalled more exactly to complete the structure. In order to accommodate this form, Brahms omitted the second stanza.

The text contains exactly those elements to which Brahms's imagination responded most readily—a tranquil nature scene shadowed by the poet's melancholy. The three stanzas that he retained constitute the poetic equivalent of an A B A form, contrasting the loneliness underlying the first and third stanzas with the image of conjugal happiness in the second. They also sharpen the focus on the hierarchic ordering of the phrases "Und die Nachtigall flötet" in the first verse, "Und die einsame Träne rinnt" in the second, and, climactically, "Und die einsame Träne bebt mir heißer die Wang' herab" in the third, which relationship is the basis for the song's expressive and dramatic architecture.

The introduction's gently moving half notes and rocking eighths evoke the text's lonely walking through quiet night. The voice's arching three-measure phrases (six half measures) are the exact equivalent of the poem's opening lines of six poetic feet. At "und die Nachtigall flötet," a two-measure phrase is inserted, the harmony takes an expressive turn to the minor, and the left hand's regular metric pulsation is temporarily displaced to the weak beats.

The second strophe opens in the key of the submediant, notated enharmonically as B major. Its derivation from the first can be seen in the vocal line's opening intervals, overall melodic contours, and the initially similar rhythm, which, however, becomes loosened as the line becomes more emotional and declamatory. Several characteristic devices appear in the accompaniment: the right hand's former rocking eighth notes have become repeated thirds in the left, portraying the comfort of sheltering foliage, while the right hand coos in duet with the voice, like the doves of the text; the dramatic *forte* rising arpeggios in the left hand stand for the poet's unresolved dreams of love; the canonic imitation at "aber ich wende mich" represents separation; at "suche dunklere Schatten," the music turns again toward E♭ minor, always a "dark" key for Brahms, while the piano's unison with the voice and decreasing rhythmic activity emphasize the sense of isolation. The key words "Und die einsame Träne rinnt" call forth a glorious five-measure soaring and falling phrase with an aching half-step dissonance on "Träne."

The piano lingers on the dominant, and the opening melody returns, this time with triplets in the accompaniment, reflecting the quickening emotion of the third stanza. The poem's climactic two-line final reference to the tear is set to the same gorgeous curve as before, followed by an even higher-arcing second five-measure curve, its crux a prolonged descent through tragic Neapolitan harmony.

The piano postlude, sad with flatted sixth and seventh, resumes its lonely walk into the night.

Ich schell' mein Horn in's Jammertal, Op. 43/3

(I Sound My Horn into the Valley of Grief)
"Old German" Text

Ich schell' mein Horn in's Jammertal,
Mein Freud ist mir verschwunden,

Ich hab gejagt, muß abelahn,
Das Wild lauft vor den Hunden.
Ein edel Tier in diesem Feld
Hatt' ich mir auserkoren,
Das schied von mir, als ich wohl spür,
Mein Jagen ist verloren.

Fahr' hin, Gewild, in Waldes Lust!
Ich will dir nimmer schrecken
Mit Jagen dein schneeweiße Brust,
Ein Ander muß dich wecken
Mit Jägers Schrei und Hundebiß,
Daß du nit magst entrinnen;
Halt dich in Hut, mein Tierle gut!
Mit Leid scheid ich von hinnen.

Kein Hochgewild ich fahen kann,
Das muß ich oft entgelten,
Noch halt ich stät' auf Jägers Bahn,
Wie wohl mir Glück kommt selten.
Mag mir nit g'bührn ein Hochwild schön,
So laß ich mich begnügen
An Hasenfleisch, nit mehr ich heisch,
Das mag mich nit betrüben.

I sound my horn into the valley of grief; my joy has vanished; I have hunted,
I must leave off; the deer is too fleet for the hounds. I had chosen a noble
beast in this field; it has gone from me, as I well see; my hunt is a loss.

Farewell, deer, and enjoy your forest! I will never frighten your snow-white
breast with hunting; another man must awaken you with huntsman's cry and
bite of hounds, so that you cannot escape; take care, my good creature! I
depart from here in sorrow.

I cannot capture any noble game, I must often suffer for that; yet I constantly tread the huntsman's path, although I seldom have good luck. If I am
not fit for a beautiful deer, I will have to be satisfied with eating hare; I
demand nothing more; that won't sadden me.

Composed in Hamburg before 1860, probably in 1859.
The first performance is not documented.
Simple strophic.
A version of the text with a melody by Arnt von Aich dates from 1519 and
is reproduced by Friedländer (*Brahms's Lieder*, 61–62); it was published in
E. N. Ammerbach's *Deutsche Tabulatur* in 1571, then in C. F. Becker's
Lieder und Weisen vergangener Jahrhunderte (Leipzig, 1849). The text
also appears in Ludwig Uhland's *Alte hoch- und niederdeutsche Volkslieder*
(Stuttgart and Tübingen, 1844–45).
Brahms's setting is deliberately archaic. A full measure is given to the first
word, and the closing phrase is somewhat melismatic, as in the sixteenth-
century melody. The harmonization avoids sevenths; its cadence chords often

lack a third; and the entire melody lies within the range of a sixth. Its chorale-like structure in long notes, the accompaniment huddled on a single staff like some sort of tablature, gives the piece the appearance of something recon-structed from centuries earlier. In performance, however, it is revealed to be a touching lament expressed with both dignity and restraint.

The text appears to be a typical hunting song, unusual only in being sung by, rather than about, the hunter, but it is in fact an allegory concerning Duke Ulrich of Württemberg (who may himself be the author). The duke as a child was betrothed to Sabina of Bavaria, a niece of the Emperor Maximilian. Though he later fell in love with the Countess Elizabeth of Brandenburg, he could not disentangle himself from the ties to the neither beautiful nor lovable Princess Sabina. The song likens Elizabeth to a noble beast that he is forbidden to hunt, being forced to content himself with rabbit.

The word "schell" means "cause to sound." Toward the end of the first verse, the 1519 version has "es scheucht ab mir" (runs shyly from me) in-stead of "das schied von mir" (it has gone from me). In the third verse the original had "Jägers Bann," referring to the enclosed hunting lands, rather than "Jägers Bahn" (hunter's path). "Hasenfleisch" (rabbit meat) is a very unflattering reference to the unattractive bride-to-be.

The version for four-part male chorus, published as Op. 41/1, preceded the solo version.

Das Lied vom Herrn von Falkenstein, Op. 43/4
(The Song of the Lord of Falkenstein)

Text from *Des Knaben Wunderhorn*

Es reit' der Herr von Falkenstein
Wohl über ein' breite Heide.
Was sieht er an dem Wege stehn?
Ein Mädel mit weißem Kleide.

"Gott grüße euch, Herrn von Falkenstein!
Seid ihr des Lands ein Herre,
Ei so gebt mir wieder den Gefangenen mein
Um aller Jungfrauen Ehre!"

"Den Gefangenen mein, den geb' ich nicht,
Im Turm muß er verfaulen!
Zu Falkenstein steht ein tiefer Turm,
Wohl zwischen zwei hohen Mauren."

"Steht zu Falkenstein ein tiefer Turm
Wohl zwischen zwei hohen Mauren,
So will ich an die Mauren stehn,
Und will ihm helfen trauren."

Sie ging den Turm wohl um und wieder um:
"Feinslieb, bist du darinnen?
Und wenn ich dich nicht sehen kann,
So komm ich von meinen Sinnen."

Sie ging den Turm wohl um und wieder um:
Den Turm wollt sie aufschließen:
"Und wenn die Nacht ein Jahr land wär',
Kein Stund' tät mich verdrießen!"

"Ei, dörft ich scharfe Messer trag'n,
Wie unser's Herrn sein' Knechte,
So tät ich mit Dem von Falkenstein
Um meinen Herzliebsten fechten!"

"Mit einer Jungfrau fecht' ich nicht,
Das wär' mir eine Schande!
Ich will dir deinen Gefang'nen geb'n,
Zieh mit ihm aus dem Lande."

"Wohl aus dem Land da zieh' ich nicht,
Hab' Niemand was gestohlen;
Und wenn ich was hab' liegen lahn,
So darf ich's wieder holen."

The Lord of Falkenstein rides over a broad heath. What does he see standing in his path? A girl with a white dress.

"Greetings, Lord of Falkenstein! If you are a lord of the land, well, then restore my imprisoned lover to me for the honor of all maidens."

"I won't release my prisoner; he must rot in the tower! At Falkenstein there stands a deep tower between two high walls."

"If at Falkenstein there stands a deep tower between two high walls, then I will stand by the walls and help him grieve."

She went around and around the tower: "Darling, are you inside? And if I can't see you, I'll lose my mind."

She went around and around the tower; she wanted to unlock the tower: "And even if the night were a year long, no hour of it would distress me!

"Yes, if I were allowed to carry sharp knives like our lord's servant, I would fight with the Lord of Falkenstein to obtain my sweetheart."

"I don't fight with girls; that would bring shame upon me! I will give you your imprisoned lover; leave the country with him."

"No, I won't leave the country; I haven't stolen anything from anyone; and if I have left anything behind, I am entitled to come and get it again."

Composed in Detmold, probably in the fall of 1857.

First performed by Heinrich Vogl on 5 December 1873 in Frankfurt.

In effect, strophic with a contrasting central section; actually, three different melodies are involved. Verses 1–3 and 8 are set to the same eleven-measure melody in C minor, the phrase structure 2 + 2 + 3 + 2 + 2. Verses 4,

7, and 9 transfer the melody to the piano's bass line and are sung to a countermelody. Verses 5 and 6 are set to a new melody in A♭ major, ten measures
phrased 3 + 2 + 2 + 3, each verse modulating to, and ending in, the dominant.

The C-minor music is vigorous and angular, the A♭ music has more stepwise melodic movement and is harmonized more warmly. The opening verse
has voice and piano in unison; thereafter, the C-minor accompaniments are
lightly varied.

The poem appears, with some differences, in *Des Knaben Wunderhorn*
(Heidelberg, 1806–1808), Johann Gottfried Herder's *Volkslieder* (Tübingen, 1778–79), Ludwig Uhland's *Alte hoch- und niederdeutsche Volkslieder*
(Stuttgart and Tübingen, 1844–45), and the Kretzschmer-Zuccalmaglio *Deutsche Volkslieder* (Berlin, 1838–40). While the *Wunderhorn* was Brahms's
principal source, his text has some aspects of a composite.

FOUR GESÄNGE, OP. 46

Lieder und Gesänge mit Begleitung des Pianoforte von Johannes Brahms (Songs with Piano Accompaniment by Johannes Brahms). Part title: *Op. 46. Vier Gesänge* (Four Songs). Published in October 1868 by Simrock in Berlin; publication number 320. The complete collection also includes the songs Opp. 47–49.

In general, the songs of these four sets represent a trend away from the dramatic character of Opp. 32 and 33 toward more intimate and personal reflections on love and life. Although strophic forms are still common, it is in these groups of songs that Brahms polishes to perfection the varied strophic form that he would continue to use so frequently and so admirably.

Op. 46 pairs two Daumer texts (in D♭ and A) and two by Hölty (both in E major).

Die Kränze, Op. 46/1 (The Wreaths)

Translated from the Greek by Georg Friedrich Daumer (1800–1875)

> Hier ob dem Eingang seid befestiget,
> Ihr Kränze, so beregnet und benetzt
> Von meines Auges schmerzlichem Erguß!
> Denn reich zu tränen pflegt das Aug' der Liebe.
> Dies zarte Naß, ich bitte,
> Nicht allzu frühe träufet es herab.
> Spart es, bis ihr vernehmet, daß sie sich
> Der Schwelle naht mit ihrem Grazienschritte,
> Die Teuere, die mir so ungelind.
> Mit einem Male dann hernieder sei es
> Auf ihres Hauptes gold'ne Pracht ergossen,
> Und sie empfinde, daß es Tränen sind;
> Daß es die Tränen sind, die meinem Aug'
> In dieser kummervollen Nacht entflossen.

Be fastened here above the doorway, you wreaths, bedewed and moistened thus by the painful outpourings of my eyes! For the eyes of love are wont to weep copiously.

119

I beg of you, do not let this tender moisture drip away too soon. Save it until you hear that she, the dear one who is so unkind to me, is approaching the threshold with her step like that of the Graces.

Then let it be poured down all at once onto the golden glory of her head, and let her realize that it is tears; that it is the tears shed by my eyes in this sorrowful night.

Composed in the spring of 1864, probably in Bonn.

First performed by Heinrich Vogl on 5 December 1873 at the fifth Museum concert in Frankfurt.

Through-composed.

The poem appears as No. 27 in Daumer's *Polydora, ein weltpoetisches Liederbuch* (Frankfurt am Main, 1855), under the title "Antike Musen: Hellas." At the words "dass sie sich der Schwelle naht," Daumer emphasized the "sie" by spaced printing. The title "Die Kränze" is Brahms's own.

The text is one of those tear-soaked reproachful messages to the beloved so dear to the minor Romantic poets. Despite its sentimentality, Brahms was moved by it to one of his most masterly creations.

The prelude itself is inspired, and the whole song seems to evolve from it. The quiet major harmonies and gently arching melody establish the mood of sadness and resignation, and the stepwise eighth notes, portraying the falling tears, form a rhythmic motive that permeates the entire song.

The irregular rhythms of the music reflect those of the poem. The climax of the first section comes with the soaring phrase at the words "das Aug' der Liebe." After a slightly varied repetition of the prelude as interlude, the music modulates to the tonic minor. (In the original key of D♭ major, this process appears more complex than it is, since the new key is notated as C♯ minor). This section is more agitated because of its increased rhythmic activity and faster harmonic rhythm. The yearned-for downpouring onto the golden head of the cruel beloved elicits the submediant key of imagination (m. 38) and a naively illustrative chromatic descent in the vocal line (mm. 40–42), while the piano sighs its reiterated falling fourth.

The return to the tonic major five bars later is a modulation unsurpassed in effectiveness even by Schubert, and is achieved by the simple means of causing the piano accompaniment, after its echo of the preceding vocal phrase, to sink a half step, soblike, at the change of key signature, carrying with it the helpless vocal line.

The voice concludes with a repetition of the climax from the first section, but unexpectedly the piano postlude extends the emotional tension by rising to a *forte* climax a whole step higher than that of the voice, immediately repeating the same gesture as if to emphasize this outburst of impassioned grief. The music then fades away in one of Brahms's most magical written-out ritards, the falling-tears motive gradually subsiding at last.

Magyarisch, Op. 46/2 (Magyar Song)

Translated from the Hungarian
by Georg Friedrich Daumer (1800–1875)

Sah dem edlen Bildnis in des Auges
    Allzusüßen Wunderschein,
Büßte so des eigenen Auges heitern
    Schimmer ein.

Herr mein Gott, was hast du doch gebildet
    Uns zu Jammer und zu Qual
Solche dunkle Sterne mit so lichtem
    Zauberstrahl!

Mich geblendet hat für alle Wonnen
    Dieser Erde jene Pracht;
All umher, so meine Blicke forschen,
    Ist es Nacht.

I gazed into the extremely sweet miraculous glow of the wondrous beauty's
eyes, and by so doing forfeited the cheerful gleam of my own eyes.
    Lord God, why, to our grief and pain, did You ever create such dark stars
with such bright magic rays?
    That splendor blinded me to all the blisses of this earth; all around, wher-
ever my eyes look, it is night.

Though the exact details are unknown, probably composed in Bonn during
the summer of 1868.
    Julius Stockhausen sang the first performance in Vienna in 1869.
    Through-composed, in three sections: the first (to m. 22) is in quietly
flowing folk-song character; the second is more dramatic and modulatory; the third contains varied references to both earlier materials, plus a
codetta.
    The text is from Daumer's *Polydora* (Frankfurt am Main, 1855).
    The poem's irregularity (stanzas of 5 + 4 + 5 + 2 poetic feet) translates
into vocal phrases of irregular length, though the piano's extensions and
overlapping phrases produce what appears to be a seamless continuity.
    Typically, whatever Hungarian flavor is present is merely suggested by a
cadence pattern here or an ornament there. The setting is more reflective
of the poem's folk style than of its smoldering passion. There are, however,
some telling dramatic effects, such as the suggestion of tolling bells when
the Deity is addressed in the middle section, the chromatic and dynamic
highlighting of "uns zu Jammer und zu Qual" in mm. 27–31, and, in the
last nine measures, the darkening of the harmony at the first mention of
night and the dying away to stillness following the second. The vocal line's

ornamentation in mm. 58–61 may be a musical synonym for the text's "all around, wherever my eyes look."

Die Schale der Vergessenheit, Op. 46/3
(The Goblet of Oblivion)

Text by Ludwig Hölty (1748–1776)

Eine Schale des Stroms, welcher Vergessenheit
    Durch Elysiums Blumen rollt,
Bring', o Genius, bring' deinem Verschmachtenden!
    Dort, wo Phaon die Sängerin,
Dort, wo Orpheus vergaß seiner Eurydice,
    Schöpf' den silbernen Schlummerquell!

Ha! Dann tauch' ich dein Bild, spröde Gebieterin,
    Und die lächelnde Lippe voll
Lautenklanges, des Haar's schattige Wallungen,
    Und das Beben der weißen Brust,
Und den siegenden Blick, der mir im Marke zuckt,
    Tauch' ich tief in den Schlummerquell.

O guardian spirit, bring a goblet of the stream that spreads forgetfulness among the flowers of Elysium, bring it to your thirsting protégé! There where Phaon forgot the poetess [Sappho], there where Orpheus forgot his Eurydice, draw the silvery sleeping potion!

Ha! Then I shall plunge your image, obstinate and imperious woman, and those smiling lips full of lute tones, the shadowy undulations of that hair, and the heaving of that white breast, and that conquering gaze which darts through me inwardly—I shall plunge them deep into the goblet of oblivion.

Probably composed in Bonn during the summer of 1868, perhaps earlier.

First performed by Julius Stockhausen (from manuscript) in 1868 in Bonn. Brahms is reported to have been unwilling to publish this song, regarding it as "desolate" and "worthless," but Stockhausen's enthusiasm finally changed his mind.

Through-composed, resembling A B A.

Hölty wrote the poem in 1776, but did not publish it. Brahms used an altered version by Johann Henrich Voss, which appeared first in Voss's *Musenalmanach* for the year 1777, then in his edition of Hölty's *Gedichte* (1804). It has alternating asclepiadic (x x – ⌣ ⌣ – – – ⌣ ⌣ – ⌣ –) and glyconaic (x x – ⌣ ⌣ – ⌣ –) lines, but these rhythmic subtleties are largely overwhelmed by Brahms's rich flood of impassioned sound.

The unrestrained eroticism of the text is nearly matched by the music's *Tristan*-like avoidance of tonic harmony and reluctance to resolve dissonance, the accompaniment's panting breathlessness, and the growing intensity of constantly increasing tempo.

An die Nachtigall, Op. 46/4 (To the Nightingale)

Text by Ludwig Hölty (1748–1776)

Geuß' nicht so laut der liebentflammten Lieder
    Tonreichen Schall
Vom Blütenast des Apfelbaums hernieder,
    O Nachtigall!

Du tönest mir mit deiner süßen Kehle
    Die Liebe wach;
Denn schon durchbebt die Tiefen meiner Seele
    Dein schmelzend Ach.

Dann flieht der Schlaf von neuem dieses Lager,
    Ich starre dann
Mit nassem Blick und totenbleich und hager
    Den Himmel an.

Fleuch', Nachtigall, in grüne Finsternisse,
    In's Haingesträuch,
Und spend' im Nest der treuen Gattin Küsse;
    Entfleuch, entfleuch!

Do not pour down the tuneful sound of your amorous songs so loudly from the blossoming twig of the apple tree, O nightingale!

You awaken love in me with your sweet throat; for your melting "Alas" is already stirring up the depths of my soul.

Then sleep once more flees this couch, then I stare at the sky with wet eyes, pale as death and haggard.

Fly off, nightingale, into the green darkness, into the shrubbery of the grove, and in your nest shower kisses on your faithful mate; fly away, fly away!

Composed in Bonn in June 1868.

First performed by Marie Fillunger on 1 December 1874 in Leipzig.

Two strophes, similar in contour but differing in detail.

The poem has as its basis a fragment, dated 1772, that was found among Hölty's papers. As usual, Brahms used a version altered by Voss, who in this case wrote at least half of the poem himself. The lines alternate eleven and four syllables; Brahms always sets the four-syllable line more broadly, often as four half notes.

It is a song of love-longing against a background of the beauty of nature. The scene of quiet dusk among the apple blossoms is set immediately by the rocking syncopations of the accompaniment, which not only evoke the poet's sighs and longing but also intensify the harmonic inflections and modulations.

In the second half of the first strophe, chromatic alterations and the sharper *sforzando* dissonances that result in the piano dramatize the increasing poignancy of the second verse; the lessening of rhythmic activity and a turn to the Neapolitan depict the hushed enchantment of the nightingale's song ("dein schmelzend Ach").

The piano interlude seems to prepare a repetition of the music from the opening, but Brahms, with his infallible variation sense, turns instead into the minor mode and the song's only *forte* climax at "den Himmel an." Syncopations in the piano lead on to the earlier second-half melody, but now the accompaniment itself has a variation; it not only breaks into triplets (perhaps in response to the idea of flight) but also sings its own countermelody (evoking the text's "faithful mate"), which rises with the vocal line to its peak on the word "Küsse" and then falls in a gradual *diminuendo*, to fade away, like the nightingale's song, into the twilight.

FIVE LIEDER, OP. 47

Lieder und Gesänge mit Begleitung des Pianoforte von Johannes Brahms (Songs with Piano Accompaniment by Johannes Brahms). Part title: *Op. 47. Fünf Lieder* (Five Songs). Published in October 1868 by Simrock in Berlin; publication number 321. The complete collection also includes the songs Opp. 46, 48, and 49.

The set comprises two Daumer translations from the fourteenth-century Persian poet Hafiz, two strophic songs, and a setting of a sonnet by Goethe. No. 3, "Sonntag," quickly became popular, achieving somewhat the status of a composed folk song.

Botschaft, Op. 47/1 (Message)

Translated by Georg Friedrich Daumer (1800–1875)
from Mohämmad Shams od-Dīn Hafiz (Persian; c.1326–c.1390)

> Wehe, Lüftchen, lind und lieblich
> Um die Wange der Geliebten,
> Spiele zart in ihrer Locke,
> Eile nicht, hinweg zu flieh'n!
> Tut sie dann vielleicht die Frage,
> Wie es um mich Armen stehe,
> Sprich: "Unendlich war sein Wehe,
> Höchst bedenklich seine Lage;
> Aber jetzo kann er hoffen,
> Wieder herrlich aufzuleben,
> Denn du, Holde, denkst an ihn."

Blow, breeze, mildly and sweetly about the face of my loved one, play tenderly with her tresses; don't hasten so to move onward!

If she then perhaps asks how things are going with me, the unfortunate man, say:

"His pain was endless, his situation extremely grave; but now he can hope to revive and be perfectly healthy, for you, lovely one, are thinking of him."

Composed in Bonn in June 1868.

First performed by Louise Dustmann on 6 January 1871 in Vienna.
A B A'.

The text is found in Daumer's *Hafis: Neue Sammlung persischer Gedichte* (Nuremberg, 1852); this poem does not appear in the 1846 and 1856 editions.

With its ripplingly urgent accompaniment and lilting melodic line, "Botschaft" rapidly became, and remains, one of Brahms's most popular songs.

It is characterized by vacillation between the minor mode and its relative major. This duality is established from the outset by the prelude, and it gives rise to the peculiarly ambiguous V^{13} chord (made up of elements from both keys) in mm. 6–7, over which the voice makes its entrance. After the quieter middle section, the same harmony recurs to support the singer's reiterated "sprich" in mm. 39 and 40, announcing and highlighting the return of the main melody.

Particularly noteworthy are the inspired extension of the melody in the final stanza at "höchst bedenklich seine Lage"; the exultant codetta; and the characteristic duplets against triplets, which affect only the piano in the first verse, but both voice and piano in the last, the duplets finally taking over completely in mm. 55–57 for the splendid climax at "denn du, Holde."

Accompanists should take care to observe the composer's *piano leggiero* indication; the writing is thick-textured and somewhat clumsy, but it depicts only a "mild breeze" until the lover's joy later becomes the dominant feature.

The Breitkopf & Härtel complete edition and the Dover reprint of it omit the fermata in the penultimate measure of the vocal line; it should appear *between* the two notes, the word "an" being sung in tempo over the piano's sustained harmony.

Liebesglut, Op. 47/2 (Blaze of Love)

Translated by Georg Friedrich Daumer (1800–1875)
from Mohammad Shams od-Dīn Hafiz (Persian; c.1326–c.1390)

Die Flamme hier, die wilde, zu verhehlen,
Die Schmerzen alle, welche mich zerquälen,
Vermag ich es, da alle Winde ringsum
Die Gründe meiner Traurigkeit erzählen?

Daß ich ein Stäubchen deines Weges stäube,
Wie magst du doch, o sprich, wie darfst du schmählen?
Verklage dich, verklage das Verhängnis,
Das waltet über alle Menschenseelen!

Da selbiges verordnete, das ew'ge,
Wie alle sollten ihre Wege wählen,

> Da wurde deinem Lockenhaar der Auftrag,
> Mir Ehre, Glauben und Vernunft zu stehlen.

Can I conceal the wild flame here, all the pains that torture me, when all the winds round about relate the causes of my sadness?

If I raise a grain of dust in your path, tell me, how have you the heart to revile me? Accuse yourself, accuse the destiny that governs all human souls!

When that eternal destiny arranged how each man should choose his path, your wavy hair was assigned the task of stealing my honor, religious faith and common sense.

Probably composed in 1868 in Bonn.

First performed on 15 February 1888 in Vienna by Julie Salter and pianist Julie Zilzer.

Through-composed, though the final segment gives the effect of augmentation of material from the first.

The poem is from Daumer's *Hafis: Eine Sammlung persischer Gedichte* (Hamburg, 1846). Daumer left the poem untitled; Brahms originally called the song "Liebeslied" but in the printer's proof he crossed out that title and substituted the present one.

The song begins at a high level of emotional intensity, its restlessness invading not only the typical two-against-three rhythm but the tonality as well. As in the preceding song, there is considerable interplay between minor and relative major, but since chromaticism and enharmonic notation are also frequent, tonal instability is the rule.

After repetition of the prelude as interlude, the idea of rising dust is illustrated in staccato broken octaves in what amount to quarter-note triplets. In stages, beginning from m. 32, the bass begins slipping down chromatically, forcing the voice to do likewise. Two identical phrases a half step apart lead, in m. 47, to bare octave triplets on a suspenseful leading tone, which is prolonged and made momentarily major. The idea of eternal destiny calls forth some fateful octave leaps, after which we arrive, via the dominant and an excursion through the minor (and angelic harp-evocative double arpeggios), at common time and a highly chromatic tonic major for the last portion of the song.

A somewhat quieter mood results from the replacement of triplets by even eighths in the accompaniment in m. 59, but soon an undercurrent of impassioned agitation returns and continues to the end of the song. In the final phrases, the voice again loses ground chromatically, as though the singer's strength had also been stolen along with "honor, faith, and common sense."

The score has an unusually "instrumental" look, like a movement from a clarinet or viola sonata, largely because of the complexity of the piano part and its independence from the vocal line.

Sonntag, Op. 47/3 (Sunday)

Text from *Volkslieder* by Ludwig Uhland (1787–1862)

So hab' ich doch die ganze Woche
Mein feines Liebchen nicht gesehn,
Ich sah es an einen Sonntag
Wohl vor der Türe stehn:
Das tausendschöne Jungfräulein,
Das tausendschöne Herzelein,
Wollte Gott, ich wär' heute bei ihr!

So will mir doch die ganze Woche
Das Lachen nicht vergehn,
Ich sah es an einem Sonntag
Wohl in die Kirche gehn:
Das tausendschöne Jungfräulein,
Das tausendschöne Herzelein,
Wollte Gott, ich wär' heute bei ihr!

After not seeing my sweetheart for a whole week, I saw her on a Sunday outside the door: the wonderfully beautiful girl, the wonderfully beautiful darling. I wish to God that I were with her today.

And so all week long I can't lose my joyous laughter; I saw her on a Sunday going into church; the wonderfully beautiful girl, the wonderfully beautiful darling. I wish to God that I were with her today.

Composed in 1859 in Hamburg.
First performed by Julius Stockhausen in London in 1871.
Simple strophic.
The text is from Ludwig Uhland's collection *Alte hoch- und nieder-deutsche Volkslieder* (Stuttgart and Tübingen, 1844–45).
The setting is one of Brahms's most charming, and it manages to sound like an authentic folk song and yet unmistakably Brahmsian. The folk quality derives from the regular four-measure phrase structure and the highly original accompaniment (based largely on a graceful figure made up of five eighth notes), which hints at rustic drones and horns.
The repetition of the final vocal phrase ("Wollte Gott," etc.), which so emphasizes the lover's longing and, serving as a kind of refrain, is one of the most memorable aspects of the song, was not in the early printings of the first edition. Brahms penciled it into his copy and instructed Simrock that it was to be included in subsequent printings.
Pianists may be persuaded by the increased complexity near the end of the postlude, which also serves as the interlude between strophes (and incidentally to soften the regularity of the phrasing), to add a ritard, but a ritard only adds to the awkwardness of the passage; to emphasize the sub-

dominant harmony in the penultimate bar, as Brahms's dynamic indication seems to prescribe, is perhaps a more graceful solution.

O liebliche Wangen, Op. 47/4 (O Lovely Face)

Text by Paul Flem[m]ing (1609–1640)

O liebliche Wangen,
Ihr macht mir Verlangen,
Dies rote, dies weiße,
Zu schauen mit Fleiße.
Und dies nur alleine
Ist's nicht, was ich meine;
Zu schauen, zu grüßen,
Zu rühren, zu küssen,
Ihr macht mir Verlangen
O liebliche Wangen!

O Sonne der Wonne!
O Wonne der Sonne!
O Augen, so saugen
Das Licht meiner Augen.
O englische Sinnen,
O himmlisch Beginnen!
O Himmel auf Erden!
Magst du mir nicht werden?
O Wonne der Sonne,
O Sonne der Wonne!

O Schönste der Schönen!
Benimm mir dies Sehnen.
Komm eile, komm komme,
Du süße, du fromme;
Ach, Schwester, ich sterbe,
Ich sterb', ich verderbe,
Komm komme, komm eile,
Komm komme, komm eile,
Benimm mir dies Sehnen,
O Schönste der Schönen!

O lovely face, you create in me the desire to look diligently upon that red and that white. And I don't mean only that; to look, to greet, to touch, to kiss—that is what you make me desire, O lovely face!

O sun of bliss! O bliss of the sun! O eyes that absorb the light of my eyes. O angelic mind! O heavenly actions! O heaven on earth! Won't you be mine, O bliss of the sun, O sun of bliss?

O fairest of the fair! take this yearning from me. Come, hasten, come, come, you sweet one, you merciful one! Ah, my sister, I am dying, I am dying, I am perishing; come, come, come, and hasten, come, come, come and hasten, take this yearning from me, O fairest of the fair!

Composed in June 1868 in Bonn.

First performed by Hermine Spies on 26 March 1887 in Vienna.

Strophic; the insertion of two measures allows for a bravura cadence in the last verse.

The poem is taken from Fleming's *Geistliche und weltliche Poemata* (Jena, 1651), where it is found in the fifth book of odes "von Liebesge-sängen." In the original the sixth line reads "das ich meine," and the third line from the end, "komm, tröste, komm, heile."

Brahms's setting is a joyously fast-moving love song, combining breathless passion with the playful juggling of the poem's successive rhymes. The structure is of three four-measure phrases, a six-measure phrase leading to the ritard and fermata, and a closing four-measure phrase. In the six-measure phrase, the piano's rocking eighth-note figure is exchanged for steady eighths with sixteenths that increase in brilliance to the end of the strophe. The varying placement in the bar of the voice's eighth notes also contributes to the effect of hurrying.

The minor-major ambivalence at the end of each verse is a musical metaphor for yearning.

Die Liebende schreibt, Op. 47/5
(A Woman in Love Writes a Letter)

Text by Johann Wolfgang von Goethe (1749–1832)

Ein Blick von deinen Augen in die meinen,
Ein Kuß von deinem Mund auf meinem Munde,
Wer davon hat, wie ich, gewisse Kunde,
Mag dem was ander's wohl erfreulich scheinen?

Entfernt von dir, entfremdet von den Meinen,
Führ' ich stets die Gedanken in die Runde,
Und immer treffen sie auf jene Stunde,
Die einzige: da fang' ich an zu weinen.

Die Träne trocknet wieder unversehens:
Er liebt ja, denk' ich, her, in diese Stille,
Und solltest du nicht in die Ferne reichen?

Vernimm das Lispeln dieses Liebeswehens,
Mein einzig Glück auf Erden ist dein Wille,
Dein freundlicher, zu mir; gib mir ein Zeichen!

A glance from your eyes into mine, a kiss of your mouth upon mine—if anyone knew those things as well as I do, would they find anything else enjoyable?

Far from you, estranged from my family, I constantly let my thoughts go straying and they always hit upon that hour, that one and only hour; then I start to cry.

My tears dry again without my noticing; I think to myself: his love surely reaches me here in this quiet spot—and can't you reach out into the distance?

Hear the murmur of this breeze of love; my only happiness on earth is your good will toward me; send me some word!

Composed in Göttingen, summer or fall 1858.

First performed by Eduard Gärtner on 22 March 1893 in Vienna.

The two four-line stanzas are treated quasi-strophically; the remaining sestet is through-composed.

The poem is found as No. 8 among the sonnets in *Sämtliche Gedichte*, the first volume of the complete works. Brahms owned *Sämmtliche Werke* (Stuttgart, 1860) and *Werke* (no date).

The text concerns itself with the emotional aftermath of a love affair's interruption, the details of which remain unspecified. Brahms's underrated setting is an insightful, compassionate psychological study of the lonely letter writer; it is profoundly touching when sensitively performed.

Throughout the song, the tonic key represents the current time and place, and the remembered love is associated with the key of the submediant.

The opening vocal line is almost studiedly matter-of-fact, with its triad-outlining rise and fall. But the yearning that aches beneath the woman's outward self-control is revealed in the sighing piano chords that introduce the first two phrases, and an anxious little rhythmic figure of two slurred eighths after a rest appears in m. 2 and persists. The second phrase's sequential rise hints at intensifying emotion and provides the first reference to the submediant. The question framed by lines 3 and 4 pours out in a flood of quickly changing harmonies and breaks off in a half-cadence on the dominant of the submediant.

Composure restored, the second strophe resumes like the first, but the harmonic addition of an insistent seventh signals a smoldering fervor that culminates in an unequivocal modulation to the submediant at the *forte* "die einzige."

At m. 24, the anxious eighth-note motive takes the form of an appoggiatura figure to suggest weeping. The drying of tears in m. 27 elicits a more cheerful version in double notes, *pianissimo*. In the setting of the poem's crucial lines 10 and 11, the accompaniment introduces continuous legato eighth notes, whose sinuous twining encompasses first single, then double, neighboring tones; as the woman implores her distant lover to reach out to her in her place of exile, a modulation brings about the return of the tonic key, and a *crescendo* leads to an ardent *forte* transition for the piano.

In the closing phrases, the anxious eighth notes assume new prominence as treble octaves. Gently pleading stepwise motion in the vocal line now replaces the triad outlines of the song's opening; the earlier forthright diatonicism is supplanted by the beseeching chromatic sequences of mm. 43–44 and the semitonal bass movement of their associated harmonies. A turn to the tender subdominant at "dein freundlicher zu mir" evokes vulnerability; a delay of the final vocal phrase and its feminine cadence, which occurs mid-phrase harmonically, seem to confirm the woman's total dependence on her lover's reassurances. As the postlude repeats the piano's closing formula in the lower octave, one can almost picture her beginning her restless wait for his message.

SEVEN LIEDER, OP. 48

Lieder und Gesänge mit Begleitung des Pianoforte von Johannes Brahms (Songs with Piano Accompaniment by Johannes Brahms). Part title: *Op. 48. Sieben Lieder* (Seven Songs). Published in October 1868 by Simrock in Berlin; publication number 322. The complete collection also includes the songs Opp. 46, 47, and 49.

Brahms's ordering within the set balances his bleak setting of Schack's somber "Herbstgefühl" against six strophic melodies to folk song, or folk song–based, texts. Though gathered and prepared for publication during the summer of 1868 in Bonn, most of the songs were composed earlier.

Der Gang zum Liebchen, Op. 48/1 (Visiting His Sweetheart)

Translated from the Bohemian by Joseph Wenzig (Czech, 1807–1876)

> Es glänzt der Mond nieder,
> Ich sollte doch wieder
> Zu meinem Liebchen
> Wie mag es ihr geh'n?
>
> Ach weh', sie verzaget
> Und klaget, und klaget,
> Daß sie mich nimmer
> Im Leben wird seh'n!
>
> Es ging der Mond unter,
> Ich eilte doch munter,
> Und eilte, daß keiner
> Mein Liebchen entführt.
>
> Ihr Täubchen, o girret,
> Ihr Lüftchen, o schwirret,
> Daß keiner mein Liebchen,
> Mein Liebchen entführt!

The moon is shining down; I really ought to go to my sweetheart again to see how she is.

Alas, she is losing courage and she laments and laments that she will never again see me while she lives!

The moon went down, but I hastened briskly, and hastened so that no one would carry off my sweetheart.

You doves, coo; you breezes, hum, so that no one carries off my sweetheart!

The date of composition is uncertain; the solo song was prepared for publication during the summer of 1868 in Bonn, but a choral version had already appeared in the part books of the Hamburg Ladies' Choir for the years 1859–1862. The same text to different music for SATB with piano was published as Op. 31/3 in July 1864.

The first performance (together with that of No. 4, "Gold überwiegt die Liebe") was given by Louise Dustmann as part of a Clara Schumann recital in Vienna on 22 December 1869.

Simple strophic; each verse comprises two eight-measure periods for the voice, separated by a six-measure interlude and followed by an eight-measure postlude.

The text is found in the "Bohemian Folk Songs" section of Wenzig's collection *Slawische Volkslieder* (Halle, 1830).

The setting is a graceful, melancholy waltz whose regularity of phrase structure and modal/minor ambivalence lend it a distinct folk flavor. The inspired stroke is the interpolation into the song itself of the material which is to become the postlude, with the disturbing effect of creating the faintest shadow of doubt. The words of the poem seems to offer reassurance; the music wistfully hints that there may be circumstances of which the boy is unaware, and that his persistent uneasiness may be justified.

Der Überläufer, Op. 48/2 (The Betrayer)

Text from Arnim and Brentano's *Des Knaben Wunderhorn*

In den Garten wollen wir gehen
Wo die schönen Rosen stehen,
Da steh'n der Rosen gar zu viel,
Brech' ich mir eine, wo ich will.

Wir haben gar öfters beisamm'n gesessen,
Wie ist mir mein Schatz so treu gewesen!
Das hätt' ich mir nicht gebildet ein,
Daß mein Schatz so falsch könnt' sein.

Hört ihr nicht den Jäger blasen
In dem Wald auf grünen Rasen,
Den Jäger mit dem grünen Hut,
Der meinen Schatz verführen tut.

Let's go into the garden where the beautiful roses are; there are many too
many roses there; I will pluck one, any one I want.

We often sat side by side; how faithful my darling was to me! I would never
have imagined that my darling could be so false.

Don't you hear the huntsman blowing in the forest on the green sward, the
huntsman with the green hat, who is taking my darling away from me?

The date of composition is uncertain; although the set was assembled for
publication during the summer of 1868, there is a copy of this song in the Library of Congress, signed and dated "1853" by the copyist, Julius Otto Grimm.

First performed by Hermine Spies on 18 January 1890 in Vienna.

Simple strophic.

The text is from the folk poetry collection *Des Knaben Wunderhorn* (Heidelberg, 1805–1808), where there is a fourth stanza that Brahms did not set:

> Hört ihr nicht den Trompeter blasen,
> In der Stadt auf der Parade?
> Den Trompeter mit dem Federbusch,
> Der meinen Schatz verraten tut.

Don't you hear the trumpeter playing, on parade in the city? The trumpeter
with the plume, who is betraying my darling. [My translation.]

The four-measure phrases and Aeolian melody of the setting recall folk
song. The accompaniment, for all its apparent plainness, is artfully evocative:
its melodic departure from unison to duet above the voice symbolizes the
girl's independence and infidelity; the imitations in the bass of the closing
phrase are particularly expressive, underlining the peak of each stanza's
accumulated resentment, their momentary suspension of meter creating
connection rather than separation between stanzas, as though the singer
had merely paused to gather his thoughts before continuing his lament. The
repetition of "mein'n Schatz" as codetta is Brahms's own, and seems a poignant reflection of the wronged lover's first full comprehension of his loss.

Liebesklage des Mädchens, Op. 48/3 (The Lovelorn Girl's Lament)

Text from *Des Knaben Wunderhorn*

> Wer sehen will zween lebendige Brunnen,
> Der soll mein' zwei betrübte Augen seh'n,
> Die mir vor Weinen schier sind ausgerunnen,
> Wer sehen will viel groß' und tiefe Wunden,
> Der soll mein sehr verwund'tes Herz beseh'n,
> So hat mich Liebe verwund't im tiefsten Grunde.

Whoever wishes to see two living fountains, should look at my two sad-
dened eyes that have almost dried up with weeping.
Whoever wants to see many large and deep wounds, should take a look at my
sorely wounded heart; that is how love wounded me to the roots of my soul.

The date of composition is uncertain, but the song is listed in an inventory
that Brahms made in April 1860 of songs not yet published.'

The first performance is undocumented.

Two strophes, differing only slightly, with a brief postlude.

In *Des Knaben Wunderhorn*, the poem is the sixth of nine under the collective title *Liebesklage des Mädchens*. For rhythmic reasons, Brahms
removed a syllable from "sehen" in line 2 and "besehen" in line 5, and added
one to "Lieb" in the last line. In line 4 the *Wunderhorn* has "Wunde" instead
of "Wunden."

The text deals unrelievedly with the intensity of a girl's suffering from unhappy love, and Brahms sets it with dignity and compassion. Borrowings
from the minor and frequent diminished-seventh harmonies depict her pain.
The unstable tonality and the accompaniment's lagging melodic doubling,
righted only for the last line's anguished outcry, evoke a kind of grief-induced
paralysis. The postlude seems to offer some small attempt at solace.

Gold überwiegt die Liebe, Op. 48/4 (Gold Prevails over Love)

Translated from the Bohemian by Joseph Wenzig (Czech, 1807–1876)

Sternchen mit dem trüben Schein,
Könntest du doch weinen!
Hättest du ein Herzelein,
O, du gold'nes Sternlein mein,
Möchtest Funken weinen.

Weintest mit mir, weintest laut
Nächte durch voll Leiden,
Daß sie mich vom Liebsten traut,
Um das Gold der reichen Braut
Mich vom Liebsten scheiden.

Little star with the veiled light, if you could only weep! If you had a little
heart, oh, you little golden star of mine, you would weep sparks.
You would weep with me, you would weep loudly through nights full of
sorrow, because they are separating me from my dear sweetheart for the sake
of the rich bride's gold.

Collected for publication during the summer of 1868, but probably composed earlier.

First performed (together with No. 1, "Der Gang zum Liebchen") by Louise Dustmann as part of a Clara Schumann recital in Vienna on 22 December 1869.

Strophic; each strophe comprises five two-measure phrases corresponding to the five lines of each stanza of the poem, plus the piano's balancing two-measure interlude, extended to three measures for the postlude.

The text is found in Wenzig's German translation in his *Slawische Volkslieder* (Halle, 1830). In line 4, Brahms changed "Sternchen" to "Sternlein."

The singer implores the little star to join her in lamenting the infidelity of her lover, lured away by the prospect of a rich dowry. Brahms depicts her grief delicately in sobbing dissonances and gasping rests, while the accompaniment gently sighs in sympathy. The strophe culminates in the voice's final long descent from its highest pitch, marked *forte* over Neapolitan harmony. The piano's intensified repetition heightens the drama.

Trost in Tränen, Op. 48/5 (Consolation in Tears)

Text by Johann Wolfgang von Goethe (1749–1832)

> Wie kommt's daß du so traurig bist,
> Da alles froh erscheint?
> Man sieht dir's an den Augen an,
> Gewiß, du hast geweint.
>
> "Und hab' ich einsam auch geweint,
> So ist's mein eig'ner Schmerz,
> Und Tränen fließen gar so süß,
> Erleichtern mir das Herz."
>
> Die frohen Freunde laden dich,
> O, komm an unsre Brust!
> Und was du auch verloren hast,
> Vertraue den Verlust.
>
> "Ihr lärmt und rauscht und ahnet nicht
> Was mich, den Armen, quält.
> Ach nein, verloren hab' ich's nicht,
> So sehr es mir auch fehlt."
>
> So raffe denn dich eilig auf,
> Du bist ein junges Blut.
> In deinen Jahren hat man Kraft
> Und zum Erwerben Mut.
>
> "Ach nein, erwerben kann ich's nicht,
> Es steht mir gar zu fern.
> Es weilt so hoch, es blinkt so schön,
> Wie droben jener Stern."

Die Sterne, die begehrt man nicht,
Man freut sich ihrer Pracht,
Und mit Entzücken blickt man auf
In jeder heitern Nacht.

"Und mit Entzücken blick' ich auf
So manchen lieben Tag,
Verweinen laßt die Nächte mich,
So lang ich weinen mag."

"How is it you are so sad while everyone seems happy? I can see from your eyes you've surely been crying." "Even if I have been crying all alone, the sorrow is my own, and my tears flow so sweetly, they relieve my heart."

"Your happy friends invite you; oh, come rest on our heart! No matter what you've lost, tell us confidently what it was." "You're noisy and uproarious and have no notion of what makes me suffer so. Oh, no, I haven't lost it, although I miss it badly."

"Then pull yourself together quickly; you're a young person. At your age people have the strength and the courage to obtain what they want." "Oh, no, I can't attain it, it's much too far away from me. It dwells so high up and twinkles as beautifully as that star way up there."

"People don't wish for the stars, but merely enjoy their splendor and look upward with delight on every clear night." "And I have been looking upward with delight so many and many a day. Let me weep the nights away for as long as I care to weep."

Composed in November 1858 in Detmold.
The first performance is undocumented.
Simple strophic.
The text was adapted by Goethe from that of a folk song, which provided the meter and the opening words. The verses were written in 1801 and appeared in print in 1804; they may be found in part 1, "Lieder," of the collected *Gedichte*.

The poem suggests that tears are as necessary as happiness and sometimes as pleasurable. It takes the form of a dialogue, with its eight short stanzas alternately allocated to the two speakers; the first attempts to convince the other to lay his sadness aside, but his friend prefers to continue weeping.

The setting follows the same format, providing robust music in the major mode (with many melodic skips) for the first speaker, and gentler, more chromatic music in the minor mode (with mostly stepwise melodic movement) for the second.

The accompaniment at first doubles the vocal melody, but its gradually increasing independence prepares the ear for the piano's assuming complete melodic responsibility when the voice pauses. The thoughtfully expressive postlude, with its rising melodic line and its prolonged dissonances resolv-

ing to major harmonies, lends characteristically Brahmsian comfort and reassurance.

"Vergangen ist mir Glück und Heil," Op. 48/6
(I Have Lost Happiness and Well-Being)

"Old German" Text

Vergangen ist mir Glück und Heil
Und alle Freud' auf Erden;
Elend bin ich verloren gar,
Mir mag nit besser werden.
Bis in den Tod
Leid' ich groß' Not,
So ich dich, Lieb, muß meiden,
Geschieht mir, Ach,
O weh der Sach'!
Muß ich mich dein verjehen,
Groß Leid wird mir geschehen.

Erbarmen tu' ich mich so hart,
Das kommt aus Buhlers Hulde,
Die mich in Angst und Not hat bracht,
Und williglich das dulde.
Um dich allein,
Herzliebste mein,
Ist mir kein Bürd' zu schwere,
Wär's noch so viel,
Ich dennoch will
In deinem Dienst ersterben,
Nach fremder Lieb' nit werben.

Um Hülf' ich ruf', mein höchster Hort,
Erhör' mein sehnlich' Klagen!
Schaff' mir, Herzlieb, dein' Botschaft schier,
Ich muß sonst vor Leid verzagen!
Main traurig's Herz,
Leid't großen Schmerz,
Wie soll ich's überwinden?
Ich sorg', daß schier
Der Tod mit mir
Will ringen um das Leben,
Tu' mir dein Troste geben.

I have lost happiness and well-being and all joy on earth; I am miserably lost
and things cannot get better for me. Until I die I will suffer great distress, if I
must be away from you, my love; sorrow befalls me, alas that it should be so!
If I must give you up, great pain will be my lot.

> I feel such great pity; it comes from a lover's kindness, which has led me into fear and distress; and I endure this willingly. For you alone, my dearest, no burden is too heavy for me; however great it may be, I still want to die in your service, and not sue for another's love.
>
> I call for help, my lofty treasure; hear my yearning lament! Send me a message, darling, or else I must despair in my sorrow! My sad heart suffers great pain; how shall I overcome this? I fear that death will come and struggle with me for my life; give me your consolation.

Collected for publication as a solo song in 1868, but composed earlier. It is listed in the 1860 catalog of unpublished songs. In an arrangement for women's voices, it was included in the part books of the Hamburg Ladies' Chorus for 1859-1862. In 1874 a version for unaccompanied mixed chorus was published as Op. 62/7.

The first performance is not documented.

Simple strophic.

The Old German text appears in Franz Ludwig Mittler's *Deutsche Volkslieder* (Marpurg and Leipzig, 1855), where it is entitled "Klage." In verse 1 it has "verlassen gar" rather than Brahms's "verloren gar," and "Geschicht mir" instead of "Gerscheiht mir"; in verse 2, "so schwere" instead of "zu schwere," and "gebracht" instead of "hat bracht." The same text is also found in C. F. Becker's *Lieder und Weisen vergangener Jahrhunderte* (Leipzig, 1849). "Verjehen" (line 10) is an archaic word meaning "give up" in the sense of "own up to" or "acknowledge."

Brahms sets the verses in a deliberately archaic style, conveyed in part by the long-note phrase beginnings and endings, and the thirdless cadences on the tonic—even the austerity of the score's appearance suggests antiquity. Formally, each strophe comprises two repeated phrases—one of five measures, the other of five and a half (the repetition of which produces a curious metric ambivalence)—plus a closing phrase extended to three full measures by a half-measure rest. The Dorian melody uses the raised seventh step only twice, both times as a neighboring tone, but the modal sound is tempered with that of a more conventional minor by the many major-dominant harmonies and, in the last phrase, a major submediant.

In performance, the song projects an appealing aura of dignity and emotional restraint, resulting at least in part from its use of root-position triads only.

Herbstgefühl, Op. 48/7 (Autumnal Mood)

Text by Adolf Friedrich von Schack (1815–1894)

Wie wenn vom frost'gen Windhauch tötlich
Des Sommers letzte Blüte krankt,

Und hier und da nur, gelb und rötlich,
Ein einzles Blatt im Windhauch schwankt,

So schauert über mein[em] Leben
Ein nächtig trüber kalter Tag,
Warum noch vor dem Tode beben,
O Herz, mit deinem ew'gen Schlag!

Sieh' rings entblättert das Gestäude!
Was spielst du, wie der Wind am Strauch,
Noch mit der letzten welken Freude?
Gib' dich zur Ruh'—bald stirbt sie auch.

As when the last blossom of summer suffers in the icy, killing blast of wind, and only here and there, yellow and reddish, a lone leaf shakes in the blast:
Thus does a cold day, somber as night, send chills through my life. Why should you still tremble at death, my heart, with your eternal beating?
See how leafless the shrubbery is all around! Why are you still playing, like the wind in the bush, with your last withered joy? Go to your rest; soon it, too, will die.

Completed on 6 May 1867 in Vienna.
The first performance is not documented.
A B A'.
The text is from Schack's *Gedichte* (Berlin, 1867); Brahms changed "vom" to "im" in the first line, and "meinem" to "mein" in the fifth.
The poem contemplates the death of nature in autumn as symbolic of man's brief life-span.
Brahms matches the poet's somber mood with music unsurpassed in sheer bleakness even by Schubert's most tragic songs. (The evocation of Schubert may not be entirely coincidental—the last vocal phrase is a reportedly deliberate reference to the ending of Schubert's "Der Doppelgänger.") The setting is filled with images of melancholy: the incessant half note-quarter note rhythm, a usual Brahmsian metaphor for isolation; the mournfully descending chain of plaintive thirds at the beginning; the numbly static vocal line; the strange occasional sighs in the bass; the floating, often halting accompaniment; the rest within the word "welken" near the end—one can almost hear the last leaf snap from its twig during the silence.
The contrasting middle section suddenly intrudes with a *forte* outburst of despair characterized by tortuous, more chromatic lines in both the voice and the bass octaves, which first double, then support the melody. The activity and agitation lessen in the quieter second half of the phrase, as the poet considers death as a perhaps desirable release from life. The accompanying triplets become stationary in m. 45, mark "Tode" with a minor inflection in m. 47, and subside in m. 57 to eighth notes in rocking thirds. As they descend, duplicating the pitches of the introduction and bolstered by a spare bass line, they make the transition to the return of the desolate opening material.

The last verse begins to music identical to that of the first, but the last line is set to new music that functions as a codetta. A change to $^6_4$ suggests the "Ruh'" of the text, as does a temporary modulation to the Neapolitan. Even the piano's closing gesture seems to symbolize death, as the bass melody slowly comes to rest in the lowest register and all motion is stilled.

In response to the gift that autumn of a copy of the song, Clara Schumann confessed to Brahms in a letter of 13 November 1867, "I have not yet been able to play through [it] without bursting into tears."

During 1867 Brahms was subject to bouts of depression that were sufficiently persistent to cause concern among his friends. Early in the year he had been passed over for the second time for a conducting post in his native Hamburg that he considered his due—a disappointment that capped a series of unhappy events, including the estrangement of his parents, the death of his beloved mother, and the subsequent news of his father's intent to marry a twice-widowed woman nearly twenty years his junior (though Brahms later became devoted to his stepmother). His pessimism was exacerbated by a sense of rootlessness, since he felt himself increasingly cut off from his Hamburg ties and had not yet found permanent lodgings in Vienna. While there is no evidence to support the connection, Clara Schumann, among others, believed that Brahms's own dark mental state stimulated his interest in Schack's shadowy poetry at that particular time—"Abenddämmerung," Op. 49/5, also bears the completion date 6 May 1867, and at least an early version of "Serenade," Op. 58/8, was composed during the same year.

FIVE LIEDER, OP. 49

Lieder und Gesänge mit Begleitung des Pianoforte von Johannes Brahms (Songs with Piano Accompaniment by Johannes Brahms). Part title: *Op. 49. Fünf Lieder* (Five Songs). Published in October 1868 by Simrock in Berlin; publication number 323. The complete collection also includes Opp. 46–48.

The set's contents are diverse, but the ordering, as in Op. 48, anchors a group of shorter songs with a large-scale Schack setting. The present opus differs from the preceding one in that it contains no strophic settings—"Wiegenlied" is an apparent exception, but its second stanza was in fact added later; the texts' implications are realized both more subtly and with greater sophistication; and a generally more elaborate treatment is evident, particularly in the writing for the piano.

Am Sonntag Morgen, Op. 49/1 (On Sunday Morning)

Text translated from the Italian by Paul von Heyse (1830–1914)

> Am Sonntag Morgen zierlich angetan,
> Wohl weiß ich, wo du da bist hingegangen,
> Und manche Leute waren, die dich sah'n
> Und kamen dann zu mir, dich zu verklagen.
> Als sie mir's sagten, hab' ich laut gelacht
> Und in der Kammer dann geweint zur Nacht.
> Als sie mir's sagten, fing ich an zu singen,
> Um einsam dann die Hände wund zu ringen.

On Sunday morning, dressed in your finery, I know exactly where you went; there were many people who saw you and then came to me to accuse you!

When they told it to me, I laughed out loud and then cried in my room at night.

When they told it to me, I started to sing; then, when I was alone, I wrung my hands till they were sore.

Probably composed in 1868 in Bonn.

First performed on 22 December 1869 in Vienna by Louise Dustmann and Clara Schumann.

Through-composed.

The text is a Tuscan popular song, found in Heyse's *Italienisches Lieder-buch* (Berlin, 1860).

The song comprises only four three-bar phrases, two of five bars, and a four-measure postlude. Though short, it is subtly constructed to reflect the girl's succession of emotions.

At the outset, her attempt to feign indifference to her lover's infidelity is exposed as false by the breaks in her voice, which are continued, multiplied, in the accompaniment. Her increasing agitation is revealed by the rising pitch of phrase 4 as compared with its counterpart, phrase 2; her reproach, by the dissonance on the word "verklagen."

Her excitement mounts as triplets conflict with duplets in the accompaniment, *animato*. As she describes her vain attempts to laugh and to sing, the vocal line rises first to an F♯ in m. 15 (C♯ in the lower key), then to G (D) in m. 20, and finally to a high A (E) as m. 22 expands to $\frac{3}{4}$ meter to accommodate her climactic outcry of overwhelming grief.

The words "geweint" in m. 17 and "wund" in m. 22 are underscored by poignant Neapolitan harmony. The accompaniment's hesitant staccatos finally yield completely to the broken, upward-leaping triplets, first introduced, like sobs, at the mention of crying in mm. 16–17. They underlie the eloquent postlude, which recalls the Neapolitan as it gradually weeps its way into the piano's low register.

An ein Veilchen, Op. 49/2 (To a Violet)

Text by Ludwig Hölty (1748–1776)

Birg, o Veilchen, in deinem blauen Kelche,
Birg die Tränen der Wehmut, bis mein Liebchen
Diese Quelle besucht! Entpflückt sie lächelnd
Dich dem Rasen, die Brust mit dir zu schmücken,
O, dann schmiege dich ihr an's Herz, und sag' ihr,
Daß die Tropfen in deinem blauen Kelche
Aus der Seele des treu'sten Jünglings flossen,
Der sein Leben verweinet und den Tod wünscht.

Conceal, O violet, in your blue calyx, conceal the tears of melancholy, until my darling visits this fountain! If she smilingly plucks you from the lawn to adorn her breast with you, oh, then press yourself to her heart, and tell her that the drops in your blue calyx flowed from the soul of the most faithful youth, who is weeping away his life and desires to die.

Composed in June 1868, probably in Bonn.

First performed by Anna Bosse on 24 October 1871 in Leipzig.

Through-composed, but with a return of opening material.

The poem is based on a song by the Italian poet Giovanni Battista Zappi (1667–1719). The Hölty version was first heard by a society of young poets at Göttingen (the Göttinger Hain) at a reading in 1772; it was published two years later in the *Göttinger Musenalmanach*. Brahms took his text from the collection of Hölty's poems issued in 1804 by Johann Heinrich Voss, whose alterations are responsible for Brahms's "entpflückt sie lächelnd dich dem Rasen" in place of Hölty's "entpflückt das Mädchen dich dem Rasen" and "ihr an's Herz" instead of "an ihr Herz."

Brahms was deeply attracted to the poetry of his fellow North German, with its undercurrent of melancholy and introspection, and his response was often, as here, a search for profundity. The poet wishes that his beloved might see the dew on the violet as the tears of longing he sheds for her; in Brahms's setting, the lightly weeping accompaniment of the opening progressively darkens and thickens until, by the end of the song, to die of love seems almost plausible.

The melody is among Brahms's most beautiful, and the piano occasionally echoes fragments of it with little sighing interludes. The accompaniment becomes more agitated in the middle section and increasingly placid in the darker return, murmuring the opening melody in the postlude before dying away. Modulations are frequent and expressive, particularly at the closing words, "der sein Leben verweinet und den Tod wünscht."

The song's dramatic weight rests on two suspenseful dominant-seventh sonorities. The first, on the dominant of the Neapolitan, is sustained from m. 26 through m. 29 and asks, "If she should pluck you, what?" The piano resolves it deceptively into tonic harmony as though it were an augmented-sixth chord; and the voice, in recitative-like fragments, rises to the song's climax in m. 36 with the answer "Press yourself to her heart!" The second, on the dominant of the home key, occurs in m. 41 and asks, "And say what?" The not-unexpected answer is provided by the weightier return of the opening melody, "Tell her that I weep for love of her."

Sehnsucht, Op. 49/3 (Longing)

Translated from the Bohemian by Joseph Wenzig (Czech, 1807–1876)

> Hinter jenen dichten Wäldern,
> Weilst du, meine Süßgeliebte,
> Weit, ach weit, weit, ach weit!
> Berstet ihr Felsen,

> Ebnet euch Täler,
> Daß ich ersehe,
> Daß ich erspähe
> Meine ferne, süße Maid!

Beyond those dense forests you tarry, my loved one, far, ah, far, far, ah, far away!

Crack, you cliffs; become smooth, valleys, so that I can manage to see, can manage to espy my faraway sweet girl!

Composed in June 1868, probably in Bonn.

The first performance was sung by Anna Bosse at a farewell concert of Clara Schumann in Vienna on 19 January 1870.

Through-composed.

The poem is found among the Bohemian folk songs in the collection *Slawische Volkslieder* (Halle, 1830).

The text deals with the anxieties arising from separation. Brahms sets its two parts in sharply contrasted sections, the first gently sentimental (*Langsam*) and the second passionately declamatory (*Lebhaft*), their difference somewhat bridged by the increasingly intense phrases "Weit, ach weit!" that connect them.

Melodic shapes and harmonic progressions in the second part recall, but do not duplicate, those in the first. Particularly noteworthy are the two falling phrases at the opening of the *Lebhaft*, which mirror both the rising bass motives that support them and the two rising phrases with which the *Langsam* began.

The song's exuberance is continued, even surpassed, by the piano postlude, marked *crescendo stringendo*.

The piece undeniably has great emotional energy, but its excitement finally seems empty and overwrought. Unlike Brahms's customary carefully plotted rise to a single late climactic pitch, the vocal line here attains the same high Ab (F in the lower key) five times during the song—the postlude reaches it yet again—resulting in a disappointing architectural shapelessness.

Wiegenlied, Op. 49/4 (Lullaby)

First stanza from *Des Knaben Wunderhorn*
Second stanza by Georg Scherer (1828–1909)
Dedicated "To B. F. in Vienna"

> Guten Abend, gut' Nacht,
> Mit Rosen bedacht,
> Mit Näg'lein besteckt
> Schlupf' unter die Deck':

Morgen früh, wenn Gott will,
Wirst du wieder geweckt.

Guten Abend, gut' Nacht,
Von Englein bewacht,
Die zeigen im Traum
Dir Christkindleins Baum:
Schlaf' nun selig und süß,
Schau im Traum's Paradies.

Good evening, good night; bedecked with roses, adorned with clove pinks, slip under the blanket. Tomorrow morning, if God so wills, you will be awakened again.

Good evening, good night, guarded by angels; in your dreams they will show you the Christ Child's tree. Now sleep blissfully and sweetly, look at Paradise in your dreams.

Composed in Bonn in July 1868, on the occasion of the birth of Bertha and Arthur Faber's second child.

First performed publicly by Louise Dustmann and Clara Schumann in Vienna on 22 December 1869.

Strophic.

The poem is very old, dating from the fifteenth century; Brahms used the version found in *Des Knaben Wunderhorn*, where it is entitled "Gute Nacht, mein Kind." "Näglein" is a colloquialism for "Nelken" ("pinks" or "carnations" in English).

The song was originally published with the first verse only, and it quickly became famous and popular. Later Brahms submitted to Fritz Simrock, the publisher, a possible second verse, written by Georg Scherer (published in his *Illustriertes deutsches Kinderbuch* [1849]), which was added in subsequent editions.

In Scherer's verse the ending is "Droben im Paradies/Schlaf nun selig uns süß." Since these two lines did not fit the rhythm of the song, Brahms himself made the revision, though several times he expressed less than complete satisfaction with it: "Since I can think of nothing better. . . ."

Despite the "folk" origins of the song, its apparent simplicity masks a technical feat. Brahms had known Frau Faber (then Bertha Porubsky) as early as 1859 in Hamburg—she was one in the succession of pretty young singers with whom he had flirtations. Her singing had made a strong impression on him, and one particular *Ländler* by Alexander Baumann that she sang had remained in his memory. Its melody dances in the accompaniment of "Wiegenlied" while the voice goes its own way against it.

Du   moanst   wohl,   du   glabst   wohl,   die   Lieb   lasst   si   zwin - ga?

On 15 July 1868 Brahms sent a copy of the song from Bonn to Arthur
Faber in Vienna, with a short note in which he wrote:

> Frau Bertha will realize that I wrote the *Wiegenlied* for her little one. She will
> however find it quite in order, as I do, that while she is singing Hans to sleep,
> a love song is being sung to her. . . . My song is suitable for either boys or girls,
> so you need not order a new one each time.

Because of the song's rapidly spreading popularity, arrangements pro-
liferated, to Brahms's great annoyance. "Why not make a new edition in the
minor for naughty or sick children?" he grumbled to Simrock. "That would
be yet another way to sell more copies."

Abenddämmerung, Op. 49/5 (Twilight)

Text by Adolf Friedrich von Schack (1815–1894)

> Sei willkommen, Zwielichtstunde!
> Dich vor allen lieb' ich längst,
> Die du, lindernd jede Wunde,
> Uns're Seele mild umfängst.
>
> Hin durch deine Dämmerhelle,
> In den Lüften, abendfeucht,
> Schweben Bilder, die der grelle
> Schein des lauten Tags gescheucht.
>
> Träume und Erinnerungen
> Nahen aus der Kinderzeit,
> Flüstern mit den Geisterzungen
> Von vergang'ner Seligkeit.
>
> Und zu Jugendlust-Genossen
> Kehren wir in's Vaterhaus;
> Arme, die uns einst umschlossen,
> Breiten neu sich nach uns aus.
>
> Nach dem Trennungsschmerz, dem langen,
> Dürfen wir noch einmal nun
> Denen, die dahingegangen,
> Am geliebten Herzen ruh'n;
>
> Und indess' zum Augenlide
> Sanft der Schlummer niederrinnt,
> Sinkt auf uns ein sel'ger Friede
> Aus dem Land, wo Jene sind.

Welcome, twilight hour! You above all I have long loved, because, soothing
every wound, you mildly enclasp our soul.

Through your dusky light, in the air damp with evening, float images that the harsh glare of the noisy day frightened away.

Dreams and memories approach from childhood days, whisper with spirit tongues of past happiness.

And we return to our father's house to see the companions of our youthful pleasures; arms that once embraced us open wide again to greet us.

After the long pain of separation, we are once again permitted to rest on the beloved heart of those who have departed.

And while slumber softly trickles down upon our eyelids, a blessed peace sinks down upon us from the land where They are.

Completed on 6 May 1867 in Vienna.

The first performance is not documented.

Rondo; A B A' C C' A".

The text is found in Schack's *Gedichte* (Berlin, 1867); it refers to lost youth and past happiness, and suggests that at day's end memories of lost loved ones come unbidden with the darkness.

The music, like the poem, is permeated with nostalgia. The accompaniment is one of the richest and most original in all of *Lieder*. From the very first sound to the last, the darkly glimmering curves in sixteenth notes, the deep-toned, endlessly tolling bell, and the solemn countermelody in the tenor register combine to make a perfect musical metaphor for the approaching nightfall, and the recurrences of these motives provide overall unity for the poem's rather diffuse thoughts.

The areas of departure from this basic texture, with their hinting at other time ratios, are perhaps even more remarkable. The second verse, in which floating images are first mentioned, is introduced in m. 21 by the slowly rising arpeggios that Brahms so often associated with the dream state; this time, they momentarily divide the $\frac{3}{4}$ measure in half as though time had slowed, which impression is bolstered by the near suspension of motion in mm. 25–26. Even more striking is the run-on setting of verses 4 and 5, beginning with the changing key in m. 44, where the softer subdominant becomes the tonality, the pianist's right hand climbs into the brighter high register, and the accompaniment's implied triplets suggest that the remembered past took place at a pace faster than the narrator's shadowy present. It is an inspired passage.

During a four-measure transition of stunning economy, the key, register, tempo, and mood all return inexorably to those of the opening. The final stanza, though a nearly exact musical repetition of the first, seems newly infused with serenity, which is confirmed by the gently rising final measures of the postlude.

The rounded-off varied rondo form and vivid imagery make of this rather long song a thoroughly satisfying aesthetic whole. The reaction among the members of Brahms's circle, however, was mixed. Though Philipp Spitta wrote to Brahms that the song was "permeated with Beethovenian mysticism," Hermann Levi characterized it in a letter to Clara Schumann as "contrived; it is like a lie." Later, he wondered, "Is it really possible to set this contemplative, descriptive poem to music?" Clara herself responded rather coolly to the song and wrote to Brahms on 13 November 1867, in a letter referring also to "Herbstgefühl," Op. 48/7, "No, dear Johannes, you, a man of talent, in your prime, life still before you, may not indulge in such melancholy thoughts. . . . Find yourself a young lady of means in Vienna . . . and you will become happier again."

LIEDER AND GESÄNGE
TO TEXTS BY G. F. DAUMER,
OP. 57

*Lieder und Gesänge von G. F. Daumer für eine Singstimme mit Be-
gleitung des Pianoforte componirt von Johannes Brahms* (Songs to Texts
by G. F. Daumer for Solo Voice with Piano Accompaniment by Johannes
Brahms), Op. 57. Published in two booklets of four songs each in December
1871 by J. Rieter-Biedermann, Leipzig and Winterthur; publication number
682ab.

The date of composition of these songs is uncertain, but they may well
have been written during the summer of 1868 at the same time as the
Liebeslieder-Walzer, Op. 52, which also have Daumer texts.

The entire set was first performed in public by Rosa Girzick in Vienna on
18 December 1872; three weeks earlier, also in Vienna, Marie Fillunger had
sung the first song only.

The undisguised sensuality of many of the texts aroused strong opposition
among Brahms's friends, who regarded them as unsuitable for performance
in the family circle. Though they are unlikely to offend many modern ears,
the poems seem to have been chosen for their explicitness.

The songs do not constitute a cycle in the usual sense, although they may
certainly be performed as one. In addition to the authorship of their texts,
they share a certain unity of style and of subject matter, essentially explor-
ing different aspects of the single situation of a lover who must restrain his
erotic yearning with patience that may after all go unrewarded.

"Von waldbekränzter Höhe," Op. 57/1
(From the forest-crowned height)

Text by Georg Friedrich Daumer (1800–1875)

Von waldbekräntzer Höhe
Werf' ich den heißen Blick

Der liebefeuchten Sehe
　　Zur Flur, die dich umgrünt, zurück.

Ich senk' ihn auf die Quelle,
　　Vermöcht' ich, ach, mit ihr
Zu fließen eine Welle,
　　Zurück, o Freund, zu dir, zu dir!

Ich richt' ihn auf die Züge
　　Der Wolken über mir,
Ach, flög' ich ihre Flüge,
　　Zurück, o Freund, zu dir, zu dir!

Wie wollt' ich dich umstricken,
　　Mein Heil und meine Pein,
Mit Lippen und mit Blicken,
　　Mit Busen, Herz und Seele dein!

From the forest-crowned height I cast the hot gaze of my love-moistened eyes back to the meadow that grows green around you.

I lower it into the stream; ah, if only I could be a wave and flow along with it back to you, to you, my friend!

I direct it [my gaze] to the processions of the clouds above me; ah, if I could fly their flights, back to you, to you, my friend!

How I would enmesh you, my well-being and my sorrow; I belong to you with my lips and eyes, with my breast, heart and soul!

The date of composition is uncertain but is earlier than autumn 1871.

First performed by Marie Fillunger in Vienna on 27 November 1872. Rosa Girzick sang the entire set in Vienna three weeks later, on 18 December.

Through-composed, but with a partial return, and unified by recurrences of the broadly arching melody first heard in the interlude between the first and second stanzas.

The text is from Daumer's collection *Frauenbilder und Huldigungen* (Leipzig, 1853) in the section "Gedichte weiblichen Ursprungs." The poem begins nonspecifically "Von . . .'s schöner Höhe," needing a two-syllable word, the name of a town or mountain with an accent on the first syllable, to complete the line. It is clear in the autograph that Brahms first tried "Dornbach" (the name of a Vienna suburb), then "Hinab von schöner Höhe," and finally settled on the present version.

The song is organized in four linked but diverse fourteen-measure sections. The first begins in G major and closes in D (E♭ and B♭ in the lower key). After the interlude in D (B♭), the voice enters over a change to the minor mode, and the section ends in B♭ (F♯) major. Another piano interlude leads to a third section that ends in B (G) minor, and yet another interlude leads back to the home key for a reprise of the first eight measures of the opening melody. Two ecstatic settings of the words "mit Busen, Herz und Seele dein" serve as an exuberant coda.

The song is filled with longing, desire, and joyous excitement. Noteworthy throughout is its freedom of both modulation and rhythm, which adds variety while increasing the effect of rhapsodic spontaneity. The voice is carried along on an impassioned torrent of piano virtuosity.

"Wenn du nur zuweilen lächelst," Op. 57/2
(If you will only occasionally smile)

Translated by Georg Friedrich Daumer (1800–1875)
from Mohammad Shams od-Dīn Hafiz (Persian; c.1326–c.1390)

> Wenn du nur zuweilen lächelst,
> Nur zuweilen Kühle fächelst
> Dieser ungemeß'nen Glut—
> In Geduld will ich mich fassen
> Und dich alles treiben lassen,
> Was der Liebe wehe tut.

If you will only occasionally smile, only occasionally fan with coolness my infinite ardor—then I will be patient and let you do all that injures love.

The date of composition is uncertain but is earlier than autumn 1871.

First performed, with the rest of the set, by Rosa Girzick in Vienna on 18 December 1872.

Through-composed.

The text is from Daumer's anthology *Hafis: eine Sammlung persischer Gedichte*, second edition (Hamburg, 1852).

Contrasting with the preceding song, the mood here is of tender longing. The poet hungers for any sign of approval from his beloved that will alleviate his suffering with hope. The lilting $\frac{9}{8}$ melody conveys perfectly his achingly combined bliss and foreboding. Warm harmonies flow gently forward while the vocal line stammers and repeats itself, finally driven as though by aroused desire to a long-breathed arching climax at "was der Liebe wehe tut." Repetition of these words is already colored by despairing resignation. The chromatic inflections on "wehe" are heartbreaking.

The eloquent postlude begins as though to repeat the song's beginning, but it leaps from the first bar to the third, which is altered to recall the poignant "wehe" just heard in the vocal line. This sighing motive is repeated twice more, restored to the major mode and falling step by step to the final tonic chord. At song's end, it seems that hope may have been restored and that the current situation is accepted, however reluctantly.

"Es träumte mir, ich sei dir teuer," Op. 57/3
(I dreamt I was dear to you)

Translated from the Spanish by Georg Friedrich Daumer (1800–1875)

Es träumte mir,
Ich sei dir teuer;
Doch zu erwachen
Bedurft' ich kaum.
Denn schon im Traume
Bereits empfand ich,
Es sei ein Traum.

I dreamt I was dear to you; but I scarcely needed to awaken, for while still dreaming, I already felt that it was a dream.

The date of composition is uncertain but is earlier than autumn 1871.

First performed, with the rest of the set, by Rosa Girzick on 18 December 1872 in Vienna.

Through-composed.

The poem is from the "Spanish" section of Daumer's *Polydora: ein welt-poetisches Liederbuch* (Frankfurt am Main, 1854), where line 5 reads "denn, ach, im Traume."

Brahms greatly extended the text by alteration and repetition in the last three lines. The first time he set the fifth line, he substituted the adverb "schon" for the more dramatic exclamation "ach" and used the line to begin (in m. 12) an increase in musical and emotional tension. After the vocal line's first climax in mm. 16–19 and the complete cessation of motion at the fermata in m. 20, the line is repeated, this time with its "ach" restored, to set in motion a brief reference to the initial vocal phrase.

Each of the first three double lines of text is set to a four-measure phrase; the treatment of the remaining short line reveals the hand of a master. The last line is repeated before the interlude, resulting in another four-measure unit obviously divisible into 2 + 2, thus avoiding the awkwardness of an abrupt short phrase. Brahms goes further by dividing the preceding phrase also into 2 + 2 measures, thereby not only deftly relating the two phrases but also introducing an element of agitation into the preparation of the climax.

By far the song's most striking feature is its extraordinary aura of suspended time. The quality of unreality is established in the introduction by dream-evocative slowly rising arpeggios, above which float disembodied chords, lacking both rhythmic and tonal definition. Many other factors play a part: much of the piece unfolds over a dominant pedal, a firm arrival at tonic harmony being postponed until the postlude; the vocal phrases often begin on the third, later on the sixth, of the measure's six eighth notes, causing some ambiguity as to the metric structure; metric rigidity is further denied by some irregular rhythmic groupings in the left-hand figure, which allow the motion to resume gradually after the fermata and to dissipate in stages at the end of the song.

Borrowings from the minor mode are associated with the last three lines of text, reflecting the lover's realization that his vision is only fantasy. The pain at which the text only hints is made explicit by the frequent melodic use of augmented and diminished intervals and the many appoggiaturas, which are particularly expressive against already dissonant harmonies, as in mm. 15 and 18.

"Ach, wende diesen Blick," Op. 57/4
(Ah, turn away your gaze)

Text by Georg Friedrich Daumer (1800–1875)

Ach, wende diesen Blick, dies Angesicht!
Das Inn're mir mit ewig neuer Glut,
Mit ewig neuem Harm erfülle nicht!

Wenn einmal die gequälte Seele ruht,
Und mit so fieberischer Wilde nicht
In meinen Adern rollt das heiße Blut—

Ein Strahl, ein flüchtiger, von deinem Licht,
Er wecket auf des Weh's gesamte Wut,
Das schlangengleich mich in das Herze sticht.

Ah, turn away your gaze, turn that face! Don't fill my heart with eternally renewed passion, with eternally renewed grief!

If for once my tortured soul is at rest, and my hot blood does not flow through my veins with such feverish wildness—

A fleeting ray of your light awakens the total fury of the pain that stings my heart like a snake.

The date of composition is uncertain but is earlier than autumn 1871.

First performed, with the rest of the set, by Rosa Girzick in Vienna on 18 December 1872.

A B A.

The source of the text is Daumer's *Frauenbilder und Huldigungen* (Leipzig, 1853). There line 2 reads "das Innere mir" and the last has "schlangenhaft" instead of "schlangengleich"; Brahms added a second "wende" in the first line.

The poem's combination of resignation and suppressed emotion is captured exactly by the single slow tempo and an eloquent simplicity of texture. As the lover's agitation begins to intensify in m. 5, wide-ranging triplets in the accompaniment support the vocal line's rise to a climax, punctuated by suffering *sforzando* dissonances in mm. 9–11. The excitement subsides, activity lessens, and the simplest of transitions leads to the richly harmonized second stanza, beginning in m. 15.

The voice refers longingly to a soul at rest, but the piano's relentless eighth notes and frequent dissonances make it clear that passion seethes just beneath the surface. Voice and piano join in a series of free rising sequences, *sempre crescendo e più agitato*, until an unexpected harmonization of the voice's outburst on "Adern" in m. 25 marks the dramatic high point of the song. A sonorous dominant-eleventh harmony in m. 26 sustains the emotional intensity, and its gradual thinning-out constitutes the transition to the return in m. 29.

The piano begins alone softly; the entrance of the voice on the third beat is affectingly dissonant against the right-hand melody. From the second measure onward, this stanza is musically identical to the first, the *sforzando* dissonances now a vividly literal representation of the snake's sting. But resentment erupts suddenly, and the two-measure postlude concludes by hurling itself *crescendo* into a full-voiced, vehement *forte* chord.

"In meiner Nächte Sehnen," Op. 57/5
(In the yearnings of my nights)

Text by Georg Friedrich Daumer (1800–1875)

> In meiner Nächte Sehnen,
>   So tief allein,
> Mit tausend, tausend Tränen,
>   Gedenk' ich dein.
>
> Ach, wer dein Antlitz schaute,
>   Wem dein Gemüt
> Die schöne Glut vertraute,
>   Die es durchglüht,
>
> Wem deine Küsse brannten,
>   Wem je vor Lust
> All' seine Sinne schwanden
>   An deiner Brust—
>
> Wie rasteten in Frieden
>   Ihm Seel' und Leib,
> Wenn er von dir geschieden,
>   Du göttlich Weib!

In the yearnings of my nights, so utterly alone, with a thousand, thousand tears, I think of you.

Ah, the man who has looked upon your face, to whom your spirit has entrusted that sweet ardor which blazes in it, for whom your kisses have burned,
who has ever lost all his senses for joy upon your bosom—
How his body and soul reposed in peace when he departed from you, you
divine woman!

The date of composition is uncertain but is earlier than autumn 1871.

First performed, with the rest of the set, by Rosa Girzick in Vienna on
18 December 1872.

A B A'.

The text is from Daumer's *Frauenbilder und Huldigungen* (Leipzig,
1853) in the section "Vermischte Formen."

The setting boils with erotic desire. The introduction begins quietly with
a melodic fragment that quickly expands to prepare the vocal entrance.
An accompaniment figure in oscillating sixteenth notes makes its appearance with the voice and persists throughout the song, representing a
pervasive but fluctuating undercurrent of unrest. Criss-cross imitation
between the vocal line and the piano's bass provides both a unifying element and a metaphor for the coupling for which the poet yearns so ardently.

The second and third verses are combined into one continuous section, a
not uncommon Brahmsian practice; as usual, the resulting compression
produces an effect of growing agitation. Rising sequences and sharp syncopations in the accompaniment underscore the poet's increasingly heated
emotional state.

A return of the opening material for the fourth verse provides only temporary relief. Although the first section ended on the dominant, the song
must conclude in the tonic, which difference enables the voice to reenter its
high register for the repeated "du göttlich Weib."

Passion ebbs somewhat during the postlude, but one senses that it is only
suppressed, not spent. Any overflow of emotional energy may be absorbed
by the succeeding song's gentler unfolding in the same key, as composed and
originally published; in the low-key edition alteration of the key relationships
lessens that opportunity.

"Strahlt zuweilen auch ein mildes Licht," Op. 57/6
(Even if occasionally a gentle light beams)

Text by Georg Friedrich Daumer (1800–1875)

Strahlt zuweilen auch ein mildes Licht
Auf mich hin aus diesem Angesicht—
Ach, es können auch wohl Huldgebärden
Machen, daß uns fast das Herze bricht.

Was die Liebe sucht, um froh zu werden,
Das verraten diese Blicke nicht.

Even if occasionally a gentle light beams at me from that countenance—
alas, gestures of grace can also make our heart almost break.
That which love seeks in order to become happy—that is not betrayed in
those glances.

The date of composition is uncertain but is earlier than autumn 1871.
First performed, with the rest of the set, by Rosa Girzick in Vienna on
18 December 1872.

A B A'.

The text is from the section "Ludoiska" of Daumer's *Frauenbilder und
Huldigungen* (Leipzig, 1853). The poet despairs that the smiles that first
won his heart are friendly but nothing more, signaling much less than the
love he desires.

The first and second couplets are set as one continuous flow occupying
thirteen measures; the cadence in the fourteenth overlaps the interlude that
initiates the setting of the third couplet, which is extended also to thirteen
measures by the repetition of its last line and the addition of a postlude.

The frequent use of the subdominant, both major and minor, colors the
entire work, and its softened harmonic color reflects the text's "gentle light."
The tone of the song is less despairing, more lyrical, more accepting than the
others in the set—a welcome relief to the ear!—but its Schubertian major-
minor inflections and chromatic harmonization, particularly in the second
couplet, reveal an ever-present underlayer of resigned suffering.

"Die Schnur, die Perl' an Perle," Op. 57/7
(The string on which pearl after pearl is arrayed)

Translated from the Sanskrit by Georg Friedrich Daumer (1800–1875)

Die Schnur, die Perl' an Perle
Um deinen Hals gereihte,
Wie wiegt sie sich so fröhlich
Auf deiner schönen Brust!
Mit Seel' und Sinn begabet,
Mit Seligkeit berauschet
Sie, diese Götterlust.
Was müssen wir erst fühlen,
In welchen Herzen schlagen,
So heiße Menschenherzen,
Wofern es uns gestattet,
Uns traulich anzuschmiegen
An eine solche Brust?

The string on which pearl after pearl is arrayed about your throat—how happily it rocks to and fro on your beautiful breast!

As if it were endowed with soul and sense, it is intoxicated with bliss by that godlike pleasure.

What, then, must we feel in whom hearts beat, such warm human hearts, whenever we are permitted to press intimately such a breast!

The date of composition is uncertain but is earlier than autumn 1871.

First performed, with the rest of the set, by Rosa Girzick in Vienna on 18 December 1872.

Through-composed.

The text is found in the "Spanish" section of *Polydora* (Frankfurt am Main, 1855).

The poem contains thirteen lines, which Brahms set in two musical sections of seven lines (twenty-five measures) and six lines (twenty-one measures) respectively, preceded by a two-measure introduction and separated by a three-measure interlude. There are several one-measure insertions in the piano part, which are important to the musical sense and continuous flow.

The music is made up of numerous similar but ever-changing patterns, varied with infinite resourcefulness. Its slow tempo, a gentle accompaniment of rocking sixteenth notes, and the intermittent love-duet texture contribute to the overall mood of caressing tenderness. But tonal unrest and the long postponement of tonic harmony are symptomatic of the passion which erupts, unrestrainable, in glowing washes of harmonic color at mention of "deiner schönen Brust!" in mm. 13–19, and, to a lesser extent, "diese Götterlust" in mm. 25–27 and "eine solche Brust" in mm. 44–46.

There is no postlude, but the voice's closing reflection on single-pitch repetitions functions as coda. The prolongation of the appoggiatura on the final "Brust" is like a sigh of almost unbearable longing.

"Unbewegte laue Luft," Op. 57/8
(Motionless, tepid air)

Text by Georg Friedrich Daumer (1800–1875)

Unbewegte laue Luft,
Tiefe Ruhe der Natur;
Durch die stille Gartennacht
Plätschert die Fontäne nur.
Aber im Gemüte schwillt
Heißere Begierde mir,
Aber in der Ader quillt
Leben und verlangt nach Leben.

Sollten nicht auch deine Brust
Sehnlichere Wünsche heben?
Sollte meiner Seele Ruf
Nicht die deine tief durchbeben?
Leise mit dem Ätherfuß
Säume nicht, daherzuschweben!
Komm, o komm, damit wir uns
Himmlische Genüge geben!

Motionless, tepid air; deep calm of Nature. Through the quiet night of the garden only the fountain splashes.

But in my mind hot desire swells, but in my veins life is flowing and longs for life.

Should not more passionate desires make your breast heave, too? Should not the call of my soul reverberate deep in yours?

Do not hesitate to float softly this way with your ethereal feet! Come, oh, come, so that we can give each other heavenly satisfaction!

The date of composition is uncertain but is earlier than autumn 1871.

First performed, with the rest of the set, by Rosa Girzick in Vienna on 18 December 1872.

Through-composed, in two sections, *Langsam* and *Lebhaft*.

The text is from Daumer's *Frauenbilder und Huldigungen* (Leipzig, 1853); it contrasts erotic turmoil with the tranquillity of nature.

The opening $\frac{9}{8}$ *Langsam* is a superb bit of tone-painting, its languorous inactivity and its Oriental lowerings of second and sixth scale-degrees evoking the oppressive, motionless air of a sultry summer night. The stillness is broken only by the quiet splashing of a fountain, portrayed by flowing triplets and gentle trills in the accompaniment.

Decreasing pace and dynamic lead, via a measure of *Adagio*, to a marked change of mood at the *Lebhaft*, where the poet articulates the desire that inflames his mind and body. The transition poses some performance problems: the change of tempo should be sudden but not startling; the *Lebhaft* half note should be approximately equal to the *Langsam* dotted quarter.

The *Lebhaft* is characterized by agitated broken chords in the accompaniment and impassioned rising vocal phrases. At the words "Sollten nicht auch deine Brust" (mm. 37–38) and again at "Sollte meiner Seele Ruf" (mm. 43–44), the opening vocal phrase from the *Langsam* is recalled in the new tempo, contributing an element of overall unity to the song. (The metric relationship recommended above enhances the unifying effect, since the distinctive flatted-sixth figure will occur at the same speed in both contexts.) At the end of m. 36 triplets replace the sixteenth-note arpeggios in the accompaniment, and a modulation in mm. 46–47 leads to an extended episode in the key of the Neapolitan.

A brief enharmonic modulation marked *crescendo molto* brings the return of the earlier key and a resumption of the agitated sixteenth notes at the words "Komm, o komm." Melodic shapes reminiscent of the first *Lebhaft* phrases further integrate the structure. The final "komm, o komm," now marked *piano molto*, is sung to another repetition of the song's initial phrase, satisfyingly rounding off the form and leading *sempre diminuendo* to a plagal cadence, through which, ever softer and slower, the music floats ecstatically away.

EIGHT LIEDER AND GESÄNGE, OP. 58

Lieder und Gesänge für eine Singstimme mit Begleitung des Piano-forte componirt von Johannes Brahms (Songs for Solo Voice with Piano Accompaniment by Johannes Brahms), Op. 58. Published in two booklets in December 1871 by J. Rieter-Biedermann, Leipzig and Winterthur; publication number 683ab.

The ordering within the set contrasts four light love songs, featuring important, virtuosic piano parts, with four heavier, more dramatic songs. Three settings of texts from Kopisch are grouped together, as are two Hebbel settings. There are no simple strophic songs.

Blinde Kuh, Op. 58/1 (Blind Man's Buff)

Translated from the Sicilian by August Kopisch (1799–1853)

> Im Finstern geh' ich suchen,
> Mein Kind, wo steckst du wohl?
> Ach, sie versteckt sich immer,
> Daß ich verschmachten soll!
>
> Im Finstern geh' ich suchen,
> Mein Kind, wo steckst du wohl?
> Ich, der den Ort nicht finde,
> Ich irr' im Kreis umher!
>
> Wer um dich stirbt,
> Der hat keine Ruh!
> Kindchen erbarm' dich,
> Und komm herzu!
> Ja, komm herzu,
> Herzu, herzu!

I am looking for you in the dark, my child; where can you be hiding? Ah, she always hides to make me die of longing!

I am looking for you in the dark, my child; where can you be hiding? I can't find the place and just turn around in circles!

The man who is dying for your sake has no repose! My child, take pity and come out to me! Yes, come out to me, come out, come out to me!

The composition date is uncertain; prepared for publication in 1871.

The first performance, together with No. 2 of the opus, "Während des Regens," was given by Louise Dustmann on 27 January 1872 at a *Künstlerabend* of the Gesellschaft der Musikfreunde in Vienna.

Binary; A A B B' with codetta.

The folk-poem text was published by Kopisch in two different versions. In his *Agrumi* of 1838, it retained in German the irregularity of the Italian structure and meter—two verses of six and five lines respectively with the second line of the first verse repeated. The *Gedichte* (Berlin, 1836) version, which Brahms used, is more regular: it has a first verse of eight lines (treated as two verses of four lines each), created by eliminating the repeat of the second line but adding a repetition of lines 5 and 6. Thus the second four-line verse in the 1836 *Gedichte* reads:

> Ich, der den Ort nicht finde,
> Ich irr im Kreis umher,
> Und ich, der den Ort nicht finde,
> Ich irr im Kreis umher!

Less than satisfied with this redundancy, Brahms chose to replace the first couplet of verse 2 with a repetition of the first couplet from verse 1. (His altered version appears at the head of this section.) He also set the third verse twice, the first time omitting lines 5 and 6, but expanding them in the codetta to "ja komm herzu, herzu, komm herzu!"

The text, which presumably is meant to be understood allegorically, describes the plight of a blindfolded lover vainly stumbling about in search of his sweetheart. The first two verses are set to a folklike tune in the minor mode against a scurrying accompaniment of sixteenth notes with bits of canonic imitation, suggestions of the outline of the vocal melody, and a certain harmonic vagueness matching the lover's disorientation.

For the third verse the music changes to the major mode, *animato*, as the lover's appeal increases in urgency. Pleading alternates with playfulness until, at the reiterations of "herzu," the voice, in growing desperation, rises a second, then a third, a fifth, and finally a seventh, while the piano's searching arpeggiations expand to cover nearly the entire keyboard.

Each section—A, B, and codetta—shows a characteristic lengthening of the last phrase.

Während des Regens, Op. 58/2 (During the Rain)

Text by August Kopisch (1799–1853)

> Voller, dichter tropft um's Dach da,
> Tropfen süßer Regengüsse;
> Meines Liebchens holde Küsse

> Mehren sich, je mehr ihr tropfet!
> Tropft ihr, darf ich sie umfassen,
> Laßt ihr's, will sie mich entlassen;
> Himmel, werde nur nicht lichter,
> Tropfen, tropfet immer dichter!

It is dripping more heavily, more forcefully, around the roof there, drops of sweet rainshowers; my darling's lovely kisses increase in number as more of you drops fall!

When you drip, I'm allowed to hug her; if you stop, she'll send me away. Sky, please don't grow brighter; drops, drip more and more heavily!

Collected for publication in 1871; the date of composition is uncertain.

The first performance, with the preceding song, was given in Vienna on 27 January 1872 by Louise Dustmann at a *Künstlerabend* of the Gesellschaft der Musikfreunde.

A A' B A".

The text is from Kopisch's *Gedichte* of 1836. It deals lightheartedly with a loving couple who have taken refuge from a shower; it is understood that the kissing may continue until the rain stops, so the boy begs the rain to fall harder.

The setting is the only one of Brahms's several *Regenlieder* in which rain is not a symbol of nostalgia or sorrow. It is also unusual in that the accompaniment is almost entirely a literal pictorialization of the falling rain, represented by staccato eighth notes that begin tentatively, become a steady showering of afterbeats, and increase for the last couplet to a downpour of constant eighths, *animato sempre*. They seem to increase in abundance as their groupings tighten from patterns of six notes (in mm. 26–28) to four notes (mm. 29–30) and finally to three (mm. 31–32).

The vocal line rises and falls in broad sweeps over the rapidly pattering accompaniment. The contrasting section beginning at m. 13 is a particularly expressive, with its entreating modulations and its soaring realizations of the words "mich entlassen" (send me away).

Die Spröde, Op. 58/3 (The Unapproachable Woman)

Translated from the Calabrian by August Kopisch (1799–1853)

> Ich sahe eine Tig'rin
> Im dunklen Haine,
> Und doch mit meinen Tränen
> Konnt' ich sie zähmen.
>
> Sah auch die harten Steine,
> Ja Marmelsteine,

Erweicht vom Fall der Tropfen
Gestalt annehmen.

Und du, so eine zarte,
Holdsel'ge Kleine,
Du lachst zu meinem Seufzen
Und bitter'n Grämen.

I saw a tigress in the dark grove, and yet with my tears I was able to tame it.
I also saw hard stones—yes, marble—when softened by dripping water,
assume various shapes.
And you, such a gentle, graceful little girl, you laugh at my sighing and
bitter sorrowing.

The date of composition is uncertain; collected for publication in 1871.
The first performance is undocumented.

A A B; an example of the varied-strophic procedure in which the demands
of the text shift the contrasting strophe to the end.

The poem is from Kopisch's *Gedichte* (Berlin, 1836), but the second and
all subsequent printings of the song use a somewhat improved version made,
at Brahms's instigation, by Paul Heyse (1830–1914), a specialist in Romance
languages.

The three verses lament that, although the poet has tamed a tigress with
his tears and has seen marble eroded by falling water, his sighing and
sorrowing elicit only derision from his unsympathetic sweetheart. Brahms
uses a Schubertian tilt to the minor to depict the wild beast and hard stone
but returns to the major for the taming and melting. The third stanza, however, offers no happy outcome, so, after some fervent pleading (with some
rather Italianate doubling at the third above in the piano at "holdsel'ge
Kleine"), it descends even more bitterly into the minor mode by way of
the always-pathetic Neapolitan. The tonic major returns darkly only at the
very end. In the first edition the song had a minor ending, which remained
in many later editions; Brahms changed it to major in his personal copy, evidently having found the minor too unrelievedly gloomy. The Breitkopf &
Härtel complete edition and its Dover reprint incorporate the revision.

The graceful across-the-beat sighs of frustration in the introduction and
interlude become, through augmentation, sorrowing cries of resignation in
the postlude.

"O komme, holde Sommernacht," Op. 58/4
(Oh, Come, Fair Summer Night)

Text by Melchior Grohe (1829–1906)

O komme, holde Sommernacht,
Verschwiegen;

Dich hat die Liebe recht gemacht
  Zum Siegen!

Da brechen manche Knospen los,
  Verstohlen,
Da öffnen ihren süßen Schoß
  Violen;

Da neigt ihr Haupt im Dämmerschein
  Die Rose,
Da wird mein Liebchen auch noch mein,
  Das lose!

Oh, come, fair summer night, you that are so discreet; love created you as
a time for conquest!
  It is then that many buds break off, in secrecy; it is then that violets open
their sweet bosom; it is then that the rose bows its head in the twilight glow;
it is then that my sweetheart will surely become mine, the wicked girl!

The date of composition is uncertain, perhaps late 1868; collected for publication in 1871.

First performed by a Fräulein Meysenheim with Carl Polko, pianist, in
Munich on 6 May 1874.

Through-composed, though the first two eight-measure periods have virtually identical melodies, and the same material returns in the key of the
subdominant at m. 26. The song comprises eight, rather than the expected
six, four-measure phrases because Brahms repeats the entire first stanza.

The poem is from Grohe's collection *Reime und Reise* (Mannheim, 1861),
where it is entitled "Sommernacht." The text is redolent with the eager
sensuality of youth, and it inspired Brahms to one of his freshest, most
exquisite creations.

Not at all the typically gloomy night piece, this is a rapturously breathless
anticipation of a night of reciprocal love, the night itself warmly inviting and
fragrant with buds and blossoms. The voice's confidently leaping line is supported by outdoorsy horn calls, and softly glittering triplets persist from
beginning to end. (The printed fingerings are Brahms's.) The dynamic is
never marked higher than *piano*, as though the youth's happiness caused
him to half-murmur the words almost to himself, like a wondrous secret. As
the postlude diminishes to *pianissimo*, he seems to disappear joyously into
the radiant darkness.

In m. 23, the early editions had a G major chord (F major in the lower key)
harmonizing the first syllable of the word "Violen"; in his own copy of the
first edition, Brahms changed it to a first-inversion B minor (A minor) triad.
The rhythmic arrangement is the same in both versions. The alteration obviously improves the preparation of the suspension in m. 24.

Maintaining the requisite walking-on-air quality makes severe demands on
both singer and pianist, particularly in the contrasting section (mm. 18–25),

with its bass octaves and thicker textures. (In all standard editions in F♯, the natural signs are missing from the piano's octave E in m. 19.) The opening of the song displays what must be a near-record number of descriptive instructions—*Lebhaft und heimlich* (lively and secretively), *molto piano, leggiero*, and *sotto voce*.

Schwermut, Op. 58/5 (Melancholy)

Text by Karl Candidus (1817–1872)

> Mir ist so weh um's Herz,
> Mir ist, als ob ich weinen möchte
> Vor Schmerz!
> Gedankensatt
> Und lebensmatt
> Möcht' ich das Haupt hinlegen in die Nacht der Nächte!

My heart hurts so much; I feel as if I could weep with pain! Full of thoughts and weary of life, I would like to lay down my head in that night of nights!

Collected for publication in 1871; the date of composition is uncertain, but could not have been earlier than 1869 because of the publication date of the text.

The first performance is not documented.

Through-composed.

The text is from Candidus's *Vermischte Gedichte* (Leipzig, 1869) and is a devastating expression of utter hopelessness. Its mood of life-weariness is matched by music of powerful simplicity by the inherently pessimistic Brahms.

The accompaniment makes use of two contrasting rhythmic constructions: the first section, depicting pain and despair, unites unrelenting slow half notes with a two-measure dirgelike motive featuring a dotted quarter and an eighth; the closing section in $\frac{4}{2}$ combines slowly rising arpeggios with half-note chords on the weak beats to represent the yearned-for sleep.

The structure of the vocal line is a detailed representation of the dramatic nuances of the text. The opening phrase, *sotto voce* and *pianissimo*, gathers itself to rise the fourth to E♭ on the word "weh," then sinks back first a step, then a fourth, like a weary sigh, ending even lower than it began. The second phrase, prodded by the piano, slowly climbs in heavy steps back up to the same E♭ and finally, after a pause for breath, attains the F, *forte*, before collapsing in exhaustion and falling *piano* to the fifth below.

The third phrase provides a turning point both textually and musically. Lower by a major third, the vocal line, "full of thoughts," ponders on a single pitch things worldly and (enharmonically) otherworldly before falling a weary third at the cadence. The piano at first listens in hushed silence (m. 18), then adds its "despair" motive in B minor (mm. 19–20), and yet again, in G minor (mm. 21–22). After a nearly motionless, dark-toned interlude, the voice rises an octave for a plaintive falling third on "möcht' ich," descends in stepwise motion for "das Haupt hinlegen," and rises in two successive skips to the climactic word "Nächte." Reversing the direction, the last phrase climbs stepwise up the fourth to "Nächte," from which it falls in two successive leaps, as though plunging into the envisioned peaceful oblivion at which the piano's major harmonies hint. Little relief is evident, however; the left-hand arpeggios sink lower and lower on the keyboard, becoming hopelessly fainter, and even the long-held final major chord seems more bleak than comforting.

In his own copy of the first edition, Brahms replaced the printed common-time symbol at the opening with the *alla breve* sign, thus reducing the possibility of confusion at the later change to $\frac{4}{2}$.

In der Gasse, Op. 58/6 (In the Narrow Street)

Text by Friedrich Hebbel (1813–1863)

Ich blicke hinab in die Gasse,
Dort drüben hat sie gewohnt;
Das öde, verlassene Fenster,
Wie hell bescheint's der Mond!

Es gibt so viel zu beleuchten;
O holde Strahlen des Lichts,
Was webt ihr denn gespenstisch
Um jene Stätte des Nichts!

I look down into the narrow street; she lived there across the way. That deserted, abandoned window—how brightly the moon shines upon it!

There is so much to illuminate; O lovely rays of light, why then do you weave in ghostly fashion around that place of nothingness?

The date of composition is uncertain, perhaps 1868; collected for publication in 1871.

The first performance is undocumented.

Through-composed; notable for the unpredictable irregularity of its phrase structure.

The poem, which Hebbel dated "Munich, 3 December 1836," first appeared under the title "Spuk" (Spectre) in the Leipzig *Musenalmanach* for 1840, edited by Friedrich Rückert. Later Hebel included it in the cycle *Ein frühes Liebesleben*. Brahms owned the *Sämtliche Werke* (Hamburg, 1865–67).

The situation calls to mind Schubert's setting of Heine's "Der Doppelgänger," but one is struck by the difference rather than by the similarity of the two songs. Schubert takes the opportunity for eloquently tortured reflection on lost love. Brahms's scene, on the other hand, is active rather than passive, an underlay of half-remembered dance and a tone of increasing vehemence suggesting a deliberate attempt to cast aside such futile dwelling on the past. The piano's silences in the last phrase symbolize the characterization of the deserted house as a "place of nothingness," but the gathering passion of the postlude casts some doubt that the matter is indeed finished.

The vocal line begins with musical material that is otherwise the exclusive property of the piano; in one variant or another, it makes up much of the accompaniment, including the introduction, the interludes, and the dramatic postlude.

Vorüber, Op. 58/7 (Gone By)

Text by Friedrich Hebbel (1813–1863)

Ich legte mich unter den Lindenbaum,
In dem die Nachtigall schlug;
Sie sang mich in den süßesten Traum,
Der währte auch lange genug.

Denn nun ich erwache, nun ist sie fort,
Und welk bedeckt mich das Laub;
Doch leider noch nicht, wie am dunklern Ort,
Verglühte Asche der Staub.

I lay down under the linden tree in which the nightingale was singing; it sang me into the sweetest dreams, which lasted a considerable time.

For now that I awaken, the bird is gone and I am covered with withered leaves. But unfortunately not yet in the same way as in that darker place, the chilled ashes are covered with dust.

Collected for publication in 1871; the date of composition is uncertain, possibly as early as 1867.

The first performance is undocumented.

Through-composed; the phrase structure is irregular and varied, vocal phrases often being continued or concluded by the piano, a hallmark of the mature Brahms's song composition.

Hebbel dated the poem "Bodenbach, 10 October 1861." It was printed in *Orion, Monatsschrift für Literatur und Kunst* (Hamburg, 1863) and, shortly after Hebbel's death, in *Friedrich Hebbel Sämtliche Werke* (Hamburg, 1865–67), of which Brahms owned a copy. Like the text of the preceding song, it was a part of the cycle *Ein frühes Liebesleben*.

The life-weary poet seeks solace in nature, but realizes that only death will bring him peace. Brahms was attracted not only by the poem's melancholy subject matter but by its indebtedness to folk art, evidenced by its simplicity of language and poetic structure, and its obvious (though vivid) imagery—protective linden tree, nostalgic nightingale song, dead leaves, cold ashes.

The gentle ebb and flow of the opening arpeggios evokes nocturnal tranquillity; over them the voice sings an expressively languid melody. The nightingale-induced dream introduces lowered sixth and seventh scale steps; it hovers suspended between minor subdominant and tonic, the bird's plaintive song sobbing in the piano part. Recognizing that the dream is both sweet and transient, Brahms set the third line twice; the harmony resumes its motion during the more restless second statement, moving through submediant to Neapolitan. Suddenly, at "Der währte," the voice abandons the stepwise enchanted melismas of "süßesten Traum" for a large melodic leap that signals the end of the nightingale's spell, though the dream state lingers in the accompaniment.

The poet's full awakening to harsh reality is marked by new accompaniment figures and the key of the mediant. To music that seems enervated, irresolute, and almost shockingly ordinary after the opulence of the earlier dream world, he realizes that the bewitching bird has flown away, leaving his despair unresolved. With rapidly mounting passion he longs for death, as the harmony undertakes its tortuous journey through the minor side toward tonic. Throbbing afterbeats quicken to pulsating triplets in m. 37, as the vocal line's soaring to "verglühte Asche," the arrival at *forte*, and dominant harmony all coincide in a climax of great power. Although the vocal line descends quickly, the dynamic level remains *forte*, and the outburst of emotion continues to reverberate in the postlude before it finally subsides to a quiet, if not completely serene, close.

(Among the very few extant sketches by Brahms are two for "Vorüber"; for a detailed study of their relation to the finished song, see Bozarth, "Lieder 1868–1872," 89–107.)

Serenade, Op. 58/8

Text by Adolf Friedrich von Schack (1815–1894)

> Leise, um dich nicht zu wecken,
> Rauscht der Nachtwind, teure Frau!
> Leise in das Marmorbecken
> Gießt der Brunnen seinen Tau.
>
> Wie das Wasser, niedertropfend,
> Kreise neben Kreise zieht,
> Also zittert, leise klopfend,
> Mir das Herz bei diesem Lied.

Schwingt euch, Töne meiner Zither,
Schwingt euch aufwärts, flügelleicht;
Durch das rebumkränzte Gitter
In der Schönen Kammer schleicht.

"Ist denn, liebliche Dolores,"—
Also singt in ihren Traum—
"In der Muschel deines Ohres
Für kein Perlenwörtchen Raum?

Denk der Laube, dicht vergittert,
Wo, umrankt von Duftgesträuch,
Ihr in Seligkeit gezittert,
Wie die Blätter über euch!

War der Platz doch still und sicher
Und kein Zeuge hat gelauscht;
Selten, daß ein abendlicher
Vogel durch das Laub gerauscht.

O dem Freund noch eine Stunde,
Wo dein Arm ihn so umschlingt,
Und der Kuß von deinem Munde
Feurig bis an's Herz ihm dringt!

Hast du ihn so ganz vergessen?
Einsam harrt er am Balkon,
Über'm Wipfel der Zypressen
Bleicht des Mondes Sichel schon.

Wie das Wasser, niedertropfend,
Kreise neben Kreise zieht,
Also zittert, leise klopfend,
Ihm das Herz bei diesem Lied."

Softly, so as not to wake you, the night wind murmurs, dear woman! Softly into the marble basin the fountain pours its dew.

As the water, dripping down, forms circle after circle, thus does my softly beating heart tremble at this song.

Arise, sounds of my lyre, arise into the air on light wings; creep through the vine-enlaced lattice into the beautiful girl's bedroom.

Sing to her thus as she dreams: "Lovely Dolores, is there then no room in the shell of your ear for a little pearly word?

"Oh, grant your friend only one hour in which your arms embrace him warmly and the kisses of your mouth pierce his heart like fire.

"Have you forgotten him so completely? He waits in solitude by your balcony. Over the tips of the cypresses the moon's sickle is already growing pale.

"As the water, dripping down, forms circle after circle, thus does his softly beating heart tremble at this song."

The date of composition is uncertain, but an early version of the closing portion appears on the last page of the manuscript of "Herbstgefühl," Op. 48/7, now in the Library of Congress, which Brahms sent to Clara Schumann for her birthday in the fall of 1867. A revision was completed in time for publication in 1871.

First performed by Louise Dustmann on 14 March 1874 in Vienna.

A B A'. The first section sets three stanzas of text, the second two, and the third also two. Of these, stanza 6 is the return and is the same as stanza 1; stanza 7 begins similarly to stanza 2, but preparation for the coda soon takes charge; stanza 3 begins independently, but its second half repeats that of stanza 1; stanzas 4 and 5 are set similarly to contrasting music.

The poem was published early in 1867 in von Schack's *Gedichte* and originally had nine verses. Brahms deleted verses 5 and 6, which speak of a former rendezvous, and thus it was necessary to change the first line of verse 7 from "O dem Freund noch eine Stunde" (Oh, grant your friend one more hour) to "... nur eine Stunde" (... only one hour). Brahms also substituted the more explicit "heiß" for the bland "so" in the next line.

The lover, in a cool moonlit setting of cypress trees, vine-covered lattice, and trickling marble fountain, sings with trembling heart of his desire, but despite his eloquence, is left waiting alone at the end of the song. Brahms provided an elegantly stylized Spanish flavor, suggesting the obligatory plucked accompaniment with refinement and subtlety.

In mm. 15–18 and 74–77, gently broken separate thirds descend in the piano, evoking the widening rings in the fountain basin. The passages that follow portray the softly beating heart in sighing thirds and voluptuous harmonies. The contrasting middle section is more intimate in tone, as love-fantasies supersede the serenade proper; it features a change to triple meter, a more conventional legato accompaniment, and improbably long chains of thirds or sixths floating down the keyboard like languorous imagined caresses.

Despite its somewhat conventional language, the song is charming and a completely convincing synthesis of music and text. The hand of a master is evident in every note, particularly in its clarity of texture and of phrase structure, its care in the reconciling of diverse materials and the placement of climaxes, and its impeccable balancing of rhythmic variety with rhythmic coherence.

EIGHT LIEDER AND GESÄNGE, OP. 59

Lieder und Gesänge für eine Singstimme mit Begleitung des Pi-anoforte componirt von Johannes Brahms (Songs for Solo Voice with Piano Accompaniment Composed by Johannes Brahms), Op. 59. Published in two booklets in December 1873 by J. Rieter-Biedermann, Leipzig and Winterthur; publication number 770a–h. Later printings of the first edition adopted some small corrections the composer made in his personal copy.

The collection comprises single settings of poems by Goethe, Karl Sim-rock, Mörike, and Daumer, and four songs on texts by Klaus Groth, Brahms's close friend. "Nachklang" functions as a kind of epilogue to "Regenlied," being linked to it by music and subject matter as well as proximity. Together, they end the first part of the opus; the other two Groth songs, the second part. The Brahms-Groth correspondence indicates that in April 1873 Brahms sent these four songs to the poet as a separate small cycle, with the two "rain" songs as the first and last. The order of the interior two cannot be determined, nor do we know the degree of completion that any of the songs had reached.

Submitting Op. 59 for publication, Brahms wrote to Rieter-Biedermann:

> There has been a frightful cleaning out at my home, and so that this does not lead to a complete nothing, I am sending you on approval some extremely lovely, recommendable, agreeable, here and there difficult, moral, god-fearing, briefly first-class songs. Op. 59, 2 volumes, is what I would like to deliver. . . . The two volumes differ in size, but I wish the order, which you will call a dis-order, to be kept.

"Dämm'rung senkte sich von oben," Op. 59/1
(Twilight Has Lowered from Above)

Text by Johann Wolfgang von Goethe (1749–1832)

> Dämm'rung senkte sich von oben,
> Schon ist alle Nähe fern,
> Doch zuerst emporgehoben
> Holden Lichts der Abendstern.

> Alles schwankt in's Ungewisse,
> Nebel schleichen in die Höh';
> Schwarzvertiefte Finsternisse
> Widerspiegelnd ruht der See.
>
> Nun am östlichen Bereiche
> Ahn' ich Mondenglanz und Glut,
> Schlanker Weiden Haargezweige
> Scherzen auf der nächsten Flut.
>
> Durch bewegter Schatten Spiele
> Zittert Luna's Zauberschein,
> Und durch's Auge schleicht die Kühle
> Sänftigend in's Herz hinein.

Twilight has lowered from above; now everything nearby is distant, but the evening star has just been raised aloft with lovely light.

Everything wavers and becomes indistinct; mists creep up the heights; the lake, reflecting dark areas with accents of deeper blackness, is at rest.

Now in the region of the east I have a presentiment of moonlight and glow; the hairlike branches of slender willows play on the surface of the nearby stream.

Through the sporting of the agitated shadows, Luna's magical rays tremble, and through the eyes, coolness soothingly steals into the heart.

The composition date is uncertain, but it is probably earlier than that of the rest of the opus, which dates from spring 1873. The biography by Kalbeck reports that Brahms became acquainted with the text through a setting by his friend Hermann Levi, who later recalled that the incident took place in "1870 or 1871." The two men were guests at a private musicale in Karlsruhe where Levi's song was performed; Brahms took Levi's manuscript copy home with him, and a few days later returned it with his own setting, into which he had incorporated four measures of Levi's music (Brahms's mm. 46–49; Kalbeck, *Brahms*, II$_1$, 146).

First performed publicly on 28 May 1894 by a Fräulein Dugge, with Julius Spengel at the piano, at a concert of the Hamburg Cäcilienverein; Hermine Spies had sung it privately as early as 5 September 1883 at the Beckeraths' in Wiesbaden.

A hybrid form, combining characteristics of strophic variation and through-composition.

The text is from *Chinesisch-Deutsche Jahres- und Tageszeiten*, a brief collection of poems written in 1827 when Goethe was seventy-eight. In these beautiful lines, the aging poet evokes a serene equilibrium between readiness for death and willingness for life through images of the shifting dim light of nightfall, the evening star, and moonrise.

The setting is among Brahms's most successful syntheses of sound and sense, the music embodying and amplifying the smallest details of the poetry. The opening image of nightfall is depicted by the piano's dark low register and the bleak repetitive rhythms. The first vocal phrase imitates the bass melody of the introduction. The evening star appears in the warm glow of the submediant major, while a new sustained-afterbeat figure reverberates gently in the accompaniment over fragments of countermelody in the tenor and bass registers. The extension to five bars of the stanza's last phrase (and its varied recurrence in mm. 37–41) amounts to a written-out *rallentando* to end the section.

The second stanza begins with the same melody as the first, but now with a solemn counterpoint in flowing sixteenths, which appears in the treble of the piano interlude and hints at two fugal entrances at four-measure intervals thereafter. The words "schwarzvertiefte Finsternisse" are set to the phrase that earlier introduced the evening star, here a third lower in the darker, more mysterious subdominant minor. "Widerspiegelnd ruht der See" recalls the rhythm and contour of the first stanza's concluding phrase, though the intervals are altered to effect a return to the tonic minor. The piano interlude duplicates the introduction but ends with a dreamily extended rising arpeggio on the dominant of the submediant major, whose aura of unreality is to relate the coming image of moonlight's glow to that of the first stanza's starlight.

The third stanza is the poem's turning point; the darkness of the first half is dispelled by the radiance of the rising moon, which initiates a growing sense of peace and acceptance. The vocal line's initial steady ascent, supported by slowly rising major triad outlines in the bass, suggests both brightening light and rising spirits. The shadowy fluttering of willows is portrayed in a little figure of three sixteenths that moves from vocal line to piano, and the quickened rhythm of the triad outlines that progress from minor to diminished.

The poetic and musical climaxes coincide at the beginning of the fourth stanza, marked by a change to the key signature of the tonic major; the crucial image of moonlight magically shimmering through silhouetted willows is set to a yet higher, brighter version of the musical phrase that underscored, in other guises, the lovely light of the evening star and the lake's blackest darkness. The wonder implied by the word "Zauberschein" is beautifully expressed by the stretching of its phrase to six measures and a turn toward the subdominant.

From that dramatic high point, the music makes a long emotional descent to the tranquillity of the ending, for which purpose Brahms repeats the last two lines. The word "sänftigend" is harmonized symbolically with subdominant gentleness (major in mm. 76–77 and 84–85, minor in mm. 86–87), mitigating the poignancy of the altered harmonies and melodic dissonances which precede it. Both alternate vocal endings are effective, but the descending one is a more convincing reflection of the music's mood of quiet resignation.

176 A Guide to the Solo Songs of Johannes Brahms

Auf dem See, Op. 59/2 (On the Lake)

Text by Karl Simrock (1802–1876)

Blauer Himmel, blaue Wogen,
Rebenhügel um den See,
Drüber blauer Berge Bogen
Schimmernd weiß im reinen Schnee.

Wie der Kahn uns hebt und wieget,
Leichter Nebel steigt und fällt,
Süßer Himmelsfriede lieget
Über der begläntzen Welt.

Stürmend Herz, tu' auf die Augen,
Sieh umher und werde mild;
Glück und Frieden magst du saugen
Aus des Doppelhimmels Bild.

Spiegelnd sieh die Flut erwidern
Turm und Hügel, Busch und Stadt,
Also spiegle du in Liedern,
Was die Erde Schönstes hat.

Blue sky, blue waves, vine-clad hills around the lake; above it, an arch of blue mountains gleaming white with untouched snow.

How the boat lifts and rocks us, how light mist rises and falls; the sweet peace of Heaven lies over the shining world.

Stormy heart, open your eyes, look around and become gentle; you can absorb happiness and peace from the double image of the sky.

See the watery mirror reflecting tower and hill, bush and town; thus should you reflect in songs the loveliest things earth has to offer.

Composed during spring 1873 in Vienna and Tutzing.

First performed on 5 December 1873 in Frankfurt by Heinrich Vogl, who sang from manuscript.

Varied strophic; A A B A'.

The text, under the title "Vevey," is found in the section "Travels in Switzerland, 1833" in Simrock's *Gedichte* (Leipzig, 1844).

The poem celebrates the beauty of nature and, from a central image of blue sky and snow-capped mountains reflected in blue water, draws implications for man's relation to the natural world. The gentle melody, supported by the undulating accompaniment, rises and falls in effortless curves, suggesting the rocking motion of a boat buoyed by the lapping waves of a lake glistening in sunlight.

The piano prelude introduces two different four-measure phrase types, the contrasting of which is a characteristic element in the song's construction: one juxtaposes two similar two-measure segments; the other sets two measures of hemiola against two of regular triple meter. Since the hemiola appears only in the accompaniment, it has an effect like the cross-tugging of some benign undercurrent, unseen beneath the placid surface.

The principal strophe reveals an asymmetric balance of diverse phrase structures: the first two lines are set to a two-segment phrase and a phrase with hemiola, with a two-measure extension for the repetition of the closing words; the last two lines (and the repetition of the final line) occupy a two-part phrase, a regular four-measure phrase, and a phrase with hemiola, plus a two-measure piano interlude.

The contrasting third strophe evolves from its predecessors; its kinship is evident in the rhythm and the rise and fall of the vocal line, and in the accompaniment's occasional interpolations of hemiola. But rising triplets in the piano signal heightened emotion, a suggestion confirmed by a shift to the tonic minor with more active, more colorful harmonies, and the stretching of key words ("werde mild," "Glück," "Frieden") in the wider-ranging vocal line.

The excitement gradually subsides during four measures of dominant harmony in the piano interlude, as triplets yield to duplets and quarter-note melodic motion gives way to the half-note activity of hemiola. The final strophe is a nearly exact repetition of the first, rounded off by the addition of a final cadence to the piano's usual two-measure closing.

Regenlied, Op. 59/3 (Rain Song)

Text by Klaus Groth (1819–1899)

Walle, Regen, walle nieder,
Wecke mir die Träume wieder,
Die ich in der Kindheit träumte,
Wenn das Naß im Sande schäumte!

Wenn die matte Sommerschwüle
Lässig stritt mit frischer Kühle,
Und die blanken Blätter tauten,
Und die Saaten dunkler blauten.

Welche Wonne, in dem Fließen
Dann zu stehn mit nackten Füßen,
An dem Grase hin zu streifen
Und den Schaum mit Händen greifen,

Oder mit den heißen Wangen
Kalte Tropfen aufzufangen,
Und den neuerwachten Düften
Seine Kinderbrust zu lüften!

Wie die Kelche, die da troffen,
Stand die Seele atmend offen,

Wie die Blumen, düftetrunken,
In dem Himmelstau versunken.

Schauernd kühlte jeder Tropfen,
Tief bis an des Herzens Klopfen,
Und der Schöpfung heilig Weben
Drang bis in's verborg'ne Leben.

Walle, Regen, walle nieder,
Wecke meine alten Lieder,
Die wir in der Türe sangen,
Wenn die Tropfen draußen klangen!

Möchte ihnen wieder lauschen,
Ihrem süßen, feuchten Rauschen,
Meine Seele sanft betauen
Mit dem frommen Kindergrauen.

Pour, pour down, rain; reawaken in me the dreams that I dreamt in childhood when the moisture foamed in the sand!

When the weary summer sultriness fought indolently against the fresh coolness, and the gleaming leaves dripped dew, and the fields of grain took on a deeper blue.

What bliss to stand in the downpour at such times with bare feet, to brush against the grass and reach out and touch the foam, or else to catch cool drops on one's flushed face and to open one's childlike heart to the newly awakened scents!

Like the calyxes that were dripping there, one's soul was wide open and breathing, like the flowers intoxicated with fragrances, sunk in the heavenly dew.

Each drop gave a thrill of pleasure and cooled you down to your beating heart, and the holy weaving of Creation penetrated the hidden sources of life.

Pour, pour down, rain; awaken my old songs, which we sang in the doorway when the drops fell noisily outside!

I would like to listen to them again, to their sweet, moist murmuring; I would like to bedew my soul gently with that holy childlike awe.

Composed in Vienna and Tutzing during the spring of 1873.

First performed publicly on 20 March 1896 in Vienna by Raimund von Zur-Mühlen; both this song and "Nachklang," which follows, had already been sung privately by Julius Stockhausen in the autumn of 1873 at Clara Schumann's home.

Through-composed with a return: A A' B C C' A A''.

The text is from Groth's 1854 collection *Hundert Blätter, Paralipomena zum Quickborn.*

The poem describes the flood of childhood memories awakened by a summer rain and the accompanying sadness for the loss of childhood's capacity for wonder.

Just as a downpour accumulates from a single first raindrop, so seem all of the materials of this song (and the next, as well) to grow out of the initial soundings of the bare dominant; its reiterations form a characteristic dotted-rhythm motive that permeates the texture (appearing successively in treble, tenor, and bass registers) and sets the vocal line in motion. It comes to symbolize the poet's sorrow, while the progress of the rainstorm itself is more realistically depicted in pattering steady eighth notes and (later) swirling triplet eighths and jagged gestures in staccato quarters.

Harmonic digressions illuminate the text's shifting moods. The words "Träume wieder" (mm. 10–11) and the parallel "alten Lieder" (mm. 101–102) and "feuchten Rauschen" (mm. 121–122) elicit a turn to the otherworldly submediant, succeeded by the poignant Neapolitan for the phrases immediately following, "die ich in der Kindheit träumte" (mm. 12–16), "die wir in der Türe sangen" (mm. 103–106), and "meine Seele sanft betauen" (mm. 123–126). The increasing excitement of the second stanza is accompanied by a gradual brightening to the relative major for the long section beginning "Welche Wonne" in mm. 45–46, which encompasses the whole of stanzas 3 and 4 and includes a further excursion (around m. 54) to the remote-sounding mediant from that key's parallel minor as the rush of memory nears its peak. In the central section in $\frac{3}{2}$, the cessation of eighth-note motion suggests that the rain has been momentarily forgotten in the face of overpowering nostalgia, and the tonality wavers between the submediant's unreality and the tonic major's comforting warmth. Toward the end of the song, an enduring shift to the tonic major underlines the remembered happiness of the poem's last line, which Brahms repeats.

Although the poem's length almost demands some contrast, the $\frac{3}{2}$ setting of stanzas 5 and 6 comes as somewhat of a disappointment, a seeming sag in the song's spontaneous flow. But the later transition to the return of the opening music is masterly. The piano postlude is another master stroke; the rain diminishes in stages and finally stops altogether, and the poet's sadness gradually dissipates in ever-larger bass augmentations of the dotted-rhythm motive as the mood resolves itself into gently intermingled resignation and regret.

Nachklang, Op. 59/4 (Lingering Sound)

Text by Klaus Groth (1819–1899)

Regentropfen aus den Bäumen
Fallen in das grüne Gras,
Tränen meiner trüben Augen
Machen mir die Wange naß.

Wenn die Sonne wieder scheinet,
Wird der Rasen doppelt grün:

Doppelt wird auf meinen Wangen
Mir die heiße Träne glühn.

Raindrops are falling from the trees into the green grass; tears from my dulled eyes are moistening my cheeks.
When the sun shines again, the lawn becomes twice as green: my hot tears will burn twice as fiercely on my cheeks.

Composed during the spring of 1873 in Vienna and Tutzing.

The first public performance is not documented, but Julius Stockhausen is known to have sung it privately at Clara Schumann's home in the autumn of 1873.

Through-composed, but with the effect of a return after contrast (A B A).

In May of 1856, Groth wrote the text on the half-title of Brahms's copy of *Hundert Blätter, Paralipomena zum Quickborn* (Hamburg, 1854). "Regenlied," WoO posth. 23, uses a slightly different version of the same text, the only poem for which there are two solo settings by Brahms; there line 5 reads "Scheint die Sonne wieder helle."

The song shares both musical materials and poetic imagery with the immediately preceding "Regenlied." This poem, however, is much shorter and more intensely emotional than the former; it explicitly compares the falling rain with the poet's bitter tears, and it hints darkly at some unspecified tragedy from the past rather than evoking general nostalgia. The result is a compellingly concentrated setting of pervading melancholy, profoundly affecting in its impact.

The opening music is nearly identical to that of the preceding song's first stanza, but the absence of an introduction adds urgency and directness, and the heightened emotion of the text motivates the painful dissonances in the piano interlude that follows. A reference to the sun's appearing prompts both a new accompaniment figure and a turn to the relative major, but the use of the minor subdominant in the interludes reminds us that the poet's sorrow is unrelieved. The last two lines of text are set to music that recalls the opening, but telling alterations provide for a welcome climactic high note for the singer and for the characteristic lengthening of the final phrase, for which purpose Brahms repeats the poem's closing line.

The song ends in the tonic major, but the postlude seems to intensify the grief rather than to relieve it. The pattering eighth notes continue and rise quickly to a dramatic *forte* as the dotted-rhythm motive from the opening sounds repeatedly and insistently in the treble. Even the three quiet major chords with which the piece ends constitute an augmentation of this rhythmic motive—a final symbolic outcry of grief.

Clara Schumann was particularly fond of the two companion "rain" songs. After receiving a manuscript copy of the G-major violin sonata (later published as Op. 78), which quotes them recognizably in its third movement and makes use throughout of their dotted-rhythm *Hauptmotiv*, she wrote to Brahms on 10 July 1879:

> I must send you a line to tell you how deeply moved I am by your Sonata. I received it today and of course played it through at once, and had to cry my heart out afterwards for you over it. You can imagine how delighted I was when after the first enchanting movement, and the second, I again came across in the third my own beloved melody, with its exquisite eighth-note movement. I say "my own" because I don't believe anyone can enjoy this melody as deeply and as thoroughly as I do. Fancy finding this last movement after all the beauties that preceded it!

The sonata was composed during the summers of 1878 and 1879, and it is likely that its references to the "rain" songs were a deliberate gesture of solicitude toward Clara during the final battle with tuberculosis of her youngest child (and Brahms's godson), Felix, who died in February 1879 at the age of 24. Although the third movement seems not to have achieved its final form until the summer of 1879, the Österreichische Nationalbibliothek in Vienna holds a manuscript copy of a version of the slow movement, on the reverse of which is a letter from Brahms to Clara, apparently dating from early February 1879. It confirmed that the *Adagio* was written to "tell you, perhaps more clearly than I otherwise could myself, how sincerely I think of you and Felix." The likelihood that the allusion to the "rain" songs in the third movement came as a surprise, while the second movement was already familiar, accounts for Clara's seemingly unequal allotment of enthusiasm in her letter of 10 July.

Agnes, Op. 59/5

Text by Eduard Mörike (1804–1875)

Rosenzeit, wie schnell vorbei,
Schnell vorbei,
Bist du doch gegangen!
Wär' mein Lieb' nur blieben treu,
Blieben treu,
Sollte mir nicht bangen.

Um die Ernte wohlgemut,
Wohlgemut—
Schnitterinnen singen.
Aber, ach! mir krankem Blut,
Mir krankem Blut,
Will nichts mehr gelingen.

Schleiche so durch's Wiesental,
So durch's Tal,
Als im Traum verloren,
Nach dem Berg, da tausendmal,
Tausendmal
Es mir Treu geschworen.

Oben auf des Hügels Rand,
Abgewandt,
Wein' ich bei der Linde;
An dem Hut mein Rosenband
Von seiner Hand,
Spielet in dem Winde.

Time of roses, how quickly you passed, quickly passed! If my sweetheart had only remained faithful, remained faithful, I wouldn't be afraid.

Cheerfully, cheerfully the women sing as they reap the harvest, but, alas! I am sick at heart, sick at heart, and nothing will go right for me any more.

I walk timidly through the meadowy valley, through the valley, as if lost in a dream, up to the mountain where a thousand times, a thousand times he promised to be true to me.

Up on the rim of the hill, turning aside, I weep by the linden tree; on my hat the ribbon of roses he made for me plays in the wind.

Composed in the spring of 1873 in Vienna and Tutzing.

First performed publicly by Amalie Joachim in Hamburg on 2 April 1875; already performed privately during the summer of 1873 by Heinrich Vogl at his home in Tutzing.

Strophic with varied accompaniment.

The poem, written in 1831 for the novel *Maler Nolten*, is found in Mörike's *Gedichte* (Stuttgart and Tübingen, 1838) with the title "Refrain-Liedchen."

Like its text, the setting is a lament in sophisticated folk-song style. Here Brahms finds an effective solution to the problem of changing emotional implication in strophic song, though he never repeated it—the vocal line repeats the same music for each verse with only slight deviation, while the accompaniment is varied with increasing complexity in each successive strophe, clarifying diverse aspects of the narrative and underlining the growing intensity of the girl's grief.

The song's folk flavor derives largely from its alternating meters of $\frac{3}{4}$ and $\frac{2}{4}$ and from its structure of three five-measure phrases, each with a central repeated $\frac{2}{4}$ bar. These reflective echoing repetitions (which are in Mörike's poem) contribute artfully to countering the seeming contradiction between vigorous rhythm and mournful text. The melody's range is relatively small, and most of the phrases descend, in keeping with the generally plaintive tone. The principal variation in the vocal line appears at the beginning of the third phrase, where in verses 2, 3, and 4 it is assigned the higher-rising melody taken in verse 1 by the piano.

The first stanza is accompanied in simple chordal style. The first interlude introduces afterbeats, which continue through verse 2 over a dancing pizzicato bass, suggesting the women's cheerful singing and contrasting ironically with Agnes' heartsickness. The interlude that follows is expanded to three measures and introduces constantly flowing eighth notes, which represent, over a mostly staccato bass, the dazed walking of verse 3. A final interlude, also of three measures, sets the stage for the weeping of verse 4 by adding increased chromaticism to longer lines of the flowing eighths, which now affect all voices of the accompaniment.

The piano's *forte* in the introduction, interludes, and postlude suggests that a streak of defiance ameliorates the pathos of the girl's abandonment.

Eine gute, gute Nacht, Op. 59/6 (A Very Good Night)

Translated from the Russian by Georg Friedrich Daumer (1800–1875)

> Eine gute, gute Nacht
>> Pflegst du mir zu sagen—
> Über dieses eitle Wort,
>> O wie muß ich klagen!
>
> Daß du meiner Seele Glut
>> Nicht so grausam nährtest;
> "Eine gute, gute Nacht,"
>> Daß du sie gewährtest!

You used to wish me a very good night; oh, how I now grieve for that simple word!

You shouldn't have fed my soul's flame so cruelly; you should have granted me a very good night!

Composed during the spring of 1873 in Vienna and Tutzing.

First performed publicly by Gustav Walter on 5 March 1874 in Vienna, at a benefit concert for the Pension Society, but already performed privately during the summer of 1873 by Heinrich Vogl at his own home in Tutzing.

A hybrid form, combining elements of strophic design and through-composition. After what amounts to a first strophe ending in the dominant, the piano seems in m. 19 to begin a repetition of the introduction, and in fact the harmonies continue as before through the first half of m. 24, but with a new vocal line superimposed. Two measures later, in the middle of m. 26, the piano presents a variant of the first strophe's opening vocal phrase, and the voice responds by recalling its own original version. In m. 31, the piano skips ahead to a parallel of m. 14, and, again with a new vocal line, the song ends with a tonic equivalent of the accompaniment of the first strophe's five-measure dominant conclusion, now (typically) expanded to six measures.

The text is from *Polydora* (Frankfurt am Main, 1855).

The self-consciously erotic poem borders on licentiousness, but Brahms sets it elegantly. The sighing tritones of the introduction, which recur at its apparent repetition between verses and again in the postlude, establish the pervading tone of earnest yearning. The sudden *fortes* in mm. 5, 30, and 33 and the *rinforzandi* in mm. 14 and 16 ring out like reproaches of the unfeeling lover. In the second stanza the change to afterbeats in the accompaniment lends a sense of increased agitation.

The entreating opening eighth-note vocal phrase is answered immediately by a piano variant in sixteenths (the order is reversed in mm. 26–30); "zu sagen" in mm. 10–11 seems to be echoed and re-echoed by the piano in mm. 12–13. Suggested imitations abound: in both introduction and postlude, the piano left hand shadows the right; the vocal line at "o wie muß ich klagen!" in mm. 16–18 alludes to the piano's arpeggios in mm. 14 and 16; the vocal arpeggios in mm. 31 and 33 are actuated by those of the piano. Slight though it may be, the song is a superb illustration of Brahms's penchant for the interrelatedness of vocal line with accompaniment.

Mein wundes Herz, Op. 59/7 (My Sore Heart)

Text by Klaus Groth (1819–1899)

Mein wundes Herz verlangt nach milder Ruh,
O hauche sie ihm ein!
Es fliegt dir weinend, bange schlagend zu—
O hülle du es ein!

Wie wenn ein Strahl durch schwere Wolken bricht,
So winkest du ihm zu:
O lächle fort mit deinem milden Licht!
Mein Pol, mein Stern bist du!

My sore heart longs for gentle rest; oh, instill that rest in it! It flies toward you weeping, beating in alarm; oh, envelop it!

As when a ray breaks through heavy clouds, thus do you beckon to it: oh, keep smiling with your gentle light! You are my pole, my star!

Composed during the spring of 1873 in Vienna and Tutzing.

First performed by Simon Weltlinger on 11 April 1878 in Vienna.

A hybrid form, combining strophic design with through-composition; two stanzas that begin alike but end differently.

The text is from the "Klänge" section of Groth's 1854 collection *Hundert Blätter, Paralipomena zum Quickborn*.

The impassioned introduction, like an upsurge of longing, avoids the tonic, but the broad opening vocal phrase defines it clearly before veering toward the relative major in response to the text. The second phrase reconfirms the tonic by means of a strong cadence on the dominant, but the third leads inexorably back toward the relative major, where the stanza ends. A condensed restatement of the introduction leads to the second stanza, where the first two lines are set identically to those in the first. But at mid-verse, the music moves (by way of the gentle subdominant) joyously into the warmth of the tonic major, where it remains through a glowing vocal climax at "mein Stern" in mm. 42–43 (echoed in inversion by the bass) and the serene ending.

The song proceeds so naturally, so compellingly, that it is surprising to find that it is also a marvel of contrapuntal ingenuity. The opening vocal phrase is imitated in diminution by the piano part's right hand and in the original note values at the sixth below by the left. The first four notes, the musical embodiment of "mein wundes Herz," constitute a motive that comes to permeate the entire texture as Brahms almost casually manipulates it with seemingly limitless imagination and skill: for example, the opening gesture of the introduction, in which the right hand pits a double statement in eighth-note broken sixths against the tenor's implied inversion; the vocal line's inversion at "Es fliegt dir weinend" in m. 13 against the piano's diminution of linked inversion and original form, answered by the bass's normal statement in the next measure; the double *Vorimitation* in m. 32 of "O lächle fort," and the piano's triple canonic response in mm. 34 with the treble in diminution, the whole pattern immediately repeated and elaborated for "mit deinem milden Licht"; and the canonic imitation in augmentation of the last vocal phrase and the bass line. Even the piano's closing chords seem to allude to the same pattern.

This pervasive motivic artifice has the effect of suggesting that the poet's heartache has become all-consuming, that his every thought is affected by it; the result is not the mere cerebration that one might presume but a heightened intensity of emotional expression.

Dein blaues Auge, Op. 59/8 (Your Blue Eyes)

Text by Klaus Groth (1819–1899)

Dein blaues Auge hält so still,
Ich blicke bis zum Grund.
Du fragst mich, was ich sehen will?
Ich sehe mich gesund.

Es brannte mich ein glühend Paar,
Noch schmerzt das Nachgefühl:
Das deine ist wie See so klar
Und wie ein See so kühl.

Your blue eyes gaze so steadily that I can see to the very depths of them.
You ask me what I expect to see? I find my well-being by looking into them.
One blazing pair of eyes scorched me; the after-feeling still hurts.
Your eyes are as limpid as a lake and as cool as a lake.

Composed during the spring of 1873 in Vienna and Tutzing.

First performed by Emma Wenzel on 25 January 1888 in Vienna.

A composite through-composed/strophic form; the effect is of a straightforward eight-measure strophe ending on the dominant plus an expanded developmental variation ending on the tonic, the whole framed by a piano prelude and postlude.

The text is found in Groth's 1854 collection *Hundert Blätter, Paralipomena zum Quickborn*. The poem, like Brahms's setting, begins as a gentle love lyric, but remembered pain brings momentary unrest; the ending is clouded by ambiguity, the words "und wie ein See so kühl" perhaps implying coldness rather than serenity.

The introduction alternates wide-ranging with nearly stable measures, establishing the song's essential vacillation between passion and tenderness. The noble vocal melody unfolds over slowly changing harmonies; the quarter-note motion in both melody and harmony at "ich blicke bis zum Grund" sounds like an acceleration, an abrupt return to reality from the languor of the opening, an effect that is heightened by the *rinforzando*. But the half-measure harmonic rhythm returns for the third line's reminiscence of the arching shape of the first. A *forte* marks the stanza's strong, octave-spanning fourth line.

At m. 13, borrowings from the minor mode and sighing melodic figures in the piano signal the poet's lingering anguish over a pair of eyes from the past. Spurred by the piano's chromatic and dissonant quarter-note harmonic movement, an apparent minor-mode repetition of the earlier melody breaks off into a repeated sobbing figure on "noch schmerzt" before an elegantly extended cadence carries the music smoothly into the relative major (the home key's mediant), a harmonic color often associated by Brahms with the unreal world of dream or memory. The half-measure diatonic harmonies return as before for the stanza's third line, though the dreamworld key remains. But the tonic reappears abruptly with the *forte* last line, which is made doubly emphatic by the repetition of its text in a closing phrase that spans a tenth. A rising tonic triad of phrase beginnings is completed by the entrance of the postlude melody on the upper fifth. The ending's obscurity of meaning is highlighted by the closing vocal phrases' puzzling angularity and *forte* indication. The postlude recedes into indecisive melodic wavering between third and fifth, leaving the ambivalence hovering.

NINE LIEDER AND GESÄNGE, OP. 63

Lieder und Gesänge für eine Singstimme mit Pianoforte von Johannes Brahms (Songs for Solo Voice with Piano by Johannes Brahms), Op. 63. Published in two books, 1–4 and 5–9, in November 1874 by C. F. Peters, Leipzig and Berlin; publication number 5704ab.

In addition to the grouping together of the four Schenkendorf texts, the two "Junge Lieder" of Felix Schumann, and the three "Heimweh" poems of Groth, the opus is further unified by its beginning and ending in the same key, A major.

Frühlingstrost, Op. 63/1 (Spring's Consolation)

Text by Max von Schenkendorf (1783–1817)

> Es weht um mich Narzissenduft,
> Es spricht zu mir die Frühlingsluft:
> Geliebter,
> Erwach' im roten Morgenglanz,
> Dein harrt ein blütenreicher Kranz,
> Betrübter!
>
> Nur mußt du kämpfen drum und tun
> Und länger nicht in Träumen ruh'n;
> Laß' schwinden!
> Komm, Lieber, komm auf's Feld hinaus,
> Du wirst im grünen Blätterhaus
> Ihn finden.
>
> Wir sind dir alle wohlgesinnt,
> Du armes, liebebanges Kind,
> Wir Düfte;
> Warst immer treu uns Spielgesell,
> Drum dienen willig dir und schnell
> Die Lüfte.
>
> Zur Liebsten tragen wir dein Ach
> Und kränzen ihr das Schlafgemach
> Mit Blüten.
> Wir wollen, wenn du von ihr gehst

Und einsam dann und traurig stehst,
Sie hüten.

Erwach' im morgenroten Glanz,
Schon harret dein der Myrtenkranz,
Geliebter!
Der Frühling kündet gute Mär',
Und nun kein Ach, kein Weinen mehr,
Betrübter!

The fragrance of narcissus wafts about me; the air of springtime says to me:
"Beloved man, awaken in the red morning glow; a wreath of blossom awaits
you in your distress!

"But you must fight for it and act, and no longer repose and dream; let your
dreams vanish! Come, dear man, come out to the field; you will find it [the
wreath] in the green house of leaves!

"We all wish you well, you poor, love-frightened child, we fragrances; you
were always a faithful playmate to us; that is why the breezes willingly and
swiftly serve you.

"We carry your sighs to your sweetheart, and we wreathe her bedroom with
blossoms. When you depart from her and then remain lonely and sad, we will
guard her.

"Awake in the morning-red glow; the myrtle wreath already awaits you,
beloved man! The spring announces good tidings, and now no more lamenting, no more weeping in your distress!"

Composed during the summer of 1874 at Rüschlikon bei Zürich.
First performed by Gustav Walter on 31 January 1875 in Vienna.
Rondo; A B A C A.
The poem, dated 12 April 1810, is found in Schenkendorf's *Gedichte*
(Berlin, 1837).

Despite its unusual length, the song seems to derive from a single flash of
inspiration, pulsating with joyous exhilaration from first note to last. The introduction's breathless triplets and soaring melodic line set the tone
immediately. The rising sixth, A–F♯ (F–D in the lower key), recurs throughout in both voice and piano as a unifying motive.

Nowhere is Brahms's rhythmic virtuosity more evident than in this song,
where it is perhaps the most striking feature. The meter signature is $\frac{6}{4}$, yet
much of the accompaniment is in $\frac{3}{2}$; its secondary pulses therefore fall on
the weak beats of the vocal line, actually propelling it forward like a spring-
board. Rests in the vocal line are bridged by the continuously melodic left
hand. The impassioned forward motion of the music is further aided by the
half-measure anticipations in the melody associated with the characteristic
lengthening at the ends of sections. The overall effects are of great ebullience
and metric elasticity.

The first contrasting section provides an example of Brahms's extraordinary gift for creating unity out of diverse elements. Although the vocal line

continues in the same vein as in stanza 1, the accompaniment introduces in m. 23 a new angular dotted figure, probably prompted by the text's exhortation to "fight and act"; though now in $\frac{6}{4}$, its stressed weak beats continue to lift and impel the melody. Suddenly, but with mercurial naturalness, this figure is replaced in mm. 27–28 by a recalling of the earlier principal $\frac{3}{2}$ figure with triplets. In quick succession there follow, with seeming inevitability, in mm. 29–30, a smoothed-out version of the previously angular figure, the dotted rhythms now reduced to even eighths; in mm. 31–32, a right-hand melody in quarters and halves in duet with the voice, accompanied by undulating eighth-note arpeggios; and in mm. 33–34, a return of the principal $\frac{3}{2}$ figure, which, in m. 35, is transformed briefly into $\frac{6}{4}$, leading to the fermata and cadence. A return of the opening material for stanza 3 is prepared by a two-measure transition, during which the accompaniment's meter is returned to $\frac{3}{2}$ by a process masked by the metrically ambiguous placement of quarter notes in the left hand.

The second contrasting section is in the gentler key of the subdominant, and its accompaniment is made up of dancing arpeggiated eighth notes; both elements are anticipated in the last bar of the transition (m. 55). In mm. 61–62, the piano melody overlaps and joins the two parts of the vocal line; in mm. 63–65, the original $\frac{3}{2}$ motive recurs, but in the left hand only. After another anticipation-filled fermata, the principal music returns to carry the song headlong to its ecstatic conclusion.

Erinnerung, Op. 63/2 (Remembrance)

Text by Max von Schenkendorf (1783–1817)

Ihr wunderschönen Augenblicke,
Die Lieblichste der ganzen Welt
Hat euch mit ihrem ew'gen Glücke,
Mit ihrem süßen Licht erhellt.

Ihr Stellen, ihr geweihten Plätze,
Ihr trugt ja das geliebte Bild,
Was Wunder habt ihr, was für Schätze
Vor meinen Augen dort enthüllt!

Ihr Gärten all', ihr grünen Haine,
Du Weinberg in der süßen Zier,
Es nahte sich die Hehre, Reine,
In Züchten gar zu freundlich mir.

Ihr Worte, die sie da gesprochen,
Du schönstes, halbverhauchtes Wort,
Dein Zauberbann wird nie gebrochen,
Du klingst und wirkest fort und fort.

Ihr wunderschönen Augenblicke,
Ihr lacht und lockt in ew'gem Reiz.
Ich schaue sehnsuchtsvoll zurücke
Voll Schmerz und Lust und Liebesgeiz.

You marvelously beautiful moments, the loveliest woman in the whole world has brightened you with her eternal good fortune, with her sweet light.

You places, you hallowed spots that bore the beloved figure, what a miracle, what treasures you revealed to my eyes there!

All you gardens, you green groves, you vineyard so sweetly adorned—the lofty, pure woman approached me with propriety but with such great friendliness!

You words that she spoke there, you most beautiful, only half-breathed word, your magic spell will never be broken; you resound and affect me constantly.

You marvelously beautiful moments, you laugh and lure with everlasting charm. I look back in longing, full of pain and pleasure and greed for love.

Composed during the summer of 1874 at Rüschlikon bei Zürich.
First performed by Albertine Hegar on 6 May 1877 at the Zürich Tonhalle.
Varied strophic; A B A B A', with varied accompaniment.
The text is found in the 1837 *Gedichte*.

The poem treats of longing for past love, but Brahms adds a further dramatic dimension by causing the tempo and rhythmic activity to increase, as though the remembered images were increasingly vivid. The final stanza brings a return to the original tempo, like the reawakening of awareness that the past exists only in memory.

The expansive opening derives much of its deceptive air of simplicity from its diatonicism, which is strengthened by the successive definition of both dominant and subdominant. The contrasting strophe borrows its rhythm from the first, and its melody begins as a transposition of the second phrase (mm. 5–8). Its first half moves effortlessly and enchantingly from the key of the dominant to that of the lowered mediant; the second half prepares the return to tonic.

The melody has the haunting rhythm of a nostalgic waltz, while the accompaniment's endless rhythmic inventiveness adds both contrast and subtle variety of mood. The absence of accompaniment downbeats lightens the first strophe, and makes it clear that these are (mostly) happy memories, without despair. The second stanza is propelled by groups of four eighth notes, first in the left hand alone, then overlapping in alternate hands. Melodic syncopations in the interlude prepare the sustained afterbeats that accompany and activate stanza 3. For the first half of stanza 4, a fifth eighth note is added as ending for the left hand's four-eighth groups, and the right hand's constant eighths are patterned in threes, simultaneously suggesting the contradictory effects of increased activity and slower tempo; the stanza's second half is as before, anticipating the broadening that is to come. The ritard and now on-beat melody of the interlude help to prepare a soberer version of the opening strophe's music for the closing stanza, this time firmly anchored by downbeat basses.

Chromatic inflections delicately tinge the last line with regret. The postlude's prolongations suggest a certain reluctance to abandon the reverie.

An ein Bild, Op. 63/3 (To a Picture)

Text by Max von Schenkendorf (1783–1817)

Was schaust du mich so freundlich an,
O Bild aus weiter Ferne,
Und winkest dem verbannten Mann?
Er käme gar zu gerne.

Die ganze Jugend tut sich auf,
Wenn ich an dich gedenke,
Als ob ich noch den alten Lauf
Nach deinem Hause lenke.

Gleich einem, der in's tiefe Meer
Die Blicke läßt versinken,
Nicht sieht, nicht hört, ob um ihn her
Viel tausend Schätze winken.

Gleich einem, der am Firmament
Nach fernem Sterne blicket,
Nur diesen kennt, nur diesen nennt
Und sich an ihm entzücket:

Ist all' mein Sehnen, all' mein Mut
In dir, o Bild, gegründet,
Und immer noch von gleicher Glut,
Von gleicher Lust entzündet.

Why do you look at me in such a friendly way, you picture from a far-off land, and why do you beckon to the exiled man? He would come only too gladly.

My whole youth reopens when I think of you, as if I were still taking the old path to your house.

Like a man who lets his gaze sink into the deep sea, and neither sees nor hears when many thousand treasures beckon all around him;

Like a man who gazes at a distant star in the sky, and knows only it, and names only it, and takes delight in it:

Thus does all my longing, all my courage, have its foundation in you, O picture, and is still enflamed with the same passion, with the same joy.

Composed during the summer of 1874 in Rüschlikon bei Zürich.

The first performance is not documented.

Varied strophic; A A B B' A'. Stanzas 1, 2, and 5 are set to the same music, with some adjustment of the final cadence. The vocal melodies of stanzas 3 and 4 are similar, with the unusual difference that the first four measures of the latter lie a third higher than those of the former, after which they coincide; the accompaniment of stanza 4 is somewhat intensified by its textural expansion into the higher octave.

The text appears in the poet's *Gedichte* (Berlin, 1837), where the editor provided the title "An ein Bild, das Porträt seiner Gattin" and the date 29 March 1816. The verses depict the poet's reliving the joys of a past love as he loses himself in contemplation of the beloved's portrait.

The introduction's slowly rising arpeggio evokes the unreal realm of memory and imagination from which the poet speaks. The frequent leaps in the main melody, often in succession and in the same direction, create an effect of fervor, to which the accompanying afterbeats add excitement. In contrast, the melody of the more meditative middle section restricts itself to stepwise movement and intervals no larger than a third, and its afterbeats are sustained.

In mm. 6–7 and analogous passages, heightened expressivity results from the use of the minor subdominant and the *rinforzando*, pointing up the poignancy associated with references to "the exiled man," "the old path," and "the same passion." There are several contrapuntal niceties: the accompaniment's treble melody in mm. 1–2 is imitated in augmentation by the bass in mm. 3–5, in diminution by the right hand in mm. 6 and 7, and in a motivic variation by the right hand of mm. 8–9 and the left hand of mm. 10–11; the vocal melody of m. 6 is imitated by the piano's bass in m. 7; the accompaniment's bass line in mm. 8–9 is imitated by its melody in mm. 10–11.

The melody for stanzas 3 and 4 develops its rhythm and takes its initial motive from the principal melody. The music of this contrasting section twice ventures deeper and deeper into flat keys before tentatively extricating itself, symbolizing the absorbed concentration of the text's "man" on the deep sea or on a remote star, to the exclusion of all else. The indicated gradual increases in animation and loudness actuate a growth in emotional intensity, which is enhanced by the thickened accompaniment of stanza 4 and by the higher pitch and more active bass line of its transposed beginning.

In a few quick strokes, the masterly transition in mm. 44–46 reintroduces the dreamworld rising arpeggio, refers to the main melodic motive in both its normal and its inverted form, and shifts from minor to major to prepare the return of the earlier music for stanza 5.

The song ends quietly and without finality, as though the poet might at any time resume his reflection on the past.

An die Tauben, Op. 63/4 (To the Doves)

Text by Max von Schenkendorf (1783–1817)

Fliegt nur aus, geliebte Tauben!
Euch als Boten send' ich hin;
Sagt ihr, und sie wird euch glauben,
Daß ich krank vor Liebe bin.

Ihr könnt fliegen, ihr könnt eilen,
Tauben, froh bergab und -an;
Ich muß in der Fremde weilen,
Ewig ein gequälter Mann.

Auch mein Brieflein soll noch gehen
Heut zu ihr, mein Liebesgruß,
Soll sie suchen auf den Höhen,
An dem schönen, grünen Fluß.

Wird sie von den Bergen steigen
Endlich in das Niederland?
Wird sich mir die Sonne zeigen,
Die zu lange schon verschwand?

Vögel, Briefe, Liebesboten,
Lied und Seufzer, sagt ihr's hell:
Suche ihn im Reich der Toten,
Liebchen, oder komme schnell!

Fly away, then, dear doves! I send you out as messengers; tell her—and she will believe you—that I am sick with love.

You can fly, you can hasten, doves, happily uphill and down; I must dwell in a strange land, a man always in pain.

My little letter, too, should go to her this very day, my love's greeting; she should seek it on the heights, by the beautiful green river.

Will she finally descend from the mountains into the valley? Will that sun finally reappear to me that has been absent far too long now?

Birds, letters, love's messengers, song and sighs, tell her this clearly: "Seek him in the realm of the dead, darling, or else come quickly!"

Composed during the summer of 1874 at Rüschlikon bei Zürich.

First performed by a Herr Seubert on 13 February 1886 in Mannheim.

Varied strophic; A B A C A'. The rondo format sets stanzas 1 and 3 to the same melody, but for stanza 5 a variant of this melody appears in the piano part, moving into the vocal line for its last three measures only; the voice meanwhile has been given new harmonizing pitches in the principal melody's rhythm.

The poem appears in the collected *Gedichte* (Berlin, 1837). Schenkendorf indicated that it was written at Koblenz in the late autumn of 1815.

The image of doves as love's messengers is far from original, but Brahms gives the longish poem an enchantingly joyous setting of such simplicity and naturalness that it almost seems to evolve on the spot. Unity is provided by the accompaniment's constant triplets, which flutter, dance, or daydream as the text requires, and which are absent only for half of m. 24, in order to call attention to the poet's tortured state.

The melody begins by rising through a tonic-triad arpeggio, from third to higher third, and much of its continuation also hints at the skeletal definition of primary triads, creating an aura of folk-song openness and innocence.

Yet much of the song's charm results from its easy and frequent modulations, which highlight the emotional implications of the text. The melodic leap upward to the flatted third on "krank" in m. 9 is an obvious example. The smooth progress to the major mediant from the parallel minor in the following measure is a delicious revelation that the "illness" is from love, and the facile immediate return to the tonic key makes it clear that this lovesickness, though not without its poignancy, is more pleasurable than painful.

At the words "ich muß in der Fremde weilen" (I must dwell in a strange land) in mm. 19–20, the second stanza, which has clearly moved into the key of the dominant, suddenly veers toward the foreign-sounding submediant of that key (the mediant of the opening tonality). A deceptive cadence in m. 22 recalls the original tonic harmony, outlined by a descending arpeggio in octaves, *forte*, in the piano's bass, which is at once imitated in inversion by the voice to announce the repetition of the phrase of text. (The curious prolongation of this harmony may be a metaphor for the word "ewig.") But as if by magic, the former tonic now functions instead as dominant of the Neapolitan in a striking cadence on the major mediant to characterize "ein gequälter Mann" (a man in pain).

The same harmonic deviation that seemed specifically designed to portray lovesickness in stanza 1 seems equally successful in evoking "beautiful green river" in stanza 3.

Stanza 4 stands apart from the rest of the poem because of its questioning character; Brahms's setting differentiates it musically as well with markedly chromatic harmonies (presaged in the preceding transition), which oscillate and drift between tender subdominant and dreamy submediant. As a symbol of the sun's long absence, the harmonies of mm. 50–51 float over a remote pedal point on the dominant of the submediant, but suddenly, as though reminded by the repetitions of "zu lange" that the home key too had been absent far too long, the dominant returns, insistently and somewhat wrenchingly.

In the last stanza, Brahms not only foregoes the opportunity of dramatizing the reference to death, but his use of major harmonies in mm. 61–62 also reveals that the sham threat, even as it is made, is only a pleasantry. The flat-key tilt of mm. 63–74 tinges the first statement of "Liebchen, oder komme schnell" with plaintiveness, which is overcome at once by the confident re-statement of the same words. The postlude seems to struggle a bit longer with its poignancy before rushing at last to its jubilant concluding gesture. (In the low key, there is some rearrangement of the final sonority.)

Junge Lieder I, Op. 63/5 (Young Songs, I)

Text by Felix Schumann (1854–1879)

> Meine Liebe ist grün wie der Fliederbusch,
> Und mein Lieb ist schön wie die Sonne;
> Die glänzt wohl herab auf den Fliederbusch
> Und füllt ihn mit Duft und mit Wonne.
>
> Meine Seele hat Schwingen der Nachtigall
> Und wiegt sich in blühendem Flieder,
> Und jauchzet und singet vom Duft berauscht
> Viel liebestrunkene Lieder.

My love is green as the lilac bush, and my loved one is as beautiful as the sun that shines down on the lilac bush and fills it with fragrance and with rapture.

My soul has the wings of the nightingale and swings in the blossoming lilacs, and exults and, made drunk by the fragrance, sings many a love-intoxicated song.

Composed in December 1873 in Vienna.

First performed (together with the following three songs of the opus) on 16 December 1874 in Munich by a Fräulein Radecke with the pianist Sophie Menter.

Strophic.

The text was an unpublished poem by Felix Schumann, the youngest child of Robert and Clara, and Brahms's godson. In a letter from Baden-Baden of 17 September 1873, Clara wrote to Brahms that she would send Felix's poems "before the end of the month, and I would be very glad if you would read them through and mark anything that you happen to like. Some of them are really very pretty." Felix at the time was at his mother's home, recuperating from an attack of the lung disease that had already manifested itself when he was barely into his teens, and to which he would succumb before his twenty-fifth birthday.

Brahms, presumably deeply touched by the request and the situation (and also no doubt genuinely attracted to the poem), responded generously and quickly—a manuscript copy of his setting of "Meine Liebe ist grün" reached the Schumanns' home in Berlin in time for Christmas. On 1 January 1874 the grateful Clara wrote to Brahms:

> The song was a delightful surprise, especially for Felix whom we had told nothing about it. When Joachim came in, in the evening, I showed it to him and we began to play it. Felix came over and asked what the words were and when he saw that they were his own he turned quite pale.

The verses' sentiments are naive and their images ordinary, but Brahms's exuberant music imbues them with the breathless impetuosity and youthful passion that they fail to express fully on their own.

The song pours forth with such spontaneity that one resists the idea of its having been "constructed"; yet specific elements in its structure contribute directly to its ardent ebullience. In the accompaniment, careening successions of left-hand eighth notes surge and recede like the desire they evoke, while the right hand's afterbeats vibrate in excitement. The tonic harmony is postponed, avoided, related temporarily to other key centers—only in the strophe's closing phrase is it allowed to establish itself firmly. The melody unfolds in sweeping arcs, first outlining the triads of the relative minor with which the initial phrase begins (ascending) and the tonic major to which it modulates (descending), then inching higher, phrase by phrase, toward the luxuriantly expansive conclusion. Each of the stanza's four lines of text is treated differently, gathering momentum: the first is set to a four-bar phrase; the second is set twice to a pair of two-bar phrases; the third is sung only once, to a two-bar phrase; the fourth is set twice, first in two bars, then climactically stretched to four.

The splendid postlude seems to carry the crux of the drama. The afterbeats are replaced by urgent incomplete triplets, and the bass line and metrically displaced melody first separate, then (under an upper pedal) converge, meeting after the fermata, like the union of two souls, on the third of the key, *piano*. The earlier rhythm then resumes to lead either to the second stanza or to the quiet ending. (Clara's New Year's Day letter continues: "How beautiful the song is, and the coda—I could go on playing that over and over again—the G♯ [low key, D] leading back to the beginning is so wonderful!")

Junge Lieder II, Op. 63/6 (Young Songs, II)

Text by Felix Schumann (1854–1879)

Wenn um den Holunder der Abendwind kost
Und der Falter um den Jasminenstrauch,
Dann kos' ich mit meinem Liebchen auch
Auf der Steinbank schattig und weich bemoost.

Und wenn vom Dorfe die Glocke erschallt
Und der Lerche jubelndes Abendgebet,

Dann schweigen wir auch und die Seele zergeht
Vor der Liebe heiliger Gottesgewalt.

Und blickt dann vom Himmel der Sterne Schar
Und das Glühwürmchen in der Lilie Schoß,
Dann lasse ich sie aus den Armen los
Und küsse ihr scheidend das Augenpaar.

When the evening breeze caresses the elders, and the night moth caresses
the jasmine bush, then I, too, hug and kiss my sweetheart on the stone bench,
shady and soft with moss.

And when the sound of the bell comes from the village, and the exultant
evening prayer of the lark, then we, too, are silent, and our soul melts with
love's sacred, divine power.

And when the troop of stars looks down from the sky and the glowworm appears in the heart of the lily, then I release her from my arms and, as we part,
I kiss her two eyes.

Probably composed in early summer 1874 at Rüschlikon bei Zürich—Clara
Schumann's diary notes in July 1874 that "Johannes sent me a setting of one
of Felix's songs, as a pleasant surprise from Rüschlikon"—though its roots
may be intertwined with those of the preceding song, which was completed
in December 1873.

First performed in Munich on 16 December 1874 by Fräulein Radecke and
Sophie Menter.

Strophic.

The text was an unpublished poem by the Schumanns' youngest child,
Felix. (See the notes to the preceding song.)

The three stanzas are set to the same vocal melody, the accompaniment
of the second altered slightly to imitate the tolling of the village bell in the
bass of mm. 15–16. The music of the introduction reappears as interlude
only between verses 2 and 3, perhaps to represent the lapse of time at that
point in the narrative.

As in "Junge Lieder I," Brahms's setting suggests the wonder and the
shoot-green freshness of first love. The melody is long-breathed and tender,
the harmonies sensuous, the total effect that of languorous yearning. An
evocation of lingering caresses is enhanced by the leisurely expansion to
three measures from the expected two of both the piano introduction and
the strophe's closing vocal phrase.

The poetic verse comprises two couplets, each set to a four-measure
phrase; the second couplet is made achingly expressive by upward leaps in
the melody and by a harmonic digression into the key of the lowered mediant. Though Brahms's repetition of the fourth line of text gives tacit license
to break the second long phrase, the first is particularly beautiful when sung
in one breath. Heed the tempo instruction, "zart bewegt" (gently animated).

Heimweh I, Op. 63/7 (Homesickness, I)

Text by Klaus Groth (1819–1899)

Wie traulich war das Fleckchen,
Wo meine Wiege ging,
Kein Bäumchen war, kein Heckchen,
Das nicht voll Träume hing.

Wo nur ein Blümchen blühte,
Da blühten gleich sie mit,
Und Alles sang und glühte
Mir zu bei jedem Schritt.

Ich wäre nicht gegangen
Nicht für die ganze Welt!—
Mein Sehnen, mein Verlangen,
Hier ruht's in Wald und Feld.

How cozy was that tiny village where my cradle rocked! There was no little tree, no little hedge, that wasn't filled with dreams.

Whenever a flower blossomed, they would at once blossom, too; and everything sang and shone for me with every step I took.

I wouldn't have gone away, not for the whole world! My yearning, my longing, dwells here in forest and field.

Composed in 1874.

The first performance of the first two of the "Heimweh" songs, together with both "Junge Lieder," was given by Fräulein Radecke and Sophie Menter in Munich on 16 December 1874.

Varied strophic; three verses, of which the first two are set to the same music, while the third begins similarly but varies the accompaniment figuration, the harmonic movement, and, in the second half, the melodic line itself.

The text, like those of the next two songs, is from *Hundert Blätter, Paralipomena zum Quickborn* (Hamburg, 1854). The three do not appear together there, but, since they share the common themes of longing for home and for childhood, Brahms joined them into one entity under the title "Heimweh," evidently intending their performance as a set. The first and third songs are similar in their relatively gentler expressiveness, and they set off the emotionally more profound second song in the same way that a sonata's outer movements frame the slow movement. (When performed in the lower key, the transposition of the first song into E♭ major from the printed E major will retain Brahms's key relationships.)

The musical language of "Heimweh I" derives from the poetic images of a rocking cradle, unspoiled nature, and the dreams of long ago. The little sixteenth-note melody of the introduction and interludes, with its swaying accompaniment, almost without dissonance, evokes the simplicity of untroubled youth. Brahms's repetition of the second line of each stanza allows the strophe to begin with an unexpectedly strong five-measure phrase; repetitions of and within the fourth lines make possible the characteristic phrase lengthening at the end of the strophe.

The second half of each stanza is set more introspectively and therefore more chromatically. Stanzas 1 and 2 veer off into the mediant from the minor mode, while the more climactic stanza 3 ventures into the seemingly more distant, but warmer and more poignant, submediant from the minor. This distinctive harmonic color seems to awaken a new deeper level of nostalgia, which affects the remainder of the song—even the postlude's attempt to return to childish innocence trails off instead into sadness.

Heimweh II, Op. 63/8 (Homesickness, II)

Text by Klaus Groth (1819–1899)

O wüßt, ich doch den Weg zurück,
Den lieben Weg zum Kinderland!
O warum sucht' ich nach dem Glück
Und ließ der Mutter Hand?

O wie mich sehnet auszuruh'n,
Von keinem Streben aufgeweckt,
Die müden Augen zuzutun,
Von Liebe sanft bedeckt!

Und nichts zu forschen, nichts zu späh'n,
Und nur zu träumen leicht und lind,
Der Zeiten Wandel nicht zu seh'n,
Zum zweiten Mal ein Kind!

O zeigt mir doch den Weg zurück,
Den lieben Weg zum Kinderland!
Vergebens such' ich nach dem Glück—
Ringsum ist öder Strand!

Oh, if I only knew the way back, the lovely path to the land of childhood! Oh, why did I seek for fortune and leave my mother's hand?

Oh, how I long to rest thoroughly, aroused by no ambition; to close my weary eyes, gently covered by love!

And to hunt for nothing, to seek out nothing, and merely to dream lightly and gently; not to see the passage of time, a child for the second time!

Oh, please show me the way back, the lovely path to the land of childhood! In vain I seek for fortune; round about me is a barren shore!

Composed in 1874.

First performed, together with "Heimweh I" and both "Junge Lieder," by Fräulein Radecke and Sophie Menter in Munich on 16 December 1874.

A B B A', with only slight variation.

The text, like those of the songs immediately preceding and following, is from Groth's *Hundert Blätter, Paralipomena zum Quickborn* (Hamburg, 1854).

This is one of those songs that are so perfect, so inseparable a fusion of text and music, that one can only rejoice that they exist. The poem itself is partly responsible for the depth of emotional intensity found here; Brahms seems to have recognized his own longings in those which Groth expressed, and they drew from him music of such nobility as to transcend any possible hint of self-pity.

The opening rolling arpeggios peak and recede with the grandeur of ocean waves; the stately bass unfolds with the fateful inevitability of some timeless passacaglia theme. The initial vocal arch establishes exactly the right tone of plaintive tenderness—the word "zurück" returns to the same pitch with which the phrase began. "Den lieben Weg zum Kinderland" prompts a gently caressing rhythmic variation, a modulation to the dominant symbolizing childhood's distance from the present. An intensification of yearning is made apparent by the move to the Neapolitan on "O warum sucht' ich nach dem Glück" and, in the middle section, by the increased chromaticism of both melody and accompaniment. In such a context, the pedal points at "Die müden Augen zuzutun" (mm. 19–20) and "Der Zeiten Wandel nicht zu seh'n" (mm. 29–30) create striking effects of drowsiness and immobility.

The parallel construction of the first and last verses is highlighted by the recalling of the opening music for the setting of verse 4. At "Vergebens such' ich nach dem Glück," however, the accompaniment changes to ominous hollow octaves in falling thirds, a figure that Brahms always associated with portentous events, usually death. (See, for example, "Feldeinsamkeit," Op. 86/2, and *Vier ernste Gesänge*, Op. 121/2 and 3.) At "Ringsum ist öder Strand," the rhythmic activity lessens and the bass line is reduced to helpless *pianissimo* doubling of the voice. These factors, together with the retention of the minor mode to the end of the vocal line, create a sense of almost para-lyzing desolation; but the postlude comforts, and its final arpeggios climb serenely into the upper register of the keyboard, like a vision of happiness beyond death. The final moments of the song are unforgettable.

Heimweh III, Op. 63/9 (Homesickness, III)

Text by Klaus Groth (1819–1899)

Ich sah als Knabe Blumen blüh'n—
Ich weiß nicht mehr, was war es doch?
Ich sah die Sonne drüber glüh'n—
Mich dünkt, ich seh' es noch.

Es war ein Duft, es war ein Glanz,
Die Seele sog ihn durstend ein.
Ich pflückte sie zu einem Kranz—
Wo mag er blieben sein?

Ich such' an jedem Blümchen nach
Um jenen Schmelz, um jenes Licht,
Ich forsche jeden Sommertag—
Doch solche find' ich nicht.

Ihr wußtet nimmer, was ich trieb?
Ich suchte meinen alten Kranz.
Es war so frisch, so licht, so lieb—
Es war der Jugendglanz.

As a boy I saw flowers blossoming; I don't know any more—what was it, actually? I saw the sun shine above them—I seem to see it still.

There was a fragrance, there was a brightness; my soul drank it in thirstily. I picked them for a wreath—what could have become of it?

I look at every little flower to rediscover that enamel-like color, that light; I hunt for them every summer day, but I don't find any like that.

You never knew what I was about? I was looking for my old wreath. It was so fresh, so bright, so dear—it was the glow of youth.

Composed in 1874.

First performed by George Henschel in Hamburg on 8 January 1875.

A B A' B'; with slight variation, verses 1 and 3 are set similarly, as are verses 2 and 4.

The text, like those of the two preceding songs, is from Groth's *Hundert Blätter, Paralipomena zum Quickborn* (Hamburg, 1854).

This is the most sweetly nostalgic of the three "Heimweh" songs. Though it is colored by introspection and poignant memory, it remains unshadowed by regret or pain.

The song bears the unmistakable stamp of Brahms at his most lyrical. Yet, perhaps more than in any other song, one is reminded of his great love for, and indebtedness to, the music of Schubert. ("There is no song of Schubert's from which one cannot learn something," Brahms is reported to have said.) The introduction, particularly its left-hand figure, sounds more Schubertian than Brahmsian. The opening vocal phrase is presumably a deliberate reference to the opening of Schubert's "Die Taubenpost," the climactic line of which is "sie heisst: die Sehnsucht" (its name is Longing). The seeming simplicity of phrase structure, the frequent appearance of warm parallel thirds or sixths, and the facile use of chromatic coloring and modulation as the essential characteristics of the harmonic language—all combine to recall the earlier composer.

Brahms repeats the last line of each verse in more thoughtful guise, always to the same melody, like a reflective refrain; it is marked with *piano* in each case except the first, where the initial *piano* indication is presumably still in effect. In verses 1 and 3, the repeated line is accompanied by expressive sighing syncopations in the piano. In verses 2 and 4 (where its *piano* contrasts sharply with the *forte* immediately preceding), the text repetition is accompanied by the affecting descent of the piano melody into the viola register, where it briefly leads the voice in a bit of quasi-canonic imitation at the sixth. In mm. 46–47, the melodies of the voice and piano from the corresponding passage (mm. 20–21) are interchanged, reflecting the higher level of emotional energy. The postlude recedes in wistful stages.

NINE GESÄNGE, OP. 69

Lieder und Gesänge mit Begleitung des Pianoforte von Johannes Brahms (Songs with Piano Accompaniment by Johannes Brahms). Part title: *Op. 69. Neun Gesänge* (Nine Songs). Published in two booklets, Nos. 1–5 and 6–9, in July/August 1877 by Simrock in Berlin; publication numbers 7951 and 7952. The complete collection also includes Opp. 70–72.

The set includes settings of five folk-song texts and four poems of compatible style—one each of Candidus, Eichendorff, Lemcke, and Keller.

Brahms himself suggested to Simrock in a letter of 18 April 1877 that the long opus might be divided into two parts. Later in the same letter he wrote, "It would not be bad if you were to advertise Op. 69 in the newspapers as *Mädchenlieder* [girls' songs]. The word is not so attractive in the title and actually doesn't even work well, since the maiden disguises herself once as a drummer-boy," presumably meaning that the female viewpoint of most of the songs should make the set attractive to female prospective buyers, but the inclusion of a "man's song" made the term "Mädchenlieder" inappropriate for use in the title of the opus. On 21 April he restated his desire that the songs be advertised as *Mädchenlieder* "even if we don't put the word in the title," but by 4 May he had changed his mind and asked that the word "be given up altogether."

Klage I, Op. 69/1 (Lament No. 1)

Translated from the Bohemian by Joseph Wenzig (Czech, 1807–1876)

> Ach, mir fehlt, nicht ist da,
> Was mich einst süß beglückt;
> Ach, mir fehlt, nicht ist da,
> Was mich erfreut!
> Was mich einst süß beglückt
> Ist wie die Well' entrückt.
> Ach, mir fehlt, nicht ist da,
> Was mich erfreut!
>
> Sagt, wie man ackern kann
> Ohne Pflug, ohne Roß?

Sagt, wie man ackern kann,
Wenn das Rad bricht?
Ach, wie solch Ackern ist,
So ist die Liebe auch,
So ist die Liebe auch,
Küßt man sich nicht!

Zwingen mir fort nur auf,
Was mit Qual mich erfüllt;
Zwingen mir fort nur auf,
Was meine Pein:
Geben den Witwer mir
Der kein ganz Herze hat;
Halb ist's der ersten Frau,
Halb nur wär's mein!

How I miss it—it no longer is here—that which once made me wonderfully happy; how I miss it—it no longer is here—that which gladdened me! That which once made me wonderfully happy has passed by like ocean waves. How I miss it—it no longer is here—that which gladdened me!

Tell me, how can one till the soil without a plough, without a horse? Tell me, how can one plough when the wheel breaks? Ah, just like that kind of ploughing is love, love too, if the lovers do not kiss!

They constantly compel me to do things that only fill me with distress; they constantly force upon me only things that pain me; they give me the widower who is completely heartless: half of him belongs to his first wife, only half would be mine!

Composed in March 1877 in Vienna.

First performed 16 December 1879 by Therese Etzelt at a Gesellschafts-konzert in Vienna.

Strophic.

The text is from Joseph Wenzig's *Westslawischer Märchenschatz* (Leipzig, 1857). In the second line of the third verse, Wenzig's version is "was mich mit Qual erfüllt." The poem flirts with pathos, but it is leavened by the homeliness—even humorousness—of its imagery.

Appropriately, Brahms's setting reverts to the invented folk-song style of a decade earlier. It too sidesteps pathos, but it is effective and expressive within the limits which the deliberate stylization imposes. Particularly touching is the modulation to the softly foreign color of the mediant for the central three-measure phrase (mm. 9–11), which marks both the middle of the musical strophe and the turning point of the poetic verse.

The melody's structure shows impressive variety while at the same time deftly illuminating the sense of the text. The first phrase, of two measures, arches up an octave and returns to the lower tonic; the second two-measure phrase rises, while the third phrase, of three measures, falls; the final phrase, of four measures, circles around the upper tonic.

The replacement of the introduction's triplets by sixteenth notes in the interludes and postlude indicates the girl's heightened agitation. Several of the accompaniment figures seem to suggest the sound of middle-European folk instruments: the two-note slurs of the first measure are concertino-like; the figure in sixteenths that appears with the entrance of the voice (and recurs frequently throughout the song in either treble or bass) recalls a hammered instrument such as the cymbalon, while the eighth notes that accompany it mimic the sound of plucked instruments, perhaps mandolins.

Though the introduction and interludes end softly to prepare the entrance of the voice, the postlude concludes strongly, like a gesture of defiance.

Klage II, Op. 69/2 (Lament No. 2)

Translated from the Slovakian by Joseph Wenzig (Czech, 1807–1876)

O Felsen, lieber Felsen,
Was stürztest du nicht ein,
Als ich mich trennen mußte
Von dem Geliebten mein?

Nimm von der eitlen Erde,
O Gott, mich auf zu dir,
Nimmt man den Heißgeliebten
Von allen Burschen mir.

O Gott, mein guter Vater,
Wie strafst du mich so schwer!
Was sonst mich süß erfreute,
Das gibst du mir nicht mehr.

Laß dämmern, Gott, laß dämmern,
Daß bald der Abend wink'
Und daß auch bald mein Leben
In Dämmerung versink'!

O Nachtigall, du traute,
O sing' im grünen Hain,
Erleichtere das Herz mir
Und meines Herzens Pein!

Mein Herz, das liegt erstarret
Zu Stein in meiner Brust,
Es findet hier auf Erden
An nichts, an nichts mehr Lust.

Ich frei' wohl einen Andern
Und lieb' ich ihn auch nicht;
Ich tue, was mein Vater
Und meine Mutter spricht.

Ich tue nach des Vaters
Und nach der Mutter Wort,
Doch heiße Tränen weinet
Mein Herz in einem fort.

O cliff, dear cliff, why didn't you crumble when I had to part from my darling?

Let twilight fall, God, let twilight fall, so that evening soon beckons and soon my life, too, can sink into twilight!

O nightingale, you dear one, sing in the green grove, relieve my heart and my heart's pain!

My heart has turned to stone within my breast; here on earth it finds no more pleasure in anything, in anything.

To be sure, I am engaged to another man even though I don't love him; I do what my father and my mother say.

I obey my father's and my mother's command, but hot tears pour forth from my heart unceasingly.

Composed in Vienna in March 1877.

The first performance is undocumented.

Strophic.

The text is from Wenzig's *Westslawischer Märchenschatz* (Leipzig, 1857); it had previously appeared in somewhat different form under the title "Mädchenklage" in his collection *Slawische Volkslieder* (Halle, 1830).

Omitting the poem's second and third verses, Brahms provided a serious but dancelike setting in $\frac{2}{4}$ meter, featuring a striking three-note ascending figure marked *sforzando*, which resembles a *Schleifer* and appears often on the fourth eighth of the measure. The majority of Slovakian folk music is in $\frac{2}{4}$; the accented second or fourth eighth is characteristic of the dance music of neighboring Moravia. Since Slovakia is situated at the intersection of the cultures of eastern and western Europe, it has accumulated a remarkable variety of folk styles, not only through assimilation and adaptation but also through the influence of Western art music. ("*Klage II* is a characteristic folk song," wrote Clara Schumann on 2 May 1877. "I like it very much.")

Initially the song may seem more placid than its passionate text, but increased familiarity reveals, within the small scale imposed by its strophic folk style, many touching features, particularly in the second half of each stanza. In the third four-measure phrase, the upbeat *Schleifer* is transferred to the voice, while the piano underlines alternate upbeats with a *sforzando* but leaves the downbeats unmarked. The harmonic rhythm seems to quicken with phrase 3 to a change on every eighth in phrase 4 (with some implied cross-relations) and to slow markedly for the last phrase. An extension in the final phrase allows for an emotionally charged keening in the vocal line in the third and fourth measures from the end. In each stanza, the dance character seems to recede as despair comes to the fore, a transition which the brief postlude reproduces in miniature.

In his own copy of the first edition, Brahms changed the "Con moto" marking over the piano part to "Comodo."

Abschied, Op. 69/3 (Farewell)

Translated from the Bohemian by Joseph Wenzig (Czech, 1807–1876)

> Ach, mich hält der Gram gefangen,
> Meinem Herzen ist so weh,
> Denn ich soll von hinnen ziehen
> Über jenes Berges Höh'!
>
> Was einst mein war, ist verloren,
> Alle, alle Hoffnung flieht;
> Ja, ich fürchte, daß, o Mädchen,
> Dich mein Aug' nicht wiedersieht.
>
> Dunkel wird mein Weg sich dehnen,
> Wenn ich scheiden muß von hier:
> Steh' ich dann auf jenem Berge,
> Seufz' ich einmal noch nach dir.

Alas, I am a prisoner of sorrow, my heart hurts so much, for I must leave this place and wander over that mountain height!

What once was mine is lost; all, all hope flees; yes, I am afraid, my dear girl, that my eyes will not look upon you again.

My path will stretch darkly before me when I must depart from here: when I then stand upon that mountain, I will sigh for you one more time.

Composed in Vienna in March 1877.
There is no record of the first performance.
Strophic.

The text appears in Wenzig's collection *Westslawischer Märchenschatz* (Leipzig, 1857). An earlier version in his *Slawische Volkslieder* (Halle, 1830) varies considerably from the later version.

In contrast to the folk music of eastern Czechoslovakia, that of Bohemia and the adjoining part of Moravia, bordering on Germany and Austria, has been strongly influenced by the music of western Europe. The typical result has regular phrase construction (two- and four-measure phrases are usual), unambiguous tonality (usually major), clearly defined rhythmic periods, and a symmetrical form. Most Bohemian melodies have a dance character, and, since the mid-nineteenth century, duple time is common. The rules of Czech prosody dictate that all songs begin on a strong beat—an unstressed initial upbeat is virtually unknown.

Brahms's miniature setting manages not only to take on the characteristics of Bohemian folk song but also to express profound emotion with great economy. Its poignancy is heightened by the flatted seventh, second, and (later) sixth scale degrees. The bass line of the prelude, in counterpoint with the plaintive dotted-rhythm melody, provides the material for the beginning of the vocal line.

Des Liebsten Schwur, Op. 69/4 (My Sweetheart's Promise)

Translated from the Bohemian by Joseph Wenzig (1807–1876)

Ei, schmollte mein Vater nicht wach und im Schlaf,
So sagt' ich ihm, wen ich im Gärtelein traf.
Und schmolle nur, Vater, und schmolle nur fort,
Ich traf den Geliebten im Gärtelein dort.

Ei, zankte mein Vater nicht wieder sich ab,
So sagt' ich ihm, was der Geliebte mir gab.
Und zanke nur, Vater, mein Väterchen du,
Er gab mir ein Küßchen und eines dazu.

Ei, klänge dem Vater nicht staunend das Ohr,
So sagt' ich ihm, was der Geliebte mir schwor.
Und staune nur, Vater, und staune noch mehr,
Du gibst mich doch einmal mit Freuden noch her.

Mir schwor der Geliebte so fest und gewiß,
Bevor er aus meiner Umarmung sich riß:
Ich hätte am längsten zu Hause gesäumt,
Bis lustig im Felde die Weizensaat keimt.

Oho, if my father were not so grumpy both waking and sleeping, I would tell him whom I met in the little garden. Just keep sulking, Father, go on sulking—I met my darling in the little garden there.

Oho, if my father wouldn't start bickering again, I would tell him what my darling gave me. Just keep bickering, Father, my little Father—he gave me a little kiss and another one to go with it.

Oho, if it wouldn't sound amazing to my father's ears, I would tell him what my darling promised me. Just be amazed, Father, and be even more amazed—all the same, you will give him my hand with pleasure one day.

My darling promised me so firmly and so surely, before he tore himself from my embrace, that I would tarry at home no longer than the time when the planted wheat merrily sprouts in the field.

Composed in March 1877 in Vienna.

Amalie Joachim sang the first known performance on 31 October 1877 at a Clara Schumann recital in Berlin.

The first three verses are simple strophic; for the beginning of the fourth verse, the melody of the piano ritornello becomes the accompaniment for a new vocal melody, though the verse ends like the others.

The text is found in Wenzig's *Westslawischer Märchenschatz* (Leipzig, 1857); a somewhat different version appeared in the 1830 *Slawischen Volkslieder*.

The charming setting dances joyously and perfectly captures not only the flavor of the folk verses but also the girl's secret delight and growing assurance.

In the middle of each stanza, the thought of the disapproving father is marked by a temporary turn to the relative minor and a two-measure extension. An attempt at mollification is suggested by the emphasis on the gentle subdominant at the third line of text and by the exclusive use of the subdominant and its own subdominant for the phrase that follows. But the idea of submission is immediately and amusingly contradicted by the piano's offbeat accents and its bold apparent shift to $\frac{3}{2}$ meter for the repetition of the last line of text.

The song's prevailing quietness is relieved at the beginning of the last stanza as the girl recalls the firmness of her sweetheart's promise and during the ecstatic postlude as she considers their approaching reunion.

Tambourliedchen, Op. 69/5 (Little Song of the Drummer)

Text by Karl Candidus (1817–1872)

Den Wirbel schlag' ich gar so stark,
Daß euch erzittert Bein und Mark!
Drum denk' ich an's schön Schätzelein.
Blaugrau,
Blau,
Blaugrau,
Blau
Ist seiner Augen Schein.

Und denk' ich an den Schein so hell,
Von selber dämpft das Trommelfell
Den wilden Ton, klingt hell und rein.
Blaugrau,
Blau,
Blaugrau,
Blau
Sind Liebchens Äugelein.

I sound a drumroll so powerfully that you all tremble in your inmost being! And so I think about my pretty sweetheart. Blue-gray, blue, blue-gray, blue is the color of her eyes.

And when I think about their bright color, the drumhead of its own accord subdues the wildness of its tone and emits a bright, pure sound. Blue-gray, blue, blue-gray, blue are my darling's dear eyes.

Composed in Vienna in March 1877.

First performed on 8 April 1878 in Vienna's Saal Bösendorfer at a soirée of the pianist Cäcilie Gaul, by either Josephine Weyringer or Louise Dustmann. Strophic.

The text is from the *Vermischte Gedichte* (Leipzig, 1869) of Candidus.

Brahms's setting is cheerful and attractive, with an atypical "popular" character and an unexpectedly gleeful indulgence in drumroll effects and dynamic surprises.

Clara Schumann disliked the song and found at least the introduction "too reminiscent of Schubert," referring, one presumes, to its piano-sonata style and texture. One might also describe as Schubertian the many harmonic colorations and seeming modulations, increasing, like the drummer's ardor, toward the end of the stanza.

The pervading military dotted rhythms of the first part are gradually softened at the thought of the sweetheart and disappear completely in the impassioned remembrance of her blue-gray eyes.

Vom Strande, Op. 69/6 (From the Beach)

Text from the Spanish by Joseph von Eichendorff (1788–1857)

> Ich rufe vom Ufer
> Verlorenes Glück,
> Die Ruder nur schallen
> Zum Strande zurück.
>
> Vom Strande, lieb' Mutter,
> Wo der Wellenschlag geht,
> Da fahren die Schiffe,
> Mein Liebster drauf steht.
> Je mehr ich sie rufe,
> Je schneller der Lauf,
> Wenn ein Hauch sie entführet,
> Wer hielte sie auf?
> Der Hauch meiner Klagen
> Die Segel nur schwellt,
> Je mehr mein Verlangen
> Zurücke sie hält!
> Verhielt' ich die Klagen:
> Es löst' sie der Schmerz,
> Und Klagen und Schweigen
> Zersprengt mir das Herz.
>
> Ich rufe vom Ufer
> Verlorenes Glück,

Die Ruder nur schallen
Zum Strande zurück.

So flüchtige Schlösser,
Wer könnt' ihn'n vertrau'n
Und Liebe, die bliebe,
Mit Freuden d'rauf bau'n?
Wie Vögel im Fluge,
Wo ruhen sie aus?
So eilige Wand'rer,
Sie finden kein Haus,
Zertrümmern der Wogen
Grünen Kristall,
Und was sie berühren,
Verwandelt sich all.
Es wandeln die Wellen
Und wandelt der Wind,
Meine Schmerzen im Herzen
Beständig nur sind.

Ich rufe vom Ufer
Verlorenes Glück,
Die Ruder nur schallen
Zum Strande zurück.

From the shore I call to my lost happiness; only the sound of the oars returns to the beach.

From the beach, dear mother, where the waves beat, there sail the ships; my sweetheart is on one. The more I call to them, the faster they travel; if a wind carries them off, who could restrain them? The wind of my lamentations merely swells the sails, the more my desire holds them back! If I kept back my lamentations, my sorrow would release them, and my heart is torn apart between lamenting and keeping silent.

From the shore I call to my lost happiness; only the sound of the oars returns to the beach.

Such fleeting castles [the ships], who could trust them and joyfully build upon them a love that would last? Like birds in flight, where do they rest? Such hurried travelers, they find no house; they destroy the green crystal of the waves and whatever they touch is completely transformed. The waves move on, the wind moves on; only the sorrows in my heart remain steadfast.

From the shore I call to my lost happiness; only the sound of the oars returns to the beach.

Composed in Vienna in March 1877.

First performed by Helene Marschall at a song recital in Vienna on 14 March 1889.

Strophic in A minor, with a ritornello for voice and piano that begins in F major (low key, F minor and D♭ major).

The poem is the third in a series to which Eichendorff gave the title "Aus dem Spanischen." The call from the shore is treated like a refrain.

The poem's length and dramatic situation invite comparison with the *Magelone* songs, Op. 33, of the preceding decade. Earlier, the various expressions of despair and passion might have been set in contrasting but related sections, but now, all is joined into a single entity by the continuous ebb and flow of the waves, which the accompaniment represents so strikingly.

The maiden's alternately hopeful and hopeless yearning find their musical equivalent in the delayed establishment of a still somewhat ambiguous tonality.

The rhythms in the accompaniment's left hand contribute greatly to expressing the girl's emotional state. The first phrase of the refrain is solidly grounded on the strong beats, but the hushed second half avoids them; and a halting figure after rests fills the weak second half of each half-measure, contradicting the prevailing triple subdivision and thereby depicting her breathless agitation. With the addition of a bass on the strong beats, this figure underlies most of the body of the song, but as the girl describes the anguish in her heart toward the end of each stanza, the six eighth notes in each measure are divided irregularly into groups of two, three, or even four, until the meter seems to have transformed itself from $\frac{6}{8}$ into $\frac{3}{4}$, but the last measure of the interlude wrests it back.

The end of the song is particularly effective dramatically. One can imagine that after her last call from the shore, the girl continues to listen as the music fades to silence, as reluctant to abandon hope as the music is to define either tonic or downbeat.

Über die See, Op. 69/7 (Over the Sea)

Text by Karl Lemcke (1831–1913)

Über die See,
Fern über die See
Ist mein Schatz gezogen,
Ist ihm mein Herz
Voll Ach und Weh,
Bang ihm nachgeflogen.

Brauset das Meer,
Wild brauset das Meer,
Stürme dunkel jagen,
Sinket die Sonn',
Die Welt wird leer,
Muß mein Herz verzagen.

Bin ich allein,
Ach, immer allein,

Meine Kräfte schwinden.
Muß ich zurück
In matter Pein,
Kann dich nimmer finden.

Over the sea, far over the sea my darling has wandered; my heart, full of sorrow and pain, has fearfully flown after him.

The ocean roars, the ocean roars wildly; storms drive darkly on; the sun sinks, the world becomes empty, and my heart must despair.

I am alone, alas, always alone; my strength is vanishing. I must go back, exhausted by sorrow; I can never find you.

Composed in Vienna in March 1877.

There is no record of the first performance.

Strophic.

The text is from Lemcke's *Lieder und Gedichte* (Hamburg, 1861). In order to preserve the rhythmic parallel with the first phrase, Brahms altered the poet's words in the ninth bar of each verse to have three syllables: in verse 1, "ist ihm mein" instead of "ist mein"; in verse 2, "sinket die" for "sinkt die"; and in verse 3, "muß ich zurück" instead of "muß zurück."

The song is placed to be heard in relation to the preceding song. The abandoned maiden is now alone on the empty shore. The tumultuous waves of "Vom Strande" have been replaced by a starker, almost skeletal texture and the dark murmuring of a sea now cold and nearly motionless. The sense of despair and desolation is pervasive.

The setting is powerful in its simplicity, and its portrayal of devastation is accomplished with economy—a few painful suspensions and the frequent use of wistful diminished-seventh harmonies suffice.

Clara Schumann disliked the song. In her letter of 2 May 1877, in which she commented on all of the songs to be published as Opp. 69–72, she remarked, "*Über die See* is one of those I should like to omit. . . . The songs which I do not consider worthy of your name make one book; I think it is far better to have two books containing only important songs, rather than three interspersed with unimportant ones."

Salome, Op. 69/8

Text by Gottfried Keller (Swiss, 1819–1890)

Singt mein Schatz wie ein Fink,
Sing' ich Nachtigallensang;
Ist mein Liebster ein Luchs,
O so bin ich eine Schlang'.

O ihr Jungfrau'n im Land,
Von dem Berg und über See!

Überlaßt mir den Schönsten,
Sonst tut ihr mir weh!

Er soll sich unterwerfen
Zum Ruhm uns und Preis!
Und er soll sich nicht rühren,
Nicht laut und nicht leis'!

O ihr teuren Gespielen!
Überlaßt mir den teuren Mann!
Er soll seh'n, wie die Liebe
Ein feurig Schwert werden kann!

If my sweetheart sings like a finch, then I sing a nightingale's song; if my darling is a lynx, oh, then I am a serpent.

O you maidens in the land, from the hills and over the sea! Leave the handsome man to me, or else you will cause me pain!

He shall acknowledge defeat, to our glory and praise! And he shall not make a move or make the slightest sound!

O my dear playmates, leave the dear man to me! He shall see how love can become a flaming sword!

Composed in Vienna in March 1877.

The first public performance was given by Ottilie Ottiker in Karlsruhe on 22 October 1877.

Strophic. The song joins verses 1 and 2 and verses 3 and 4 of the poem, setting the two pairs as two like strophes; verses 1 and 3 are set to the same music, as are verses 2 and 4.

The text is from Keller's *Neuere Gedichte* (Brunswick, 1851) in the 1846 series *Von Weibern*. In verse 4 Brahms changed Keller's "den stolzen Mann" to "den teuren Mann."

"Salome" is lively and effective in performance and seems all of a piece; but with study, one discovers somewhat unexpectedly that subtle variations in the musical style reveal several different facets of this willful girl's character.

The music for the first half of the strophe features squarish rhythms (including a rebounding figure like that of "Der Schmied," Op. 19/4), and mainly diatonic harmonies over a bass that is reluctant to move, conveying the impression that the girl is both high-spirited and determined. The first melodic phrase includes outlines of the dominant, tonic, and supertonic triads, but the second phrase uses more small intervals and stepwise movement; some chromatic alterations appear, aiding the modulation to the dominant and exposing a streak of capriciousness.

The third phrase, in which Salome addresses herself directly to "you maidens" in the first strophe and "dear playmates" in the second, introduces persistent dotted rhythms and coaxing two-note slurs over a chromatic bass line, ending with a fermata over a dominant-seventh chord. The effect of the phrase, heightened by the drop to *piano*, is to suggest a gentler, more seductive quality.

The final phrases reinforce the idea of stubbornness with a bass pedal, this time on the dominant, but the constant *crescendo*, the excitement generated by the piano's conflicting triplets against the voice's duple rhythms, and particularly the many upward-resolving chromatic alterations evoke a sensuality of considerable passion and intensity.

Mädchenfluch, Op. 69/9 (A Girl's Curse)

Translated from the Serbian by Siegfried Kapper (Czech, 1821–1879)

Ruft die Mutter, ruft der Tochter
Über drei Gebirge:
"Ist, o Mara, liebe Tochter,
Ist gebleicht das Linnen?"
Ihr zurück die junge Tochter
Über neun Gebirge:
"Nichts in's Wasser, liebe Mutter,
Taucht' ich noch das Linnen,
Denn, o sieh', es hat das Wasser
Jawo mir getrübet.—
Wie dann erst, o liebe Mutter,
Hätt' ich es gebleicht schon!
Fluch' ihm, Mutter, liebe Mutter!
Ich auch will ihm fluchen.
Gäbe Gott im hellen Himmel,
Daß er sich erhänge—
An ein böses Bäumchen hänge,
An den weißen Hals mir!
Gäbe Gott im hellen Himmel,
Daß er lieg' gefangen—
Lieg' gefangen tief im Kerker,
An der weißen Brust mir!
Gäbe Gott, der Herr im Himmel,
Daß er Ketten trage—
Ketten trage, festgeschlungen,
Meine weißen Arme!
Gäbe Gott im hellen Himmel,
Daß ihn nähm' das Wasser—
Daß ihn nähm' das wilde Wasser,
Mir in's Haus ihn bringe!"

The mother calls, calls her daughter, across three mountain chains: "O Mara, dear daughter, is the linen bleached?"

Back to her calls the young daughter, across nine mountain chains: "Dear Mother, I have not yet dipped the linen into the water; for see Javo has muddied the water.

"How then, dear Mother, could I have already bleached it! Curse him, Mother, dear Mother! I will curse him, too!

"May God in the bright heavens grant that he should hang himself on a fatal tree—on my white neck!

"May God in the bright heavens grant that he should be imprisoned deep in a dungeon—on my white breast!

"May God, the Lord in heaven, grant that he should wear chains wrapped tightly around him—my white arms!

"May God in the bright heavens grant that the waters should seize him, that the wild waters should seize him—and bring him to my house!"

Composed in April 1877.

The first performance was given on 10 January 1878 in the Leipzig Gewandhaussaal by Magdalene Kölle-Murjahn with Brahms at the piano; the program also included Op. 69/4.

Strophic, with an introductory section and a coda with which it shares material.

The text is from Kapper's collection *Die Gesänge der Serben* (Leipzig, 1852), where it is entitled "Fluch ihm, Mutter, ich auch will ihm fluchen."

The setting contrasts dramatic, expressive music in $\frac{3}{4}$ meter with faster, dancelike music in $\frac{2}{4}$, a practice with many precedents in the folk music of central Europe. There are other dualities as well—both A and F♯ (F and D in the low key) are used as tonal centers, and minor/major ambiguity is prevalent.

The notions of duality and ambiguity are already suggested by the piano's spiraling triplets that introduce the poem's two purely narrative lines, mm. 3–6 and 15–18; both phrases are set to the same music, but the change of a single interval subtly emphasizes "neun" in the second over "drei" in the first.

The mother's question (mm. 7–12) lies in the lower register and is characterized musically by the move to the dominant and the rising third at the cadence. The daughter's response begins in m. 19 with music that is similar rhythmically and harmonically, but an immediate upward leap of a perfect fourth replaces the analogous whole step in m. 7, throwing her words into the singer's higher register, where the rest of the song remains.

That Javo has aroused responses in the girl other than the annoyance implied by her words is made evident by the change to the major mode, the *più dolce sempre* marking, the decreasing dynamic, and the gradual smoothing-out of both vocal line and accompaniment. She pauses, her indecision echoed by the piano.

Suddenly, with a return to the minor mode and to the rhythm of the opening, she implores her mother to curse the rascal, and, with increasing excitement, vows to add condemnation of her own.

In each of the next three strophes, marked *Schnell und sehr lebhaft*, the girl suggests in F♯ (D) minor, a punishment, of which she then, in a parallel but extended passage in A (F) minor/major, offers her own erotically charged interpretation.

The borrowing of music from the earlier introductory section for the final climactic curse both emphasizes its culminating effect and rounds out the form in the manner of a coda. The prayer that God might cause the wild waters to seize Javo (mm. 101–110) is set to the music that first introduced the ideas of "curse" (mm. 39–42) and "water" (mm. 19–23). But the girl's thought that the waters might in fact bring him home to her prompts the return of the same impassioned music that ended the other strophes. The vocal line is swept joyously along to its brilliant conclusion, the girl's exhilaration reinforced by the piano postlude.

Brahms's setting is bold and masterly, simultaneously illuminating the meaning of the text and capturing its folk flavor. In her letter of 2 May 1877, Clara Schumann wrote: "*Mädchenfluch* is one of my favorites; the music is so full of swing and interesting from beginning to end, which makes me forget the ugliness of the words."

FOUR GESÄNGE, OP. 70

Lieder und Gesänge mit Begleitung des Pianoforte von Johannes Brahms (Songs with Piano Accompaniment by Johannes Brahms). Part title: *Op. 70, Vier Gesänge* (Four Songs). Published, together with Opp. 69, 71, and 72, in July/August 1877 by N. Simrock in Berlin; publication number 7953.

The four songs share an aura of sadness for past loss. An increasing terseness of expression is particularly evident in the first two.

Im Garten am Seegestade, Op. 70/1
(In the Garden by the Seashore)

Text by Karl Lemcke (1831–1913)

Im Garten am Seegestade
Uralte Bäume steh'n,
In ihren hohen Kronen
Sind kaum die Vögel zu seh'n.

Die Bäume mit hohen Kronen,
Die rauschen Tag und Nacht,
Die Wellen schlagen zum Strande,
Die Vöglein singen sacht.

Das gibt ein Musizieren
So süß, so traurig bang,
Als wie verlor'ner Liebe
Und ewiger Sehnsucht Sang.

In the garden by the seashore stand old, old trees; in their high tops the birds can barely be seen.

The trees with their high tops rustle day and night; the waves beat upon the beach; the birds sing softly.

That creates a music so sweet, of such sad anxiety, like a song of lost love and eternal longing.

Composed in February 1877 in Vienna.

First performed by Gustav Walter on 9 December 1877 in Vienna at the season's third Philharmonic concert.

Varied strophic; A B A'; unity is achieved through consistency of style and similar rhythms.

The text is from Lemcke's *Lieder und Gedichte* (Hamburg, 1861).

The poem treats of sadness for lost love, and Brahms captures its delicate mood perfectly. The melody is quietly pensive. The accompaniment is based on gentle arpeggios, suggesting the sound of waves lapping at the shore, and a descending countermelody, which, with its variants, introduces, overlaps, and comments upon the vocal phrases.

In the second stanza, arpeggios in triplets represent the beating of the waves, low afterbeats and pedal points suggest rustling, and the transfer of the afterbeats to the upper register in single notes to evoke the softly singing birds provides one of the song's most enchanting moments. The birdsong elides with the descending countermelody from before, now also in afterbeats and *forte*, to prepare the return of the opening material for the third verse.

At the end of the song, the reference to eternal longing prompts a turn to the poignant Neapolitan, which, together with the lengthened note values of the falling final vocal line (echoed by the piano postlude), provides a moving summation of the nostalgic character of both poem and setting.

Lerchengesang, Op. 70/2 (Song of the Larks)

Text by Karl Candidus (1817–1872)

Ätherische ferne Stimmen,
Der Lerchen himmlische Grüße,
Wie regt ihr mir so süße
Die Brust, ihr lieblichen Stimmen!
Ich schließe leis' mein Auge,
Da zieh'n Erinnerungen
In sanften Dämmerungen
Durchweht vom Frühlingshauche.

Voices far off in the sky, the heavenly greetings of the larks; how sweetly you stir my heart, you lovely voices!
I gently close my eyes, and memories pass by in a quiet dusk pervaded by the breath of spring.

Composed in Vienna in February or March of 1877.

Together with No. 3 of the opus, first performed by Gustav Walter on 15 December 1877 in Vienna, at a *Künstlerabend* of the Gesellschaft der Musikfreunde.

Through-composed, unified in style and spirit.

The text was published by Candidus in 1869 in his *Vermischte Gedichte*.

The exquisite setting is one of Brahms's most atmospheric and original, with near-Debussian colors and textures. The poem's opening clearly inspired the musical materials—the piano's wide intervals spreading and resolving high above tethered, swaying harmonies and the free-floating vocal line are a perfect metaphor for a vast twilit sky, its stillness broken only by the singing of unseen larks.

The unusual sparseness of the accompaniment places particular emphasis on the vocal melody. In the first part of the song, its quarter-note triplets and absence of angularity contribute greatly to the mood of spellbound rapture. In the second half, the pain of regretful memory intrudes, bringing subtle chromatic inflections and compliance with the prevailing rhythm, but "memories pass by," and the earlier ecstatic contemplation of quiet spring dusk returns—mm. 28–37 are only slightly varied from mm. 9–18.

The postlude reestablishes exactly the crepuscular hush of the opening, the distant birdsong now gradually fading.

Serenade, Op. 70/3

Text by Johann Wolfgang von Goethe (1749–1832)

> Liebliches Kind,
> Kannst du mir sagen,
> Sagen, warum
> Einsam und stumm
> Zärtliche Seelen
> Immer sich quälen,
> Selbst sich betrüben
> Und ihr Vergnügen
> Immer nur ahnen
> Da, wo sie nicht sind;
> Kannst du mir's sagen,
> Liebliches Kind?

> Lovely girl, can you tell me, tell me why delicate souls always torment themselves, lonely and silent, cause their own vexation and always feel that they can only find pleasure in some different place? Can you tell me that, lovely girl?

Composed in May 1876.

First performed, together with Op. 70/2, by Gustav Walter on 15 December 1877, at a *Künstlerabend* of the Gesellschaft der Musikfreunde in Vienna.

Through-composed.

The text is an amiable little extract from the play *Claudine von Villa Bella*; the hero, Rugantino, accompanying himself on a zither, sings the words to Claudine and Lucinde, addressing each in turn as "Liebliches Kind" and asking why happiness always seems to elude those who are sensitive. Brahms somewhat rearranged Goethe's words. Beginning with line 3, the original is:

> Sagen warum
> Zärtliche Seelen
> Einsam und stumm
> Immer sich quälen,
> Selbst sich betrügen

Instead of "betrügen" (deceive) Brahms wrote and printed "betrüben" (afflict). The title is derived from a collection of songs by Beethoven's teacher Christian Gottlob Neefe (1748–1798), called *Serenaden*, which Brahms knew and in which a setting of this text appears.

Brahms provides charming music that captures the lighthearted, amorous tone, the strumming accompaniment, and the question that remains unanswered. Like the text, the song seems a pleasant trifle but upon analysis proves to be profound. The question is asked lightly but the answer probes the depths of human nature; the melody lilts graciously while the accompaniment ponders with contrapuntal complexity.

For the first half of the song, the right-hand figure imitates in diminution the shape of the vocal line; in mm. 17–19, it imitates in canon; in mm. 20–23, in canon by diminution. Each of the first nine lines is set within one measure, but the tenth is extended first to two measures, then a half-measure more. The closing lines of text, which reverse those of the opening, are set to units of three half-measures rather than two. Beginning in m. 17, and including the canonic imitation in the piano and the customary extension to end, the concluding phrases lengthen from three through four to five half-measures.

Particular harmonies characterize specific words and ideas: the Neapolitan for "zärtliche" (delicate) in m. 6; the sharp dissonance of augmented triad plus major seventh for "betrüben" (afflict) in m. 8; the minor mode with appoggiaturas for "immer nur ahnen da, wo sie nicht sind" (always feel [that they can find pleasure] only in some different place) in mm. 10–16.

The simple postlude seems to function like a retrograde form of the introduction, gradually bringing to a stop the activity that the introductory measure sets in motion.

Abendregen, Op. 70/4 (Evening Rain)

Text by Gottfried Keller (Swiss, 1819–1890)

> Langsam und schimmernd fiel ein Regen,
> In den die Abendsonne schien;

Der Wand'rer schritt auf engen Wegen
Mit düst'rer Seele drunter hin.

Er sah die großen Tropfen blinken
Im Fallen durch den gold'nen Strahl;
Er fühlt es kühl auf's Haupt ihm sinken
Und sprach mit schauernd süßer Qual:

Nun weiß ich, daß ein Regenbogen
Sich hoch um meine Stirne zieht,
Den auf dem Pfad, so ich gezogen,
Die heit're Ferne spielen sieht.

Und die mir hier am nächsten stehen,
Und wer mich scharf zu kennen meint,
Sie können selber doch nicht sehen,
Wie er versöhnend ob mir scheint.

So wird, wenn and're Tage kamen,
Die sonnig auf dies Heute seh'n,
Ob meinem fernen, bleichen Namen
Der Ehre Regenbogen steh'n.

Slowly, gleaming, fell a rain through which the evening sun shone; under it the traveler trod along on narrow paths with a gloomy soul.

He saw the big drops shine in the golden ray as they fell; he felt their cool touch on his head, and said with tremblingly sweet sorrow:

"Now I know that high over my brow there arches a rainbow which, on the path I have wandered, can be seen by those in the happy distance.

"And those who are closest to me here and think they know me perfectly, nevertheless cannot themselves see how it shines above me redeemingly.

"Thus, when other days have come which will look back sunnily upon today, above my distant, pallid name the rainbow of honor will stand."

Composed during the summer of 1875 at Ziegelhausen bei Heidelberg.

The first performance was given by Adolf von Schultner on 12 January 1879 at a concert of the Singakademie in Vienna.

The setting consists of two sections comprising verses 1–2 and 3–5, the first in minor, the second in the relative major. Verses 1 and 2 are set similarly, as are verses 3 and 5, the music for verse 4 ranging farther afield harmonically.

Before the song was included in his Op. 70, Brahms had submitted it to the Leipzig publisher E. W. Fritsch for publication in *Blätter für Hausmusik*, where it appeared in October 1875.

The text is from Keller's *Neuere Gedichte* (Brunswick, 1851). There, the last two lines read: "Um meinen fernen blassen Namen/Des Friedens heller Bogen steh'n."

In the poem, the sorrowing traveler sees in the rain at sunset a vision of his own immortality, a future in which others will see him as somehow vindicated, his whole life marked by the rainbow of honor. The metaphors seem somewhat forced and the whole poem a bit pompous, even defensive. Clara Schumann disliked the song, and in her letter of 2 May 1877, she tactfully blamed the text: "The text seems to me bombastic, the whole lacks spontaneity and is labored. A text like this is utterly uninspiring."

One wonders why Brahms was attracted to the subject. Kalbeck's biography (*Brahms*, II₁, 121) claims a connection with an unpleasant misunderstanding concerning Wagner, as a result of which Brahms seemed to have felt that his integrity had been questioned. On 10 June 1864, Brahms had received a holograph full score of Wagner's *Tannhäuser* from Peter Cornelius and Karl Tausig and believed it to be a gift; the following year, on 18 August, Cornelius reclaimed the score as his property in order to put it at Wagner's disposal for a new production in Munich. Though the score had become the showpiece of his growing collection of autograph scores, Brahms of course returned it, but he and Cornelius became estranged. In June 1875 (just before the composition of this song), Wagner sent Brahms a deluxe first edition of *Das Rheingold*, bound in leather richly embossed in gold, which had been displayed at the 1873 Vienna World's Fair, with the handwritten dedication "To Mr. Johannes Brahms as a substitute in good condition for a battered manuscript. Bayreuth 27 June 1875, Richard Wagner." The affair was finally over, but Brahms may well have felt himself to have been wronged and perhaps composed the song in an effort to heal the wound.

For whatever reasons, it is undeniable that this song lacks the organic unity typical of Brahms's song composition at this time, or that much of it sounds more Wagnerian than Brahmsian. On the other hand, one cannot deny the beauty of individual passages.

It begins with a shower of the staccato eighths that Brahms so often associated with falling rain. Legato eighths represent the traveler's weary footsteps in m. 7 and the cool touch of raindrops in m. 16.

A modulation to the relative major and a slower tempo mark the appearance of the noble melody associated with the rainbow—the transition's arpeggiated overlapping layers of harmonic color are a particularly apt metaphor.

The perceived inability of those closest to the traveler to recognize the purity of his reputation brings increased agitation, evidenced by lightly syncopated rhythms, tonal instability, and numerous suspensions, particularly near the end of the section. After the fermata in m. 49, the *Langsamer* melody returns, this time varied to allow richly altered harmonies (including the Neapolitan, the lowered submediant, and the German sixth) to express the emotional intensity of the poem's closing lines.

The postlude's slightly varied recalling of this melody in an inner voice is hauntingly lovely and nearly succeeds in expressing the benediction of exoneration that has eluded the body of the song.

FIVE GESÄNGE, OP. 71

Lieder und Gesänge mit Begleitung des Pianoforte von Johannes Brahms (Songs with Piano Accompaniment by Johannes Brahms). Part title: *Op. 71. Fünf Gesänge* (Five Songs). Published, together with Opp. 69, 70, and 72, in July/August 1877 by N. Simrock in Berlin; publication number 7954.

Rather than sadness over love lost, it is the joys and pains of love current or sought that unite this group of songs. All five date from March 1877.

Es liebt sich so lieblich im Lenze, Op. 71/1
(Love Is So Delightful in the Spring)

Text by Heinrich Heine (1797–1856)

Die Wellen blinken und fließen dahin—
Es liebt sich so lieblich im Lenze!
Am Flusse sitzet die Schäferin
Und windet die zärtlichsten Kränze.

Das knospet und quillt und duftet und blüht—
Es liebt sich so lieblich im Lenze!
Die Schäferin seufzt aus tiefer Brust:
"Wem geb' ich meine Kränze?"

Ein Reiter reitet den Fluß entlang;
Er grüßet so blühenden Mutes!
Die Schäferin schaut ihm nach so bang,
Fern flattert die Feder des Hutes.

Sie weinet und wirft in den gleitenden Fluß
Die schönen Blumenkränze.
Die Nachtigall singt von Lieb' und Kuß—
Es liebt sich so lieblich im Lenze!

The waves gleam and flow by—love is so delightful in the spring! By the river sits the shepherdess and weaves the daintiest wreaths.

Amid the buds, the running water, the fragrance, the blossom—love is so delightful in the spring! The shepherdess heaves a deep sigh: "To whom shall I give my wreaths?"

A horseman rides along the river; he greets her with such youthful bold-
ness! The shepherdess looks after him so nervously; in the distance flutters
the plume on his hat.

She weeps and throws the beautiful wreaths of flowers into the flowing
river. The nightingale sings of loving and kissing—love is so delightful in the
spring!

Composed in March 1877.

First performed by Louise Dustmann on 8 April 1878 at the Saal Bösendorfer in Vienna, at a soirée of the pianist Cäcilie Gaul.

A A' B A''; interestingly, since it does not always fall at the same place in
the stanza, the line of text that provides the title is set to the same musical
phrase at each appearance except its repetition at the end.

The text is from Heine's *Romanzen* (1839), where it has the title "Frühling." In the first edition, the second verse reads:

> Das knospet und quillt und duftet und blüht—
> Es liebt sich so lieblich im Lenze!
> Die Schäferin seufzt aus vollem Gemüt:
> Wem geb' ich meine Kränze?

In later editions, however, Heine changed the first and third lines to: "Das
knospet und quillt, mit duftender Lust,—" and "Die Schäferin seufzt aus
tiefer Brust." Brahms disliked the revised "mit duftender Lust," and even
more the original version of the third line, "seufzt aus vollem Gemüt." So he
decided on the compromise version (given above), which spoils the rhyme.
In the first and third verses he added a syllable to Heine's "sitzt" and "grüßt,"
and he substituted "Reiter" for "Ritter" in verse 3. Originally he used Heine's
title "Frühling" but changed it in the fair copy for the printer.

The poem treats folk-song subject matter with sophistication and irony,
all also captured by the charming setting. The background of spring flowers,
flowing waters, and youthful longing for love are reflected in the high-
spirited vocal line and the fast-moving piano part.

The prelude's flowing eighths, which grow from simple doubling at the
octave through doubling at the double octave to fullfledged melody with bass
line, serve equally well to evoke the spring-swollen stream of verse 1 and, as
interlude, the more generic flowing and flowering of verse 2.

The first phrase of the vocal line outlines triads and comprises consonances
only, as in a folk song, while the second phrase—the recurring title phrase—
introduces some sighing dissonances. The third and fourth phrases, which
speak of the shepherdess and her wreaths, continue the yearning appoggiaturas and introduce an element of breathlessness as well. In verse 2
these phrases subtly increase their chromaticism to characterize the shepherdess's "deep sigh" and the eroticism implied in her naive question "To
whom shall I give my wreaths?" The repetition of the inquiry elicits a

half-measure extension, and the vocal line's questioning fall from the fifth to the third degree of the scale is intensified by the piano's mirroring repetitions.

The young horseman's appearance is greeted by a new key and with joyous leaps in the vocal line, as the accompaniment breaks into galloping staccato triplets. He greets the shepherdess, but passes by without stopping, and the vocal line reflects the wistfulness of her gazing after him as he rides away. The piano's triplets become quieter, and against them, the flowing eighths of the introduction appear as if by magic, first in the left hand, then in the right.

They lead to a minor-inflected restatement of the opening vocal phrase, which introduces the last stanza. The wreaths are discarded to a richly harmonized and emotionally intensified development of the appoggiaturas of phrase 2. Suspended in the tenderly unreal world of the subdominant, the nightingale sings briefly of love, oblivious of the girl's tears. As the now ironic title phrase recurs refrainlike to end the stanza, the piano's triplets give way to lighthearted sixteenth notes that race *forte* to the end of the song, though the postlude sighs in sympathy with the girl whom love has eluded.

An den Mond, Op. 71/2 (To the Moon)

Text by Karl Simrock (1802–1876)

Silbermond, mit bleichen Strahlen
Pflegst du Wald und Feld zu malen,
Gibst den Bergen, gibst den Talen
Der Empfindung Seufzer ein.
Sei Vertrauter meiner Schmerzen,
Segler in der Lüfte See:
Sag' ihr, die ich trag' im Herzen,
Wie mich tötet Liebesweh.

Sag' ihr, über tausend Meilen
Sehne sich mein Herz nach ihr.
"Keine Ferne kann es heilen,
Nur ein holder Blick von dir."
Sag' ihr, daß zu Tod getroffen
Diese Hülle bald zerfällt;
Nur ein schmeichlerisches Hoffen
Sei's, das sie zusammenhält.

Silver moon, you are wont to paint forest and field with your pale rays; you inspire the sigh of sentiment in mountains and valleys.

Be the confidant of my sorrows, you that sail in the sea of the sky: tell the woman who dwells in my heart how the pain of love is killing me.

Tell her that my heart longs for her over a distance of a thousand miles. "No distance can heal it, only a loving look of yours."

Tell her I am fatally wounded and my body will soon perish; that only a flattering hope keeps me alive.

Composed in March 1877.

First performed by Louise Dustmann at a soirée of the pianist Cäcilie Gaul in the Saal Bösendorfer in Vienna on 8 April 1878.

Through-composed. Disregarding the poem's form but observing its content, Brahms allots six lines each to two contrasting sections; the apparent return that begins in m. 46 sets two of the remaining four lines to each musical idea; a postlude derived from the opening rounds out the form.

The text appeared in the poet's collected *Gedichte* (Leipzig, 1844); Brahms owned the 1863 edition.

The three-measure introduction sets a phrase-structure pattern that is unbroken until the final vocal phrase expands to four measures and its tonal ambiguity establishes the song's characteristic harmonic wavering.

The setting is wonderfully atmospheric. The sinuous opening melody evokes the lover's suffering; the walking accompaniment, his sleepless pacing in the moonlight; and the fluctuation between major and minor, his longing and lack of assurance.

The contrasting section, beginning in the key of the dominant, seems more resolute. The melody's regular rhythms and triad-outlining intervals are supported by the accompaniment's bass movement by fifth and outdoorsy hints of horns. But the constantly flowing legato eighths undermine the effect of strength, chromaticisms creep in, and at the climactic cry "Keine Ferne kann es heilen, nur ein holder Blick von dir" a deceptive resolution to the foreign-sounding submediant strikingly depicts the "distance which cannot heal."

At the textually analogous "Nur ein schmeichlerisches Hoffen sei's das sie zusammen hält," a similar deceptive movement initiates a gorgeous succession of key relationships suggesting the life-sustaining hope of the poet—the home key's submediant in m. 55, then the Neapolitan in m. 58, and, finally, the tonic major as the repetition of the line is set to music recalling, but surpassing, the earlier climax.

The long postlude, its melody enriched by chromaticism and doublings in sixths or thirds, and its harmonies softened by references to the minor subdominant, gradually winds down, but a sense of uncertainty lingers after its end.

Geheimnis, Op. 71/3 (Secret)

Text by Karl Candidus (1817–1872)

O Frühlingsabenddämmerung!
O laues, lindes Weh'n!
Ihr Blütenbäume, sprecht, was tut
Ihr so zusammensteh'n?

Vertraut ihr das Geheimnis euch
Von uns'rer Liebe süß?

Was flüstert ihr einander zu
Von uns'rer Liebe süß?

O twilight of a spring evening! O warm, gentle breeze! You blossoming trees,
tell me, why are you standing together like that?
　Are you confiding to one another the secret of our sweet love? What are you
whispering to one another about our sweet love?

Composed in March 1877.
　The first performance was sung by Gustav Walter at the third concert of
the Vienna Philharmonic's season on 9 December 1877.
　Through-composed, though somewhat resembling varied strophic.
　The text is found in the *Vermischte Gedichte* (Leipzig, 1869) of Candidus.
　The setting is among Brahms's most beautiful, with a quietly ecstatic
dreamlike aura all its own. The mood is actually enhanced by the many
(even for Brahms) repetitions of text; it is as though the lover, in breathless
disbelief, were obliged to keep trying to convince himself that his love could
not only be accepted, but returned.
　The principal accompaniment figure—a rocking divided arpeggio, one
note in each hand languorously prolonged before resolving or moving—is a
musical depiction of the shimmering of blossoming trees in the gentle breeze
of a spring twilight. The numerous bass pedals contribute to the song's distinctive hovering quality, as does the absence of any modulation other than
that to the dominant at the midpoint.
　As the "secret" of the title is identified in the second stanza, chromaticism
increases the sensuous beauty of both melody and accompaniment. The delicately embellished return of the opening vocal phrase in mm. 16–20 is particularly lovely. New melodic material is assigned to the piano, bridging the
rests in the vocal line and culminating in a doubling-enriched chromatic
countermelody to the voice, beginning in m. 23. The impression of suspended time is bolstered by a constantly slowing tempo and the awed
statement with three repetitions of the words "uns'rer Liebe" to similar
melodic contour, the last two over a throbbing afterbeat pulse of dominant
bass pedal. Another iteration of the same words brings an actual cessation
of motion in the final phrase. The postlude's tender little flurry of excitement
and rising pitch match the lifting spirits of the happy lover.
　As was his frequent custom, on 23 April 1877 Brahms sent a copy of the
songs of Opp. 69–71 to his friends the Herzogenbergs in Leipzig, asking for
their comments. On 27 April, Henrich Herzogenberg wrote to Brahms in
Vienna:

　　A curious thing happened with *Frühlingsabenddämmerung*. We had sung
　　it through many times with all possible fervor, when my eye . . . fell casually
　　on the tempo mark. We were struck dumb, and exchanged conscience-
　　stricken glances. . . . How slowly we had taken it[!] . . . We had dwelt upon

every suspension in the left hand, we had lingered in blissful awe . . . and all wrong! . . . We will in future play the song with the desired lively tempo. But the discovery rather pained us, and we cherish a hope that Röder [the engraver] made a mistake which you overlooked in the proof, and we may yet see it publicly marked *Langsam und heimlich.*

With characteristic pseudo-humility, Brahms replied on 29 April:

In return for your very kind letter, I must tell you at once that, although *Belebt und heimlich* is the tempo mark for *Frühlingsdämmerung* in the manuscript, I set it down practically in desperation, thinking the song very tedious. But later on there is *immer langsamer, Adagio,* and finally actually a fermata over the whole bar!

The fermata in question (in the last full bar of the final vocal phrase) is missing in the voice part in the complete Breitkopf & Härtel edition and the Dover reprint; it should appear over what would be the fifth quarter in the bar, prolonging the E (low key, B) rather than its resolution. The piano's sixth-beat fermata is correct.

Theodor Billroth characterized the song as evoking "the most exquisite scent of lilies in the moonlight!" Clara Schumann described it simply as "glorious," the second half "enchanting."

Willst du, daß ich geh'?, Op. 71/4 (Do You Want Me to Go?)

Text by Karl Lemcke (1831–1913)

Auf der Heide weht der Wind—
Herzig Kind, herzig Kind—
Willst du, daß trotz Sturm und Graus
In die Nacht ich muß hinaus—
　　Willst du, daß ich geh'?

Auf der Heid' zu Bergeshöh'
Treibt der Schnee, treibt der Schnee;
Feget Straßen, Schlucht und Teich
Mit den weißen Flügeln gleich.
　　Willst du, daß ich geh'?

Horch, wie klingt's herauf vom See
Wild und weh, wild und weh!
An den Weiden sitzt die Fei
Und mein Weg geht dort vorbei—
　　Willst du, daß ich geh'?

Wie ist's hier in deinem Arm
Traut und warm, traut und warm;
Ach, wie oft hab' ich gedacht:

So bei dir nur eine Nacht—
Willst du, daß ich geh'?

On the heath the wind blows, charming girl, charming girl; do you want me to go out into the night in spite of the storm and horror? Do you want me to go?

On the heath the snow piles up, the snow piles up as high as mountains; it brushes roads, gorges and ponds to an even height with its white wings. Do you want me to go?

Listen, what a wild and sorrowful, wild and sorrowful sound arises from the lake. By the willows sits the [malicious] fairy, and on my way I would have to pass them. Do you want me to go?

How comfortable and warm, comfortable and warm it is here in your arms; ah, how often I have thought: if I could just spend one night with you! Do you want me to go?

Composed in March 1877.

First performed by Julius Spengel in Hamburg on 18 March 1878.

Strophic, but treated so freely as to appear through-composed. The same rhythm is retained for all four stanzas (except at the end), but only strophes 1 and 2 are identical.

The poem is from Lemcke's *Lieder und Gedichte* (Hamburg, 1861), where it is entitled "Auf der Heide saust der Wind." Brahms altered the first line, changing "saust der Wind" to "weht der Wind"; he originally left the song untitled, adding the present title only in the fair copy for the printers.

The situation depicted is similar to that in the more familiar "Vergebliches Ständchen," Op. 84/4, but here there is no dialogue, only the boy's attempts at persuasion. The erotic intensity of the verses finds its equivalent in Brahms's impassioned setting, with its fast tempo, its panting afterbeats, and its questioning rising inflections. Clara Schumann found the text tasteless, but "all the same I should like to hear a good singer sing it some time" (2 May 1877).

The keyboard-spanning introduction immediately evokes the raging storm, and the surging dynamics and incessant turbulence of the opening stanzas' accompaniment portray it vividly. Toward the end of each stanza the motion becomes quieter, and coaxing chromaticisms in the piano's canonic melody anticipate the young man's pleading refrain; during the closing *poco ritardando*, one can imagine his searching intently for signs of the girl's reaction, the storm momentarily forgotten.

In stanza 3, which shifts to consideration of supernatural forces, the fluctuating dynamics yield to a *sempre piano* indication, and the minor subdominant and major submediant harmonies are stressed. At first, legato lines in broken octaves or with pedal points, moving generally in contrary motion with the voice, replace the detached chords and afterbeats of stanzas 1 and 2, but the earlier texture returns softly to portray the fear aroused by the prospect of nearing the lake's malevolent spirits. The imploring refrain, seemingly more eloquent at each recurrence, returns as before.

As Platt points out (*Text-Music*, 205ff.), a change to the tonic major for stanza 4 signals a marked revision in strategy. The yearning lover, his growing confidence revealed in strong circle-of-fifth harmonies in mm. 32–33, subtly shifts the emphasis from "whether" to "how long" he will stay—the winsome half steps of "ich muß" in stanza 1 are here transformed into whole steps plus emphatic upward leaps on "nur eine," first a fifth in m. 36, then a seventh, to the song's highest pitch in m. 37. The refrain asks its question once, then waits expectantly. Suddenly *lebhaft* and *forte* after the fermata, the accompaniment's ascending and descending melodies converge on the dominant in m. 42 as though in agreement at last, while the anxious afterbeats cease and the concluding vocal phrase is triumphantly extended, no longer interrogatory in effect. As the final chords ring out joyously, there seems little doubt that the door has closed with both lovers snug and warm inside.

Minnelied, Op. 71/5 (Love Song)

Text by Ludwig Hölty (1748–1776)

> Holder klingt der Vogelsang,
> Wenn die Engelreine,
> Die mein Jünglingsherz bezwang,
> Wandelt durch die Haine.
>
> Röter blühen Tal und Au,
> Grüner wird der Wasen,
> Wo die Finger meiner Frau
> Maienblumen lasen.
>
> Ohne sie ist alles tot,
> Welk sind Blüt' und Kräuter;
> Und kein Frühlingsabendrot
> Dünkt mir schön und heiter.
>
> Traute, minnigliche Frau,
> Wollest nimmer fliehen,
> Daß mein Herz, gleich dieser Au,
> Mög' in Wonne blühen!

The song of the birds sounds more lovely when the angelically pure woman who conquered my young heart walks through the grove.

Valley and meadow blossom in a deeper red, the lawn becomes greener where my lady's fingers have picked May flowers.

Without her everything is dead; blossoms and plants wither, and no spring sunset appears beautiful or happy to me.

Beloved, charming woman, please never depart, so that my heart, like this meadow, may bloom in rapture!

Composed in March 1877.
First performed by Julius Spengel in Hamburg on 29 October 1877.
Varied strophic; A A B A'.
The text was taken from the 1804 collection of Hölty's poems edited by Johann Heinrich Voss, who had made here, as generally, numerous revisions. Hölty's original version, though written in 1773, was first published in 1890.

The poem is striking in its simplicity of expression, but Brahms's elegant setting endows it with transcendent beauty. Both the melody and its accompaniment exude tenderness, and their lack of rhythmic congruity is one of the song's great charms. The opening melody refers to Joseph Gungl's "Styrian Waltz," a song then popular in Vienna.

The accompaniment is at first languorously tethered to a tonic pedal; the second half of the strophe is notable for the chromaticisms, melodic and harmonic, that seem both to postpone and to caress the phrase's key pitches.

In the key of the dominant, the contrasting third strophe derives its melodic rhythm from that of the earlier melody. Both voice and piano sink into their lower registers in response to the text's darkened mood, and the harmonies remain firmly anchored to the bass pedal. Little hints and murmurs of canonic imitation become more clearly defined in anticipation of the return of the main melody. Clara Schumann criticized this segment as lacking "melodic significance" (2 May 1877), apparently failing to understand (or perhaps to appreciate) the aptness of its relative characterlessness in symbolizing the drabness of the poet's world without his beloved.

The fourth verse is set to an exact repetition of the amiable opening strophe, with the last line of text repeated to provide the opportunity for a characteristically lengthened (and ecstatically climactic) concluding phrase.

The piano begins its lovely postlude with a waning remembrance of the pedal-bound introduction. The superb closing phrase recalls the pitches of the vocal line's recent melodic climax, while combining augmentation with a *ritardando* in one of Brahms's most exquisite, seemingly nonmetric, decelerations—the left hand's rhythmic units increase in value from the equivalent of two eighth notes (in mm. 47–49) through three (m. 50) and four (mm. 51–52) to six (mm. 53–54), while the length of the right hand's melodic groups decreases from a span of five quarter notes (mm. 47–48) through four (mm. 49–51) to three (mm. 52–54). The song ends simply with a gently sonorous chord, sounded twice.

FIVE GESÄNGE, OP. 72

Lieder und Gesänge mit Begleitung des Pianoforte von Johannes Brahms (Songs with Piano Accompaniment by Johannes Brahms). Part title: *Op. 72. Fünf Gesänge* (Five Songs). Published, together with Opp. 69–71, in July/August 1877 by N. Simrock in Berlin; publication number 7955.

These five songs, for which Clara Schumann expressed unqualified praise in her letter of 2 May 1877, represent a kind of pinnacle of Brahms's song composition to date. Their synthesis of text and music is close to perfection, vocal lines are integrated into organically evolved textures, the musical language is concise, and the expression of emotion is sincere and compelling.

Alte Liebe, Op. 72/1 (Old Love)

Text by Karl Candidus (1817–1872)

Es kehrt die dunkle Schwalbe
Aus fernem Land zurück,
Die frommen Störche kehren
Und bringen neues Glück.

An diesem Frühlingsmorgen,
So trüb', verhängt und warm,
Ist mir, als fänd' ich wieder
Den alten Liebesharm.

Es ist, als ob mich leise
Wer auf die Schulter schlug,
Als ob ich säuseln hörte,
Wie einer Taube Flug.

Es klopft an meine Türe
Und ist doch niemand draus;
Ich atme Jasmindüfte
Und habe keinen Strauß.

Es ruft mir aus der Ferne,
Ein Auge sieht mich an,

Ein alter Traum erfaßt mich
Und führt mich seine Bahn.

The dark swallow returns from a far-off country; the faithful storks return and bring renewed good fortune.

On this spring morning, so gloomily overcast and warm, I seem to find once more my old love-sorrow.

It is as if someone touched me lightly on the shoulder, as if I heard a rustling like that of a dove's wings. There is a knock at the door, but no one is outside. I smell the fragrance of jasmine, but I have no bouquet. I hear a voice calling me from far away; a pair of eyes are looking at me.

An old dream takes hold of me and leads me off in its own direction.

Composed in May 1876.

First performed by Amalie Joachim on 18 January 1878 at the Grosser Saal des Conventgartens in Hamburg.

Through-composed.

The text is from the poet's *Vermischte Gedichte* (Leipzig, 1869).

The poem is simple in structure—five verses, each with four lines of alternately seven and six syllables, the six-syllable lines rhyming. It deals with the lingering sorrow over a lost love; the signs of spring's return awaken increasingly painful memories.

Brahms observes the poem's content rather than its structure to devise a modified A B A form. The first two verses are straightforward statements and are set to complementary sections of similar phrase structure, each extended to ten measures by the repetition of the closing words of text. Then follows a succession of "it is as if" statements, comprising stanzas 3, 4, and the first half of 5. Brahms sets them as a unit, without interlude, to music that is modulatory, increasingly animated, and developmental in style and function, twice recalling the melody of the opening phrase (mm. 34–35 and 38–39). The return to narrative near the end of the poem prompts a return to the original key and tempo, and to music that recalls and balances that of the opening, although the melody goes "off in its own direction" after only one phrase, symbolic of the text. Again the section is stretched to ten measures by repetition of text, this time of both complete lines plus an internal repetition in the last.

There are deft illustrative touches throughout the song. A tonality-dissolving chromatic bass portrays "fernem Land" in m. 4. In m. 9, a move to the major subdominant illuminates "neues Glück." The spring morning blossoms in the key of the submediant, and the vocal line's falling seventh in m. 16 caresses the word "warm." The striking shift from major to minor (and from *piano* to *pianissimo*) in m. 23 transports the listener in one stroke into the realm of memory, where unreality is reflected in the elusively shifting tonality.

A grouping into threes of the accompaniment's prevalent eighth notes is often implied by their distribution between the hands or by their contour; when this arrangement becomes overt, as in mm. 16–21, a slower $\frac{4}{4}$ meter is in effect superimposed on the prevailing $\frac{6}{4}$, suggesting that the time scale of imagination is independent of that of reality.

At the end of the song, the repetition of the poem's closing line is pensively elongated, while the accompaniment's right hand slows to reflective quarter notes, shadowing the vocal line. In support, the left hand introduces dream-evocative rising arpeggios, which continue through the piano postlude's wistful slow remembrance of the song's opening melody.

"How glorious it is!" remarked Clara Schumann of "Alte Liebe" in her letter of 2 May 1877.

Sommerfäden, Op. 72/2 (Gossamer)

Text by Karl Candidus (1817–1872)

Sommerfäden hin und wieder
Fliegen von den Himmeln nieder;
Sind der Menschen Hirngespinste,
Fetzen goldner Liebesträume,
An die Stauden, an die Bäume
Haben sie sich dort verfangen;
Hochselbsteigene Gewinste
Sehen wir darunter hangen.

Threads of gossamer fly down from heaven to and fro; they are people's brain-spinnings, remnants of golden dreams of love.

They have caught themselves there on the bushes, on the trees; we see hanging below them winnings of our very, very own.

Composed in May 1876.
The first performance is not documented.
Modified strophic.
The text is found in the poet's *Vermischte Gedichte* (Leipzig, 1869).
The obscure poem strains to find a comparison between threads of gossamer and the detritus of human hopes of love. At first, Brahms's idea of spinning strands of two-part piano counterpoint around the vocal melody seems scarcely less forced; the importance and harmonic complexity of the polyphony contradict weightlessness, and the prevalent use of the middle register frustrates attempts at delicacy. But one soon realizes that the composer's principal concern is not the literal depiction of drifting cobwebs

caught in the shrubbery, but rather the sadness resulting from the unrealized dreams that they symbolize. The song's mood darkens as it progresses, and its unusually strong emphasis on the dominant subtly conveys a sense of unfulfillment.

The vocal melody begins simply, embellished only by occasional little floating roulades of eighth notes. But pensiveness accumulates as the strophe proceeds, peaking in the last line's anguished repetition, which is extended to embrace five strong beats rather than four, and which connects its opening tritone and cadential diminished third with a chain of sobbing eighth notes.

The soberly expressive five-measure introduction establishes the constant eighth-note rhythm and the obsessive contrary motion that characterize the accompaniment. The left hand's initial melodic motive recurs significantly, as, for example, in the right hand as the voice enters in m. 6, in the left hand to define the beginning of the second phrase in m. 10, and in the bass of the interlude, mm. 18 and 19.

The second strophe begins like the first, but after a few notes of the second phrase the melody plunges down a scalewise minor ninth. In the piano, a *pianissimo* and the cessation of harmonic motion in m. 30 signal that the song's emotional climax is at hand. Hovering, barely moving harmonies in a new oscillating figuration and the bass line's descent into the low register of the piano illustrate the text's "darunter hangen." The vocal line climbs by half steps to a symbolically prolonged dissonance on "hangen," the word's impact dramatized by the quickly achieved *forte*. The phrase's repetition is made even more poignant by the additional prolongation of "darunter."

In m. 34 the bass line initiates a return to figuration resembling that appearing earlier in the song, a process that culminates in the repetitive recalling of key motives and rhythms in mm. 36–37. The postlude's closing gesture—an unanchored rising arpeggio from which key pitches are caught by ties—is a final metaphor for the ensnared floating strands of gossamer.

In her 2 May 1877 letter, Clara Schumann pronounced "Sommerfäden" "beautiful! But the word 'Fetzen' [rags] jars on me. Can't you find some other word?"

O kühler Wald, Op. 72/3 (O Cool Forest)

Text by Clemens Brentano (1778–1842)

> O kühler Wald,
> Wo rauschest du,
> In dem mein Liebchen geht?
> O Widerhall,
> Wo lauschest du,
> Der gern mein Lied versteht?

> O Widerhall,
> O sängst du ihr
> Die süßen Träume vor,
> Die Lieder all,
> O bring sie ihr,
> Die ich so früh verlor!—

Im Herzen tief,
Da rauscht der Wald,
In dem mein Liebchen geht;
In Schmerzen schlief
Der Widerhall,
Die Lieder sind verweht.

> Im Walde bin
> Ich so allein,
> O Liebchen, wandre hier,
> Verschallet auch
> Manch Lied so rein,
> Ich singe andre dir!

Where do you murmur, O cool forest in which my darling walks? Where do you listen, O echo that gladly understands my song?

Deep in my heart, there murmurs the forest in which my darling walks; the echo has fallen asleep in sorrows; the songs are dispersed.

Composed in March 1877.

First performed by Adele Assmann on 22 October 1878 in Breslau at the opening concert of the Orchesterverein.

Through-composed.

The poem is found in Brentano's *Gesammelte Werke* (Frankfurt am Main, 1852–55). Brahms used only the first and third verses, thereby clarifying and simplifying its dramatic import. The poet mourns his beloved's absence, the cause of which is left unspecified, by summoning up shadowy memories of her walking in cool woodlands while his songs echo sadly. His lament is rendered even more touching by Brahms's compassionate and unsentimental setting. The song requires impeccable phrasing from the singer and interpretative finesse from both performers.

The first stanza's quarter-note chords pulsate like heartbeats, as noble as the stately trees they evoke. The eighth-note figuration of the second stanza intensifies the emotion and suggests the rustling of leaves or the dappling of sunlight on the shaded forest floor. The questioning first stanza is led inexorably toward the dominant, culminating in the piano's unresolved dominant-seventh chord in mm. 10–11, which evaporates into silence; the answering second stanza moves with equal inevitability toward a somewhat elusive tonic. The dramatic crux of the song occurs in mm. 12–13, where it is revealed, in *pianissimo* slow-moving harmonies from the key of the minor mode's major submediant (Brahms's key of unreality), that the entire scene exists only in the depths of the poet's heart and mind.

There are many masterly examples of the illumination or amplification of meaning. The piano's continuations of the vocal line in mm. 5 and 17 seem to reaffirm "mein Liebchen." The hinted large hemiola in mm. 8–9 combines with the reiteration a third lower of "mein Lied" to evoke the echoing described by the text. In mm. 18–19, "Schmerzen" is darkly harmonized with the tonic minor, while "Widerhall" elicits that key's seemingly reverberated relative major. The ending portion of the song is dominated by the influence of the word "verweht" (scattered, dispersed), first sung to pitches that recall the piano's questioning tenor in m. 10: rather than resolving, harmonies spin on a dominant axis; the tonic major, although it has obviously returned in m. 20, is allowed to drift rootless, evading firm establishment until the final measure; the vocal line's closing chromatic rise, as the last words are repeated thoughtfully, seems to dissipate into musing.

The piano concludes with a more sonorous restatement of the gesture with which the song began. Clara Schumann declared the setting simply "wonderful!" (2 May 1877).

Verzagen, Op. 72/4 (Despondency)

Text by Karl Lemcke (1831–1913)

Ich sitz' am Strande der rauschenden See
Und suche dort nach Ruh',
Ich schaue dem Treiben der Wogen
Mit dumpfer Ergebung zu.

Die Wogen rauschen zum Strande hin,
Sie schäumen und vergeh'n,
Die Wolken, die Winde darüber,
Die kommen und verweh'n.

Du ungestümes Herz sei still
Und gib dich doch zur Ruh',
Du sollst mit Winden und Wogen
Dich trösten, —was weinest du?

I sit by the shore of the roaring sea, and seek there for repose; I watch the movement of the waves with numb devotion.

The waves roar onto the beach; they foam and disappear, the clouds and winds above them come and are blown away.

You stormy heart, be still and finally go to rest; you should be consoled by the winds and the waves; why do you weep?

Composed in March 1877.

First performed by Amalie Joachim and Clara Schumann on 31 October 1877 in Berlin.

Modified strophic; the third strophe begins differently, but ends like the other two.

The text is from Lemcke's *Lieder und Gedichte* (Hamburg, 1861). On a stormy seashore, the despairing poet seeks consolation but, unlike the waves that foam and recede or the clouds that dissipate before the wind, his nameless grief persists, undiminished.

In Brahms's turbulent setting, the poet's pain becomes at the same time more personal and more universal. The virtuosic piano writing vividly suggests the incessant motion of the dark sea as waves break on the bleak shore, leaving behind little ripples of backwash. Since the few modulations in the principal strophe are only transient, the strong emphasis on the dominant at the beginning of the third strophe dramatically underlines the poet's turning inward at that point.

Carried on the powerful surge and swell of piano sound, the vocal line rises in stages, like a wave gathering force, to a climax at the repetition of the second line, from which it declines into the third line's undulating wavelets. Perhaps the most striking feature of the melody is the long descending scale to which the fourth line is first set, leading to its hushed, thoughtful repetition.

Rhythmic augmentations are characteristic of this song; they lend variety to the phrase structure and gravity to the impact of the text. In all three strophes, the fourth line is elongated upon repetition, as is the second line of strophes 1 and 2. In the third strophe, the first two lines are set in larger note values than before so that, even without text repetition, they again occupy six measures. The broadened metrics are a metaphor for the text's plea for quietude and solace; the melody takes on enhanced expressive significance because its rhythm and pitch contour are reminiscent of those of the strophe's pensive closing phrase.

Performers should observe the composer's dynamic indications with care—so active an accompaniment invites over-loudness. The requested wide range of dynamics helps to clarify the song's dramatic shape.

Unüberwindlich, Op. 72/5 (Unconquerable)

Text by Johann Wolfgang von Goethe (1749–1832)

Hab' ich tausendmal geschworen
Dieser Flasche nicht zu trauen,
Bin ich doch wie neugeboren,
Läßt mein Schenke fern sie schauen.
Alles ist an ihr zu loben,

Glaskristall und Purpurwein;
Wird der Pfropf herausgehoben
Sie ist leer und ich nicht mein.

Hab' ich tausendmal geschworen,
Dieser Falschen nicht zu trauen,
Und doch bin ich neugeboren,
Läßt sie sich in's Auge schauen.
Mag sie doch mit mir verfahren,
Wie's dem stärksten Mann geschah.
Deine Scher' in meinen Haaren,
Allerliebste Delila!

I've sworn a thousand times not to trust this bottle; and yet I feel as if born anew when my innkeeper appears with it at a distance.

Everything about it is praiseworthy, its crystal and its purple wine; when the cork is drawn out, the bottle becomes empty and I am no longer master of myself.

I've sworn a thousand times not to trust that false one; and yet I am born anew when I can gaze lovingly upon it (her).

Let it (her) treat me as the strongest of men was treated—your scissors in my hair, most lovely Delilah!

Composed in May 1876.

The first performance was given by Julius Stockhausen in Hamburg in December 1878.

Varied strophic. The poem's two verses are set as four musical sections: sections 2 and 4 are nearly alike; the second half of section 3 is a variant of the corresponding portion of section 1; and sections 1 and 3 begin dissimilarly although the texts are parallel.

Brahms owned Goethe's *Sämmtliche Werke* (Stuttgart, 1860) and his *Werke* (without date), in both of which the text is found.

From Goethe's witty and racy drinking song, Brahms fashioned a brilliant and powerful *aria buffa*. The poem compares women with wine—both irresistible despite all good intentions, and both with the ability to render one helpless! The sense depends upon the clever exchange of "Flasche" (bottle) in the first stanza for "Falsche" (false one) in the second; not only is the similarity of sounds amusing, but the use as a noun of the feminine adjective "falsche" can refer ambiguously either to the bottle or to an unfaithful woman.

The music is as playful as the poem and as winning, filled with hiccuping bass octaves and staccato cork-poppings. (Presumably to heighten its percussiveness, Brahms changed Goethe's onomatopoeic "Pfropf" to "Propf.") A particularly delightful touch is Brahms's use as introduction of a motive (transposed) from the harpsichord sonata in D, L. 214, by Domenico Scarlatti, which glistens with the clarity of a fine sparkling Burgundy. The motive reappears at the end of each large strophe to generate the bass line of music that humorously depicts the poet's wine-induced fuzzy-headedness (and slurred speech) in the first case and his easy surrender to feminine wiles in the second. The immediately preceding section, with its curious metric telescoping, also derives its bass from the Scarlatti motive.

At the beginning of the second half of the song, the mock solemnity of the poet's oft-repeated vows of abstinence is underscored by pompous canonic imitation between bass line and voice, both in doubled note values.

Music and text fit hand in glove—the poem could have been written for the setting as well as the reverse. "A great favorite," wrote Clara Schumann on 2 May 1877. "How absolutely original!"

FIVE ROMANZEN AND LIEDER FOR ONE OR TWO VOICES, OP. 84

Romanzen und Lieder für eine oder zwei Stimmen mit Begleitung des Pianoforte von Johannes Brahms (Romances and Songs for One or Two Voices with Piano Accompaniment by Johannes Brahms), Op. 84. Published in July 1882 by N. Simrock in Berlin; publication number 8298.

The ordering of the group joins three settings of texts from Hans Schmidt's *Gedichte und Übersetzungen*, probably composed during summer 1881 at Pressbaum bei Wien, with two from the Kretzschmer-Zuccalmaglio collection *Deutsche Volkslieder mit ihren Original-Weisen*, probably composed at Pörtschach during the summers 1877–1879.

The indication "for one or two voices" is more an acknowledgment of their dialogue format than an invitation to their performance as duets; there is, however, an *ad libitum* harmonizing second part at the end of the fifth song, "Spannung."

Sommerabend, Op. 84/1 (Summer Evening)

Text by Hans Schmidt (1856– ?)

Geh' schlafen, Tochter, schlafen!
Schon fällt der Tau auf's Gras,
Und wen die Tropfen trafen,
Weint bald die Augen naß!

"Laß weinen, Mutter, weinen!
Das Mondlicht leuchtet hell,
Und wem die Strahlen scheinen,
Dem trocknen Tränen schnell!"

Geh' schlafen, Tochter, schlafen!
Schon ruft der Kauz im Wald,
Und wen die Töne trafen,
Muß mit ihm klagen bald!

> "Laß klagen, Mutter, klagen!
> Die Nachtigall singt hell,
> Und wem die Lieder schlagen,
> Dem schwindet Trauer schnell!"

THE MOTHER: Go to sleep, daughter, go to sleep! The dew is already falling on the grass, and whoever is touched by the drops will soon cry his eyes wet!

THE DAUGHTER: Let him cry, Mother, let him cry! The moonlight gleams brightly, and the one for whom its beams shine will soon dry his tears!

THE MOTHER: Go to sleep, daughter, go to sleep! Soon the screech owl will hoot in the forest, and whoever hears that sound must soon lament with the owl!

THE DAUGHTER: Let him lament, Mother, let him lament! The nightingale sings brightly, and the one for whom its songs are sung will lose his mourning quickly!

Probably composed at Pressbaum bei Wien during the summer of 1881.

First performed on 21 May 1895 in Hamburg by Ida Seelig with Julius Spengel as accompanist.

Strophic. Except for slight differences in the accompaniment, the mother's two verses are set to the same music in minor and the daughter's two are set alike to different music in the major; the two sections are related by rhythm and phrase structure.

The text (without the indications "Die Mutter" and "Die Tochter") appears in Schmidt's *Gedichte und Übersetzungen* (Offenbach am Main, n.d.).

The text's weeping and lamenting are evoked by the piano's sustained afterbeats (sometimes notated as sighing quarter and eighth only, without prolongation over the barline), which are replaced briefly by the *animato* rising triplets against rising eighths of the daughter's cheery response. Expressive touches of Neapolitan harmony color the mother's verses, and a gentle caress of minor subdominant softens the music of the interlude and postlude.

The melody of the mother's strophe is a particularly masterly example of graceful symmetry, with its framing similar pairs of phrases that rise to dominant and fall to tonic, separated by a little phrase in which the piano departs from the vocal line to complete the sequence. Elisabet von Herzogenberg wrote to Brahms from Graz on 24 July 1882, "I can hardly imagine anything prettier or daintier than the lines of the mother's melody in *Sommerabend*."

Der Kranz, Op. 84/2 (The Wreath)

Text by Hans Schmidt (1856– ?)

> Mutter, hilf mir armen Tochter,
> Sieh' nur, was ein Knabe tat:

Einen Kranz von Rosen flocht er,
Den er mich zu tragen bat!

"Ei, sei deshalb unerschrocken,
Helfen läßt sich dir gewiß!
Nimm den Kranz nur aus den Locken,
Und den Knaben, den vergiß."

Dornen hat der Kranz, o Mutter,
Und die halten fest das Haar!
Worte sprach der Knabe, Mutter,
An die denk' ich immerdar!

THE DAUGHTER: Mother, help your poor daughter; just look at what some boy did: he wove a wreath of roses and asked me to wear it!
THE MOTHER: Ho, don't let that frighten you; there is definitely a remedy for that! Just take the wreath out of your hair, and forget the boy!
THE DAUGHTER: The wreath has thorns, Mother, and they cling firmly to my hair! The boy said things to me, Mother, that I think about all the time!

Probably composed during the summer of 1881 at Pressbaum bei Wien.
First performed by Amalie Joachim on 17 February 1884 in Berlin.
Through-composed, although the last verse begins like the first.

The text is from the poet's undated *Gedichte und Übersetzungen*. The mother-daughter dialogue was such a convention in German poetry at the time that Schmidt did not find it necessary to identify the speakers.

The two women are clearly differentiated in Brahms's setting, both by tessitura and by the character of the music assigned to them.

The daughter's emotional unease is revealed in her melody's many little sighing dissonances and in the tremulous twittering of the accompaniment. The powerful significance of the wreath is made apparent by the expansion to three measures of the gorgeously harmonized phrase in which she first mentions it, and by a modulation to the relative major, in which key her quiet repetition of the revelation that the boy has asked her to wear it is also expanded to three measures.

The mother's music, on the other hand, suggests her outward firmness, with functional harmonies and a melody that often outlines triads. But it is clear that she too recognizes the wreath's import; her reference to it borrows the daughter's quavering melody and accompaniment and it changes her previously major key of the dominant to the minor. Even the expanded repetition of her admonition to forget the boy seems not completely to reestablish her authority.

The daughter begins her response to the same music as before, but with quickly burgeoning assurance and independence she remembers the boy's persuasive words in the major mode, *animato* and *forte*. Expansive phrases in the high register and a joyously rocketing piano postscript bring the song to a brilliant conclusion.

In den Beeren, Op. 84/3 (Among the Berries)

Text by Hans Schmidt (1856–?)

Singe, Mädchen, hell und klar,
Sing' aus voller Kehle,
Daß uns nicht die Spatzenschar
Alle Beeren stehle!

"Mutter, mag auch weit der Spatz
Flieh'n vor meinem Singen,
Fürcht' ich doch, es wird den Schatz
Um so näher bringen."

Freilich, für so dreisten Gauch
Braucht es einer Scheuche,
Warte nur, ich komme auch
In die Beerensträuche!

"Mutter, nein, das hat nicht Not:
Beeren, schau, sind teuer,
Doch der Küsse, reif und rot,
Gibt es viele heuer!"

THE MOTHER: Sing, my girl, brightly and clearly, sing with all your might, so that the flock of sparrows doesn't steal all the berries from us!
THE DAUGHTER: Mother, even if the sparrow flies far away when I sing, still I'm afraid my singing will bring my sweetheart all the nearer.
THE MOTHER: You're right, for such an impudent cuckoo a scarecrow is needed; just wait, I'll come into the berry bushes, too!
THE DAUGHTER: Mother, no, there's no need of that: look, berries are dear, but kisses ripe and red are plentiful this year!

Probably composed during the summer of 1881 at Pressbaum bei Wien. The first performance is undocumented.

Strophic; the mother's two verses are set to similar music as are, with somewhat more variation, the two of the daughter.

The text is found in Schmidt's *Gedichte und Übersetzungen* (Offenbach am Main, n.d.). Brahms inserted the designations "Die Mutter" and "Die Tochter," which are absent in the original poem.

The mother's ebullient music modulates twice to the dominant, the second time moving on to a somewhat surprising cadence in that key's relative minor. The piano softly restores the dominant and, in sighing quarter-note chords, works its way artlessly through the tonic E♭ minor to the (visually) even more astonishing key of B major—"that chameleon-like key with its D♯," as Elisabet von Herzogenberg remarked in her letter of 24 July 1882, "so perplexing at first reading!" (The low key's change from B♭ minor to F♯ major is no less intimidating in appearance.)

The daughter's response begins in the new key (enharmonically, the submediant from the minor—Brahms's "dreamworld" key), which joins the frequent chromatic inflections and expressive dissonances to suggest that her thoughts are not on berry picking alone. At the first mention of her sweetheart, the swinging afterbeat figure in the accompaniment gives way to tender flowing eighth notes, and soon, almost imperceptibly, the tonic key returns, and with it the earlier carefree mood.

The only significant change in the mother's second verse is the lowered sixth scale step, which shadows her references to the "impudent cuckoo," perhaps a fleeting premonition of her daughter's leaving home.

The mention of "ripe red kisses" in the third line of the daughter's response prompts repetition of the text and the expansion of the phrase to eight measures by means of varied augmentation; the accompanying eighths become even more caressing in their elaborated form. The characteristic lengthening of the final vocal phrase stretches the song's highest pitch to its longest duration, providing a brilliant ending.

The girl's evident happiness is confirmed by the piano's insouciant postlude, which rounds out the form by recalling, like a ritornello, the music of the introduction.

Vergebliches Ständchen, Op. 84/4 (Fruitless Serenade)

Text by Anton Wilhelm Florentin von Zuccalmaglio (1803–1869)
Based on a Folk Song from the Lower Rhine

Guten Abend, mein Schatz,
Guten Abend, mein Kind!
Ich komm' aus Lieb' zu dir,
Ach, mach' mir auf die Tür,
Mach' mir auf die Tür!

"Meine Tür ist verschlossen,
Ich laß dich nicht ein;
Mutter die rät' mir klug,
Wär'st du herein mit Fug,
Wär's mit mir vorbei!"

So kalt ist die Nacht,
So eisig der Wind,
Daß mir das Herz erfriert,
Mein' Lieb' erlöschen wird;
Öffne mir, mein Kind!

"Löschet dein Lieb',
Lass' sie löschen nur!
Löschet sie immerzu,

> Geh' heim zu Bett zur Ruh',
> Gute Nacht, mein Knab'!"

HE: Good evening, darling, good evening, sweet child! I come from love of you; ah, open the door for me, open the door for me!

SHE: My door is locked, I won't let you in; Mother gives me good advice; if you were permitted inside it would be all over for me!

HE: The night is so cold, the wind is so icy, that my heart will freeze and my love will be extinguished; open for me, sweet child!

SHE: If your love is extinguished, let it go out! If it keeps going out, go home to bed and rest; good night, my boy!

Probably composed during one of Brahms's summers in Pörtschach, 1877–1879.

First performed on 23 February 1883 at a song recital by the tenor Gustav Walter in the Saal Bösendorfer in Vienna, with Brahms at the piano. Kalbeck's assertion (*Johannes Brahms*, III$_2$, 339), repeated elsewhere by others, that Amalie Joachim sang it the preceding December in Strasbourg seems to be in error.

Strophic, with varied accompaniment; most of the third strophe is in the minor mode.

Brahms found the poem in his favorite collection, *Deutsche Volkslieder mit ihren Original-Weisen* (Berlin, 1838–40), edited by Kretzschmer and Zuccalmaglio. He assumed that it was an authentic folk-song text, but it is an almost entirely new interpretation by Zuccalmaglio of the content of an old folk song. The reworking is masterly however, and the result is one of Brahms's most beloved songs. The composer himself, customarily so self-deprecating about his work, was unusually pleased with it; Kalbeck reports (III$_2$, 337) that, in response to the critic Eduard Hanslick's singling the song out for praise, Brahms wrote, "It was really something special for me and I am in a particularly good humor about it. . . . For this one song I would sacrifice all the others." The indications "Er" and "Sie" were added by Brahms.

The song's breezy good humor stems from its lack of harmonic complexity, the many reiterations of text, its repetitive rhythms, and, above all, the extraordinary economy of its melodic construction. Upward leaps of a fourth highlight the sixth, fifth, and fourth scale steps in mm. 3, 4, and 5, and again in mm. 7, 8, and 9; the order is reversed in mm. 12, 14, and 15. Apart from chord outlines, the scalewise third that those three pitches define is the only other significant motive: downward, it completes the sequences in the opening pair of phrases and forms the cadences in mm. 5–6, 9–10, 15–16, and, with a dominant interpolated, 19–20; upward, it provides the sequences of mm. 17 and 18.

Over rising eighth-note arpeggios, the piano introduction anticipates the opening vocal melody, which it doubles in unison octaves until the cadence.

The piano alone then begins a lightly harmonized repetition, joined midway by the voice and gracefully varied in the second strophe.

The lover's pleading in the third strophe is made more pathetic by the change of mode and by the interplay between the raised and lowered fourth scale step. A running eighth-note counter-melody evokes the chill wind, accompanying the voice in bare octaves and continuing as bass support for the piano's legato takeover of the tune. Forceful second-beat accents in the second half of the strophe give way to little entreating imitations as the major mode returns in the last phrase.

Suddenly the tempo quickens and a new chordal version of the interlude, cross-rhythmed and rising melodically to the upper tonic, predicts the cheery resolve with which the girl proceeds to dismiss the boy's suit. The eighth notes that smoothly accompany the strophe's now fully harmonized opening phrases dance lightly to accompany the remainder, suggesting her merry laughter. The window is slammed firmly shut to a *sforzando* chord in the piano, and a decisive cadence quickly concludes the matter. One suspects that it is for neither the first time nor the last.

Spannung, Op. 84/5 (Tension)

Folk Song from the Lower Rhine[?]

Gut'n Abend, gut'n Abend, mein tausiger Schatz,
Ich sag' dir guten Abend;
Komm' du zu mir, ich komme zu dir,
Du sollst mir Antwort geben, mein Engel!

Ich kommen zu dir, du kommen zu mir?
Das wär' mir gar keine Ehre;
Du gehst von mir zu andern Jungfrauen,
Das hab' ich wohl vernommen, mein Engel!

Ach nein, mein Schatz, und glaub' es nur nicht,
Was falsche Zungen reden,
Es geben so viele gottlose Leut',
Die dir und mir nichts gönnen, mein Engel!

Und gibt es so viele gottlose Leut',
Die dir und mir nichts gönnen,
So solltest du selber bewahren die Treu'
Und machen zu Schanden ihr Reden, mein Engel!

Leb' wohl, mein Schatz, ich hör' es wohl,
Du hast einen Anderen lieber,
So will ich meiner Wege geh'n,
Gott möge dich wohl behüten, mein Engel!

Ach nein, ich hab' kein' Anderen lieb,
Ich glaub' nicht gottlosigen Leuten,

> Komm' du zu mir, ich komme zu dir,
> Wir bleiben uns beide getreue, mein Engel!

HE: Good evening, good evening, my precious treasure; I give you a good evening; come to me, I will come to you; you must answer me, my angel!

SHE: I should come to you, and you to me? That would be no honor for me; you go to other girls when you leave me; that I have heard from good sources, my angel!

HE: Oh, no, darling, don't believe what false tongues say; there are so many godless people who begrudge the two of us everything, my angel!

SHE: And if there are so many godless people who begrudge the two of us everything, then you yourself should keep your faith and put their gossip to shame, my angel!

HE: Goodbye, darling; I can tell from what you say that you prefer another man to me; so I will go my way; may God keep you well, my angel!

SHE: Oh, no, I don't love anyone else; I don't believe godless people; come to me, I will come to you; we will both be faithful to one another, my angel!

Probably composed during one of the summers at Pörtschach, 1877–1879.

First performed by Ida Huber-Petzold and Adolf Weber, as a duet, in Basel on 23 January 1883.

Varied strophic; A A B B A' A". Stanzas 1 and 2 are set to the same music, as are stanzas 3 and 4, the two settings being related by their phrase structure and some rhythmic correspondences. Stanza 5 has the same melody as 1 and 2 but a different accompaniment, and stanza 6 is an expanded variation in the major of the same music.

The text is from the Kretzschmer-Zuccalmaglio collection *Deutsche Volkslieder mit ihren Original-Weisen* (Berlin, 1838–40). Brahms had already made an arrangement of the supposed folk song that would be published in 1894 as No. 4 of the forty-nine *Deutsche Volkslieder*, but it is likely that the text, and virtually certain that the melody, had been subjected to Zuccalmaglio's usual tampering. In the forty-nine *Deutsche Volkslieder* version, the second verse retains Zuccalmaglio's fourth line, "Das kann ich an dir wohl spüren" (I can tell it by looking at you); for the Op. 84 setting, Brahms changed the line to the less accusatory "Das hab' ich wohl vernommen" (That have I heard from good sources). The third verse has "und glaub' es mir nicht" in the *Volkslieder*, but "und glaub' es nur nicht" in Op. 84. Brahms added the designations "Er" and "Sie."

The setting has the same meter and phrase structure as the folk-song arrangement, including the plaintive expansion of the last phrase to five measures. Both have a section with a contrasting accompaniment in flowing sixteenth notes, but the insertion of secondary material, the changing tempo, the melodic use of diminished and augmented intervals, and especially the developmental concluding section with its optional additional voice, all combine to position the song nearer to dramatic *scena* than to folk song style.

The use of rhythm is particularly imaginative. The right hand's rest-isolated, gasping rhythmic figure imbues the opening pair of strophes with unrest. As the tempo quickens for the contrasting strophes 3 and 4, the grouping in threes of the left hand's sixteenths in effect superimposes a slower duple meter upon the prevailing lively $\frac{3}{8}$, symbolizing the conflicting viewpoints of the lovers. As the voice enters, the process expands—the piano's hemiola, which is temporarily dropped near the end of the second phrase but reappears for the fourth, implies $\frac{3}{4}$ at half the speed of the voice. In strophe 5, a left-hand figure of three sixteenth notes begins and ends off the beat, increasing the agitation, but for the transition to strophe 6, it shifts reassuringly onto the beat, heralding the coming rapprochement. Another metaphorical use of metric duality occurs near the end of the song: at the words "komm' du zu mir, ich komme zu dir" and again at their repetition, the left hand suggests duple meter and the right hand imitates the vocal melody by inversion (first following, later leading). These devices emphasize the individuals' separateness, but all of the musical elements coalesce as the conflict is resolved with the words "wir bleiben une Beiden getreue."

In her letter of 24 July 1882 from Graz, Elisabet von Herzogenberg wrote that she found *Spannung* "strangely touching. 'Du sollst mir Antwort geben, mein Engel' is so urgent, so sweetly persuasive—indeed, it goes straight to my heart."

SIX LIEDER, OP. 85

Sechs Lieder für eine Stimme mit Begleitung des Pianoforte von Johannes Brahms (Six Songs for Solo Voice with Piano Accompaniment by Johannes Brahms), Op. 85. Published in July 1882 by N. Simrock in Berlin; publication number 8299.

The ordering juxtaposes settings of two related Heine texts (further integrated by their shared musical materials), two Kapper folk-song translations, and single poems by Geibel and Lemcke.

Sommerabend, Op. 85/1 (Summer Evening)

Text by Heinrich Heine (1797–1856)

Dämmernd liegt der Sommerabend
Über Wald und grünen Wiesen;
Gold'ner Mond im blauen Himmel
Strahlt herunter, duftig labend.

An dem Bache zirpt die Grille,
Und es regt sich in dem Wasser,
Und der Wand'rer hört ein Plätschern
Und ein Atmen in der Stille.

Dorten, an dem Bach alleine,
Badet sich die schöne Elfe;
Arm und Nacken, weiß und lieblich,
Schimmern in dem Mondenscheine.

The summer evening dusk lies over forest and green meadows; the golden moon in the blue sky shines down, fragrantly and refreshingly.

By the brook the cricket chirps, and there is a stirring in the water; and the traveler hears a splashing and a respiration in the silence.

There, alone by the brook, the beautiful fairy is bathing; her arms and neck, white and lovely, gleam in the moonlight.

Composed in Pörtschach in May 1878.
First performed by Lenar Bolzani on 4 February 1896 in Vienna.

Varied strophic; A B A.

The poem was first published in 1826 in *Reisebilder von Heinrich Heine*, then included as No. 85 of the cycle *Heimkehr* in the *Buch der Lieder* (1826/27). Brahms owned Heine's *Sämliche Werke* (Hamburg, 1861–84).

The evocative text creates a mood of hushed serenity through images of healing moonlight, dark woods and quiet water, and the magical vision of a solitary sprite bathing. Brahms's nocturnal setting, with its *sempre pianissimi* and its pulsating sustained afterbeats, matches it perfectly.

Two quiet long-held chords, tonally equivocal, set the song in motion. The principal strophe is a languidly sensuous duet between the vocal melody, which begins with falling triad outlines, and the piano's twining countermelody, whose phrases begin with a counterbalancing rising arpeggio. The setting of the last couplet is stretched to six measures from the expected four by the elongation of the final four syllables; the internal phrase structure is ambiguous—here it divides 3 + 3, but in the third strophe repetition it falls 2 + 4.

The contrasting melody of the second strophe is developed from a motive in the piano's countermelody in the first strophe, which appears first in m. 4 and more frequently in the third and fourth phrases. The prevailing pattern of two-measure phrases with a culminating expansion (though slight) is retained. Unlike the principal strophe, the second is modulatory, passing through D minor and G minor to end on the dominant of F minor (low key, B, E, and D), which makes possible the re-sounding of the two harmonies that began the song, with poignant long appoggiaturas superimposed, as transition to the third strophe.

The vocal melody returns exactly as before, but the piano's countermelody appears an octave higher in the right hand, where it assumes added importance, sometimes crossing over to sound higher than the voice. The left hand of the accompaniment is assigned a new figure of rocking, noncontinuous triplets, which Brahms seemed to associate with quietude or contentment.

In the postlude, the slow arpeggios of dream rise through tender seventh-chord harmonies, while the melody recalls the lingering appoggiaturas of the earlier interlude before transferring their rhythm to the final cadence in a low register.

Mondenschein, Op. 85/2 (Moonlight)

Text by Heinrich Heine (1797–1856)

Nacht liegt auf den fremden Wegen,
Krankes Herz und müde Glieder;—

Ach, da fließt, wie stiller Segen,
Süßer Mond, dein Licht hernieder;

Süßer Mond, mit deinen Strahlen
Scheuchest du das nächt'ge Grauen;
Es zerrinnen meine Qualen,
Und die Augen übertauen.

Night lies on the unfamiliar paths; a sick heart and weary limbs; ah, then,
like a silent blessing, your light pours down, sweet moon; sweet moon, with
your rays you dispel the horror of night; my torments melt away and my eyes
run over with tears.

Composed in Pörtschach in May 1878.
The first performance is not documented.
Through-composed.
The poem first appeared in *Rheinische Flora*, No. 12 (20 January 1825),
and was later included as No. 86 of the cycle *Heimkehr* in the *Buch der
Lieder* (1826/27).

The song is meant to be paired with the preceding "Sommerabend," with
which it shares both musical material and the central image of moonlight as
assuager. The two texts are found in succession in *Heimkehr*; Brahms's
treatment dramatizes their kinship. Together the two songs in effect constitute a rondo with two episodes and a coda.

Over the piano's slow descent by thirds of octaves a third apart—a motive
that in bare unison octaves often represented death for Brahms—the voice,
without introduction, begins a despairing nine-measure quasi-recitative.
Following the sustained major-mode ending of "Sommerabend," the effect
of the entrance on the minor third is desolate. There are three freely
sequential phrases: the first begins in the tonic minor and moves to the
submediant, which is retained for the second; the third shifts enharmonically to the home key's relative minor, in which key the voice cries out
agonizingly in the only *forte* of the two songs. The vocal line's closing phrase
is greatly elongated and overlaps the piano's astonishing recollection of
the harmonies and appoggiaturas from mm. 23–24 and 34–35 of the preceding song.

There then follows an exact restatement of the vocal melody of the earlier
song's principal strophe, to which are set the last two lines of the poem's verse
1 and the first two of verse 2. The piano's countermelody, *dolcissimo*, is
placed yet another octave higher than before, where it sounds above the voice
almost constantly. The left hand's sustained afterbeats evoke those of the
former song, but their contour inverts the rise and fall of the right hand's line.
As the strophe nears its end, the texture thins, the afterbeat line becomes
fragmented, the dominant pedal over which the harmonies have drifted is

abandoned, and the voice and piano resolve together on the tonic pitch, unharmonized.

The poem's closing lines are set to a moving coda-like section that slows and softens continuously to the end. The vocal melody arches over affective harmonies, its cadences marked by melting appoggiaturas; the throbbing afterbeats yield to the discontinuous arpeggiated triplets that connote contentment; the piano has an elegant variant of the countermelody's initial rise and curve, compressed into a single octave and divided between two contrapuntal voices. The resulting figure ascends by fourths as the voice sings its concluding phrases; as postlude, its second half falls quickly by fifths over a tonic pedal. Finally in the low register are heard, like a memory, the two motto-like chords that began the former song. As they resolve to the long-delayed tonic harmony, all earthly care seems to dissolve like the poet's torment.

Mädchenlied, Op. 85/3 (Girl's Song)

Translated from the Serbian by Siegfried Kapper
(Czech, 1821–1879)

Ach, und du mein kühles Wasser!
Ach, und du mein rotes Röslein!
Was erblühst du mir so frühe?
Hab' ja nicht, für wen dich pflücken!
Pflück' ich dich für meine Mutter?
Keine Mutter hab' ich, Waise!
Pflück' ich dich für meine Schwester?
Ei doch, längst vermählet ist sie!
Pflück ich dich für meinen Brüder?
Ist gezogen in die Feldschlacht!
Pflück' ich dich für den Geliebten?
Fern, ach, weilet der Geliebte!
Jenseit dreier grünen Berge,
Jenseit dreier kühlen Wasser!

Ah, my cool river! Ah, my red rose! Why are you blooming so early? I have no one to give you to if I pick you!
Shall I pick you for my mother? I am an orphan and have no mother!
Shall I pick you for my sister? No, she got married long ago!
Shall I pick you for my brother? He has gone off to the battlefield!
Shall I pick you for my sweetheart? Ah, my sweetheart is far away from here! Across three green mountains, across three cool rivers!

Composed in Pörtschach in May 1878.

First performed by Gustav Walter and Brahms on 23 February 1883 at the Saal Bösendorfer in Vienna.

Strophic, with a sung coda based on the music of the introduction and interlude.

The text is from Kapper's *Gesänge der Serben* (Leipzig, 1852), where it is entitled "Röslein, was erblühst du mir so frühe." The maiden of the poem touchingly expresses her loneliness to a red rose, having no one for whom to pick it.

Until its final measures, the song is in $\frac{5}{4}$ meter, subdivided 3 + 2. The mournful introduction establishes the pattern of like-rhythmed one-measure phrases of small range. Its harmonies digress to the relative major, then return to the tonic minor via the subdominant—the vocal strophe's tonal design in miniature.

The first two vocal phrases differ only in their cadences, the former ending on the dominant, the latter on the dominant of the relative major. The dramatic crux of the strophe is the vocal line's octave leap upward (defining both extremes of its range) to begin the third phrase, where the harmonies briefly establish the subdominant before recalling the preceding cadence chords. The fourth phrase begins a step lower than the third, but with a sharp dissonance, revealing the anguish that will gradually abate as the phrase proceeds. In the third strophe, each of these last two phrases is marked with a *rinforzando*, underlining that the primary cause of the girl's pain is the absence of her sweetheart.

As interlude between the strophes, the melody of the introduction returns, doubled in sixths as before, but with a different, less-assured accompaniment. Unlike the earlier on-beat rising triplets with their suggestion of drone, the triplets, now connected by little melodic descents, begin after the beat, and the figure ends with a resigned falling fifth in even eighths. The coda uses both versions: first the poem's closing lines are sung to the melody of the interlude, then the last line is repeated to a wistful new melody that floats over the piano's *pianissimo* remembrance of the introduction. Longer note values and the change to $\frac{6}{4}$ lend gravity to the concluding vocal phrase. The piano's additional rests heighten the sense of loss, and its resigned echo of the girl's last word dramatizes her sadness.

Time has blunted the unique character of Serbian folk music by exposing it to various cultural influences, but ethnomusicological studies in the twentieth century have shown that autochthonous Serbo-Croation melodies characteristically are heterometric, lack upbeats, are of narrow range, and may enlarge their structures by the (sometimes varied) repetition of phrases, either at pitch or sequential. Brahms was always more interested in the spirit of folk song than in its authenticity, and he preferred to suggest, rather than to imitate, ethnicity. It is therefore likely that his setting was intended to evoke a generalized folkloric feeling, and that its identifiably Serbian characteristics result not from intent but from a discriminating aural imagination and felicitous coincidence.

Ade!, Op. 85/4 (Goodbye!)

Translated from the Bohemian by Siegfried Kapper
(Czech, 1821–1879)

> Wie schienen die Sternlein so hell, so hell
> Herab von der Himmelshöh'!
> Zwei Liebende standen auf der Schwell',
> Ach, Hand in Hand: "Ade!"

> Die Blümlein weinten auf Flur und Steg,
> Sie fühlten der Liebenden Weh',
> Die standen traurig am Scheideweg,
> Ach, Herz an Herz: "Ade!"

> Die Lüfte durchrauschen die Waldesruh',
> Aus dem Tal und von der Höh'
> Weh'n zwei weiße Tücher einander zu:
> "Ade, ade, ade!"

How brightly, how brightly the little stars shone down from the heights of heaven! Two lovers stood in the doorway, alas, hand in hand: "Goodbye!"

The little flowers were weeping in the meadow and on the path; they felt the sorrow of the lovers who stood sadly at the crossroads, alas, heart by heart: "Goodbye!"

The winds rustle through the silence of the forest; from the valley and from the mountaintop two white handkerchiefs wave toward each other: "Goodbye! Goodbye! Goodbye!"

Probably begun in Pörtschach during summer 1877 and completed in Vienna in early 1882.

The first performance is not documented.

Strophic; a rhythmic alteration in the third strophe accommodates the text's run-on connection of lines 2 and 3.

The poem appears in Kapper's *Slawische Melodien* (Leipzig, 1844). Its subject is the sadness arising from the reluctant parting of two lovers.

The melodies of Bohemian folk song have been strongly influenced by the music of western Europe, particularly instrumental dance music. Regular four-measure phrase construction, definite tonality, repeated rhythmic patterns, and triad outlines are characteristic and, perhaps by coincidence, are features of Brahms's setting as well. The strophic formal design and the almost-pentatonic melody also are evocative of folk song, but the elaborate rippling accompaniment and the last line's codalike repetition in the major both lean toward art music.

The piano's notated decreasing activity as the strophe nears its end is particularly noteworthy. In m. 13, the grouping of the right hand's six sixteenths changes from implied twos to implied threes; the implication is confirmed four measures later when the left hand abandons its triplet eighths for a rhythmic figure in normal eighths and quarters over a sustained bass, and the right hand's double-stemming highlights a melody in even eighth notes. In m. 19 the sixteenth notes are abandoned entirely, and the melodic motion slows to harmonized quarters in quasi-imitation of the preceding eighths.

The two options for the vocal ending are equally satisfying but different in effect—the lower seems to emphasize the sorrow of the situation, while the higher points up the phrase's function as major-mode echo. The singer's dramatic conviction and individual voice type should be the bases for choice. One reasonable possibility is to end the first two strophes low but the third high to illustrate the echoing farewells of the text.

Frühlingslied, Op. 85/5 (Spring Song)

Text by Emanuel Geibel (1815–1884)

Mit geheimnisvollen Düften
Grüßt vom Hang der Wald mich schon,
Über mir in hohen Lüften
Schwebt der erste Lerchenton.

In den süßen Laut versunken
Wall' ich hin durch's Saatgefild,
Das noch halb vom Schlummer trunken
Sanft dem Licht entgegenschwillt.

Welch' ein Sehnen! welch' ein Träumen!
Ach, du möchtest vor'm Verglüh'n,
Mit den Blumen, mit den Bäumen,
Altes Herz, noch einmal blüh'n.

With mysterious fragrances the forest already greets me from the slope; above me, high in the sky soars the first note of the lark.

Enraptured by that sweet sound, I wander through the field of grain that, still half dazed with slumber, gently swells toward the daylight.

What a yearning! What a dreaming! Ah, before you burn out, old heart of mine, you would like to blossom one more time with the flowers, with the trees.

Composed in March 1878 in Vienna.

The first performance is not documented.

Varied strophic; A B A, with an extension at the end.

The text is from a section called "Lieder aus alter und neuer Zeit" in the *Spätherbstblätter*. Surrounded by signs of spring's return, the poet yearns for his own reflowering.

From its ecstatic rising-seventh beginning, the vocal melody swoops and soars in ardent arcs, culminating in the long quarter-note descent (mm. 7–8) from the song's highest pitch on "Lüften." The intervals that begin the second four-measure phrase furnish the pattern from which the contrasting strophe derives its first two phrases; its last two rise slowly from a relatively static beginning, suggesting the newly burgeoning grain's stretching upward toward the light. At the end of the third strophe, the climactic descent in quarter notes (mm. 26–27) is echoed by the piano and reechoed in modified augmentation by the voice, creating, in combination with the repetition of the poem's last line, a multiple metaphor for "noch einmal blüh'n."

The song takes on exuberance from the piano's nearly constant triplets; restlessness from the right hand's conflicting, panting eighth-note figures; and emotional intensity from the frequent, often surprising, changes of harmony. The shift of the right hand's eighth notes onto the beat in m. 5 begins a terraced lessening of their agitating effect, and they disappear entirely four measures later. Meanwhile a hovering new melodic figure emerges—an upper pedal activated by dotted rhythms and neighboring-tone alternations. Here and in the interlude to come (mm. 9–10), after a digression to double the vocal line in thirds, it seems to represent the forest's elusive aromas; the same figure at higher pitches depicts the song of the lark in the succeeding strophe. An oscillating wide-interval variant lags sleepily behind the beat in mm. 15–18, illustrating the text.

At the *animato* in m. 19, the afterbeat passage is crowned by a series of chords that descend *forte* over dominant harmony; they give way in the next measure to breathless upward-resolving dissonances as the returning tonic heralds the start of the third strophe. At the end of the song, the rising-dissonance figure reappears, expanded, in the rapturous piano postlude, like an irrepressible eruption of hopeful longing.

The dramatic impact of the song will be enhanced if performers observe the opening *mezza voce* and withhold their *forte* until the final strophe, as indicated.

In Waldeseinsamkeit, Op. 85/6
(In the Loneliness of the Forest)

Text by Karl Lemcke (1831–1913)

Ich saß zu deinen füßen
In Waldeseinsamkeit;
Windesatmen, Sehnen
Ging durch die Wipfel breit.

In stummem Ringen senkt' ich
Das Haupt in deinen Schoß,

Und meine bebenden Hände
Um deine Knie ich schloß.

Die Sonne ging hinunter,
Der Tag verglühte all,
Ferne, ferne, ferne
Sang eine Nachtigall.

I sat at your feet in the loneliness of the forest; the breathing of the wind, and a yearning, stirred the treetops all around.

In silent struggle I laid my head in your lap and closed my trembling hands around your knee.

The sun went down, the daylight vanished completely; far away, far away, far away a nightingale sang.

Composed in May 1878 in Pörtschach.

First performed on 23 February 1883 in Vienna's Bösendorfer Hall by Gustav Walter with Brahms at the piano.

Through-composed, with a partial return at the third verse.

The text is from Lemcke's *Lieder und Gedichte* (Hamburg, 1861); Brahms supplied the title.

One would be hard-pressed to invent an image more representative of the Romantic movement's mystic bond with nature than that of Lemcke's lovers in the lonely forest at twilight along with the sound of a distant nightingale. The poem verges on sentimentality, but Brahms's haunting setting ennobles it by its sincerity and depth of feeling. Elisabet von Herzogenberg, in her letter of 24 July 1882, called the song "a glorious thing, full of lofty emotion, and yet so human in its appeal, born as it is of deep personal experience. The man who can listen to it dry-eyed is surely past saving!"

The opening measures establish an almost tangible sense of stillness. The harmonies, bound by pedal points, move reluctantly; the vocal line languidly repeats an expansive tonic-triad outline, varying its embellishment; eighth notes quietly begin to stir, like leaves in the wind-ruffled treetops; canonic echoes of the vocal melody surface and recede in the flow of the accompaniment.

But emotion begins to intensify as the minor mode intrudes and the eighth notes' rustling yields to the sighing of dissonances and their resolution. The vocal line quickly spans a minor ninth to rise to the high note of "Sehnen" and falls a diminished seventh later in the phrase, suggesting the pain caused by the mounting desire.

The second verse's "silent struggle" brings increasing agitation. The vocal line introduces anxious slurred pairs of eighth notes and superimposes its own dissonances in aching quarter notes over those ongoing in the piano's eighths. The emotional tension reaches a climax with the third line, for which the unstable tonality settles temporarily in the key of the minor's mediant and the vocal line doubles its declamation speed, to eighth notes with

gasping eighth rests, inserting a single triplet for the onomatopoeic "bebenden." The bass's half-step descent for the fourth line initiates a return to
tranquillity; it is continued by the lowered pitch of the repetition of the third
line and confirmed by the gradual relaxation of rhythmic activity into the
return of the opening music.

The sun sets and night falls to a hushed restatement of the first phrase.
Constantly softer and slower, the passage that follows is among the most exquisite in all of art song. The word "ferne" is sung and repeated to a plaintive
rising third, which the piano inverts in diminution with echoes an octave
higher in the minor mode, like reverberations distorted by distance. (When
the complete opus is sung, an additional layer of association accrues from
the use of the same pitches for the major/minor reiterations of "ferne" here
as for those of "ade!" in the fourth song.) The third "ferne" begins a half step
lower; reharmonized, it leads to the key of the lowered submediant, whose
foreignness combines with the left hand's rising arpeggios to bathe the scene
in a dreamlike haze. The high pitch of "sang" and the triadic descent of
"Nachtigall" somehow recall the phrase to which "Sehnen" was sung earlier,
and the poignancy of the moment is heightened by that added resonance.
The return of the rising third to conclude the lower repetition of the line
hints that longing persists. (Use the lower ending only if absolutely necessary.) A new flowing countermelody in the piano is tinged with minor-mode
coloration, contributing to the bittersweet aura that remains as the last
chords die away.

SIX LIEDER FOR LOW VOICE, OP. 86

Sechs Lieder für eine Tiefere Stimme mit Begleitung des Pianoforte von Johannes Brahms (Six Songs for Low Voice with Piano Accompaniment by Johannes Brahms), Op. 86. Published in July 1882 by N. Simrock in Berlin; publication number 8300.

Despite the diversity of texts, the general designation "for low voice" and the contrasting moods that result from the ordering suggest that Brahms regarded the group of songs as an entity. His continual striving toward a more detailed synthesis of music and text led him increasingly toward a blurring of the traditional distinctions between formal types—a feature that is characteristic to some extent of all six.

Therese, Op. 86/1

Text by Gottfried Keller (Swiss, 1819–1890)

> Du milchjunger Knabe,
> Wie schaust du mich an?
> Was haben deine Augen
> Für eine Frage getan!
>
> Alle Ratsherrn in der Stadt
> Und alle Weisen der Welt
> Bleiben stumm auf die Frage,
> Die deine Augen gestellt!
>
> Eine Meermuschel liegt
> Auf dem Schrank meiner Bas':
> Da halte dein Ohr d'ran,
> Dann hörst du etwas!

You young, young boy, what way is that to look at me? What a question your eyes asked!

261

All the councillors in the town and all the wise men in the world would remain silent if asked the question your eyes asked!
There is a seashell on my cousin's cabinet: put your ear to it, and you will hear something!

Composed in Pörtschach in May 1878.

First performed on 23 February 1883 by Gustav Walter and Brahms on a Brahms-Schubert program in Vienna.

Through-composed, with strophic elements; the first two verses are set to the same vocal melody, but the accompaniment differs.

The text is found in Keller's *Neuere Gedichte* (Brunswick, 1851), where it forms part of the cycle *Von Weibern: Alte Lieder: 1846*. The subject of the set is the love of an inexperienced young man for a more mature women, who is beautiful but spoiled. At first she scornfully rejects his advances; later she tries to rekindle the affair, but he no longer loves her. "Therese" appears in the context of his still-active desire. Later in his life, Keller considerably reworked the poem's third stanza.

Brahms's setting explores both the poem's directness and its obscurity, and it combines disparate elements into an affecting small masterpiece.

In the introduction the stepwise melody is animated by triplets, and its cadence is repeated twice; each repetition begins with a higher pitch, suggesting the youth's mounting ardor, and the last broadens to a pensive pause.

The vocal melody of the first two verses is almost like a folk song in its simplicity, though it ends on an enigmatic prolonged dominant of the relative minor. The piano provides amiable counterpoint, belying the text's reproving tone.

For the third verse, there is an unexpected shift to the submediant major, which seems tinged with enchantment. Hushed and sustained, the music of the introduction returns in the piano in a new chordal guise. First the bass line, later, the melody, sounds after the beat. A new, wider-ranging vocal line soon trails away to entranced near-recitative at "Da halte dein Ohr d'ran"; the piano's afterbeats become a suspended, expectant throbbing, and a mysterious chromatic bass line rises and recedes like a wave in some distant ocean. Seven measures before the end of the song, all the strands meet on the dominant of the home key. The final vocal phrase then recalls the falling octave and rising triad of this verse's opening, and the piano expressively restates the introduction in its chordal version, now extended to become a short postlude, filled with longing.

An exchange in the Brahms-Herzogenberg correspondence reveals that Brahms at one point favored a melody for the first and second verses that bore more resemblance to that of the third. In April of 1882, while the song was being prepared for publication, he wrote from Vienna:

I hope you still have my song, *Therese*? I should be particularly pleased if you could honestly give your approval to the following version:

and

One version is as old as the other, though not, perhaps so simple to sing. But although this one has been more generally copied and sung, I cannot get used to it, and am puzzled to know what to do.

Sing the song through again, both of you, and let the poor youth languish at the piano meanwhile; then send me a line.

Elisabet replied from Leipzig on 26 April 1882:

With the best will in the world, I cannot take to the old-new version, and Heinrich feels the same about it. I should feel quite sad if you insisted on it. The simpler form

seems to me to go much better with the counterpoint in the piano than the other jagged version, and to be much more in keeping with the song, where clear diction matters far more than vocal display. Just try singing to yourself, in the light manner that suits the piece, that jump to the octave below! Is it not clumsy compared with the simple repetition of the three notes?

I do beg of you don't meddle with the dear little song any more, but rest satisfied with the simpler version.

Brahms had already sent a request to his copyist in Berlin to change the vocal part, but he rescinded it immediately upon his receipt of Elisabet's objection.

Feldeinsamkeit, Op. 86/2 (The Loneliness of the Field)

Text by Hermann Allmers (1821–1902)

Ich ruhe still im hohen grünen Gras
Und sende lange meinen Blick nach oben,

Von Grillen rings umschwirrt ohn' Unterlaß,
Von Himmelsbläue wundersam umwoben.

Die schönen weißen Wolken zieh'n dahin
Durch's tiefe Blau, wie schöne stille Träume;
Mir ist, als ob ich längst gestorben bin
Und ziehe selig mit durch ew'ge Räume.

I lie quietly in the high green grass and gaze fixedly upward; crickets chirp around me without interruption; the blue of the sky weaves around me wondrously.

The beautiful white clouds pass by through the deep blue like beautiful quiet dreams; I feel as if I had died long ago and was passing blessedly along with them through eternal space.

Probably composed in May 1879.

First performed by Gustav Walter and Brahms on 23 February 1883 in Vienna.

Modified strophic; the two strophes begin and end alike, but the settings of the intervening lines differ.

Allmers's *Dichtungen* (Bremen, 1860) is the source of the text. There, line 1 reads "Ich liege still"; line 5, "Und schöne weiße Wolken."

The poem epitomizes Romanticism's fundamental striving toward spiritual union with nature. Brahms interprets its images with almost pictorial vividness. In this splendid song, the music and the verses are inseparably fused.

The contemplative, gently arching vocal line stresses ascents in each strophe's first line, descents in the third. Irregularity of phrase length and a leisurely expansion at the end of each half-strophe contribute to the song's aura of timelessness.

The musical texture is grounded in the quiet throbbing of the piano's bass pedal points. Static chords float above, continually fluctuating like the changing cloud shapes the poet watches so raptly. In the introduction and interlude, rootless right-hand chords drift upward, their melody anticipating the vocal line's beginning; later, as postlude, they seem to symbolize the soul's passage into eternity.

Snatches of canonic imitation between the piano's tenor and bass near the end of the strophe illustrate "unwoben" in the first and "ziehe mit" in the second. "Wie schöne stille Träume" elicits a tinge of submediant harmony and a chromatic bass line that slowly climbs from tonic to dominant. The notion of death is depicted in Brahms's usual unison octaves descending in thirds; the texture change, the minor-mode coloration, and the stretching of "gestorben bin" highlight the phrase, dramatizing its function as the psychological turning point of the song.

Of the melody that sets the fourth line of each verse, Elisabet von Herzogenberg wrote (26 April 1882) that "it tears at my very heartstrings."

Nachtwandler, Op. 86/3 (Sleepwalker)

Text by Max Kalbeck (1850–1921)

Störe nicht den leisen Schlummer
Dess', den lind ein Traum umfangen!
Laß ihm seinen süßen Kummer!
Ihm sein schmerzliches Verlangen!

Sorgen und Gefahren drohen,
Aber keine wird ihn schrecken,
Kommst du nicht, den Schlafesfrohen
Durch ein hartes Wort zu wecken.

Still in seinen Traum versunken
Geht er über Abgrundtiefen
Wie vom Licht des Vollmonds trunken,
Weh' den Lippen, die ihn riefen!

Do not disturb the quiet slumber of one who is gently embraced by a dream!
Leave him his sweet anxiety, his painful longing!
Cares and dangers threaten, but none of them will frighten him, if you avoid
awakening by some rough word the man who is so happy in his sleep.
Similarly lost in his dream, he walks over yawning chasms as if intoxicated
by the light of the full moon; woe to the lips that would call out to him!

The date of composition is uncertain, probably 1877.

The first performance was given on 23 February 1883 on a Brahms-Schubert program in Vienna by the tenor Gustav Walter, with Brahms at the piano.

A A B; the first two stanzas are set to the same music, the third to a variant in which the voice overlaps the piano interlude.

The text was printed in the section "Aus Heimat und Fremde" of Kalbeck's collection *Nächte* (Hirschberg, 1878), but Brahms had received it earlier in manuscript.

The poem somewhat obscurely compares a lover to a sleepwalker, oblivious of the dangers to which he is exposed so long as he is not awakened. The setting goes far beyond that image to create a dreamy drifting between the real and the unreal, the conscious and the subconscious, which is unique among Brahms's songs.

The equivocal tone is set immediately by the introduction's Mahlerian thirds and sixths, vacillating between major and minor. The rhythms lack energy; the accompaniment's sustained afterbeats suggest motion but not direction.

The marvelous bass line quietly walks in deliberate quarters and half notes, which ascend and descend without obvious goal. At times it doubles the voice to symbolize isolation; at others the two lines diverge like the twin states of dreaming and waking. Sometimes the bass moves in support of the melody, sometimes it seems to hover protectingly.

Over the music of the piano interlude, the third stanza begins, as though in a trance, in a dazed murmur of new melody. The afterbeats move to the left hand as low bass notes and irresolute harmonies evoke both the yawning chasms of the text and the depth of the subconscious. At last the piano regains familiar territory—the music that ended the other strophes. The voice, however, has a new final phrase that climbs a full octave before trailing off to end, like the others, indecisively on a dominant unresolved (until later) by the accompaniment.

As postlude, the piano repeats the music of the introduction, returning, like the undisturbed somnambulist, to the same safe place from which the journey began.

Über die Heide, Op. 86/4 (Over the Heath)

Text by Theodor Storm (1817–1888)

Über die Heide hallet mein Schritt;
Dumpf aus der Erde wandert es mit.

Herbst ist gekommen, Frühling ist weit—
Gab es denn einmal selige Zeit?

Brauende Nebel geisten umher,
Schwarz ist das Kraut und der Himmel so leer.

Wär' ich nur hier nicht gegangen im Mai!
Leben und Liebe—wie flog es vorbei!

Over the heath my step resounds; a muffled echo from the earth follows me.
Autumn has come, spring is far away; was there really once a happy time?
Steaming mists encircle me like ghosts; the vegetation is black and the sky so empty.
If only I hadn't walked here in May! Life and love—how they flew by!

The date of composition is unknown.

The first performance is undocumented.

Varied strophic; A A B A'.

The text appears in Vol. 7 of Storm's *Gesammelte Schriften* (Brunswick, 1868–89).

The setting is dominated by stark octaves in the bass that recur throughout, relieved only by a sighing falling third (in answer to the same figure in the right hand) that punctuates the end of the strophe. The somber sound evokes not only the traveler's tread and his melancholy but also the bleak, deserted landscape with its rising mists and frost-blackened vegetation.

The octaves' predominant motive is a scalewise third, which also dominates the vocal line. Either rising or falling, it appears twice in each phrase of the principal strophe; extended, and with skips interposed, it makes up the contrasting third strophe as well.

In the second strophe, the right hand's staccato afterbeats are shifted to the second half of the bar; there, their melodic imitations of the bass first duplicate, then invert, the segment of the vocal line they accompany, and finally double it in thirds. The resulting emotional intensification is accelerated in the succeeding section, where the change from short to sustained afterbeats and the quasi-sequential structure combine to build quickly to a climax in m. 15. The elongated repetition of the verse's second line of text is particularly effective—the larger rhythmic values suggest the emptiness to which the text refers, and the long descending line is like a wail of grief. The fourth strophe combines the afterbeat patterns of strophes 1 and 2. The typical broadening of the final phrase is achieved by stretching the word "Liebe," which makes necessary the insertion of a $\frac{9}{8}$ measure.

The postlude extends and fills the sighing-third motive that concludes the strophe, clarifying its kinship to the same interval in the initial bass octaves. At the very end, the scalewise third is heard both ascending in the right hand and descending in the left as the lonely wayfarer disappears into the distance.

The conciseness and structural economy that are so striking here increasingly characterize Brahms's later songs.

Versunken, Op. 86/5 (Enraptured)

Text by Felix Schumann (1854–1879)

> Es brausen der Liebe Wogen
> Und schäumen mir um das Herz;
> Zwei tiefe Augen zogen
> Mich mächtig niederwärts.
>
> Mich lockte der Nixen Gemunkel,
> Die wunderliebliche Mär',
> Als ob die Erde dunkel
> Und leuchtend die Tiefe wär'!
>
> Als würde die seligste Ferne
> Dort unten reizende Näh',
> Als könnt' ich des Himmels Sterne
> Dort greifen in blauer See.

Nun brausen und schäumen die Wogen
Und hüllen mich allwärts ein,
Es schimmert in Regenbogen
Die Welt von ferne herein.

The waves of love rage and foam about my heart; two deep eyes drew me powerfully downward.

I was lured by the whispers of the water sprites, by their miraculously lovely narrative, as if the earth were dark and the watery deeps were aglow with light.

As if down there the most blissful distant things became alluringly near, as if I could grasp the stars of the sky there in the blue sea.

Now, the waves rage and foam and envelop me all around; from afar off the world sends gleams down to me in the rainbows.

Composed in May 1878 in Pörtschach.

The first performance is not documented.

Varied strophic; verses 1 and 4 are set to the same music, as are, after their first four measures, verses 2 and 3.

The unpublished poem in manuscript had been sent to Brahms by Clara Schumann. (See the notes to "Junge Lieder I," Op. 63/5.)

The central image of engulfment in a stormy sea of passion seems a bit meager to warrant the young poet's enthusiastic treatment of it, but it provided Brahms with the germ of an effective song.

The form of the setting is dictated by that of the poem: both verses 1 and 4 begin with references to the waves' "raging and foaming" and end with suggestions of downward movement; verses 2 and 3 are "as if" constructions, primarily concerned with the contrasting of darkness with light.

The song is set in motion by two impetuous chords in the piano, like a flash of realization. The beginning accompaniment figure in sixteenth notes shares its contour with that of the opening vocal phrase in eighths. The text's first pair of lines is set to two breathless two-measure phrases, rapid-moving and wide-ranging. The second pair, joined, stretch to five measures, their melody inclining ever-downward; harmonic colorations from the minor and three melodic tritones lend poignancy, and the right hand's changing distribution of sixteenth notes hints at a conflicting cross rhythm.

The contrasting middle section sets verses 2 and 3 as two somewhat dissimilar strophes. They both begin in the key of the submediant—minor for verse 2, major (notated enharmonically) for verse 3—before continuing in the subdominant, signaling that their subject matter originates in the realm of imagination. The initial phrases of both, though different, adopt the rhythm of the first strophe's opening. Throughout the entire section, the odd-numbered lines are set syllabically in two-bar phrases, but the even-numbered ones are handled more freely and extended to three measures. In the third and fourth phrases (common to both strophes) the vocal and bass lines are doubled in *pianissimo* octaves before they diverge in a bright *forte*, dramatically highlighting the text's points of contrast. Their concluding lines are then repeated to new music, the final vocal cadence of verse 3 slightly altered.

The music of the first strophe returns for the fourth verse. In the postlude, the piano, reflecting the "rainbow" imagery of the final phrase, recalls its earlier wavelike accompaniment figure (in the vocal line's eighth-note rhythm and in octaves divided between the two hands on and after the beat) to outline a broad arch of melody that rises from the depths of the keyboard and returns, slowing and softening, and tinted affectingly by a lingering minor-major ambivalence.

Todessehnen, Op. 86/6 (Longing for Death)

Text by Max von Schenkendorf (1783–1817)

Ach, wer nimmt von meiner Seele
Die geheime, schwere Last,
Die, je mehr ich sie verhehle,
Immer mächtiger mich faßt?

Möchtest du nur endlich brechen,
Mein gequältes, banges Herz!
Findest hier mit deinen Schwächen,
Deiner Liebe, nichts als Schmerz.

Dort nur wirst du ganz genesen,
Wo der Sehnsucht nichts mehr fehlt,
Wo das schwesterliche Wesen
Deinem Wesen sich vermählt.

Hör' es, Vater in der Höhe,
Aus der Fremde fleht dein Kind:
Gib', daß er mich bald umwehe,
Deines Todes Lebenswind.

Daß er zu dem Stern mich hebe,
Wo man keine Trennung kennt,
Wo die Geistersprache Leben
Mit der Liebe Namen nennt.

Ah, who will take away from my soul the secret, heavy burden that, the more I conceal it, grips me more and more powerfully?

I wish you could finally break, my tortured, anxious heart! Here with your infirmities and your love, you find nothing but sorrow.

You will become completely well only there where nothing more is lacking to satisfy your yearning, where the sisterly being is wedded to your being.

Hear it, Father up above, Your child is weeping in a strange land: grant that the life-giving wind of Your death may soon waft around me.

That it may raise me to the star where separation is unknown, where the language of spirits calls life by the name of love.

Composed in May 1878 in Pörtschach.

The first performance is not documented.

Through-composed, with strophic elements; the common-time settings of verses 1 and 2 are similar, as are the settings of verses 4 and 5 in $\frac{3}{4}$ meter.

Schenkendorf's poem was first published in 1837, but dates from 1807.

Perhaps empathizing with the poet and his "secret, heavy burden" of unfulfilled yearning, Brahms composed a moving, large-scaled song of great power and beauty.

The dirgelike opening comprises two related but differing strophes in F♯ minor. The first comes to a cadence on the dominant; the second moves to the relative major, where it too closes on the dominant. In both cases, a long anguished dissonance in the bass undermines any sense of finality. The first four measures, which are common to both strophes, convey the idea of pain by means of recurring accented passing tones in the bass and dissonant harmonies on strong beats; the augmented triad on the downbeat of m. 2 is particularly telling, in part because Brahms used that sonority so rarely. In the remainder of strophe 1, sequences build quickly to the climactic repetitions of both motive and text at "immer mächtiger mich faßt"; the quieter equivalent segment of strophe 2 interrupts its chromatic melodic movement only to highlight "deiner Liebe."

The poem's third verse, in which death is contemplated as a welcome release from grief, serves as a transition from the earlier lament to the prayer that is to come, and Brahms sets it accordingly. After a hesitant, but decreasingly troubled, short interlude, the tempo brightens, like the poet's spirits. Accompanying afterbeats add emotional animation to mollifying A-major music. There is a modulation to F♯ major toward the end of the section, as the broadening vocal line and slowing harmonic rhythm herald the return to *Langsam*.

The splendid concluding portion balances the opening with an equivalent pair of strophes, akin, but identical only in their first halves. The earlier desperation is now exchanged for a joyous serenity that approaches spiritual ecstasy. (Neither that emotion nor the chromatic language in which it is expressed seems typically Brahmsian—one is likely to be reminded of Hugo Wolf.)

Along with its changed meter and mode, the piano interlude ushers in a new calm. The harmonic slowing that began at the end of verse 3 with the shift from quarters to half notes is carried a step further as the dotted half becomes the norm. A lazily rising figure in eighth notes replaces the preceding afterbeats, suggesting the dissipation of turmoil. The slow-moving chords (mm. 33–35) that emerge from the sustained dominant seventh seem to echo the vocal line's recently heard cadence before they evaporate into silence.

The floating unaccompanied entrance of the voice for the invocation "Hör' es" is only one of many noteworthy details: augmented-sixth resolution of dominant-seventh sonorities lends wondrous emphasis to "Todes" in the fourth verse and "Liebe" at the end of the fifth; the piano interlude between the strophes reflects on the vocal line's "Todes Lebenswind" (mm. 51–52) before proceeding; and "Geistersprache" in verse 5 elicits a spectral melodic mirroring in the bass. From that point onward, the right hand's eighth notes are grouped in threes instead of twos (even expanding to fours to accommodate the vocal line's hemiola at "Liebe" in the last phrase), implying yet greater serenity in the spirit world. In a characteristic broadening at the end, repetition of the last line is stretched from four to seven measures; the rapturous phrase that results is linked to the slowly abating postlude by the piano's *espressivo* evocation (mm. 77–80) of "Vater in der Höhe" from the beginning of the section. The singer should be aware that the piano's overlapping phrase postpones the song's climax and that the temptation to diminish as the vocal line turns downward for the cadence should therefore be resisted.

TWO GESÄNGE FOR ALTO VOICE WITH VIOLA, OP. 91

Zwei Gesänge für eine Altstimme mit Bratsche und Pianoforte von Johannes Brahms (Two Songs for Solo Alto Voice with Viola and Piano by Johannes Brahms), Op. 91. Published in December 1884 by N. Simrock in Berlin; publication number 8474.

The publication of the two songs was a well-intentioned but fruitless attempt by Brahms to reconcile the estranged Amalie and Joseph Joachim, at least on the concert stage. Amalie had separated from her husband at the time, his attempt to divorce her having failed, largely because of a letter in which Brahms appeared to support her side of the dispute. Her making the letter public caused a rift in the lifelong friendship of the two men that was never fully repaired.

Though Amalie sang the songs many times, including the first Viennese performance on 7 January 1886, it was never in collaboration with her husband; in the Vienna première, Joseph Hellmesberger played the viola part.

The Op. 91 songs are elegant studies in color, the timbre of the viola being subtly exploited for both its similarity to and its difference from that of the alto voice. The two are treated with equal importance, and their frequent and facile interchange of register and material is one of the songs' most engaging characteristics.

Finely shaded sonority and compositional refinement combine to enhance the meaning of the poetry, resulting in two of Brahms's greatest songs. Both are unusually extended, comparable in scale to instrumental slow movements.

Gestillte Sehnsucht, Op. 91/1 (Satisfied Longing)

Text by Friedrich Rückert (1788–1866)

In gold'nen Abendschein getauchet,
Wie feierlich die Wälder stehn!
In leise Stimmen der Vöglein hauchet
Des Abendwindes leises Weh'n.

Was lispeln die Winde, die Vögelein?
Sie lispeln die Welt in Schlummer ein.

Ihr Wünsche, die ihr stets euch reget
  Im Herzen sonder Rast und Ruh!
  Du Sehnen, das die Brust beweget,
  Wann ruhest du, wann schlummerst du?
  Beim Lispeln der Winde, der Vögelein,
  Ihr sehnenden Wünsche, wann schlaft ihr ein?

Was kommt gezogen auf Traumesflügeln?
Was weht mich an so bang, so hold?
Es kommt gezogen von fernen Hügeln,
Es kommt auf bebendem Sonnengold.
Wohl lispeln die Winde, die Vögelein:
Das Sehnen, das Sehnen, es schläft nicht ein.

Ach, wenn nicht mehr in gold'ne Fernen
  Mein Geist auf Traumgefieder eilt,
  Nicht mehr an ewig fernen Sternen
  Mit sehnendem Blick mein Auge weilt;
  Dann lispeln die Winde, die Vögelein
  Mit meinem Sehnen mein Leben ein.

Dipped in golden evening glow, how solemnly the forests stand! Mingled with the soft voices of the little birds is the soft breath of the evening wind. What are the winds and the little birds whispering? They are whispering the world into slumber.

You desires of mine, always stirring in my breast without letup! You longing of mine that makes my breast heave, when will *you* rest, when will *you* slumber? To the whispering of the winds and little birds, you longing desires, when will you fall asleep?

Ah, when my spirit no longer hastens toward golden faraway places on the wings of dreams, when my eyes no longer gaze at eternally distant stars with longing looks; then the winds and little birds will whisper my life away together with my longing.

Probably composed in the summer of 1884 in Mürzzuschlag.

A B A, with instrumental introduction, the melody of which is taken up by the voice for the fifth line of each stanza.

The first public performance was given by Auguste Hohenschild at a chamber music evening for the charitable foundation of the Singverein in Krefeld on 30 January 1885.

The text is from the first book of the "Jugendlieder" section (written 1807–1810) of Rückert's *Werke*, Vol. 2 (1816). It deals with the images of sunset, birdsong at evening, the whispering of wind, and the approach of sleep, all magically evoked in the music by wide-ranging arpeggios in the piano and the expressive *adagio* melody in the viola. Brahms did not set the poem's third verse.

After the long introductory viola passage, the voice enters simply and quietly, as though lost in contemplation of the "golden evening." The viola resumes its melody in counterpoint to the voice; as the vocal line becomes more active, the viola becomes more accompanimental until, at the mention of "whispering winds and little birds," the voice takes up the original viola melody while the viola borrows triplet arpeggios from the piano to imitate the murmuring sounds of nature.

The second stanza's consideration of erotic turmoil is expressed in restless harmonies and rhythmically intensified figuration. The agitation recedes temporarily for the questions "wann ruhest du, wann schlummerst du?" which the voice and the piano's bass line ponder together in reversed order; it intrudes itself again into the voice's ritornello-like recalling of the viola's opening melody near the end of the verse and dissipates completely into silence following the final question, "wann schlaft ihr ein?"

The music of the first stanza is repeated for the last; a characteristic lengthening in the final vocal phrase and an instrumental postlude that gradually resolves any remaining unrest are sufficient to transform into longing for death what earlier had been serene observation of nature.

The song is deeply affecting. Rückert's fine poem in Brahms's noble setting is an exemplary summation of German Romantic metaphysical thought.

Geistliches Wiegenlied, Op. 91/2 (Religious Lullaby)

Text by Emanuel Geibel (1815–1884)
after Lope Felix de Vega Carpio (Spanish, 1562–1635)

Die ihr schwebet
Um diese Palmen
In Nacht und Wind,
Ihr heiligen Engel,
Stillet die Wipfel!
Es schlummert mein Kind.

Ihr Palmen von Bethlehem
Im Windesbrausen,
Wie mögt ihr heute
So zornig sausen!
O rauscht nicht also!
Schweiget, neiget
Euch leis' und lind;
Stillet die Wipfel!
Es schlummert mein Kind.

Der Himmelsknabe
Duldet Beschwerde;
Ach, wie so müd' er ward

Vom Lied der Erde.
Ach, nun im Schlaf ihm
Leise gesänftigt
Die Qual zerrinnt,
Stillet die Wipfel!
Es schlummert mein Kind.

Grimmige Kälte
Sauset hernieder,
Womit nur deck' ich
Des Kindleins Glieder!
O, all' ihr Engel,
Die ihr geflügelt
Wandelt im Wind,
Stillet die Wipfel!
Es schlummert mein Kind.

Altes Lied (Old Song)

Josef, lieber Josef mein,
Hilf mir wieg'n mein Kind'lein fein,
Gott, der wird dein Lohner sein,
Im Himmelreich,
Der Jungfrau Sohn, Maria.

Text of the "old song": Joseph, my dear Joseph, help me rock my lovely baby; in Heaven you will be rewarded by God, the Son of the Virgin, Mary.

Main text: You that hover about these palms in night and wind, you holy angels, silence the treetops! My child is slumbering.

You palms of Bethlehem in the roar of the wind, how can you rustle so angrily today? Do not make so much noise! Be quiet, bow down softly and mildly; silence the treetops! My child is slumbering.

The heavenly infant is suffering hardships; oh, how he has been wearied by the earth's sorrow.

Ah, now softly soothed in sleep, his distress fades away. Silence the treetops! My child is slumbering!

Cruel coldness whirs down; whatever can I use to cover the child's limbs? O all you angels that wander winged in the wind, silence the treetops! My child is slumbering.

Composed 1863/1864, revised 1884.

A B C A B; A and B end with the same music, and the old carol provides the material for the introduction, ritornello, and postlude.

The first public performance, together with the preceding song, was given by Auguste Hohenschild on 30 January 1885 at a chamber music evening for the benefit of the Singverein in Krefeld.

In the Geibel-Heyse *Spanisches Liederbuch* (Berlin, 1852), where Brahms found the text, the original poem is listed in the index of first lines as "Pues andais in las palmas" by Lope de Vega.

At the time of Joseph Joachim's marriage to the contralto Amalie Weiss (née Schneeweiss), Brahms wrote to his old friend on 13 April 1863: "In due course I shall send you a wonderful old Catholic song for singing at home; you will never discover a more beautiful lullaby." His reference was to the old Christmas song "Josef, lieber Josef mein," upon which he based his "Geistliches Wiegenlied," an early version of which he sent to the Joachims later in the same year. Apparently not completely satisfied with the piece, Brahms soon asked for the return of the manuscript. In September 1864, Joachim wrote to ask for the lullaby, which he would "now shortly need," as the birth of their first child was imminent; Brahms indeed fulfilled his request before the child's christening.

Even before its publication, the song was familiar within Brahms's circle of friends. In addition to the Joachims and Clara Schumann, Hermann Levi owned a manuscript, from which he made a copy for the Herzogenbergs at the beginning of 1878, and Theodor Billroth received a manuscript in April 1882 with permission to have it copied.

"Josef, lieber Josef mein" was known as early as the fifteenth century. Johann Walther included it in his *Wittemburgisch Deudsch Geistlich Gesangbüchlein* of 1544. Brahms found it in Corner's *Groß-Catolischem Gesangbuch* (1631) and (in Walther's setting) in Karl Severin Meister's *Das Katholische Kirchenlied* (1862). Its use for the viola's introduction imparts to the song a flavor of archaic legend, and its rocking rhythms evoke the image of swaying palm trees as well as the cradle-song character.

Brahms's portrait of the mother and child is a rather reserved one; even the premonitions of the suffering to come seem to elicit solemnity rather than anguish.

The gentle opening vocal line evolves effortlessly from the introductory old carol; only the word "Nacht" and the plea to the angels, "stillet die Wipfel," are darkened by chromatic inflection. Increased chromaticism and rhythmic activity depict the growing agitation of verse 2 and the corresponding verse 4. The first half of verse 3 is the emotional climax of the poem, marked by a change to the minor mode and to $\frac{3}{4}$ meter; the scalar instrumental motive in descending eighth notes suggests the future final journey to Golgotha. (At the $\frac{3}{4}$, the tempo of the quarter notes should equal that of the preceding dotted quarters, so that the constant pace of the rocking triplet figure provides unity.)

A return to the major mode temporarily dispels all foreboding and brings with it a repetition of the music of the earlier part of the song. The postlude features a full, only slightly varied restatement of the "Josef" melody in the viola and a final long rising arpeggio in the piano, which seems to portray both the peacefully sleeping child and the angels who keep watch overhead.

FIVE LIEDER FOR LOW VOICE, OP. 94

Fünf Lieder für eine tiefe Stimme mit Begleitung des Pianoforte von Johannes Brahms (Five Songs for Low Voice with Piano Accompaniment by Johannes Brahms), Op. 94. Published in December 1884 by N. Simrock in Berlin; publication number 8488.

The title specifies a low voice, and the first song (only) actually appears with a bass clef; Brahms, however, also consented to a simultaneous publication in a higher key. Op. 94 was presumably composed with Julius Stockhausen in mind, its subject matter appropriate to a dark-toned voice. All the songs treat of lost youth or lost love (or both) except "Sapphische Ode," and even it may in fact recall a love from the past. Brahms's surgeon-friend Theodor Billroth described the five songs as "a sort of autumn or winter journey" (6 August 1884), referring, of course, to Schubert's bleak *Winterreise* cycle.

Mit vierzig Jahren, Op. 94/1 (At Forty)

Text by Friedrich Rückert (1788–1866)

Mit vierzig Jahren ist der Berg erstiegen,
　　Wir stehen still und schau'n zurück;
　　Dort sehen wir der Kindheit stilles liegen
　　Und dort der Jugend lautes Glück.

Noch einmal schau', und dann gekräftiget weiter
　　Erhebe deinen Wanderstab!
　　Hindehnt ein Bergesrücken sich, ein breiter,
　　Und hier nicht, drüben geht's hinab.

Nicht atmend aufwärts brauchst du mehr zu steigen,
　　Die Eb'ne zieht von selbst dich fort;
　　Dann wird sie sich mit dir unmerklich neigen,
　　Und eh' du's denkst, bist du im Port.

> At forty, the mountain has been climbed; we stand still and look back; there
> we see lying the quiet happiness of childhood, and there the noisy happiness
> of youth.
> Take one more look, and then with renewed strength lift your walking staff
> and continue! A mountain ridge stretches before you, a broad one, and not
> here, but beyond, the way leads downward.
> You will no longer need to climb upward taking deep breaths; the plain will
> draw you onward of its own accord; then it will imperceptibly slope downward
> along with you; and before you realize it, you will be in port.

Composed during 1883/84.

First performed at a *Lieder* recital with Olga Alberta and Richard Dannenberg (presumably by Dannenberg) in Hamburg on 25 April 1894.

Modified strophic with varied accompaniment.

The poem was first published posthumously in the 1883 *Deutscher Musenalmanach* but is believed to date from 1832, when Rückert was in his mid-forties.

The poet at middle age assesses his life and finds strength in the belief that the hardest part of the journey is nearly over; Brahms at middle age shifts the emphasis, finding solace in contemplation of the peace that lies at journey's end.

In form the setting is a hybrid of the sort that Brahms began to favor in the late 1870s, combining the rigor of strophic recurrence with the freedom of through-composition. Here, because of his detailed interpretation of the text's meaning, every phrase is subjected to some degree of alteration at each reappearance; the contours of the strophe's first and third phrases, however, remain recognizable throughout, contributing to a sense of order and unity as the song progresses.

The opening vocal line climbs stepwise in vigorous dotted rhythms to a peak on "Berg," then eases downward in longer note values amid calming piano chords, pausing reflectively on the lower dominant. The piano re-examines this succession of harmonies, then proceeds toward the relative major in longer chords that are tied across the strong beats, depicting the quiet happiness of childhood. The resumption of quicker rhythms in both voice and piano evokes the noisier joys of youth; the last words are repeated thoughtfully in doubled note values as the piano sighs over a restless bass pedal. A sustained dominant seventh in m. 14 reconfirms the home key and ushers in the next strophe.

With renewed strength the music resumes as at first, but submediant harmonies intrude, reminding us that what lies ahead is cloaked in mystery. In the third phrase, converging, mostly chromatic lines in the piano convey the obscurity of the future. "Breiter" elicits the vocal line's first white note; "hier nicht," an enharmonic digression into (visually, at least) foreign tonal territory, where Brahms's symbolic bare octaves descend in thirds to reveal that it is death that waits at the end of the path downward.

The home key is restored for the third strophe by means of the reinterpretation of B♭ as A♯. The piano's descending melody and sustained afterbeats confirm that the need for the hard-breathing climb upward is past. The harmony drifts onward as though of its own accord, lingering on the dominant's dominant. Melodic falling fifths anticipate and continue those of the vocal line's third phrase, and the bass line's midphrase downturn is made less perceptible ("unmerklich") by its rising one step for each skip downward.

The song's glorious conclusion affectingly depicts the serenity of the traveler's final haven by shifting not only to the tonic major, but on to the Neapolitan and back, while the vocal line arches broadly over a rolling accompaniment of discontinuous upward arpeggios in triplets—Brahms's customary symbol for contentment. The postlude adds a comforting, richly sonorous plagal cadence as benediction. One can easily accept Kalbeck's report (*Brahms*, I$_2$, 227n, and III$_2$, 522) that Julius Stockhausen, for whom the song was written, was so moved when he first sang through it with Brahms that he broke down, overcome by emotion.

Steig' auf, geliebter Schatten, Op. 94/2
(Arise, Beloved Ghost)

Text by Friedrich Halm (Austrian, 1806–1871)

> Steig' auf, geliebter Schatten,
> Vor mir in toter Nacht,
> Und lab' mich Todesmatten
> Mit deiner Nähe Macht!
>
> Du hast's gekonnt im Leben,
> Du kannst es auch im Tod.
> Sich nicht dem Schmerz ergeben,
> War immer dein Gebot.
>
> So komm! Still' meine Tränen,
> Gib meiner Seele Schwung,
> Und Kraft den welken Sehnen,
> Und mach' mich wieder jung.

Arise before me, beloved ghost, in the dead of night, and refresh me in my deathly weariness with the power of your presence!

You were able to do so when alive, you can do it again now that you are dead. Not to give in to sorrow, was always your commandment.

So come! Dry my tears, give energy to my soul, and strength to my withered sinews, and make me young again.

Probably composed during 1883/84—the exact date is unknown.
The first performance is not documented.

A B A; a deviation in the vocal line at the end of the third phrase of verse 3 enhances the declamation.

The text is found in the "Vermischte Gedichte," in Vol. 9 of the poet's *Gesammelte Werke* (Vienna, 1856–72).

The poet, grieving for lost youth and seeking revitalization, summons an unidentified "beloved ghost," presumably a past love. In E♭ minor, Brahms's favored key of mourning, the setting is atmospheric and enigmatic, like the poem. Terseness and lean textures intensify the emotion.

The vocal line's striking beginning is propelled by the piano's arpeggiated chords and supported by a bass motive that will come to dominate the music of the outer verses—a descending seventh-chord outline with an interior dotted rhythm. It is heard at the beginning of every bass line entrance, always a fourth lower in pitch (although the very last is displaced up an octave). Usually altered, it is also a prominent feature of the vocal melody: there are three seeming imitations of the figure in each of the outer sections, only the third of which is exact; the contrasting section reduces the idea from four successive pitches to three in even eighth notes, once descending and twice rising.

In the second verse, the poet finds hope for refreshment in his memories of the invoked spirit in life; Brahms finds several musical metaphors for this rather abstruse notion. The first and third lines, which reflect life and hope, have an active triplet accompaniment and vocal lines animated by conflicting eighth notes, while the second and forth, which evoke death and the past, move in quiet quarters and half notes—the bass line's spectral octave doublings of the voice are a particularly arresting effect. An astonishingly variegated (but aurally logical) succession of harmonies exploits the dream-world connotation of submediant relationships, moving enharmonically from the relative major to its submediant, and thence to the home key's dominant by way of its own submediant. In the interlude between verses 1 and 2, the piano introduces a new melodic idea—two rising stepwise slurs, the second a step lower than the first—that seems to symbolize the possibility of the assuagement of sorrow. It first appears in the tenor register in mm. 12–13 and is immediately repeated an octave higher; back in the tenor, it underscores "Tod" in mm. 20–21 and (in quarter notes) the succeeding line "Sich nicht dem Schmerz ergeben." Varied, it seems to lurk within the triplets of mm. 16–17 and 22–23, and it affects the retransition to verse 3; finally, it forms the basis for the mournful postlude, where its hopefulness seems dispersed rather than fulfilled.

Mein Herz ist schwer, Op. 94/3 (My Heart Is Heavy)

Text by Emanuel Geibel (1815–1884)

Mein Herz ist schwer, main Auge wacht,
Der Wind fährt seufzend durch die Nacht;

Die Wipfel rauschen weit und breit,
Sie rauschen von vergang'ner Zeit,

Sie rauschen von vergang'ner Zeit,
Von großem Glück und Herzeleid,
Vom Schloß und von der Jungfrau d'rin—
Wo ist das Alles, Alles hin?

Wo ist das Alles, Alles hin,
Leid, Lieb' und Lust und Jugendsinn?
Der Wind fährt seufzend durch die Nacht,
Mein Herz ist schwer, mein Auge wacht.

My heart is heavy, my eyes enjoy no sleep, the wind rides sighing through the night; the treetops rustle on all sides; their rustling speaks of times past.

Their rustling speaks of times past, of great happiness and sorrows of the heart, of the castle and of the maiden within it—where did all that, all that go?

Where did all that, all that go—sorrow, love and pleasure and youthful thoughts?

The wind rides sighing through the night, my heart is heavy, my eyes enjoy no sleep.

Composed during 1883/84.

The first performance is not documented.

Varied strophic, with some elements of through-composition; A B B' A'.

The text is from the section "Lieder aus alter und neuer Zeit" in the poet's *Spätherbstblätter*. The last line of each verse is repeated as the first line of the next, and the poem's closing pair of lines reverses the order of the opening pair.

Brahms sets the outer couplets to similar music, treats line 3 as a transition (using the repeated-chord motive that ends the introduction and reappears in the retransition and codetta), and adapts lines 4–7 and 8–10 to two developmental strophes that derive their rhythms from those of the framing material. The repeated lines are handled sequentially. In order to complete an eighth phrase, inserted for balance and begun by the piano alone, the ending words of line 10 are also repeated; their expanded rhythmic values cause a characteristic broadening of the section's concluding phrase. Similarly, the end of the song repeats the final line of text in modified rhythmic augmentation, increasing the span of the last phrase from four strong beats to eight.

Every element seems to contribute to a sense of restlessness, which is pervasive. The piano's hushed alternating octaves in contrary motion rustle like the whispering leaves, and its anxious seventh-chord repetitions sigh like the night wind. (Most pianists will find the requisite murmuring effect easier to achieve if they omit the optional notes in small print.) The vocal line begins in gasping short phrases with jagged rhythms. The stretching at "Die Wipfel rauschen weit und breit," like that of the corresponding phrase at the end of the song, adds gravity to the text's impact.

The juxtaposition in mm. 10–11 of dominant sevenths on G and E is a harbinger of the wide-ranging harmonic (and enharmonic) exploration that is one of two prominent features of the contrasting middle section. The other is a process of constant metric intensification, of which the change from $\frac{9}{4}$ to $\frac{6}{4}$ and the instruction *Nach und nach lebhafter* are signals. The phrases that set lines 4 and 8 of the poem are each extended to three measures by the piano, but their sequential repetitions as lines 5 and 9 each occupy only two measures. Though it is somewhat ambiguous, the movement of the piano's bass line and the introduction of hemiola at three-measure intervals in mm. 16 and 19 suggest that the accompaniment through m. 25 comprises segments of three measures (or thereabouts), independent of the vocal phrase structure. With the arrival of verse 3 in m. 26, the accompanying sustained afterbeats give way to continuous eighth-note motion.

A *poco ritardando*, a rise from F to F♯ in the reiterated repeated-chord motive, and an arresting silence herald the return of the opening key and tempo for the concluding section. An adaptation of the initial vocal line now bridges its gaps (but retains its uneasy rhythms) and leads to tonic rather than to dominant. Despite a shift to the major mode, the progressive slowing and softening toward the end combine with the minor-tinged quasi-Phrygian cadences to cast a shadow of despair over the already portentous final phrase.

Sapphische Ode, Op. 94/4 (Sapphic Ode)

Text by Hans Schmidt (1856– ?)

Rosen brach ich Nachts mir am dunklen Hage;
Süßer hauchten Duft sie, als je am Tage;
Doch verstreuten reich die bewegten Äste
Tau, der mich näßte.

Auch der Küsse Duft mich wie nie berückte,
Die ich Nachts vom Strauch deiner Lippen pflückte:
Doch auch dir, bewegt im Gemüt gleich jenen,
Tauten die Tränen!

I picked roses at night by the dark hedge; they emitted a sweeter fragrance than they ever do during the day; but the branches, when moved, richly sprinkled dew, which moistened me.

Similarly I was bewitched as never before by the kisses that I picked at night from the rosebush of your lips: But you, too, moved in your mind as those branches were, found your eyes all dewy with tears.

Composed summer 1884.
First performed by Gustav Walter on 9 January 1885 in Vienna.
Strophic; the second strophe is slightly varied.

The text is found in Schmidt's *Gedichte und Übersetzungen* (Offenbach, n.d.) in the section "In antiker Form," where it has the title "Gereimte sapphische Ode."

A sapphic strophe, named for Sappho (fl. c.600 B.C.), the Greek lyric poet who used the form, comprises four lines. Three of them contain five equal beats of which the middle one is a dactyl ($-\smile\smile$) and the others are trochees ($-\smile$). The shorter fourth line is a dactyl followed by either a trochee or a spondee ($--$). Each of Schmidt's two strophes has the following plan:

$$
\begin{array}{ll}
(1) & -\ \smile\ -\ \smile\ -\ \smile\ \smile\ -\ \smile\ -\ \smile \\
(2) & -\ \smile\ -\ \smile\ -\ \smile\ \smile\ -\ \smile\ -\ \smile \\
(3) & -\ \smile\ -\ \smile\ -\ \smile\ \smile\ -\ \smile\ -\ \smile \\
(4) & -\ \smile\ \smile\ -\ \smile
\end{array}
$$

Brahms's setting beautifully follows, even enhances, the meter of the poem, although the last trochee of each of the first three lines is stretched to span two strong beats (albeit the first and second beats in *alla breve*) for a total of six. His penchant for broadening toward the end also leads him to expand the fourth line to include a corresponding six strong beats.

The song is one of Brahms's most universally loved, indeed is among the greatest love songs ever written. Not surprisingly, it is elegant in its simplicity—triad outlines and scalar motion make up most of the melody, and although the third phrase turns to the minor mode, there is no modulation. Several slight but significant alterations in the second strophe (mm. 21–22, 24–25, and 26) create an even more detailed fusion of words with music.

In the piano part, the right hand accompanies in afterbeats throughout, usually throbbing quietly in legato, sometimes detached like individual droplets of dew or tears, and finally sighing ardently in pairs. The harmonies are suffused with the warmth of chromatic alterations and secondary dominants; rich sonorities in the middle and low registers predominate; a perceptible aura of tenderness results from a discreet emphasis on the subdominant side of the key. Scalewise tenor melodies in quarter notes bridge and predict the vocal phrases, and bass lines in half notes introduce and participate in the augmentation in the fourth phrase of each strophe. The postlude touchingly revisits the minor subdominant that earlier had darkened the images of dewfall and teardrops.

Kein Haus, keine Heimat, Op. 94/5 (No House, No Homeland)

Text by Friedrich Halm (Austrian, 1806–1871)

Kein Haus, keine Heimat,
Kein Weib und kein Kind,

> So wirbl' ich, ein Strohhalm,
> In Wetter und Wind!
>
> Well' auf und Well' nieder,
> Bald dort und bald hier;
> Welt, fragst du nach mir nicht,
> Was frag' ich nach dir?

No house, no homeland, no wife and no child; thus I am whirled like a straw in storm and wind!

A rising wave, a falling wave, now here and now there; world, if you don't ask about me, why should I ask about you?

Probably composed during 1883/84.

The first performance is not documented.

Strophic; the closing phrase has an authentic cadence in strophe 1 but a plagal cadence in strophe 2.

The text is from the rather grisly dramatic poem "In der Südsee" in Vol. 7 of Halm's *Gesammelte Werke* (Vienna, 1856–72), not from a play, as the score's indication implies. There is a first verse that Brahms did not use:

> Meine Jacke ist ganz noch
> Und mein Glas noch voll Gin!
> Welt, geh' deiner Wege,
> Ich frag' nicht, wohin?

My jacket is still whole and my glass still full of gin! World, go your own way, I don't ask where. [My translation.]

The three verses constitute a song that is identified with the hero, a Negro sailor, formerly a slave. Early in the poem, he sings the complete song; he repeats the third stanza only at the end of the opening scene; and finally, the two-stanza version appears near the end of the narrative, just before the man sacrifices his life for the sake of others.

The setting is not heard often, probably because its appearance on the page seems un-Brahmsian and, at least initially, is misleading. The simplicity of the vocal melody suggests folk song, the waltzy-looking accompaniment invites playfulness—*giusto* (strict) is widely misinterpreted as connoting liveliness, perhaps through unthinking association with *gioia* or *gioco*—and one can easily be led to find the setting disappointingly flippant, incongruous with its desolate text.

In fact, these twenty measures epitomize the terseness for which Brahms strived in his late songs, and while the spare textures may call to mind Webern or the Schoenberg of the Op. 19 piano pieces, they contain the seeds of a powerful dramatic scene. This song repays careful study, but it requires performers who are gifted tragedians as well as sensitive musicians. Of prime importance is the tempo, which must be slow enough to accommodate the singer's projection of impending disaster and to imbue the melody's plainness with a kind of childlike directness. At the same time, it must be rigidly, even mechanically, strict, so that every staccato sound in the piano reverberates with the inevitability of harsh fate. The several augmented-triad sonorities should seem agonizingly painful, the silences bleak. The piano's unpredictable cross-metric punctuations in the second half of the strophe suggest the disorder that has marked the wretch's life, and they take on a grotesque, nightmarish quality. A change to the major and a crescendo to the final ringing chord color the concluding phrase with audacity.

SEVEN LIEDER, OP. 95

Sieben Lieder für eine Singstimme mit Begleitung des Pianoforte von Johannes Brahms (Seven Songs for Solo Voice with Piano Accompaniment by Johannes Brahms), Op. 95. Published in December 1884 by N. Simrock in Berlin; publication number 8489.

The group brings together settings of three poems by Halm and translations by Kapper (two), Heyse, and Daumer. All have an aura of folk song, whether authentic or invented. Their progression by related keys (aided by the modulatory introduction of No. 3) and their predominantly female viewpoint contribute internal unity to the set.

Das Mädchen, Op. 95/1 (The Girl)

Translated from the Serbian by Siegfried Kapper
(Czech, 1821–1879)

Stand das Mädchen, stand am Bergesabhang,
Widerschien der Berg von ihrem Antlitz,
Und das Mädchen sprach zu ihrem Antlitz:
"Wahrlich, Antlitz, o du meine Sorge,
Wenn ich wüßte, du mein weißes Antlitz,
Daß dereinst ein Alter dich wird küssen,
Ging hinaus ich zu den grünen Bergen,
Pflückte allen Wermut in den Bergen,
Preßte bitt'res Wasser aus dem Wermut,
Wüsche dich, o Antlitz, mit dem Wasser,
Daß du bitter, wenn dich küßt der Alte!
Wüßt' ich aber, du mein weißes Antlitz,
Daß dereinst ein Junger dich wird küssen,
Ging hinaus ich in den grünen Garten,
Pflückte alle Rosen in dem Garten,
Preßte duftend Wasser aus den Rosen,
Wüsche dich, o Antlitz, mit dem Wasser,
Daß du duftest, wenn dich küßt der Junge!"

The girl stood, stood on the mountain slope; the mountain reflected her
face, and the girl spoke to her face:
"Truly, my face, you sorrow of mine, if I were to know, you white face of mine,
that some day an old man will kiss you: I would go out to the green mountains,
I would pick all the wormwood in the mountains, I would squeeze bitter fluid
out of the wormwood, and I would wash you, my face, with the fluid, so you
become bitter when the old man kisses you!
"But if I were to know, you white face of mine, that some day a young man
will kiss you: I would go out into the green garden, I would pick all the roses
in the garden, I would squeeze fragrant fluid out of the roses, and I would
wash you, my face, with the fluid, so you are fragrant when the young man
kisses you!"

Composed in April 1883; the song is probably earlier than the SATB version, also published in 1884 as Op. 93a/2.

First performed by Helene Marschall on 14 March 1889 at a *Lieder* recital
in Vienna.

Through-composed, with some recurrence of similar material.

The text appeared in Kapper's *Die Gesänge der Serben* (Leipzig, 1852),
where the seventh line has "nach" instead of "zu," and the title is "Wüßt
ich, Antlitz, wer dich einst wird küssen."

A distinct folk flavor derives from the alternation of $\frac{3}{4}$ and $\frac{4}{4}$—indeed, alternating meters are typical of certain Slovakian and Bohemian dances. In
the earlier setting of Kapper's "Mädchenlied," Op. 85/3, $\frac{3}{4}$ and $\frac{2}{4}$ alternate
regularly to form $\frac{5}{4}$; here, however, Brahms chooses to break the pattern occasionally for particular effect. The retention of $\frac{3}{4}$ for "wenn ich wüßte" in m.
10 and the analogous "wüßt ich aber" in m. 30, for example, stresses their
conjectural quality by removing them from the recurring rhythm of dance.
In each case the missing beat is reinserted three bars later, converting an
expected $\frac{3}{4}$ bar to $\frac{4}{4}$, as the words seem to tumble forth in excitement. The
substitution of $\frac{4}{4}$ for $\frac{3}{4}$ in m. 65 accomplishes the customary broadening of
the final phrase.

The first half of the song, in which the girl contemplates the kiss of an old
man, is in the minor mode, though there is some quasi-modal interchange
with major harmonies. The mention of bitter wormwood juice elicits sharp
chromatic dissonances.

The parallel situation, the thought of a young man's kiss, calls forth similar music in the parallel major mode. The intention of rose-gathering in
the young lover's honor is expressed in a giddy $\frac{2}{4}$ *Animato grazioso*, in
which five- and six-measure vocal phrases bridge the joins of alternating
four-measure skippings and two-measure whirlings in the piano.

At the end of the song, music reminiscent of the opening is recalled joyously, this time in the major mode and *Lebhaft*.

Bei dir sind meine Gedanken, Op. 95/2
(My Thoughts are with You)

Text by Friedrich Halm (Austrian, 1806–1871)

Bei dir sind meine Gedanken
Und flattern um dich her;
Sie sagen, sie hätten Heimweh,
Hier litt es sie nicht mehr.

Bei dir sind meine Gedanken
Und wollen von dir nicht fort;
Sie sagen, das wär' auf Erden
Der allerschönste Ort.

Sie sagen, unlösbar hielte
Dein Zauber sie festgebannt;
Sie hätten an deinen Blicken
Die Flügel sich verbrannt.

My thoughts are with you and flutter around you; they say they are home-sick, and can't stand it here any more.

My thoughts are with you and don't want to leave you; they say that that is the most beautiful spot on earth.

They say your magic has cast an unbreakable spell on them; that they burned their wings in the flame of your eyes.

Probably composed early 1884.

The first performance is not documented.

Strophic.

The text is found in the section "Lieder und Liebe" in Vol. 7 of Halm's *Gesammelte Werke* (Vienna, 1856–72).

Brahms provides a delicate setting with a gently arching melody and a murmuring accompaniment whose fluttering alternate-hand sixteenth notes evoke the flight of thoughts to the absent beloved.

Varying phrase lengths lend an almost recitative-like suppleness to the declamation of the text. The irregularity is the result of the occasional inser-tion of an "extra" measure in the piano part, an interior repetition of two syllables in line 2, an interruption after the first two words of line 3, and an elongated repetition of line 4. In strophe 3, the omission of the interior repe-tition in line 2 makes possible the metaphorical held note for the first syllable of "festgebannt" (literally, riveted to the spot).

All three verses of the poem have the same structure, which suggests both the strophic design and its distinctive harmonic scheme. The initial couplet constitutes a direct statement (allegorical though it may be), which Brahms sets unadornedly in the tonic key with a modulation to the domi-nant. The last two lines counterbalance by detailing an obviously fanciful notion, which, in Brahms's psycho-harmonic language, virtually demands a digression into the key of the lowered submediant, here reached via its own dominant. The return to the tonic during the last phrase is almost equally enchanting.

In general, the composer's performance indications suggest lightness and intimacy—a single, short-lived *forte* marks the point of departure from the tonic key toward foreign territory. At the end of the song, two evanescent concluding chords are added to the usual between-strophe music.

Beim Abschied, Op. 95/3 (At Parting)

Text by Friedrich Halm (Austrian, 1806–1871)

> Ich müh' mich ab und kann's nicht verschmerzen
> Und kann's nicht verwinden in meinem Herzen,
> Daß ich den und jenen soll sehen
> Im Kreis um mich herum sich drehen,
> Der mich nicht machte froh noch trübe,
> Ob er nun ging oder bliebe,
> Und nur die Eine soll von mir wandern,
> Für die ich ertragen all' die Andern.

I try and try but can't get over the sorrow—and can't overcome it in my heart—of seeing this person and that person circling around me, none of whom could make me happy or sad whether they went or stayed—while just that very woman must depart from me for whose sake I have put up with all the other people.

Presumably composed in early 1883—the exact date is unknown.

First performed on 30 October 1886 at a special Musikverein concert in Hermannstadt in Siebenbürgen.

A hybrid form, combining quasi-strophic repetition with elements of through-composition.

The text appears in Vol. 1 of Halm's *Gesammelte Werke* (Vienna, 1856–72) in the section "Lieder der Liebe."

The poem's lines have four metric feet but are stretched to accommodate five-measure musical phrases.

The same pair of such phrases sets lines 1 and 2 and is repeated for lines 3 and 4, lines 7 and 8, and, in an expanded variant, the repetition of lines 7 and 8 at the end of the song. The first phrase leads to the subdominant, the second proceeds to a half-cadence on the dominant; the pair therefore repeats itself easily, but lacking a full cadence, is not a closed unit like a normal strophe. The lowered sixth degree of the scale figures prominently (though the major mode is never seriously in doubt); it is introduced in the piano prelude, appears frequently in the accompaniment, and invades the second vocal phrase. The resulting minor tinge symbolizes the inner hurt that underlies the poet's complaint.

Tonal contrast is provided by two new phrases for lines 5 and 6, which progress from the dominant to the submediant. A varied restatement of line 6 contracts the vocal phrase to four measures, allowing it a fifth measure of rest.

The song's concluding variation of its basic phrase pair expands the first phrase to seven measures, the second to six. The former, which speaks of the departure of the beloved, dwells on the mournful minor subdominant and gradually slows, pausing at a fermata; the latter restores the previous tempo and changes to major those segments of its contour that have heretofore been minor. The effect is brilliant, but a suggestion of aggrievedness lingers in the postlude.

As the song was originally published, the meter of the accompaniment (only) changed to $\frac{2}{4}$ at m. 41, for the last four phrases and the postlude. Apparently pleased with the agitation produced by the metric conflict and wishing to extend it to the entire song, Brahms indicated in his own copy of the first edition that the change should occur immediately after the introduction. In the Breitkopf & Härtel edition and its Dover reprint, the song appears in both formats; since it represents a later decision, the revised version is recommended.

Der Jäger, Op. 95/4 (The Huntsman)

Text by Friedrich Halm (Austrian, 1806–1871)

> Mein Lieb ist ein Jäger,
> Und grün ist sein Kleid,
> Und blau ist sein Auge,
> Nur sein Herz ist zu weit.

> Mein Lieb ist ein Jäger,
> Trifft immer in's Ziel,
> Und Mädchen berückt er,
> So viel er nur will.

> Mein Lieb ist ein Jäger,
> Kennt Wege und Spur,
> Zu mir aber kommt er
> Durch die Kirchtüre nur.

My darling is a huntsman; his jacket is green and his eyes are blue; only, his heart has too much room.

My darling is a huntsman; he always hits the mark and captivates as many girls as he wishes.

> My darling is a huntsman; he knows paths and tracks, but will come to me
> only by way of the church door.

The composition date is uncertain, probably early 1884.

First performed by Hermine Spies on 18 January 1890 in Vienna.

Strophic.

The text appeared in the first draft of the play *Wildfeuer* as a song for the peasant girl Margot, but was subsequently replaced by another, shorter song. "Der Jäger" is printed as the second of two poems under the title "Margot's Lieder 1 & 2" in the general section "Vermischte Gedichte" in Vol. 9, *Neueste Gedichte* (Vienna, 1872), of Halm's *Gesammelte Werke*.

One can hardly imagine a more amiable song than this, with its sunny major mode, its dancing rhythms, and its ingenuous diatonic melody. There are many felicitous details: in the piano's prelude and postlude, the accumulation of voices in stages evokes the solo-and-response style of folk-song performance, and the unharmonized beginning predicts the unaccompanied entrance of the voice. The stretched first syllable of "Jäger" lengthens that phrase to three measures, giving it particular emphasis in its context of two-measure units—the immediately subsequent drop to *piano* highlights it even more sharply. The piano's echoing of the second vocal phrase is balanced by the repetition of the fourth line of text, which itself functions as a substitute for Brahms's characteristic broadening toward the end. The unusually frequent choice of subdominant and secondary harmonies contributes to the song's distinctive aura of tenderness. Considerable rhythmic interest accrues from the diverse accompaniment figures and patterns of articulation, particularly in the bass line—the bass's staccato afterbeats and the implied hemiola in mm. 12–13 are especially striking.

It is not clear how Brahms intended the grace note to be treated, although it is certainly short. Neatness in vertical alignment of the text would argue for placing the grace on the beat to start the syllable.

Vorschneller Schwur, Op. 95/5 (Hasty Oath)

Translated from the Serbian by Siegfried Kapper
(Czech, 1821–1879)

> Schwor ein junges Mädchen:
> Blumen nie zu tragen,
> Blumen nie zu tragen,
> Niemals Wein zu trinken,
> Niemals Wein zu trinken,
> Knaben nie zu küssen.
>
> Gestern schwor das Mädchen—
> Heute schon bereut es:

> "Wenn ich Blumen trüge,
> Wär' ich doch noch schöner!
> Wenn ich Rotwein tränke,
> Wär' ich doch noch froher!
> Wenn den Liebsten küßte,
> Wär' mir doch noch wohler!"

A young girl swore never to wear flowers, never to wear flowers, never to drink wine, never to drink wine, never to kiss boys.

The girl swore that oath yesterday, and already regrets it today:

"If I wore flowers, I would look more beautiful! If I drank red wine, I would be merrier! If I kissed my sweetheart, I would feel happier!"

The date of composition is uncertain; possibly April 1883, along with "Das Mädchen," the other Kapper translation from the Serbian in the set.

First performed by Hermine Spies on 15 April 1886 in Vienna.

The form is an amalgamation of strophic and through-composed elements.

The text appears in Kapper's *Gesänge der Serben* (Leipzig, 1852) in the "Frauenlieder" section, where it is entitled "Wie das Mädchen vorschnell schwört."

The setting's appearance suggests its folkloric origins, not only in its regular four-measure phrases, clear cadences, and little triplet melismas, but particularly in its minor-mode opening and faster concluding section in the major, a common formula in Slavic folk song and dance. Beneath its seeming simplicity, however, is an elegantly detailed, sophisticated structure, filled with psychological insights.

Brahms sets the poem's first verse of six lines as a strophe of three periods, the first two lines of the second verse as a transition, and the girl's six lines as a variant three-period strophe; the last couplet is repeated as a coda, balancing the transition in the first part and equalizing the two halves with a total of eight phrases each.

The essence of the song lies in the differences between the two strophes, which describe the girl's hasty oath and her reconsideration of it respectively. That she has already gladly renounced the ill-considered vow is made clear by the second strophe's brighter mode and tempo, higher tessitura, and increased (and mounting) sense of elation. In both strophes, every period begins with a rising third followed by a drop to the lower dominant; what remains of the antecedent phrases hovers around that dominant in the first strophe, but in the second, it centers on the upper tonic instead. The accompaniment of the first strophe starts each period in unison octaves with the voice and withholds downbeat basses, suggesting the girl's weak resolve; but in the second strophe, each period is fully harmonized from the outset and bass notes sound confidently on every downbeat. In order to accommodate the poem's lines of three metric feet to musical phrases of four measures, stretching is necessary somewhere in the line; some relatively weak words are affected in the first strophe, but in the second it is the im-

portant nouns and adjectives that receive the added emphasis. In both strophes, the second period differs only slightly from the first, but the third is
varied considerably, indicating that the forswearing of kissing is the most
consequential aspect of the vow. In fact, the girl's eagerness to retract it carries the vocal line to the upper dominant for the first time, adds touching
appoggiaturas to "Liebsten küßte," and elicits the song's longest embellishment on "wohler." As a result, that vocal phrase is extended to five measures,
overlapping the piano's *forte* start of a new period, which the voice joins in
its second measure.

Platt observes (*Text-Music*, 199) that the vocal line's climactic attainment
of the upper dominant (it appears first as an eighth note in m. 52, then as a
quarter in m. 60, and finally as a dotted quarter in m. 66) has great structural
significance, since it at long last completes the triad implied by the many initial rising thirds. The piano's sounding of the upper-octave tonic in its
concluding gesture satisfyingly rounds off the full ascending arpeggio.

Mädchenlied, Op. 95/6 (Girl's Song)

Translated from the Italian by Paul von Heyse (1830–1914)

Das Ufer ist so morgenstill,
Noch kaum ein Fischlein springen will.
Am Bänkchen schon, in Rohr und Ried,
Ein Wäschermägdlein emsig kniet.

O Jugendblut, kaum fünfzehn Jahr,
Verschlafen noch ihr Augenpaar,
Das Röckchen dürftig, hochgeschürzt,
Mit Singen sie die Zeit sich kürzt.

"Am jüngsten Tag ich aufersteh'
Und gleich nach meinem Liebsten seh',
Und wenn ich ihn nicht finden kann,
Leg' wieder mich zum Schlafen dann.

"O Herzeleid, du Ewigkeit!
Selbander nur ist Seligkeit!
Und kommt mein Liebster nicht hinein,
Mag nicht im Paradiese sein!"

On Judgment Day I will be resurrected and will immediately look for my
sweetheart, and if I can't find him, I will lie down and sleep again.

O heart's sorrow, how eternal you are! Happiness comes only for two! And
if my sweetheart doesn't enter, I don't want to be in heaven!

Probably composed in early 1884—the exact date is uncertain.
First performed by Gustav Walter on 9 January 1885 in Vienna.

Strophic; verse 2 has a varied accompaniment at the beginning and an augmentation at the end.

The text is a portion of a poem called "In der Bucht" in the section "Landschaften und Staffage" in Heyse's *Gedichte*. There are two introductory verses that Brahms did not use, apparently regarding them as superfluous or distracting from the girl's song itself. My English version follows:

> The shore is so morning-silent, hardly a tiny fish yet wants to leap. Already
> on the little bank, amid cane and reed, a laundrymaid is busy on her knees.
> O blush of youth!—barely fifteen, still sleepy-eyed, her little frock shabby,
> tucked up high, she passes the time by singing.

The setting is charming, with an amiable melody and an unobtrusive accompaniment. By varying the rhythms to highlight key words, Brahms avoids the jingly effect of the poem's constant iambs and at the same time clarifies the meaning. For example, relatively high pitch and long duration combine to stress "ihn" in m. 6 ("Liebster" in the second strophe); the additional factor of placement on a downbeat underlines "Liebsten" in m. 4 as the focal point of the first two lines ("Seligkeit" in the second strophe). A changed metric structure also alters the meaning of the fourth line upon repetition—the first strophe heightens "schlafen," then "mich" and "dann," while the second strophe's augmentation adds emphases on "nicht" and "sein" to that on "Paradiese" retained from the first statement.

The vocal line in mm. 1 and 2 imitates the piano's downward fourths and embellishes them with a caressing little chromatic inflection. The third phrase seems to develop itself gradually out of the piano's repeated one-measure melodic pattern. The accompaniment's straightforward doubling of the voice at the beginning of the second strophe bolsters the song's only *forte* and makes the sequential construction more apparent. In the last phrase, it was an inspired stroke to separate the individual harmonies of the accompaniment by the insertion of rests, without a ritard: it allows the piano not only to participate in the process of elongation (which continuing the figure on every beat would have prevented) but also to reinforce the conviction of the girl's closing assertion (which a ritard would have undermined).

Schön war, das ich dir weihte, Op. 95/7
(It Was Beautiful, My Solemn Gift to You)

Translated from the Turkish by Georg Friedrich Daumer (1800–1875)

> Schön war, das ich dir weihte,
> Das goldene Geschmeide;
> Süß war der Laute Ton,
> Die ich die auserlesen;

Das Herze, das sie beide
Darbrachte, wert gewesen
Wär's zu empfangen einen bessern Lohn.

It was beautiful, the golden jewelry I solemnly gave to you; sweet was the
note of the lute that I chose for you; the heart that offered them both up to
you, would have been worthy to receive a better reward.

The date of composition is uncertain, probably early 1884.

The first performance is not documented.

The form resembles varied strophic, with elements of through-composition;
the same four-measure phrase provides the material for lines 1–2, 3–4, and
the repetition of line 7, and inspires the developmental contrasting section.

The text is from *Polydora, ein weltpoetisches Liederbuch* (Frankfurt
am Main, 1855).

The setting has often been criticized for its failure to observe the structure of the poem and for its faulty declamation. One might argue that
Brahms's fidelity to the poem's enjambments rather than to its lineation aids
comprehension of the meaning of the sung text, and that a sensitive singer
can ameliorate any awkwardnesses in accentuation.

In fact, the music is closely attuned to the text's injured tone, reproachful
but not petty. Almost constant afterbeats throb in discontent, the minor mode
frowns, the quasi-appoggiatura descending pairs of quarter notes sigh un-
happily, and pain erupts in augmented and diminished melodic fourths. The
text's turn in m. 10 into the nonliteral world of the heart elicits a characteristic shift into the key of the submediant major. Chromatically derived minor
harmonies at "wert gewesen wär's" reveal that the poet's resentment has a
surprisingly bitter core—it is symbolic of the rift separating the lovers that
the piano here leaves off its doubling of the melody and goes its independent
way. Increasing vehemence brings sobbing eighth notes and a quickening harmonic rhythm to "einem bessern Lohn." The anguished sequential repetitions
of "wert gewesen" rising to culminate in the opening music's return in m. 19
are profoundly affecting. Like an outcry of righteous indignation, the principal phrase rings out *forte*, harmonized more sonorously than before and
embellished with aching suspensions and appoggiaturas. But passion wanes
midphrase, and the song ends in quiet, albeit reluctant, resignation.

FOUR LIEDER, OP. 96

J. Brahms Vier Lieder für eine Singstimme mit Begleitung des Pianoforte (J[ohannes] Brahms, Four Songs for Solo Voice with Piano
Accompaniment), Op. 96. Published, with an imaginative drawing by Max
Klinger on the title page, in March 1886 by N. Simrock in Berlin; publication
number 8626.

The set was originally intended to contain only Heine songs, but possibly
because of Elisabet von Herzogenberg's negative criticism of a setting of
"Wie der Mond sich leuchtend dränget" in manuscript, Brahms suppressed
it and substituted the Daumer "Wir wandelten."

Der Tod, das ist die kühle Nacht, Op. 96/1
(Death Is the Cool Night)

Text by Heinrich Heine (1797–1856)

Der Tod, das ist die kühle Nacht,
Das Leben ist der schwüle Tag.
Es dunkelt schon, mich schläfert,
Der Tag hat mich müd' gemacht.

Über mein Bett erhebt sich ein Baum,
Drin singt die junge Nachtigall;
Sie singt von lauter Liebe,
Ich hör' es sogar im Traum.

Death is the cool night, life is the sultry day. It is already growing dark; I am
sleepy; the day has wearied me.
Over my bed rises a tree; in it the young nightingale is singing; it sings of
nothing but love; I hear it even in my dreams.

Composed in Vienna and Mürzzuschlag during the spring and early
summer of 1884.
The first performance is not documented.
Through-composed.

The poem appears as No. 87 in *Die Heimkehr* (1823–24), part 3 of the *Buch der Lieder* (1826/27). Brahms owned the *Sämtliche Werke* (Hamburg, 1861–84).

Often praised as one of the supreme examples of the synthesis of music and text, Brahms's setting achieves its perfection with such economy as to seem near-miraculous. Exact repetition is minimal. The accompaniment's pervasive eighth-quarter rhythm provides unity; a distinctive, gradually widening melodic figure in the piano, combined with a scalewise-descending cadence for the voice occurs twice in the first stanza (initially in mm. 4–5) and twice more in the second, providing at least an aural link between the two verses—a link that is left enigmatic by the words alone. (The close association of that melody with the notion of "der Tag" in the first verse implies that Brahms intended some association of meaning as well, but it is not obvious what that connection might be.)

The song's opening contrasts a vocal line that floats upward to symbolize the comforting night with another that works its way downward to suggest oppressive day. The impeding dissonance on "schwüle" is recalled seven measures later on "müd'," intensified by its higher pitch and its minor coloration. The commas in the poem's second couplet become long rests in a vocal line that is made coherent and carried along to a plaintive climax on "der Tag" by the piano's astonishing succession of chromatic harmonies.

Like the song's first pair of phrases, the entire second stanza unfolds over pedals on the dominant or tonic. The accompaniment's rising left-hand arpeggios evoke dream, and the repeated notes at the top of the right hand's chords suggest the nightingale's singing. The vocal line is higher and brighter than that of the first verse, and more continuously lyric—melody in the piano fills any gaps. Bittersweet dissonances underscore "Nachtigall" and the climactic "Liebe." A gradual ebbing of emotional tension is begun by the lower repetition of "von lauter Liebe." Each half of the final line of text is repeated, the segments framing the last full vocal phrase; the postlude begins with seeming reminiscences of fragments of the piano's cadence phrase, which give way to increasingly tranquil recallings of the song's initial sonority.

Wir wandelten, Op. 96/2 (We Were Walking)

Translated from the Magyar
by Georg Friedrich Daumer (1800–1875)

> Wir wandelten, wir zwei zusammen,
> Ich war so still und du so stille;
> Ich gäbe viel, um zu erfahren
> Was du gedacht in jenem Fall.

> Was ich gedacht—unausgesprochen
> Verbleibe das! Nur Eines sag' ich:
> So schön war alles was ich dachte,
> So himmlisch heiter war es all.
>
> In meinem Haupte die Gedanken,
> Sie läuteten wie gold'ne Glöckchen;
> So wundersüß, so wunderlieblich
> Ist in der Welt kein and'rer Hall.

We were walking, we two together; I was so silent and you so silent; I would give a lot to find out what you were thinking at that moment.

What I was thinking—let it remain unspoken! I will say one thing: everything I was thinking was so beautiful, it was all so divinely cheerful.

In my head my thoughts tinkled like little golden bells: so wonderfully sweet, so wonderfully lovely was the sound that it does not have its equal in the world.

Composed during the spring and summer of 1884 in Vienna and Mürz-zuschlag.

The first performance is not documented.

Through-composed, but ternary in effect.

The poem appears in Daumer's *Polydora, ein weltpoetisches Lieder-buch* (Frankfurt am Main, 1855).

The piano introduction establishes the song's extraordinary atmosphere of serenity and spiritual harmony, as two lovers stroll aimlessly in effortless canon, floating between pedal points above and below. The vocal line begins as though the singer were lost in reverie, recalling the scene in separated phrases of irregular length. The structure of the phrases is obscured by overlapping imitations, which appear intermittently, the whole underlaid by the gentle walking of continual eighth notes.

As the poem's second verse moves from narrative into the realm of unspoken thought, the imitations and eighth notes gradually recede, and a $\frac{3}{2}$ bar disrupts the sense of regular motion. A modulation as subtle as shifting light leads to the key of the lowered submediant—the key that Brahms so often associated with the unreal world of dream or imagination—here notated enharmonically in sharps, a further symbol of removal. The effect is breathtaking, an apt metaphor for the text's "so schön war alles was ich dachte."

Portraying the "little golden bells" of the third verse by quiet octave afterbeats in the accompaniment is particularly enchanting. The afterbeats persist, helping to bridge the return to the home key and there assuming the stabilizing role of the earlier double pedal.

The poem's closing lines are set to music which resembles that of the opening, but the vocal line is now embellished with long successions of little sighing appoggiatura figures, as if the moment's sweetness had in remembrance become almost overwhelmingly poignant. The piano here only hints at canonic imitation, in the left hand's quarter notes in mm. 38–39. But in the postlude, fragments of imitation proliferate, at smaller intervals of both time and pitch than before, symbolic of the lovers' being drawn even closer together by their shared silence.

Clara Schumann wrote to Brahms on 14 May 1886, after the publication of Opp. 96 and 97, "Just a word today about your beautiful songs. . . . I like all the songs in Op. 96, and think the second one particularly fine and full of feeling." Elisabet von Herzogenberg, who had seen the songs in manuscript, wrote from Leipzig in a letter dated 21/22 May 1885, "[*Wir wandelten*] must be one of the most glorious songs in the world." Many share her opinion.

Es schauen die Blumen, Op. 96/3 (Flowers Look)

Text by Heinrich Heine (1797–1856)

> Es schauen die Blumen alle
> Zur leuchtenden Sonne hinauf;
> Es nehmen die Ströme alle
> Zum leuchtenden Meere den Lauf.
>
> Es flattern die Lieder alle
> Zu meinem leuchtenden Lieb—
> Nehmt mit meine Tränen und Seufzer,
> Ihr Lieder, wehmütig und trüb!

All flowers look up to the beaming sun; all rivers run down to the gleaming sea.
All songs fly to my radiant sweetheart. Take along my tears and sighs, you melancholy and sad songs!

Composed in Vienna and Mürzzuschlag during the spring and early summer of 1884.

The first performance is not documented.

Through-composed.

The text was first printed in the Berlin periodical *Gesellschafter oder Blätter für Geist und Herz* in 1822; in the *Sämtliche Werke*, it appears in an appendix to the *Buch der Lieder* under the heading "Zu 'Lyrisches Intermezzo.'"

The song's pervading unrest is reflected in the accompaniment's conflicting sixteenth-note triplets and duplets; its melancholy undercurrent is revealed in the morose little melody that is indicated by the introduction's double-stemming and often implied thereafter in the right hand's figuration.

The quick tempo and rapidly moving vocal melody make the song almost scherzo-like, particularly in comparison with its weightier peers in the opus. But a certain seriousness accrues from the scraps of canonic imitation, the bass pedal in afterbeats that supports the concluding couplet's long diminuendo, and particularly the augmentation of the last phrase.

The melodic fragment in the vocal line of m. 9 is imitated by the piano in the following measure and takes on added significance when the process is repeated in mm. 13–14. When it reappears in the codalike concluding section, where it sounds in four successive measures in the piano's tenor and provides the basis for the voice's soaring "wehmütig und trüb," it has become a metaphor for the flight of the poet's sorrow-laden songs.

Elisabet von Herzogenberg described "Es schauen die Blumen" as "a gem indeed, a marvel of compactness!" (Leipzig, 21/22 May 1885). Upon her receipt of the published songs, Clara Schumann wrote on 14 May 1886, "Oh, how the third moves one with its cry of despair at the end!"

Meerfahrt, Op. 96/4 (A Boat Ride on the Sea)

Text by Heinrich Heine (1797–1856)

> Mein Liebchen, wir saßen beisammen
> Traulich im leichten Kahn.
> Die Nacht war still, und wir schwammen
> Auf weiter Wasserbahn.
>
> Die Geisterinsel, die schöne,
> Lag dämm'rig im Mondenglanz;
> Dort klangen liebe Töne
> Und wogte der Nebeltanz.
>
> Dort klang es lieb und lieber
> Und wogt' es hin und her;
> Wir aber schwammen vorüber
> Trostlos auf weitem Meer.

My darling, we were sitting together snugly in a small, light boat. The night was quiet and we floated on a broad watery path.

The beautiful isle of the spirits lay dusk-clad in the moonlight; there lovely music was heard and the dance of the mists rocked to and fro.

There the music sounded more and more lovely and the rocking motion came and went, but we floated past, disconsolate on the wide sea.

Composed during the spring and early summer 1884 in Vienna and Mürzzuschlag.

First performed by Gustav Walter on 8 January 1886 in Vienna.

Through-composed; A B A in effect, though lacking an exact return.

The poem is No. 42 in the "Lyrisches Intermezzo" from the *Buch der Lieder* (1827); it was first published in 1823 in *Tragödien nebst einem lyrischen Intermezzo*.

In Heine's evocative verses, the lovers in their little boat approach the beautiful moonlit isle of spirits, with its ever-lovelier music and dancing mists, but they are carried past it to drift, inconsolable, on the open sea. Brahms translates the text's despairing fatalism into an ominous, relentless barcarolle that encloses a snatch of the fervid waltz music emanating from the island.

The song's most striking feature is the anguished *forte* dissonances, filled with foreboding—"those strangely affecting hornblasts," as Elisabet von Herzogenberg described them in her letter of 21/22 May 1885—that appear in mm. 3, 29, 54, and 58 to mark the statements of the piano's principal melody. When the voice twice joins in toward the end, it is with the word "trostlos."

The long, atmospheric piano prelude and the first vocal stanza are firmly anchored to the tonic key, their harmonic richness notwithstanding; the middle section, on the other hand, is carried far afield on iridescent ripples of modulation. Gradually growing animation leads to the dramatic climax of the song, when the listener is set adrift, like the lovers, on a powerful swell of ambiguous diminished-seventh harmony. Slowing, it melts into the key and tempo of the opening, and the song recedes despairingly into an increasingly bleak night.

The setting is impressive, even daring, and its depiction of helpless longing for the unattainable lingers in the memory. Frau Herzogenberg not only praised the song in painstaking detail in her letter of 21/22 May 1885 (and begged for a manuscript copy as a Christmas gift) but also returned to it repeatedly in subsequent correspondence: "We are all quite intoxicated with your A-minor song—such gems do not fall from heaven every day" (24 May 1885); "The A-minor song, with its final 'trostlos,' still haunts me perpetually. It follows me to bed, and, once I begin, I have to go through with it to the glorious ending" (3 June 1885).

SIX LIEDER, OP. 97

J. Brahms Op. 97. 6 Lieder für eine Singstimme mit Begl. d. Pianoforte (Six Songs for Solo Voice with Piano Accompaniment). Published, with a drawing by Max Klinger on the cover, in March 1886 by N. Simrock in Berlin; publication number 8627.

The group joins settings of two poems by Reinhold (pseudonym for Christian Köstlin, the father of Marie Fellinger, who was a close friend of Brahms and made many informal photographs of him during his last years), two folksong texts from the Kretzschmer-Zuccalmaglio collection, and single poems by Alexis (pseudonym for Wilhelm Häring) and Klaus Groth. The ordering juxtaposes related keys. Five of the six were given their first performance by the tenor Gustav Walter.

Nachtigall, Op. 97/1 (Nightingale)

Text by Christian Reinhold
(Christian Reinhold Köstlin, 1813–1856)

O Nachtigall,
Dein süßer Schall,
Er dringet mir durch Mark und Bein.
Nein, trauter Vogel, nein!
Was in mir schafft so süße Pein,
Das ist nicht dein—
Das ist von andern, himmelschönen,
Nun längst für mich verklungenen Tönen,
In deinem Lied ein leiser Widerhall!

O nightingale, your sweet sound penetrates my inmost being. No, dear bird, no! what causes such sweet pain in me is not your singing; it is a soft echo within your song of other music, divinely beautiful, but long silenced for me!

Composed earlier in 1885 than 6 May, when a manuscript copy was sent to the Herzogenbergs.

First performed (from manuscript) by Gustav Walter on 8 January 1886 at a *Lieder* recital in Vienna.

Through-composed, with a reference toward the end to material from the beginning.

The text is from Reinhold's *Gedichte* (Stuttgart, 1853).

Evidently inspired by the idea of the awakening of memories of lost, past happiness by a nightingale's singing, Brahms wedded the poem's plaintive lines to music of heartbreaking poignancy, creating yet another of the supreme masterpieces of the art song repertoire.

The rhythmically similar, three-note melodic figures that make up the piano's ardent introduction evoke the bird's yearning song. The vocal line begins by imitating in short phrases, first repetitive, then sequential. A further sequence in the piano interlude invokes the pathos of Neapolitan harmony before giving way to rhythmic calming.

Reflecting the poet's intensifying emotion, a tender, more expansive vocal melody in the major soars ever-higher to a blossoming climax at "nun längst für mich." ("It can never be broad enough for me," Brahms is said to have remarked when Alice Barbi's pronounced broadening of the tempo was praised in his presence.) The even-paced accompaniment, with its melodic bass line, suggests the unhurried strolling of harmonious lovers. As that "other music" from the past is recalled, hushed quarter-note chords yield to the wondrous rising arpeggios of dream. The rapturous harmonization of "himmelschönen" is indeed "divinely beautiful," and the wistful minor inflection at "verklungenen Tönen," as both voice and piano trail off into silence, is deeply affecting.

The accompaniment's soft remembrance of fragments from the opening is a graphic illustration of "in deinem Lied ein leiser Widerhall," as is also the appoggiatura figure that reverberates in three different registers during the concluding major-mode phrase.

Improbable as it seems of such a hand-in-glove setting, Kalbeck reports (*Brahms*, III$_2$, 531–532) that the melody of "Nachtigall" is adapted from one composed originally for another Reinhold text, "Ein Wanderer," later published with new music as Op. 106/5. In fact, a group of manuscript songs that Brahms sent to Elisabet von Herzogenberg for comment on 6 May 1885 included both "Nachtigall" and the early version of "Ein Wanderer," with a note describing them as "more or less twins—on whom I am now trying all sorts of experiments." Her response to "Ein Wanderer" was cool, and Brahms is presumed to have destroyed that version.

For "Nachtigall," on the other hand, Elisabet had nothing but praise, calling it "delicious as the first tender green of the woods" and "inspired from first to last." Of its borrowed melody, she wrote that it "has the bittersweet of the real nightingale's song; they seem to revel in augmented and diminished intervals, passionate little creatures that they are!"

Auf dem Schiffe, Op. 97/2 (On the Ship)

Text by Christian Reinhold
(Christian Reinhold Köstlin, 1813–1856)

Ein Vögelein
Fliegt über den Rhein
Und wiegt die Flügel
Im Sonnenschein,
Sieht Rebenhügel
Und grüne Flut
In gold'ner Glut.—
Wie wohl das tut,
So hoch erhoben
Im Morgenhauch!
Beim Vöglein droben,
O, wär' ich auch!

A little bird flies over the Rhine and cradles its wings in the sunshine; it sees vine-clad hills and the green river in a golden glow.

What a good feeling that is, to be so high up in the morning breeze! I wish I too were with the little bird up there!

The composition date is uncertain, probably early 1885—a copy was sent to Elisabet von Herzogenberg on 6 May of that year.

First performed by Gustav Walter on 11 February 1887 at an all-Brahms concert in Vienna.

Through-composed; only the music for the voice's first eight measures is repeated.

The text is from Reinhold's 1853 *Gedichte*.

The introduction pictures the darting flight of the lone bird—surely a swallow!—in a flapping accompaniment figure of atypical literalness. The vocal line too seems to circle and soar as it deftly evades alighting on tonic harmony.

In the second part of the poem, the flying bird is seen as a symbol of happy release from earthly care. At "Wie wohl das tut" the music suddenly finds itself, like a flight of imagination, in the distant key of C major (A♭ in the low key), with a new flowing accompaniment which is to predominate hereafter. The line's repetition is elongated in a rapturous outcry supported by the piano with a rising left-hand arpeggio, which Brahms so often associated with dream or wishful vision.

The two vocal phrases that follow are constructed entirely from repetitions of a yearning resolving-appoggiatura figure, which begin a step higher with each measure of the first phrase, a third higher with each measure of the second.

The tonic key returns, and the earlier accompaniment figure is recalled as the text refers once more to the little bird. Aching dissonances point up the longingly reiterated "O wär' ich auch." At the end of the song, a gentler variant of the flapping figure evokes an image of the bird hovering briefly overhead, suddenly circling to disappear into the sky above. Two *forte* punctuations bring the enchanting song to a cheerful close.

Entführung, Op. 97/3 (Abduction)

Text by Willibald Alexis (Wilhelm Häring, 1798–1871)

> O Lady Judith, spröder Schatz,
>> Drückt dich zu fest mein Arm?
> Je zwei zu Pferd haben schlechten Platz
>> Und Winternacht weht nicht warm.
>
> Hart ist der Sitz und knapp und schmal,
>> Und kalt mein Kleid von Erz,
> Doch kälter und härter als Sattel und Stahl
>> War gegen mich dein Herz.
>
> Sechs Nächte lag ich in Sumpf und Moor
>> Und hab' um dich gewacht,
> Doch weicher, bei Sankt Görg ich's schwor,
>> Schlaf' ich die siebente Nacht!

O Lady Judith, my stubborn sweetheart, is my arm pressing you too tightly? It isn't comfortable for two on one horse, and a winter night's wind isn't warm.

The seat is hard and scant and narrow, and my suit of metal is cold, but colder and harder than saddle and steel was your heart to me.

Six nights I lay in the bog and heath keeping vigil for your sake, but softer—by Saint George I swore it—will be my sleep on the seventh night!

The composition date is uncertain; a manuscript version existed in May 1885, and the song was given its final form sometime between late May 1885 and its publication in March 1886.

The first performance is not documented.

Strophic, with an elongated final phrase.

The text is from Alexis's *Balladen* (Berlin, 1836).

The introductory trumpet call imparts a certain chivalric flavor and sets the galloping accompaniment in motion; at the end of the strophe, it serves to complete the four-measure phrase begun by the voice's repetition of the closing line of the verse.

The wide-ranging vocal melody is notable for its unusual upward leaps of a tenth, which appear at the end of the first phrase and, filled with intervening pitches, join the last two phrases. The conflict of the voice's duplet eighths with the piano's triplets adds restless excitement.

In keeping with its folkloric tone, the song stays close to its home key, venturing only to the dominant in the first four-measure phrase and to the relative major (via its own dominant) in the second. The accompaniment pattern's perfectly placed slur defines the horse's gait exactly. Toward the end of the strophe, a single slurred appoggiatura figure in the bass expressively underscores "warm" and "Herz," and in the last verse, suggests the anticipated pleasure of "Nacht." The perpetual motion is finally brought to a halt by two *forte* chords, without ritard.

Brahms's expansion of the third strophe's conclusion is presumed to have been influenced, at least in part, by Elisabet von Herzogenberg's dissatisfaction with the version he sent to her in manuscript on 6 May 1885. In her lengthy letter of 21/22 May, she wrote of "Lady Judith":

> The words are splendid and the music delicious. It is too short, though. One almost wishes you had not made a strophic song of it, or had made some alteration or extension of the last verse. It is over so quickly, and there is so much concentration in the poem that one feels it all the more.

And further, on 3 June 1885:

> I have been wondering what could be done with Judith, and whether you could not add a train to the proud lady's robe. . . . It seems so painfully abrupt and scanty. Do think it over again, please!

Dort in den Weiden, Op. 97/4 (There among the Willows)

Text, a "Folk Song from the Lower Rhine," by
Anton Wilhelm Florentin von Zuccalmaglio (1803–1869)

Dort in den Weiden steht ein Haus,
Da schaut die Magd zum Fenster 'naus!
Sie schaut stromauf, sie schaut stromab:
Ist noch nicht da mein Herzensknab'?
Der schönste Bursch' am ganzen Rhein,
Den nenn' ich mein!

Des Morgens fährt er auf dem Fluß
Und singt herüber seinen Gruß,
Des Abends, wenn's Glühwürmchen fliegt,
Sein Nachen an das Ufer wiegt,
Da kann ich mit dem Burschen mein
Beisammen sein!

Die Nachtigall im Fliederstrauch,
Was sie da singt, versteh' ich auch,
Sie saget: Über's Jahr ist Fest,

> Hab' ich, mein Lieber, auch ein Nest,
> Wo ich dann mit dem Burschen mein
> Die Froh'st' am Rhein!

There among the willows stands a house; there the girl looks out the window! She looks upstream, she looks downstream: isn't my beloved boy here yet? The handsomest fellow on the whole Rhine I call my own!

Every morning he sails on the river and sings a greeting to me; every evening when the glowworm flies and his boat rocks by the riverbank, then I can be together with my lover!

What the nightingale sings in the lilac bush, I can understand too; it says: a year from now will be celebration time and I too, my dear, will have a nest, where with my lover I will be the happiest girl on the Rhine!

The date of composition is uncertain, but earlier than May 1885.

The first performance was sung (from manuscript) by Gustav Walter on 8 January 1886 in Vienna.

Strophic.

The text is from the Kretzschmer-Zuccalmaglio *Deutsche Volkslieder mit ihren Original-Weisen* (Berlin, 1838–40).

Neither the poem nor the tune there associated with it is authentically from the lower Rhine; both were fabricated by Zuccalmaglio. Brahms innocently included an arrangement of the double counterfeit as No. 31 in his forty-nine *Deutsche Volkslieder* (1894), which has many similarities to his own setting of the text. Both have the same meter signature, accompaniment style, and opening melodic contour; both feature two parallel phrases at the beginning but sequential construction toward the end, both insert a dominant-directed interlude between strophes, and both somewhat vary the accompaniment of the third strophe. But Brahms's original melody comprises only fourteen measures rather than sixteen, avoiding the effect of breathlessness by adding a beat to mm. 4 and 8; where the other song repeats text in its opening phrases, this one repeats a melodic motive instead, reserving its own text repetitions for the ascent to the climax at the close. In the earlier version the alterations to the third strophe are only rhythmic and sonorous, contributing to a brilliant conclusion, but those in the later setting provide a contrasting countermelody and new harmonies.

Elisabet von Herzogenberg did not much like "Dort in den Weiden." Although it had been among the manuscripts that were the subject of her letter of 21/22 May 1885, she failed to mention it. When Brahms questioned her about it, suggesting that it may have been overlooked "on the back of *Lady Judith,*" she replied (3 June 1885):

> The song somehow failed to captivate me. I thought to myself how much I should like it if I did not know the other Brahms songs; knowing them, I realized how spoilt I was! It seemed to me that you had given us much the same

message before, only told more prettily and weighing heavier in the golden scales; while everything that charms me most in the other songs is, I feel, being said for the first time. . . .

Over and above this I consider the little *Willow Song* unvocal, and I never like the accompaniment to follow the notes of the melody—it rarely fails to embarrass the singer.[!]

Komm bald, Op. 97/5 (Come Soon)

Text by Klaus Groth (1819–1899)

Warum denn warten
Von Tag zu Tag?
Es blüht im Garten
Was blühen mag.

Wer kommt und zählt es,
Was blüht so schön?
An Augen fehlt es,
Es anzuseh'n.

Die meinen wandern
Vom Strauch zum Baum;
Mir scheint, auch Andern
Wär's wie ein Traum.

Und von den Lieben,
Die mir getreu,
Und mir geblieben,
Wär'st du dabei!

Why should we wait from day to day? In the garden everything that feels like blossoming is doing so.

Who comes to count all the beautiful blossoming things? There aren't enough eyes to look at it all.

My eyes wander from bush to tree; I think others too would find it to be like a dream.

And among the loved ones who are faithful to me and still remain to me, I wish you were here!

Composed in May 1885.

First performed publicly on 8 January 1886 at a Vienna song recital by Gustav Walter, who sang from manuscript.

A A B A'; varied strophic.

Groth gave the poem in manuscript to Brahms for his fifty-second birthday and sent a copy to their mutual friend the contralto Hermine Spies. By the following day, Brahms had finished setting it to music, and he also posted a copy of the song to the fortunate Mme Spies.

The text amounts to little more than an elegantly expressed greeting card message, but its Viennese gentility elicited a love song of compelling beauty, suffused with tenderness and glowing with sincerity of feeling.

The rich doublings of the chordal accompaniment are presaged by the serene introduction with its wide-spaced voicing in the piano's middle register and its tenor-range interior melodic counterpoint. The vocal line is simplicity itself, but unexpectedly wide in range. The first strophe comprises two rhythmically identical four-measure phrases of only nine notes each; the first phrase spans an octave, the second a tenth. The same music is repeated for the second stanza. In the piano, a little turning motive in eighth notes binds weak measures to strong throughout.

The third stanza is set to a melody derived by a process of development and variation from motives heard earlier. Obvious examples are the eighth-note idea, appearing here in the vocal line for the first time, and the melodic curve of "von Strauch zum Baum" in mm. 18–19 and "wär's wie ein Traum" in mm. 22–23, which expands the intervals of "von Tag zu Tag" in mm. 7–8. Downbeat rests in the accompaniment shift importance to the melody. The sequential construction accommodates the introduction of the warmly affecting major harmonies from the minor side of the key, including the mediant (implied by its dominant) and the submediant. A particularly exquisite effect is achieved at the repetition of "wär's wie ein Traum," where a hushed *pianissimo* and hemiola lift the passage temporarily into unreality, as the harmony surefootedly wends its way, with only three suspension-embellished chords, back to the dominant to begin the transition to the final strophe.

The fourth stanza begins like the first, but an alteration in the second phrase allows for a climactic high note for the voice in m. 36 (reinforced in *forte* by the piano in m. 40) as well as a musically satisfying emphasis on the hitherto largely absent subdominant. The wistful repetitions of "wär'st du dabei" touchingly evoke the poet's loneliness.

Trennung, Op. 97/6 (Separation)

Swabian Folk Song

Da unten im Tale
Läuft's Wasser so trüb,
Und i kann dir's net sagen,
I hab di so lieb.

Sprichst all'weil von Liebe,
Sprichst all'weil von Treu',
Und a bissele Falschheit
Is auch wohl dabei.

Und wenn i dir's zehnmal sag',
Daß i di lieb' und mag,

> Und du willst nit verstehen, muß i
> Halt weiter geh'n!
>
> Für die Zeit, wo du g'liebt mi hast,
> Da dank' i dir schön,
> Und i wünsch', daß dir's anderswo
> Besser mag geh'n.

Down in the valley there, the water in the river is troubled, and I can't tell you how much I love you.

You always talk about love, you always talk about constancy, but there's a bit of falseness in you too.

And if I tell you ten times that I love you and care for you, and you refuse to understand, I'll just have to travel on.

I thank you kindly for the time that you loved me and I hope that things go better for you elsewhere.

Composed in March 1885 or earlier; Maria Fellinger was given a manuscript copy (of an earlier version, in E♭ rather than F) on 9 March.

The first performance was sung (from manuscript) by Gustav Walter on 8 January 1886 in Vienna.

Strophic.

The text is from the Kretzschmer-Zuccalmaglio *Deutsche Volkslieder mit ihren Original-Weisen* (Berlin, 1838–40); both the poem and its melody are presumed to be authentic Swabian folklore.

An arrangement of the folk song appears as No. 6 in Brahms's forty-nine *Deutsche Volkslieder* (1894). It is instructive to compare it with his own setting of the text. There are the obvious similarities of meter, texture, and the flowing eighth-note accompaniment, but the two melodies also correspond sufficiently in rhythm, mood, and overall contour that the same music can serve as postlude for both.

By means of text repetitions, Brahms's melody expands the original eight measures to twelve; the second line is restated as a poignantly harmonized echo, the fourth as a wider-ranged confirmation. The folk-song arrangement gains immediacy from its lack of an introduction, but the art-song version's expressiveness is enhanced by its less rigid bass line.

The poem is cast in the form of a dialogue between a pleading, probably duplicitous, lover (verses 1 and 3) and a spirited maiden (verses 2 and 4), who dismisses him smartly at the end. Brahms ignores the situation's potential for lighthearted treatment and imbues both versions with an undercurrent of sadness; the resulting aura of wistful tenderness accounts for much of their effectiveness.

EIGHT ZIGEUNERLIEDER
FOR SOLO VOICE, OP. 103

Translated from the Hungarian by Hugo Conrat

Acht Zigeunerlieder für eine Singstimme mit Begleitung des Pi-anoforte von Johannes Brahms (Eight Gypsy Songs for Solo Voice with Piano Accompaniment by Johannes Brahms), Op. 103. Published in April/May 1889 by N. Simrock in Berlin; publication number 9046.

The original Op. 103 was eleven *Zigeunerlieder* for vocal quartet (SATB) with piano, composed during the winter of 1887/88 in Vienna and published in October 1888, also by Simrock; this is the composer's arrangement of Nos. 1–7 and 11, presumably dating from early 1889.

The first performance of the solo version is not documented. As quartets, the first public performance was given at the Berlin Singakademiesaal on 31 October 1888 by Frau Schmidt-Köhne, Amalie Joachim, Raimund von Zur-Mühlen, and Felix Schmidt; there had been earlier private performances within the circle of Brahms's friends, for whom they were intended.

The texts were brought to Brahms's attention by Hugo Conrat, a cultured Viennese businessman (and a correspondent for the *Neue Musikzeitung*) in whose home Brahms was later a frequent guest. Conrat, with the help of Fräulein Witzl, a Hungarian nanny employed in his household, had prepared rhyming German translations of twenty-five presumed Hungarian folk songs (*Ungarische Liebeslieder*) with piano accompaniments by Zoltan Nagy, to be published in Budapest and Leipzig, and had submitted them to Brahms—the composer of the vastly popular Hungarian Dances—for his appraisal. After his return from a brief winter holiday in Budapest, Brahms set eagerly to work on the *Zigeunerlieder*.

The project seems to have been undertaken for sheer pleasure, perhaps to counterbalance the simultaneous labor of completing the Double Concerto, published in May/June 1888 as Op. 102. (Brahms characterized the new quartets to Elisabet von Herzogenberg as "excessively gay stuff" [March 1888] and suggested to Clara Schumann that she might find them "a little too rollicking" [April 1888].) Gypsy music exerted a strong fascination throughout his life, and Brahms returned to it again and again, particularly in his lighter moments.

The Gypsy Songs combine characteristics of two of Brahms's most popular (and profitable) works; like the *Liebeslieder*, they are a succession of sung dance-pieces of the same type, but instead of the waltz, they glorify the $\frac{2}{4}$ csárdás style of the Hungarian Dances—there are changes of tempo, but not of meter. Not unpredictably, the popularity of the Op. 103 quartets spread rapidly also, and their success led to a demand for the solo version and to the composition of four more Conrat gypsy-song quartets, which were published in 1892 as Op. 112/3–6.

The musical settings are pure Brahms, with only an occasional hint of a rhythm or a melodic contour from the original Hungarian tunes. While there is little that an ethnomusicologist would identify as authentic, one is seldom unaware of an underlay of ethnicity of a sort, albeit of that citified, universalized gypsy language familiar from the Liszt Hungarian Rhapsodies and from the Hungarian Dances of Dvořák and of Brahms himself. (When Elisabet von Herzogenberg first saw the *Zigeunerlieder* in manuscript, she remarked that "the line of the melodies often strikes me as being more Bohemian-Dvořákesque than Hungarian" [25 March 1888].)

It is somewhat surprising that only the first two songs are in the minor mode, and that the characteristic reversed dotted-rhythm figure (short-long) is entirely lacking. There are suggestions of the sounds of cimbalom, concertina, gypsy violin, and zither. The principal elements that contribute to the redolence of nationalism are the extraordinary vigor and variety of the rhythmic treatment within the constant $\frac{2}{4}$ meter, and the frequent avoidance of regular four-measure phrases, either by the writing of phrases of six measures (as in No. 1) or five measures (last part of No. 7), or by the addition of measures of echo (No. 3) or of interlude (No. 5). Sometimes the procedure is reversed, and an added measure evens an odd-measured phrase (Nos. 2, 7, and 8). The bar of silence before the returns in Nos. 3, 4, and 6 has a distinctively "authentic" ring, as does the fermata after the short introduction to No. 5.

The piano provides humorous wrong-octave echoes in No. 3 and implied imitations by diminution in the last part of No. 7. No. 3 presents the dilemma of a man's first verse but a woman's second; Brahms provided an optional second voice in the refrain in case two singers should opt to share the song. The final song of the set, with its enticing key changes and infectious rhythms, cannot fail to captivate.

Upon her reacquaintance with the Gypsy Songs, newly published, Elisabet von Herzogenberg's opinion of them warmed:

> The more I play the *Zigeunerlieder*, the more I love them. . . . They are so gloriously alive—rushing, throbbing, stamping along, then settling down to a

smooth, gentle flow. We cannot try them properly in this beautiful uncivilized spot [the Herzogenbergs were vacationing in Nice], and it is a sore deprivation. Yet I have a vivid idea of how they all sound; the two first numbers aglow with life, the charming humor of No. 6, the durable melancholy fervor of [No. 7]—I am always moved to tears by the second part. . . . How delightful it would be to arrange a really good performance of this fine work by a few music-lovers! I look forward to next winter for this sort of enjoyment. [28 October 1888]

1.

He, Zigeuner, greife in die Saiten ein!
Spiel' das Lied vom ungetreuen Mägdelein!
Laß die Saiten weinen, klagen, traurig bange,
Bis die heiße Träne netzet diese Wange!

Hey, Gypsy, play your violin! Play the song of the unfaithful girl! Let the strings weep, lament, sadly and anxiously, until hot tears moisten my cheek!

2.

Hochgetürmte Rimaflut, wie bist du so trüb',
An dem Ufer klag' ich laut nach dir, mein Lieb!
Wellen fliehen, Wellen strömen,
Rauschen an den Strand heran zu mir;
An dem Rimaufer laßt mich ewig weinen nach ihr!

River Rima with your towering banks, how troubled you are; by its edge I loudly moan for you, my love! Waves dash by, waves rush along and rumble up to the riverbank where I stand; by the banks of the Rima let me weep eternally for her!

3.

Wißt ihr, wann mein Kindchen
Am allerschönsten ist?
Wenn ihr süßes Mündchen
Scherzt und lacht und küßt.
Mägdelein,
Du bist mein,
Inniglich
Küß' ich dich,
Dich erschuf der liebe Himmel
Einzig nur für mich.

Wißt ihr, wann mein Liebster
Am besten mir gefällt?
Wenn in seinen Armen
Er mich umschlungen hält.
Schätzelein,
Du bist mein,
Inniglich
Küß' ich dich,
Dich erschuf der liebe Himmel
Einzig nur für mich!

Do you know when my darling is most beautiful? When her sweet little mouth jokes and laughs and kisses. Dear little girl, you are mine, I kiss you fervently; loving heaven created you for me alone!

Do you know when I like my sweetheart best? When he holds me close in his arms. Dear lover, you are mine, I kiss you fervently; loving heaven created you for me alone!

4.

Lieber Gott, du weißt, wie oft bereut ich hab',
Daß ich meinem Liebsten einst ein Küßchen gab.
Herz gebot, daß ich ihn küssen muß,
Denk', so lang' ich leb', an diesen ersten Kuß.

Lieber Gott, du weißt, wie oft in stiller Nacht
Ich in Lust und Leid an meinen Schatz gedacht.
Lieb' ist süß, wenn bitter auch die Reu',
Armes Herze bleibt mir ewig, ewig treu.

Dear God, you know how often I have regretted the kiss I once gave my sweetheart. My heart commanded me to kiss him; I will think about that first kiss as long as I live.

Dear God, you know how often in the silence of the night I have thought about my loved one in pleasure and pain. Love is sweet, even if repentance is bitter; my poor heart will remain eternally, eternally true to him.

5.

Brauner Bursche führt zum Tanze
Sein blauäugig schönes Kind,
Schlägt die Sporen keck zusammen,
Czardas-Melodie beginnt;
Küßt und herzt sein süßes Täubchen,
Dreht sie, führt sie, jauchzt und springt;

Wirft drei blanke Silbergulden
Auf das Cimbal, daß es klingt.

A suntanned lad leads his beautiful blue-eyed sweetheart to the dance;
he boldly strikes his spurs together; a csárdás melody begins; he kisses and
caresses his sweet loved one, turns her around, leads her, rejoices and leaps;
he throws three bright silver coins onto the cimbalom to make it twang.

6.

Röslein dreie in der Reihe blüh'n so rot,
Daß der Bursch' zum Mädel geht, ist kein Verbot!
Lieber Gott, wenn das verboten wär',
Ständ' die schöne weite Welt schon längst nicht mehr,
Ledig bleiben Sünde wär'!

Schönstes Städtchen in Alföld ist Ketschkemet,
Dort gibt es gar viele Mädchen schmuck und nett!
Freunde, sucht euch dort ein Bräutchen aus,
Freit um ihre Hand und gründet euer Haus,
Freudenbecher leeret aus!

Three little roses in a row blossom so red; there's no law against a young
man's visiting a young girl! Dear God, if that were forbidden, the beautiful, wide world would have been gone long ago; to remain unmarried is
a sin!
The prettiest little town in Alföld is Kecskemét; there are really a lot of
good-looking and nice girls! Friends, find yourselves a bride there, ask for her
hand and establish your household; drain the cup of joy!

7.

Kommt dir manchmal in den Sinn,
Mein süßes Lieb,
Was du einst mit heil'gem Eide
Mir gelobt?
Täusch' mich nicht, verlaß' mich nicht,
Du weißt nicht wie lieb ich dich hab',
Lieb' du mich, wie ich dich,
Dann strömt Gottes Huld auf dich herab.

Do you sometimes recall to mind, my darling, what you once promised me
with a sacred oath? Don't deceive me, don't abandon me; you don't know how
much I love you; love me as I love you, and then God's grace will pour down
on you!

8.

Rote Abendwolken zieh'n
Am Firmament,
Sehnsuchtsvoll nach dir, mein Lieb,
Das Herze brennt;
Himmel strahlt in glüh'nder Pracht
Und ich träum' bei Tag und Nacht
Nur allein von dem süßen Liebchen mein.

Red evening clouds pass by in the firmament; my heart burns longingly for you, my darling. The sky beams in glowing splendor, and I dream, by day and night, only of my sweet lover.

FIVE LIEDER FOR LOW VOICE, OP. 105

Fünf Lieder für eine tiefere Stimme mit Begleitung des Pianoforte von Johannes Brahms (Five Songs for Low Voice with Piano Accompaniment by Johannes Brahms), Op. 105. Published in October 1888 by N. Simrock in Berlin; publication number 9042.

The fifteen songs published as Opp. 105–107 in October 1888 show the sure hand of a master. Though the performance of Op. 105 as a set by a single performer is almost precluded by the diversity and changing gender-specificity of its texts, the progression of keys is compatible.

Simrock owns a manuscript—a booklet with page numbers in Brahms's hand—that shows that originally the five songs Op. 105/3 and 4, Op. 106/3 and 4, and Op. 107/5, in that order, were to have formed a single set.

Wie Melodien zieht es mir, Op. 105/1
(As If Melodies Were Moving)

Text by Klaus Groth (1819–1899)

> Wie Melodien zieht es
> Mir leise durch den Sinn,
> Wie Frühlingsblumen blüht es,
> Und schwebt wie Duft dahin.
>
> Doch kommt das Wort und faßt es
> Und führt es vor das Aug',
> Wie Nebelgrau erblaßt es
> Und schwindet wie ein Hauch.
>
> Und dennoch ruht im Reime
> Verborgen wohl ein Duft,
> Den mild aus stillem Keime
> Ein feuchtes Auge ruft.

I feel as if melodies were moving faintly through my mind; they seem to blossom like spring flowers and waft away like fragrance.

> But when words come and capture them and bring them before my sight,
> they grow pale like the grayness of a mist and vanish like a puff of breath.
>   And yet, a fragrance surely does remain enclosed within my rhymes, a fragrance that tear-dampened eyes gently evoke from the silent bud.

Composed at Thun in August 1886.

First sung publicly (from manuscript) by Gustav Walter on 11 February 1887 at an all-Brahms concert in Vienna; Hermine Spies had sung the song earlier, in September 1886, in a private performance at Brahms's house in Thun.

Modified strophic.

The text is from *Hundert Blätter, Paralipomena zum Quickborn* (Hamburg, 1854).

Groth's poem muses enigmatically on the elusive ability of the poet to communicate feelings, implying that the power of his words to move is enhanced when, by attaching themselves to the evanescent melodies in his mind, they become lyric poetry. It is not difficult, particularly when Brahms's affective setting is at hand, to extend that notion to include the art of the song composer as well—to suggest that the fusion of poetry and music has greater power to arouse emotion than does either alone.

Each of the song's three strophes begins with a nobly arching melodic phrase with an atypical three-beat anacrusis. A sense of underlying vagueness rather than firmness is conveyed by movement through subdominant and Neapolitan harmonies, usually associated in Brahms's vocabulary with gentleness and tenderness respectively. Subsequent phrases are dominated by the dotted rhythms that first appear in the fourth measure.

Wide-ranging arpeggios in the accompaniment waft freely through the texture. Toward the end of each strophe, a piano melody in legato thirds, symbolizing the fragrance or breath that is a part of each stanza's imagery, floats through the vocal silence that postpones the concluding repetition of text.

The first strophe modulates to a close on the dominant, but its successors are altered to reflect more precisely the changing implications of the text. The second avoids the dominant, but moves instead to the subdominant and on to a cadence in the relative minor, mirroring the poet's frustrated intentions. The third stanza's misty-eyed hopefulness prompts even greater harmonic digression, to the lowered submediant, to the Neapolitan, and at last tortuously back to the tonic, like the poet groping about in search of reassurance. Expanded text repetition and a final arching phrase that calls to mind that of the opening provide a sense of closure. In the brief postlude, a spiraling arpeggio melody, indecisive rhythmic interjections, and a delayed and extended plagal cadence seem to summarize the whole song's tone of wistful introspection.

Concerning "Wie Melodien zieht es mir," Elisabet von Herzogenberg wrote to Brahms (2 December 1886): "The warm flow of melody of the A major song, with its unusually abstract text, gives me the greatest pleasure, and I love singing it."

"Immer leiser wird mein Schlummer," Op. 105/2
(My Slumber Grows More and More Peaceful)

Text by Hermann Lingg (1820–1905)

Immer leiser wird mein Schlummer,
Nur wie Schleier liegt mein Kummer
   Zitternd über mir.
Oft im Traume hör' ich dich
Rufen draus vor meiner Tür,
Niemand wacht und öffnet dir,
   Ich erwach' und weine bitterlich.

Ja, ich werde sterben müssen,
Eine Andre wirst du küssen,
   Wenn ich bleich und kalt,
Eh' die Maienlüfte weh'n,
Eh' die Drossel singt im Wald:
Willst du mich noch einmal seh'n,
   Komm', o komme bald!

My slumber grows more and more peaceful; my anxiety lies tremblingly over me merely like a thin veil. Often in my dreams I hear you calling outside my door; no one is awake to let you in; I wake up and weep bitterly.

Yes, I shall have to die; you will kiss another woman when I am pallid and cold, before the May breezes blow, before the thrush sings in the forest. If you want to see me once more, come, oh, come quickly!

Composed at Thun in August 1886.

First performed publicly on 4 January 1889 at a Museumskonzert in Frankfurt am Main by Hermine Spies, for whom this and the preceding song were intended, and who had sung them both privately at Brahms's Thun house in September 1886.

Modified strophic, resembling through-composition.

The text is from Lingg's *Gedichte* (Stuttgart and Augsburg, 1857), where it is titled simply "Lied."

Brahms included the song among some manuscripts he sent from Thun in mid-August 1886 to a friend in Vienna, the surgeon Theodor Billroth. Billroth responded (18 August 1886):

> H. Lingg's poem about the dying girl in your illuminating setting affected me
> most of all. I imagined it sung quite simply in a touching girlish voice, and I am
> not ashamed to say that I could not finish playing it for weeping.

The lines are indeed moving. The speaker knows that she is near death, and that her lover will eventually find someone else; her only wish is to see him once more, but when she cries out in anguish that he should come quickly, it is death instead that responds. Brahms's setting is one of the supreme syntheses of words and music, ennobling the poetry and transforming its sentiment into genuine pathos.

The song begins in a hushed murmur, without a prelude, over a somber repeated left-hand rhythmic figure, like muffled drumbeats. The initial melodic motive—a pitch enclosed by its lower and upper neighbors—and its various permutations provide most of the material for the first half of the strophe. The opening's doublings in thirds and sixths and its prevalent appoggiaturas—particularly the double appoggiaturas—generate the poignant harmonic language that is characteristic. The girl's losing battle with death is depicted symbolically by descending phrases, which predominate, and by the many breathless short phrases separated by rests.

Rising left-hand arpeggios in m. 9 herald the appearance of a tender new "dream" melody that modulates to the relative major. Over the right hand's throbbing afterbeats, the melody tries three times to rise, beginning in m. 15. But the effort is so taxing that the first two rising thirds break off into silence; each attempt to resume begins a step lower in pitch than its predecessor, and the harmonies drift unpredictably from E major to G major, F major, and E minor. The third attempt succeeds, and the line ascends to a short-lived *forte* climax before trailing off into gasping, falling fragments. The pain of "weine bitterlich" is strikingly conveyed by the D♯–A tritones in mm. 21–22, their dissonant impact strengthened by their placement on strong beats, in contrast with the preceding weak-beat rising thirds.

The piano alone begins the second strophe, as though allowing the weakening girl to recover her strength. The voice reenters for the second phrase and is given some additional melodic material, which falls into the lowest part of the song's range as the girl speaks of her approaching death. Her vision of the summer she knows she will not live to see elicits the return in m. 37 of the dream melody from the first strophe.

As before, short-breathed phrases with rising thirds follow, but this time, seemingly by sheer strength of will, they mount ever higher to the song's highest pitch and principal climax. Increasingly ecstatic harmonies rise from E major to G, to B♭, and finally to D♭ major. The vocal line, spent, sags and sinks as the last line is repeated, and the excitement wanes quickly. The change to the major mode, particularly in its enharmonic notation in flats, implies the attainment of some degree of repose, or at least of acceptance, at the end. The postlude's grieving syncopations subside, concluding the scene.

Klage, Op. 105/3 (Lament)

Folk Song from the Lower Rhine [?]

> Fein's Liebchen, trau' du nicht,
> Daß er dein Herz nicht bricht!
> Schön' Worte will er geben,
> Er kostet dein jung' Leben,
> Glaub's sicherlich!
>
> Ich werde nimmer froh,
> Denn mir ging es also:
> Die Blätter vom Baum gefallen
> Mit den schönen Worten allen,
> Ist Winterzeit!
>
> Es ist jetzt Winterzeit,
> Die Vögelein sind weit,
> Die mir im Lenz gesungen—
> Mein Herz ist mir gesprungen
> Vor Liebesleid.

Sweet girl, don't trust him so he won't break your heart! He will give you fine words and they will cost you your young life, take it for a fact!

I will never be happy again, because that is what happened to me: the leaves have fallen from the trees together with all the fine words, and it is wintertime!

It is now wintertime; the birds that sang to me in the spring are far away; my heart is broken with love's pain.

The date of composition is uncertain, probably 1887 or early 1888.

The first performance was given (from manuscript) on 6 March 1888 by Adele Mandlich at a concert of new music in Vienna.

Simple strophic.

The text is found in the second volume of Brahms's favorite folk-song collection, later shown to be highly unreliable, the Kretzschmer-Zuccalmaglio *Deutsche Volkslieder mit ihren Original-Weisen* (Berlin, 1838–40). It is probable that the text is not traditional but was written by Zuccalmaglio himself. In the third verse, Brahms removed the final "e" from the source's "Lenze" for rhythmic consistency, and substituted "gesprungen" for "zersprungen."

The poem laments the fragility of love, so easily betrayed. Since the emotional progression is similar in each verse, the unvaried strophic form is appropriate.

The setting exemplifies Brahms's supreme ability to dramatize the meaning through the structure of the melody: the first two phrases are nearly alike and lack any feature sufficiently distinctive to inhibit their straightforward narrative function; the next two phrases add poignant cadential appoggiaturas and descend sequentially in deepening grief; the fifth line's climax is reflected musically in a phrase, suddenly *forte*, that contains the melody's highest pitch and longest note values; the last line of text is repeated in a balancing phrase which trails off to the octave below, with the effect of thoughtful reinforcement of the culminating idea. The strophe begins in the major mode, but the relative minor intrudes with increasing conviction as the emotion intensifies.

The simple accompaniment assists without overpowering. Its repeated dotted rhythm propels and, together with the bass pedal, unifies the first part of the strophe. At the climactic fifth phrase, the eighth notes of the melody's basic rhythmic pattern are transferred to the piano, where they are developed and extended into a secondary climax underlying the sixth phrase. Augmented-triad sonorities underscore the pain that these two phrases express.

The postlude returns to *piano* to echo the vocal line's final cadence. Rising through sequential repetition, it comfortably reestablishes the major mode in a modified augmentation that duplicates the rhythms of the earlier vocal climax, as expressive reiterations of the eighth-note motive subside below.

Auf dem Kirchhofe, Op. 105/4 (In the Churchyard)

Text by Detlev von Liliencron (1844–1909)

> Der Tag ging regenschwer und sturmbewegt,
> Ich war an manch vergeß'nem Grab gewesen,
> Verwittert Stein und Kreuz, die Kränze alt,
> Die Namen überwachsen, kaum zu lesen.
>
> Der Tag ging sturmbewegt und regenschwer,
> Auf allen Gräbern fror das Wort: Gewesen.
> Wie sturmestot die Särge schlummerten,
> Auf allen Gräbern taute still: Genesen.

The day was heavy with rain and disturbed by storms; I had visited many a forgotten grave; stone and cross were weathered, the wreaths were old, the names were overgrown so they could hardly be read.

The day was disturbed by storms and heavy with rain; on all the graves the word "departed" froze. The coffins slumbered as if in the deadness of the storm; on all the graves there appeared, in a silent thaw: "healed."

The date of composition is uncertain, probably 1887 or 1888.
First performed on 30 November 1888 by Filip Forstén in Vienna.
Modified strophic.

The text is from Liliencron's *Adjutantenritte und andere Gedichte* (Leipzig, 1883).

The song, like the poem, has two stanzas; they begin similarly but end in markedly contrasting moods.

The introduction's sweeping arpeggios and crashing chords, ominously dissonant over their tonic pedal, portray the driving rainstorm that rages over the churchyard. The recitative-like vocal line adopts the rhythms and inflections of the text. In recognition of the more regular accentuation in lines 3 and 4, the meter changes from $\frac{3}{4}$ to common time, and at mid-strophe, the melody gradually submits to the piano's increasingly lyrical influence as the closing cadence on the dominant nears. But with a pungent minor ninth the piano overruns the vocal ending, and a descending arpeggio leads to the reintroduction of the stormy music from the opening.

The second strophe begins exactly like the first, pointing up the similarity of their initial lines of text. But in its second phrase, a chromatic bass line leads inexorably upward to linger on the subdominant, whose harmony is embellished and prolonged before the close on the dominant. Because of their similarity in rhythm and contour, the vocal line's descending arpeggio on the key word "Gewesen" and the piano's echo of it recall the dramatic diminished-seventh arpeggio that joins the two strophes.

Again there is a change to common time at mid-strophe, but now, tempestuous C minor gives way to serene C major. In solemn quarter notes, the vocal line quotes the first six pitches of the chorale melody "O Haupt voll Blut und Wunden," originally by Hassler but inextricably identified with Bach's *St. Matthew Passion*; the succeeding phrase imitates a third higher. A quarter rest's delay enhances the impact of the climactic word "Genesen"; the piano underlines it by recalling in the major its flowing cadential melody from the first strophe. A reverent postlude is crowned by a radiant C-major sonority, impeccably spaced. (Under no circumstances should the final chord be broken; because of the bass octave sustained by the pedal, the lowest note in the left hand may be omitted if absolutely necessary.)

Brahms eschewed religious dogma and was reticent about his beliefs, but he concerned himself throughout his life with questions of human purpose, of life, death, and the hereafter. His association of the word "Genesen" with a familiar chorale tune adds an unmistakeable spiritual dimension—the implication of resurrection—to its usual connotation of convalescence or restoration to health. The poem's affirmative conclusion is therefore substantially strengthened by its musical setting.

The arrival in October 1888 of a packet of that month's new Brahms publications—the Op. 103 *Zigeunerlieder*, the Op. 104 unaccompanied choruses, and the Opp. 105–107 songs—provided a welcome distraction for the Herzogenbergs, on holiday in Nice. Elisabet responded at length on the 28th, singling out "Auf dem Kirchhofe" with particular enthusiasm and returning to it later in the letter:

I must say some more about the glorious thing, with its distinctive coloring, its perfect co-operation of words and music. . . . It is all so powerful, so original, and so mature, such real music of so superior an order, that one would be content to hear nothing else for a long time.

Theodor Billroth also selected "Auf dem Kirchhofe" from the new songs as having "made the deepest impression. . . . Only you understand how to contrive the immortal with such power, even in the very small forms" (16 October 1888).

Verrat, Op. 105/5 (Betrayal)

Text by Karl Lemcke (1831–1913)

Ich stand in einer lauen Nacht
An einer grünen Linde,
Der Mond schien hell, der Wind ging sacht,
Der Gießbach floß geschwinde.

Die Linde stand vor Liebchens Haus,
Die Türe hört' ich knarren.
Mein Schatz ließ sacht' ein Mannsbild 'raus:
"Laß morgen mich nicht harren;

Laß mich nicht harren, süßer Mann,
Wie hab' ich dich so gerne!
An's Fenster klopfe leise an,
Mein Schatz ist in der Ferne!"

Laß ab vom Druck und Kuß, Feinslieb,
Du Schöner in Sammetkleide,
Nun spute dich, du feiner Dieb,
Ein Mann harrt auf der Heide.

Der Mond scheint hell, der Rasen grün
Ist gut zu unsrem Begegnen,
Du trägst ein Schwert und nickst so kühn,
Dein' Liebschaft will ich segnen!—

Und als erschein der lichte Tag,
Was fand er auf der Heide?
Ein Toter in den Blumen lag
Zu einter Falschen Leide.

On a warm night I stood by a green linden tree; the moon shone brightly, the wind blew gently, the torrent flowed rapidly.
The linden tree stood in front of my darling's house; I heard the door creak. My loved one quietly let a man out of the house:

"Don't keep me waiting tomorrow; don't keep me waiting, dear man; how I love you! Tap gently at the window; my sweetheart is far away!"

Leave off hugging and kissing, ardent man, you handsome one in velvet garb; now make haste, you fine thief; a man is waiting on the moor.

The moon shines brightly, the green turf is suitable for our encounter; you wear a sword and nod so boldly; I will bless your wooing!

And, when the light of day appeared, what did it find on the moor? A dead man lay in the flowers, to a false woman's sorrow.

Composed in August 1886 at Thun.

First performed by Gustav Walter on 5 December 1888 in Vienna.

Varied strophic, so freely handled as to approach through-composition.

The text is from the poet's *Lieder und Gedichte* (Hamburg, 1861).

The setting combines the styles of ballad and operatic *scena*, and a composite formal structure results. The settings of verses 1, 2, and 6 begin similarly, as (to different music) do those of verses 4 and 5. The opening phrases of the two melodies have the same rhythm, and they roughly resemble retrograde inversions of each other; in verse 5, the piano's bass line actually quotes the other melody. The speech of the unfaithful woman, comprising the last line of verse 2 and the whole of verse 3, is set continuously to a contrasting, more flowing melody that lies markedly higher in the singer's range than what precedes; some tonal contrast is provided by modulations to the relative major (D) and to the home key's dominant (F♯). This F♯ major is the enharmonic relative of the E♭ minor of the *Lebhafter* section; the eventual return to the home tonic is also enharmonic, and it comes about when the vow of vengeance in verse 5 prompts a shift to the submediant (C♭), Brahms's customary key relationship to depict a desired unreality. The dramatic crux of the song and, indeed, of the macabre narrative, is the massive diminished-seventh chord in m. 59, after whose fermata the tempo resumes as at first. The piano, however, chooses to ponder the initial melodic motive, which it recalls at the dominant level, first in the bass, then in the tenor register in augmentation. When the music of the opening returns, after another fermata, its accompaniment is in a more sustained style, its melody is slightly varied to intensify "zu einer Falsche Leide," and its final phrase is elongated. The shocking contrast of the piano's mordant final chord and its pale predecessors seems to symbolize the immensity of the song's emotional range.

Much of the folk flavor of the principal strophe derives from the repetition of the last word and the five-measure phrase that results; to balance, the piano has a one-measure insertion at mid-strophe with a bass line that refers to the opening motive of the vocal melody. The text repetitions do not appear in Lemcke's poem; Max Friedländer asserts (*Brahms's Lieder*, 181) that the use of this device was inspired by a folk song on a similar subject, "Es reit ein Herr und auch sein Knecht" (No. 28 in the forty-nine *Deutsche Volkslieder*), with which Brahms was occupied at the same time.

Elisabet von Herzogenberg reacted to the song with the verbal equivalent of a shudder (28 October 1888):

> But to turn the page and be confronted with that *Mannsbild*, that skulking figure of a man, is to be brought back to earth with a thump. Oh, how could you think this poem worthy of being composed by you! I cannot understand. An unattractive, dry, cheaply popular ditty with its barren heath—barren enough it seems to me! Are all the good poems really so used up that you must fall back on such skim milk[?]

On the other hand, the less easily offended Billroth wrote with enthusiasm (16 October 1888), "And the ballad, *Verrat*—what a treasure for all bassos[!]"

FIVE LIEDER, OP. 106

Fünf Lieder für eine Singstimme mit Begleitung des Pianoforte von Johannes Brahms (Five Songs for Solo Voice with Piano Accompaniment by Johannes Brahms), Op. 106. Published in October 1888 by N. Simrock in Berlin; publication number 9043.

Ständchen, Op. 106/1 (Serenade)

Text by Franz Kugler (1808–1858)

> Der Mond steht über dem Berge,
> So recht für verliebte Leut';
> Im Garten rieselt ein Brunnen,
> Sonst Stille weit und breit.
>
> Neben der Mauer im Schatten,
> Da steh'n der Studenten drei
> Mit Flöt' und Geig' und Zither
> Und singen und spielen dabei.
>
> Die Klänge schleichen der Schönsten
> Sacht in den Traum hinein,
> Sie schaut den blonden Geliebten
> Und lispelt: "Vergiß nicht mein!"

The moon is over the mountain, just right for people in love; in the garden a fountain babbles; otherwise there is silence all around.

Next to the high wall in the shadows, three students stand with flute and fiddle and zither and sing and play.

The tones steal softly into the beautiful girl's dream; she sees her blonde sweetheart and whispers: "Don't forget me!"

Probably composed at Thun during the summer of 1886 or 1887.

First performed (from manuscript) by Gustav Walter on 27 February 1888 in Vienna.

A B A.

The text may be found in the collected *Gedichte* (Stuttgart and Tübingen, 1840), but it originally appeared in the 1830 *Skizzenbuch*, which included musical compositions and illustrative drawings by Kugler in addition to his poetry.

Among poems called "Ständchen," this one is unusual in describing a serenade rather than itself constituting one. The setting is infinitely charming, with a genial melody that at first hearing seems already in the memory.

Stanzas 1 and 3 are virtually identical; the second offers both melodic and tonal contrast, with frequent modulations. The accompaniment adroitly suggests the sound of the students' instruments without imitating them literally. The turn to the submediant major at the vocal melody's fifth measure was probably suggested by the dreaming girl in verse 3, but it conveys with equal aptness the enchanting effect of the moonlit babbling fountain in verse 1. The piano's reminiscence of the original melody in the new key is a source of particular delight.

The postlude begins by recalling the ritornello-like music of the introduction, then becomes a tender echo of the closing vocal phrase. At the end, one can almost see the musicians, their instruments stilled, stealing away into the shadows.

Elisabet von Herzogenberg had only qualified praise for the song (28 October 1888):

> What shall I say about *Ständchen*? As I glance over it, I see it stamped with the charm and originality which you are always able to impart with a turn of the hand; and yet it seems more of a Brahms manufacture than a Brahms inspiration. I cannot warm to it.

Auf dem See, Op. 106/2 (On the Lake)

Text by Christian Reinhold
(Christian Reinhold Köstlin, 1813–1856)

An dies Schifflein schmiege,
Holder See, dich sacht!
Frommer Liebe Wiege,
Nimm sie wohl in Acht!

Deine Wellen rauschen;
Rede nicht so laut!
Laß mich ihr nur lauschen,
Die mir viel vertraut!

Deine Wellen leuchten,
Spiegeln uns zurück

$$\left[\begin{array}{l} \text{Tausendfach die feuchten} \\ \text{Augen voller Glück.} \end{array} \right]$$

Deine Wellen zittern
Von der Sonne Glut;
Ob sie's heimlich wittern,
Wie die Liebe tut?

Weit und weiter immer
Rück' den Strand hinaus!
Aus dem Himmel nimmer
Laß uns steigen aus!

Fern von Menschenreden
Und von Menschensinn,
Als ein schwimmend Eden
Trag dies Schifflein hin!

Nestle closely and quietly to this little boat, O lovely lake! It is the cradle of virtuous love, so take good care of it!

Your waves are blustery; don't talk so loud! Let me listen only to the girl who is telling me so much in confidence!

Your waves tremble in the glow of the sun; do they secretly sense how love makes one feel?

Push the shore farther and farther away! Don't ever let us leave heaven!

Far from people's talking and from people's thoughts, carry this boat along like a floating Eden!

Composed in 1885.

First performed by Gustav Walter on 5 December 1888 in Vienna.

Through-composed.

The text, untitled, appears among the "Seelieder" in Reinhold's *Gedichte* (Stuttgart, 1853). Brahms omitted the third verse.

The poem is an ardent love song in which the sea is the symbol of protection, seclusion, and serene rapture. Brahms set it as a flowing barcarolle, radiating warmth and glowing with shifting harmonic color.

The spirit of strophic song hovers nearby; the separate verses are clearly defined, and until the last, which functions like a coda, each begins with a similarly lilting melody in the same rhythm. The melody of the vocal line's first four measures or a variant of it returns to end the second verse and to provide all the material for verse 4.

Two-measure phrases result almost inevitably from the poem's singsong rhythms. Brahms manages at times to break out of the pattern, particularly later in the song, but his principal asset in the avoidance of saccharine excess is his superbly inventive use of the piano—to disrupt rhythmic regularity, to vary the metric substructure, to diversify the textures and figurations, and to bridge the gaps between vocal phrases.

Harmonic turbulence and rhythmic unrest symbolize the blustery waves of verse 2, and they yield to an unruffled tonic major. Similarly, a turn to the mediant from the minor side of the key in verse 3 highlights the waves' sunlit shimmer. At the end of verse 3, "wie die Liebe tut" prompts a *sempre poco più animato* marking, and the piano surmounts the voice's cadence in a panting, ecstatic arch of melody.

For the concluding stanza, phrases of three measures replace those of two as the norm; extensions and internal repetitions of text accommodate the stretching of the next-to-last phrase to four measures and the last to five. The broadening process also affects the accompaniment. In m. 53, at the indication *sempre più tranquillo*, the piano's prevailing sixteenth notes give way to eighths, which group themselves first in twos, then in threes, in effect twice enlarging the size of the metric unit. The waning postlude recalls the rhythm and the tonic-subdominant alternation of the opening measure.

Since the song was already in print, Elisabet von Herzogenberg's appraisal of 28 October 1888 seems oddly carping:

> Amanda Röntgen and I play *Auf dem See* together; it sounds charming on the violin—better than sung, I almost think. . . . For my part, I should picture a "floating Eden" less bristling and without this array of obstacles in the harmony.

She did, however, point out the omission of an accidental, which was corrected in subsequent editions—D♮ in the bass (low key, B♭) on the fifth eighth of m. 54 (eighteenth from the end).

Es hing der Reif, Op. 106/3 (Hoarfrost Hung)

Text by Klaus Groth (1819–1899)

Es hing der Reif im Lindenbaum,
Wodurch das Licht wie Silber floß.
Ich sah dein Haus, wie hell im Traum
Ein blitzend Feenschloß.

Und offen stand das Fenster dein,
Ich konnte dir in's Zimmer seh'n—
Da tratst du in den Sonnenschein,
Du dunkelste der Feen!

Ich bebt' in seligem Genuß,
So frühlingswarm und wunderbar:
Da merkt' ich gleich an deinem Gruß,
Daß Frost und Winter war.

Hoarfrost hung in the linden tree, and through it the light flowed like silver. I saw your house, like a sparkling fairy castle brightly in a dream.

And your window was open; I could see into your room; then you stepped into the sunlight, you darkest of fairies!

I shuddered in blissful enjoyment, so springtime-warm and wonder-filled; then I noticed immediately when you greeted me that it was frosty win-tertime.

Composed at Thun during summer 1888.

The first performance is not documented.

Varied strophic, somewhat modified.

The text is from Groth's *Hundert Blätter, Paralipomena zum Quick-born* (Hamburg, 1854).

A warm vision of his beloved deludes the poet into imagining a thawing of the emotional winter that separates them, but her chilly greeting dispels the notion. Brahms's setting exactly captures the poem's sense of suspended time and reality—the only performance instruction is *träumerisch*—and it delicately contrasts warmth with cold, expectancy with rejection, and hope with despair.

Two of Brahms's most enduring metaphors recur with hypnotic persist-ence throughout the song—the repetitive rhythm of alternating half notes and quarters, representing isolation (particularly through abandonment), and the rising left-hand arpeggios, symbolizing dream. Significantly, the vocal line shares the left hand's eighth-note rhythm only at the words "se-ligem Genuß."

The prelude introduces the song's characteristic downward stepwise melodic movement and major-minor modal ambivalence. The principal stro-phe's bass line sinks continually lower, as though weighed down by sorrow, and the vocal line is hard-pressed to resist its pull. Mentions of the hoarfrost are tinged with minor; those of the linden tree and the light shining through it, with major. The vision of the house is at first accompanied by a tilt toward the minor; but with its transformation into a fairy castle, the harmonies, after a fleeting observation of its foreignness, gradually brighten to a prolonged, unequivocally major-mode dominant seventh.

The vocal line of the contrasting strophe develops the rhythm of the pre-vious cadential phrase before it resumes the prevailing short-long patterns. The accompaniment's discreet interjections, separated by silences, evoke the airiness of the envisioned room; they darken warily as the room's owner-ship becomes evident. The dreamy left-hand arpeggios return with the image of the beloved, but as though spellbound, they remain fixed in the en-chanted key of the submediant of the parallel minor. The setting of the words "der Feen" brings to mind the opening gesture from the introduction; tentatively, the piano remembers the next gesture, and as though hardly daring to breathe, the music of the principal strophe returns.

Hushed, the singer reminisces, "Ich bebt," and breaks off as though overcome with emotion; the piano echoes. The remainder of the phrase is altered to include the song's highest pitch as an upbeat, and the piano repeats that melody also. Both vocal line and bass then begin their long, slow descent as before, but the hopeful upturn at the end of the first strophe is lacking. The vocal line's octave leaps underscore "Winter" and "Frost"; its final phrase becomes a heartbreaking wail of inconsolable sorrow, supported by the piano's bleak chords.

The postlude's drawn-out lament seems an ironic mockery of this strophe's initial "Ich bebt"; even the dreamy arpeggio becomes distorted. Ringing out in the prescribed *mezzo forte*—the only dynamic indication stronger than *piano* in the entire song—its plangent sound pierces the senses like a dagger.

Meine Lieder, Op. 106/4 (My Songs)

Text by Adolf Frey (Swiss, 1855–1920)

> Wenn mein Herz beginnt zu klingen
> Und den Tönen löst die Schwingen,
> Schweben vor mir her und wieder
> Bleiche Wonnen, unvergessen,
> Und die Schatten von Zypressen—
> Dunkel klingen meine Lieder!

When my heart begins to make music and frees the wings of melody, there hover back and forth before me pale blisses, unforgotten, and the shadows of cypress trees. My songs have a dark sound!

Composed at Thun during summer 1888.
First performed by Gustav Walter on 26 January 1889 in Vienna.
Through-composed.
The text is from Frey's *Gedichte* (Leipzig, 1886).
One can readily imagine Brahms's identifying himself with the poet who recognizes the inescapable influence of life's transient joys and unfulfilled promises on the creative process. The setting is thoughtful and tender, but it has a pervasive undercurrent of melancholy. It radiates a sense of simple honesty that makes it instantly appealing.

The melodies of the vocal line and the piano are curiously intertwined—sometimes separate, sometimes joined—and are constructed with astonishing economy. One of three basic melodic ideas is nearly always discernible in one or both. The prelude introduces all three in succession: motive *a*, the scalewise descent of a fourth, usually in dotted halves and quarter notes; motive *b*, four quarter notes that often include the outline of a triad; and motive *c*, a hovering around the dominant (C♯ in the high key, A♯ in the low), usually sounding one or both neighboring tones and often in a dotted rhythm. Phrases 1 and 2 use all three in order—*a* appears in the piano only and loses its last note in phrase 2. Three statements of *a* make up the interlude and phrase 3. Phrase 4 comprises two statements of *b* (while the piano recalls the rhythm of *a*) and a variant of *c* that defines the new temporary dominant a half-step lower. Phrase 5 spans its falling fourth in successive half-steps that alternate with the original pitch. Motives *a*, *b*, and *c* in succession constitute phrase 6. In phrase 7, *a* subsumes *b* and the beginning of *c*, and *c* is expanded into a closing cadence. The postlude recalls the introduction in slightly enriched form, repeating and elaborating *c* with wistful insistence.

Brahms often associated falling arpeggios with the notion of separation and rising arpeggios with dreaming or imagination; it is therefore not unreasonable to infer that it is separation that saddens the hovering memories of "pale blisses" and, as a result, darkens the "songs' sound." Certainly it is significant that it is the key of the submediant, itself usually evocative of some sort of unreality, that ushers in the "bleiche Wonnen, unvergessen" and prompts the reversal of direction in the arpeggios, acknowledging the text's progression from statement to fantasy. The idea of darkness is suggested in the last two vocal phrases by the addition of a supporting bass line that initially doubles the voice, then continues its descent alone.

The song has a distinctive fragility, a haunting beauty all its own. Performers should carefully choose a tempo that precludes any hint of ponderousness. Writing about "Meine Leider" (28 October 1888), Elisabet von Herzogenberg declared it "quite my favorite in Op. 106. Who could resist anything so dainty, [with] its fine gold tracery and the added fervor which those sustained bass notes give to the closing sentences."

Ein Wanderer, Op. 106/5 (A Traveler)

Text by Christian Reinhold
(Christian Reinhold Köstlin, 1813–1856)

> Hier, wo sich die Straßen scheiden,
> Wo nun geh'n die Wege hin?
> Meiner ist der Weg der Leiden,
> Dess' ich immer sicher bin.
>
> Wand'rer, die des Weges gehen,
> Fragen freundlich: wo hinaus?
> Keiner wird mich doch verstehen,
> Sag' ich ihm, wo ich zu Haus.
>
> Reiche Erde, arme Erde,
> Hast du keinen Raum für mich?

Wo ich einst begraben werde,
An der Stelle lieb' ich dich!

Here where the ways diverge, where do the paths now lead? Mine is the road of sorrows; I am always sure of that.

Travelers who pass along the road ask in a friendly manner: "Where are you heading?" But no one will understand if I tell him where I dwell.

Rich earth, poor earth, have you no room for me? Where I shall be buried one day, in that place I shall love you!

Composed in 1885.

The first performance is not documented.

Varied strophic; verses 1 and 3 are set to the same music with only slight variance, and verse 2 begins similarly.

The text is from Reinhold's *Gedichte* (Stuttgart, 1853).

A compelling falling-third motive begins the song and recurs after each stanza; the gesture evokes both sorrow and weariness, and its reappearance in bare octaves before verse 3 reveals that, in Brahms's customary metaphor, it symbolizes approaching death. The wanderer's pain is evident in the tortured vocal line, with its dissonances and its many diminished and augmented intervals. Whatever its rhythmic notation, an implied slow-paced walking bass seems to drive the music inexorably forward.

The accompaniment's sixteenth-note pairs in contrary motion at the opening suggest the diverging paths of the text. In the fifth measure of each stanza, the piano echoes the vocal line, as though pondering the question just posed. A more assured vocal melody sets the third line in the principal strophe; the bass line imitates at first, but it sinks ever lower into the pathos of Neapolitan harmony as the voice rises in anguish for the fourth line. Response to "Weg der Leiden" (or "Wo ich begraben werde" in strophe 3) impels the piano's melody downward into its low bass register to conclude the strophe with a sighing *pianissimo* reminder of the death motive.

With a new trudging accompaniment, the second strophe begins like the first, but motivated by the text's "freundlich," the harmonies soon veer toward the major mode and a cadence on the Neapolitan—that "beautiful modulation on the second page," as Elisabet von Herzogenberg called it (28 October 1888). The piano then takes on an agitated dotted rhythm, and the vocal melody mounts in rising sequence toward the song's dramatic climax, the expanded repetition of "wo ich zu Haus." As the vocal line's 4-3 suspension resolves, the piano's minor ninth impacts, resolving a measure later.

The falling-third motive returns after the fermata, shadowed by an afterbeat bass, to introduce the third strophe; it extends itself, harmonized, as the voice resumes. A final recurrence over a rising left-hand arpeggio ends the song with a moving symbolic longing for death.

FIVE LIEDER, OP. 107

Fünf Lieder für eine Singstimme mit Begleitung des Pianoforte von Johannes Brahms (Five Songs for Solo Voice with Piano Accompaniment by Johannes Brahms), Op. 107. Published in October 1888 by N. Simrock in Berlin; publication number 9064.

The five songs share an aura of folklore and the masterly adaptation of strophic form for dramatic purpose.

An die Stolze, Op. 107/1 (To a Haughty Woman)

Text by Paul Flem[m]ing (1609–1640)

Und gleichwohl kann ich anders nicht,
Ich muß ihr günstig sein,
Obgleich der Augen stolzes Licht
Mir mißgönnt seinen Schein.
Ich will, ich soll, ich muß dich lieben,
Dadurch wir Beid' uns nur betrüben,
Weil mein Wunsch doch nicht gilt
Und du nicht hören wilt.

Wie manchen Tag, wie manche Nacht,
Wie manche liebe Zeit
Hab' ich mit Klagen durchgebracht,
Und du verlachst mein Leid!
Du weißt, du hörst, du siehst die Schmerzen,
Und nimmst der' keinen doch zu Herzen,
So daß ich zweifle fast
Ob du ein Herze hast.

Bist du denn harter Stein und Stahl
Die man doch zwingen kann?
Feld, Wiesen, Wälder, Berg und Tal
Seh'n meine Wehmut an.
Die Vögel seufzen, was ich klage.
Der hohle Busch ruft, was ich sage.

Du nur, du Stolze du,
Hältst Ohr und Augen zu.

Ach denke, denke, was du tust.
Ich kann nicht anders sein.
Ich hab' an meinem Leiden Lust,
Du hassest meine Pein.
Kann ich denn keine Huld erlangen,
So laß' mich die Gunst nur empfangen
Und wolle doch mit mir,
Daß ich stracks sterbe hier.

But all the same, I can't help it, I must be well-disposed to her, even though the prideful light of her eyes begrudges their own glowing. I want to, I shall, I must love you, and thereby we will only make each other miserable, because my wishes have no force and you refuse to listen.

How many days, how many nights, how much precious time I have spent in lamentations, and you laugh at my sorrow! You know, you hear, you see my sufferings, but you take none of them to heart, so that I almost doubt whether you have a heart at all.

Composed at Thun during the summer of 1886.
The first performance is not documented.
Strophic.
The text is from Flemming's *Geistliche und weltliche Poemata* (Jena, 1651), where there are two additional verses that Brahms chose not to set.

The bitter reproach of the poem is belied by the warmth and passion of the musical setting. ("The 'proud one' gives me the unshakeable impression that old Flemming conceived of her as quite a different person. I can't reconcile words and music," observed Elisabet von Herzogenberg in her letter of 28 October 1888.)

The vocal line pleads and cajoles in coaxing appoggiaturas and suspensions, while the piano's flowing melody intertwines independently. Their contrapuntal relationship symbolizes the contrast between the singer's ardor and the coolness of the object of his desire. The nearly constant quarter-note movement is like the steadfastness of the love, which resists even the beloved's unyielding indifference. Tension mounts and chromatic inflections multiply as the first section approaches its climax, the dissonant whole note of "lieben" in the first strophe, "Schmerzen" in the second.

There ensues a brief antiphonal exchange between voice and piano. Finally a degree of reproach gradually asserts itself, in phrases that rise in pitch and increase in impact to the vocal line's concluding expanded outcry of accusation. The growing excitement is depicted in the accompaniment by quarter notes with afterbeats, each passage longer and denser than the last. Three closing chords restore calm.

Except for the piano melody's short-lived excursion into the higher octave at the beginning, the second strophe is musically identical to the first.

Salamander, Op. 107/2

Text by Karl Lemcke (1831–1913)

Es saß ein Salamander
Auf einem kühlen Stein,
Da warf ein böses Mädchen
In's Feuer ihn hinein.

Sie meint, er soll verbrennen,
Ihm ward erst wohl zu Mut,
Wohl wie mir kühlem Teufel
Die heiße Liebe tut.

A salamander sat on a cool rock; then a malicious girl threw it into the fire. She thought it would burn up but it just began to feel good—just as I, a cool devil, get a good feeling from fiery love.

Composed at Thun in July 1888.

First performed by Amalie Joachim on 31 October 1888 at the Singakademiesaal in Berlin.

Modified strophic.

The text is from Lemcke's *Lieder und Gedichte* (Hamburg, 1861).

The first strophe's melody, clearly tonal and comprising two-measure phrases only, resembles folk song, but the accompaniment, with its diverse figurations and its canonic echo (m. 4) and anticipation (m. 8), derives from art song. (Many of Brahms's folk-song settings are based on a similar juxtaposition.) A rhythmically disguised variant of the opening melody underlies the interlude—the left hand's octaves recall the opening triadic ascent, and the right hand's staccato chords quote m. 3.

With the change to the major mode for strophe 2 comes additional structural liberty. A measure inserted after the first phrase allows the piano to echo the vocal line's "verbrennen" (and its own bass melody). At "die heiße Liebe tut," a new phrase develops the chromatic motive that was associated with "ins Feuer" in strophe 1, appearing initially in m. 8, interjected *forte* by the piano. Now a descending piano melody and an ascending vocal line converge on their fourth note, and after another *forte* interjection by the piano, the two lines are interchanged for a broadened repetition of the line. In somewhat extended format, the postlude recalls the earlier interlude's contrast of a vigorous beginning with a quietly cheerful close.

Heinrich Schenker wrote admiringly of "Salamander" in his review of Brahms's Op. 107 for the Leipzig *Musicalisches Wochenblatt*, calling it "a perfect art work. . . . I think Brahms has here set his own laughter to music." Elisabet von Herzogenberg, on the other hand, disliked it intensely, considering its text unworthy of Brahms's attention. "How glad I am to think that I always detested Lemcke," she wrote (28 October 1888). "I now know why." If the song was ever truly humorous, time has dulled its edge; it remains, however, an artful, pleasant diversion.

Das Mädchen spricht, Op. 107/3 (The Girl Speaks)

Text by Otto Friedrich Gruppe (1804–1876)

> Schwalbe, sag' mir an,
> Ist's dein alter Mann,
> Mit dem du's Nest gebaut?
> Oder hast du jüngst erst
> Dich ihm vertraut?
>
> Sag', was zwitschert ihr,
> Sag', was flüstert ihr
> Des Morgens so vertraut?
> Gelt, du bist wohl auch noch
> Nicht lange Braut?

Swallow, tell me, was it with your old husband that you built your nest, or was it just recently that you entrusted yourself to him?

Tell me, what do the two of you twitter about? Tell me, what do the two of you whisper so confidentially in the morning? I bet you haven't been marrried long either!

Composed at Thun during the summer of 1886.

First performed (together with the following song, "Maienkätzchen") on 11 February 1887 in Vienna by the tenor Gustav Walter, who sang from manuscript.

Strophic.

The text is found in Gruppe's collected *Gedichte* (Berlin, 1835).

The irrepressible happiness of a new bride overflows into conversation with a female swallow that has caught her attention. Each stanza begins with questioning about the mundane, but after three lines nuptial concerns intrude irresistibly. The recurrent structure suits the verses ideally to Brahms's favored simple strophic treatment, used here for the last time; the result is one of his most endearing songs.

The paired complementary rhythms of the introduction dart and flicker like the bird's flight and continue through the song, interwoven delicately with the voice and often capriciously displaced within the meter.

The girl's breathless joy is revealed in the vocal line's short phrases, at first sprightly, later thoughtful.

Despite the elegance of the figurations, the harmonies are robust and straightforward, evoking a folkloric earthiness. The strophe's first section comprises mostly primary triads and culminates in a hemiola-supported modulation to the dominant as the third line of text is repeated. But thoughts of conjugal bliss rush in, and the distant, otherworldly key of the major mediant of the parallel minor suddenly interrupts *forte*; it alternates with its own amiable subdominant as the vocal line's ꞌhythms broaden and its earlier lively leaps yield to scalewise descents with appoggiaturas. Gradually the music slows and softens, and an affecting chromatic modulation brings, seemingly reluctantly, the plagal return of the tonic key, and with it, the everyday world.

Performers should take care that the *poco ritardando* does not overreach the song's small scale; the pianist may find it more graceful to resume the tempo gradually during the measure preceding its marked return. Note the second strophe's *pianissimo*.

Maienkätzchen, Op. 107/4 (Catkins)

Text by Detlev von Liliencron (1844–1909)

> Maienkätzchen, erster Gruß,
> Ich breche euch und stecke euch
> An meinen alten Hut.

> Maienkätzchen, erster Gruß,
> Einst brach ich euch und steckte euch
> Der Liebsten an den Hut.

Catkins, spring's first greeting, I break you off and stick you in my old hat.
Catkins, spring's first greeting, once I broke you off and stuck you in my darling's hat.

The date of composition is uncertain, probably late 1886.

First performed (from manuscript) by Gustav Walter on 11 February 1887 in Vienna.

Modified strophic. The two strophes' identical first lines are set to the same music, and the melodies of their closing phrases comprise the same pitches in different rhythms; what appears between, however, is so much altered and extended in the second strophe that the song might also be classified defensibly as through-composed.

The text is from Liliencron's *Adjutantenritte und andere Gedichte* (Leipzig, 1883), where it is entitled "Tiefe Sehnsucht" (Deep Longing).

The verses' folkloric simplicity and emotional neutrality inspire a charming miniature, an homage to remembered youthful love. Despite the implied undercurrent of loss, Brahms's setting smiles rather than weeps, recalls with affection rather than laments what might have been.

A tender, cheerful little dotted-rhythm motive in the introduction seems to suggest both the swaying catkins and the happy return of spring that they represent. It reappears to form the interlude between strophes, first in a jaunty *forte* in the bright key of the dominant's dominant, conjuring up a proud parading of the catkin-bedecked hat, then *piano* and restored to the home key's dominant, but with its melody pitched a third higher than before, predicting the mounting of nostalgia as memories awaken. When the motive finally enters the voice part for the twice-stated second line of the second strophe, its rhythm so aptly fits the words "einst brach ich euch und steckte euch" that they almost seem still to be heard during its textless final appearance in the postlude.

Each of the song's first two lines is set to the same arching melody, bridged by the piano's partial imitation. After the second strophe's initial phrase, the vocal line reflects on "erster Gruß," *sostenuto*, then bursts forth in ardent recollection of past pleasures. At the repetition of the second line, the piano replaces its right-hand doubling of the dotted-rhythm motive with a duetting tenor line, evoking the pair's tête-à-tête. The second "einst" is highlighted by the song's highest pitch, and as though pulled back into the present by the emphasis, the vocal line descends sequentially through expressive harmonies and returns to *piano* for its broadened concluding phrase.

The postlude, seemingly reluctant to relinquish remembrance, dwells on warm subdominant harmony, whose prolongations earlier in the strophe had underlined "den Liebsten." Two *forte* chords of punctuation put an end to the reverie.

Mädchenlied, Op. 107/5 (Girl's Song)

Text by Paul von Heyse (1830–1914)

> Auf die Nacht in der Spinnstub'n,
> Da singen die Mädchen,
> Da lachen die Dorfbub'n,
> Wie flink geh'n die Rädchen!
>
> Spinnt Jedes am Brautschatz,
> Daß der Liebste sich freut.

Nicht lange, so gibt es
Ein Hochzeitgeläut.

Kein Mensch, der mir gut ist,
Will nach mir fragen;
Wie bang mir zu Mut ist,
Wem soll ich's klagen?

Die Tränen rinnen
Mir über's Gesicht—
Wofür soll ich spinnen?
Ich weiß es nicht!

At night in the spinning rooms the girls sing and the village lads laugh; how nimbly the wheels turn!

Every girl is spinning something for her trousseau, so that her lover is glad. It won't be long before wedding bells ring!

Nobody cares for me or asks about me; I feel so distressed in my mind; to whom can I pour out my sorrow?

The tears trickle down my face; what's the good of my spinning? I don't know!

The date of composition is uncertain, probably late 1886 or 1887.

First performed by Hermine Spies on 4 January 1889 in Frankfurt am Main.

Modified strophic; the coda-like final section is a development of the main strophe, though it seems to bear little resemblance to it.

The poem appears among other "Mädchenlieder" in the section "Jugendlieder" in Heyse's *Gedichte* (Berlin, 1885).

The song exemplifies that Brahmsian specialty, the combination of folksong's directness with the subtlety of art song; the result is as touching a depiction of a lonely girl's despair as the song literature offers.

The melody is constructed economically, with scalewise thirds ascending and fourths descending as its principal materials. With an upturn at the end, the joined third and fourth rise sequentially to form the initial pair of phrases. Phrase 3 begins as though to continue the sequence but ends with a descending arpeggio. Phrase 4 echoes phrase 1, but the start of the descending fourth itself replaces the rising third as upbeat, and the insertion of an upper neighbor before the concluding upturn stretches the phrase to three measures.

The accompaniment's two-measure rotating figure suggests the turning of spinning wheels; the overlapping successions of detached eighths in the interlude hint at quietly falling tears. When the third verse shifts the focus from the group to the forlorn girl herself, a change in the turning figure's direction exposes the vocal line. At "wie bang mir zu Mut ist," the piano's hemiola depicts the girl's unease; at "wem soll ich's klagen," rests in the accompaniment evoke the emptiness of her life.

The vocal line of the fourth strophe is derived from the melodic materials of the first. The opening phrase sets two lines of text to two overlapping scalewise descending fourths; the next chromatically alters phrase 3 to fit its new harmony. "Ich weiß es nicht" is set twice to the contour of the original phrase 4 without its first and last notes, and finally, to a broadened scalar descent of a fourth.

The distinctive tone of compassion in the song's concluding portion results, at least in part, from the frequent use of the tonic major and from a particular emphasis on subdominant harmony. The plaintive first phrase touches both major and minor subdominant in succession, and the piano's detached-eighth teardrops echo the plagal phrase ending quietly. But suddenly, "wofür soll ich spinnen?" rings out agonizingly, its effect of desperation arising from the combination of its strange submediant-minor harmony, the hemiola in the piano, and the appearance of the song's first *forte* indication. The pain of "ich weiß es nicht" is conveyed by a piercing minor-major seventh, *sforzando*; two increasingly despondent repetitions of the line follow, the last drawn out like a sigh of grief almost too heavy to bear. The postlude weeps in sympathy.

FOUR ERNSTE GESÄNGE, OP. 121

Vier ernste Gesänge für eine Bassstimme mit Begleitung des Piano-forte von Johannes Brahms (Four Serious Songs for Bass Voice with Piano Accompaniment by Johannes Brahms), Op. 121. *Max Klinger zugeeignet* (Dedicated to Max Klinger). Published in July 1896 by N. Simrock in Berlin; publication number 10679.

The dedication to Klinger (1857–1920) was in acknowledgment of his cycle *Brahms-Phantasie* (1885–1894), forty-one engravings, etchings, and lithographs inspired by Brahms's works.

On 7 May 1896, his sixty-third (and last) birthday, Brahms showed the manuscript of the *Four Serious Songs* to Max Kalbeck with the remark, "This is what I have given myself for my birthday." Within days he had offered them to Simrock for publication, playfully referring to them as his "*Schnadahüpferl* of 7 May"—"Schnadahüpferl" is a South German name for a lively dance-song performed at harvesters' festivals, and Brahms enjoyed using the term facetiously to describe the Serious Songs, often adding the adjective "godless."

Although Brahms completed composition of the *Four Serious Songs* during Clara Schumann's final illness (she died on 20 May 1896 from the effects of a stroke suffered on 26 March), that does not seem to have been a conscious stimulus to their creation, as has been suggested. It is more likely that an awareness of the inevitability of her death (and perhaps also some unacknowledged inkling of the nascent cancer in his own body) merely contributed to an increasingly elegiac mood brought on by the deaths of many of those closest to Brahms—Elisabet von Herzogenberg in 1892, Hermine Spies in 1893, both Theodor Billroth and Hans von Bülow in 1894. In fact, in alerting Clara's daughter Marie that she would soon receive a copy of the songs, Brahms wrote on 7 July 1896:

> Some such words as these have long been on my mind, and I did not think that worse news about your mother was to be expected—but deep in the heart of man something often whispers and stirs, quite unconscious perhaps, which in time may ring out in the form of poetry or music. You will not be able

to play the songs yet, because the words would affect you too much, but I beg you to regard them and to lay them aside merely as a death offering to the memory of your dear mother.

The *Vier ernste Gesänge* stand apart from Brahms's (or any other) previous songs. With their symphonic concentration and expressive declamation, they represent the culmination of a lifelong process of refinement. They expand the concept of art song to accommodate the exploration at the level of the individual of those ethical and spiritual matters that the *Requiem* and the motets ponder on a more universal scale. The biblical texts are chosen to comfort the bereaved and the miserable, and they epitomize Brahms's own undogmatic, earthly religious beliefs—that death is certain, that a life well lived is its own reward, that love and compassion for one's fellow man are the greatest human virtues. The simple strength of Luther's German found a perfect match in the terseness and sincerity of Brahms's music. The Serious Songs (deliberately not "Sacred" Songs) stand like a monument at the end of the nineteenth century, facing the twentieth.

Overall, there is progressively greater use of the major mode from the totally minor first song to the totally major fourth, matching the progression from the pessimism of the Ecclesiastes texts to the warmth of St. Paul's discourse on love in his first letter to the Corinthians. The songs' extraordinary sense of organic growth and unity derives at least in part from their shared development of common motives, most notably the melodic chain of descending thirds that symbolized death in the Brahms lexicon.

Brahms himself played and sang the first documented performance, a private one on 25 May 1896 at an estate near Honnef on the Rhine for a circle of friends with whom he was spending a few days after Clara Schumann's funeral in Bonn on the 24th. The first public performance was sung by Anton Sistermans on 9 November 1896 at the Saal Bösendorfer in Vienna, with Anton Rückauf at the piano.

"Denn es gehet dem Menschen wie dem Vieh," Op. 121/1
(For that which befalleth the sons of men befalleth beasts)

Text from Ecclesiastes 3:19–22

Denn es gehet dem Menschen wie dem Vieh, wie dies stirbt, so stirbt er auch; und haben alle einerlei Odem; und der Mensch hat nichts mehr denn das Vieh; denn es ist alles eitel.

Es fährt alles an einen Ort; es ist alles von Staub gemacht, und wird wieder zu Staub.

Wer weiß, ob der Geist des Menschen aufwärts fahre, und der Odem des Viehes unterwärts unter die Erde fahre?

Darum sahe ich, daß nichts besser's ist, denn daß der Mensch fröhlich sei in seiner Arbeit; denn das ist sein Teil. Denn wer will ihn dahin bringen, daß er sehe, was nach ihm geschehen wird?

19. For that which befalleth the sons of men befalleth beasts; even one thing befalleth them: as the one dieth, so dieth the other; yea, they have all one breath; so that a man hath no preeminence above a beast: for all is vanity.

20. All go unto one place; all are of the dust, and all turn to dust again.

21. Who knoweth the spirit of man that goeth upward, and the spirit of the beast that goeth downward to the earth?

22. Wherefore I perceive that there is nothing better, than that a man should rejoice in his own works; for that is his portion; for who shall bring him to see what shall be after him?

Completed in May 1896.

First performed in public by Anton Sistermans and pianist Anton Rückauf on 9 November 1896 in the Saal Bösendorfer in Vienna.

Andante alternating with *Allegro*, A B A' B'.

The text is from the Old Testament.

Against a knell of reiterated dominant, the piano introduces a dirgelike melody reminiscent of the second chorus from *Ein deutsches Requiem*, "Denn alles Fleisch es ist wie Gras." The first measure becomes a quasi-ostinato accompaniment to the vocal line, which imitates the melody of the introduction, then proceeds in solemn quarter notes with expressive sighing inflections. A broadened cadence modulates to the dominant, where doublings in sixths and tenths, canonic imitations, and increased activity provide contrast before the opening key and music return to round out the tripartite initial *Andante*.

In the ensuing *Allegro*, rising scales and spiraling diminished-seventh arpeggios in triplets evoke swirls of rising dust. The text's sense of doubt is reflected in the accompaniment's open downbeats and quickened harmonic rhythm at "wer weiß" (m. 46) and, later, by the movement of the piano's chords downward while the voice has "aufwärts" (mm. 50–52) and upward at "unterwärts" (mm. 64–65, 68–69). In various guises, this section introduces the falling-thirds motive that is to be developed so importantly in the remaining songs in the set, particularly in the second and third. The figure is of course enclosed within the right hand's diminished-seventh triplets, but it appears more obviously in the vocal line at "einem Ort," "Staub gemacht," and (with some passing tones) "und wird wieder zu Staub." In the descending-triad form in which it begins the next song, and at the same pitches, it constitutes the bass line at "Wer weiß, ob der Geist des Menschen" and, a half-step lower, "Und der Odem des Viehes."

The dirgelike music returns, its opening abbreviated to two measures; at "denn daß der Mensch fröhlich sei in seiner Arbeit," a short-lived brightening results from the transposition up to the tonic major of the vocal phrase that appeared in the dominant in mm. 13–15.

But with the ominous question of what of man's works may remain after him, the swirling dust of the *Allegro* returns in overlapping eddies. Gradually the activity lessens into a deliberate trill over a tolling pedal point and, further, to a motionless empty fifth. Two *forte* chords break the bleak mood to end the song resolutely.

"Ich wandte mich und sahe," Op. 121/2
(So I returned, and considered)

Text from Ecclesiastes 4:1–3

Ich wandte mich und sahe an alle, die Unrecht leiden unter der Sonne; und siehe, da waren Tränen derer, die Unrecht litten und hatten keinen Tröster, und die ihnen Unrecht täten, waren zu mächtig, daß sie keinen Tröster haben konnten.

Da lobte ich die Toten, die schon gestorben waren, mehr als die Lebendigen, die noch das Leben hatten;

Und der noch nicht ist, ist besser als alle beide, und des Bösen nicht inne wird, das unter der Sonne geschieht.

1. So I returned, and considered all the oppressions that are done under the sun: and behold the tears of such as were oppressed, and they had no comforter; and on the side of their oppressors there was power; but they had no comforter.

2. Wherefore I praised the dead which are already dead more than the living which are yet alive.

3. Yea, better is he than both they, which hath not yet been, who hath not seen the evil work that is done under the sun.

Completed in May 1896.

All four songs were first performed in public by Anton Sistermans on 9 November 1896 in Vienna's Saal Bösendorfer.

Through-composed.

The text is from the Old Testament.

In the piano introduction, the pitches of the tonic G-minor triad, starting from the D that ended the preceding song, descend, unharmonized, in slow succession. The vocal line follows their lead, confirming Brahms's lifelong metaphor for death as the song's principal motive.

There are two additional important melodic ideas. The first, introduced by the vocal line at m. 7, is distinguished by initial repeated notes that culminate in a suspension, while the piano's supporting bass transforms the descending-arpeggio motive into a chain of falling thirds; it appears four times in the song's first half, always in association with the word "Unrecht." The second appears in the piano in m. 15, deriving some of its compassionate tone from the warmth of the relative major key; the voice's subsequent imitation of it leads to an affecting melisma on "Tränen." Later, a higher-pitched variant of the phrase laments "daß sie keinen Tröster haben konnten," capping the section's mounting emotional intensity (and harmonic adventurousness) with a *sforzando* cadence on the dominant.

Suddenly hushed, three similar phrase pairs follow, constituting the dramatic climax of the song. The voice solemnly intones "Da lobte ich die Toten" to the descending-arpeggio motive, with hollow octaves in the piano; terse harmonies bring "die schon gestorben waren" to a cadence on D. "Mehr als die Lebendigen" is set to an extended chain of bare falling thirds; the balancing harmonized phrase cadences on A. Finally, "und der noch nicht ist" is whispered to a tonally ambiguous diminished-seventh descent that breaks off into silence; a mysterious A♯ octave in the piano's bass interrupts the stillness and leads to an enigmatic cadence on B as dominant of E minor. The gradual revelation of E minor as a bridge to G major solves the enigma.

The concluding section is dominated by the repetition-plus-suspension motive in the vocal line, supported by the piano's descending chains of thirds. The change to the major mode is oddly comfortless, its cheering effect being undermined by chromatic inflections and harmonic borrowings from the minor.

"O Tod, wie bitter bist du," Op. 121/3
(O death, how bitter is the remembrance of thee)

Text from Ecclesiasticus 41:1–2

O Tod, wie bitter bist du, wenn an dich gedenket ein Mensch, der gute Tage und genug hat und ohne Sorge lebet; und dem es wohl geht in allen Dingen und noch wohl essen mag!

O Tod, wie wohl tust du dem Dürftigen, der da schwach und alt ist, der in allen Sorgen steckt, und nichts Besser's zu hoffen, noch zu erwarten hat!

1. O death, how bitter is the remembrance of thee to a man that liveth at rest in his possessions, unto the man that hath nothing to vex him, and that hath prosperity in all things: yea, unto him that is yet able to receive meat!

2. O death, acceptable is thy sentence unto the needy, and unto him whose strength faileth, that is now in the last age, and is vexed with all things, and to him that despaireth, and hath lost patience!

Completed in May 1896.

First sung publicly by Anton Sistermans, with Anton Rückauf at the piano, on 9 November 1896 in the Saal Bösendorfer in Vienna.

Through-composed.

The text is from the Apocrypha.

The death-evocative motive in falling thirds that appears throughout the opus reaches the peak of its development in this song. The first four pitches of the vocal melody are the same as those that begin the opening theme of the Fourth Symphony, and, as in the symphony, nearly everything that follows seems to evolve from that initial cell. Through Brahms's contrapuntal mastery, the seminal descending thirds are imitated, inverted, extended, filled, and augmented—finally they permeate every aspect of the song, melodic or harmonic. (Note, as an example, that the piano's chords in m. 1 are derived from a vertical realignment of the pitches of the descending vocal line that they accompany.) The climactic instance is one of the most magical transformations in all of music; it occurs toward the end of the song with the return to $\frac{3}{2}$ meter, when the thirds that fell in the minor mode to depict the bitterness of death are inverted to rise as sixths in the warm glow of E major to portray death's promise of comfort. The song has been much dissected and often written about; for greater detail, see particularly Schoenberg's motivic analysis in "Brahms the Progressive" (*Style and Idea*, 90–93).

There are other noteworthy features. The words "wie bitter" elicit painful cross-relations between C♯ and C♮, and a disquieted diminished-seventh harmony in m. 4; when the words are repeated, the phrase's beginning is transferred from an upbeat to a downbeat, subtly shifting the emphasis. A similar variance of accentuation exists between the piano melody that begins on the third beat of m. 5 and its canonic imitation beginning on the following downbeat. The rhythmic activity that suggests the man who "hath prosperity in all things" in the song's first half contrasts markedly with the lassitude of the second half's "feeble and old" man, who is further characterized by alternations between the tender subdominant and poignant, minor-tinged secondary harmonies. "Noch zu erwarten hat" prompts a long vocal melisma over sustained harmonies, which shift temporarily to the minor mode, and fermatas on both pitches of the dominant 4-3 suspension that ends the section expectantly. In the $\frac{3}{2}$ closing portion, not only are the earlier falling thirds of "O Tod" changed to rising sixths but also the labored rhythms and tortured cross-relations of the opening's "wie bitter bist du" are metamorphosed into the most serene of benedictions at "wie wohl tust du."

"Wenn ich mit Menschen- und mit
Engelzungen redete," Op. 121/4
(Though I speak with the tongues of men and of angels)

Text from I Corinthians 13:1–3, 12–13

Wenn ich mit Menschen- und mit Engelzungen redete, und hätte der Liebe nicht, so wär' ich ein tönend Erz, oder eine klingende Schelle.

Und wenn ich weissagen könnte und wüßte alle Geheimnisse und alle Erkenntnis, und hätte allen Glauben, also, daß ich Berge versetzte; und hätte der Liebe nicht, so wäre ich nichts.

Und wenn ich alle meine Habe den Armen gäbe, und ließe meinen Leib brennen; und hätte der Liebe nicht, so wäre mir's nichts nütze.

Wir sehen jetzt durch einen Spiegel in einem dunkeln Worte, dann aber von Angesicht zu Angesichte. Jetzt erkenne ich's stückweise, dann aber werd' ich's erkennen, gleichwie ich erkennet bin.

Nun aber bleibet Glaube, Hoffnung, Liebe, diese drei; aber die Liebe ist die größeste unter ihnen.

1. Though I speak with the tongues of men and of angels, and have not charity, I am become as sounding brass, or a tinkling cymbal.

2. And though I have the gift of prophecy, and understand all mysteries, and all knowledge; and though I have all faith, so that I could remove mountains, and have not charity, I am nothing.

3. And though I bestow all my goods to feed the poor, and though I give my body to be burned, and have not charity, it profiteth me nothing.

. . .

12. For now we see through a glass, darkly; but then face to face: now I know in part; but then shall I know even as I am known.

13. And now abideth faith, hope, charity, these three; but the greatest of these is charity.

Completed in the present form in May 1896; Kalbeck asserts that it originated earlier in sketches for a different project, left unfinished (*Brahms*, IV$_2$, 445–54).

First performed in public by Anton Sistermans, with Anton Rückauf at the piano, on 9 November 1896 in the Saal Bösendorfer in Vienna.

Through-composed, with some features of strophic variation.

The text is from the New Testament.

Though the eye may at first find if difficult to relate this final song's key of E♭ major to what came before, the ear readily accepts the enharmonic correspondence of the opening A♭ with the concluding G♯ preceding. The thirds and triad shapes that descended to reflect the earlier songs' concern with death now often rise instead, reinforcing the affirmative tone of this hymn to the power of love. The upward melodic motion of the piano's first three chords is recalled to accompany the vocal entrance, and it recurs frequently thereafter. After an initial octave descent, the vocal melody itself features rising intervals, including the sixths that came into prominence in the third song and recur here to lift the line importantly to "redete" in m. 6 and "Liebe" in m. 7.

The song's overall form—a three-sectioned *Andante con moto*, a contrasting *Adagio*, and a coda that refers to both—reflects the structure of the text as excerpted. (Brahms's choice in the coda of the less rigorous indications *Più moto* and *Sostenuto un poco* seems to imply, and experience confirms, that the actual difference in tempo between the original *Andante con moto* and *Adagio* should not be extreme.) Verses 1, 2, and 3 are similar in format and subject; the tone of verse 12 differs sharply; verse 13 summarizes and draws a conclusion.

Parallelisms in the text prompt quasi-strophic recurrences of similar musical materials. There is an obvious resemblance between the phrases in mm. 3–6 and 15–18, which set the beginnings of verses 1 and 2; the kinship also of mm. 30–32 is masked by a turn to the flatted submediant, evoking the tone of compassion in verse 3, but it is revealed by the rhythm and opening contour of the vocal line and by the accompaniment figure. An additional "and though" clause in verses 2 and 3 elicits the kindred musical passages that are inserted at mm. 19–23 and 33–37. "Und hätte die Liebe nicht" is given like settings in each of its three appearances, in mm. 7–8, 24–25, and 38–40, although the last is expanded in order to effect the return to the tonic key. The closing thoughts of all three verses—their assessments of the negative results of charity's absence—are set to the same musical idea, in mm. 9–12, 26–29, and 41–43; the phrase's concluding melodic descent, which in the third instance is assigned to the piano alone, recalls the set's germ-motivic chains of falling thirds, here contracted into uneasy diminished sevenths. A broadened repetition of "so wäre mir's nichts nütze" and a slowing modulation to the dominant of C♭ major (foreshadowed by the excursion at m. 30) prepare the enharmonic arrival of the *Adagio* in B major.

The accompaniment's serenely rocking triplets suggest angelic harps. Perceptible relatednesses exist between the two six-measure antecedent phrases at mm. 48–52 and 60–65 (despite the latter's division between the piano and voice, and its move to the dominant) and between the two soaring consequent arches of mm. 54–60 and 66–72.

Another enharmonic shift, accelerating, brings back the tonic E♭ major for the coda. The first line of verse 13 is set to an extended variant of the song's opening phrase. The closing line is sung twice, to versions of the *Adagio*'s two phrase shapes, accompanied as before by serene triplets. In the former instance, the piano has the principal melody, while the vocal line doubles sumptuously at the lower sixth or tenth; in the latter, the vocal melody blossoms forth in a nobly expansive, ecstatic curve. Many have observed that the end of the phrase duplicates the familiar intervals of the final "wonnevoll" of "Wie bist du, meine Königin," Op. 32/9; whether or not the resemblance is intended, the song indeed concludes "rapturously," the fitting culmination of a lifetime of lyric innovation, refinement, and mastery.

Mondnacht, WoO 21 (Moonlight Night)

Text by Joseph von Eichendorff (1788–1857)

Es war, als hätt' der Himmel
Die Erde still geküßt,
Daß sie im Blütenschimmer
Von ihm nur träumen müßt'.

Die Luft ging durch die Felder,
Die Ähren wogten sacht,
Es rauschten leis die Wälder,
So sternklar war die Nacht.

Und meine Seele spannte
Weit ihre Flügel aus,
Flog durch die stillen Räume,
Als flöge sie nach Haus.

It was as if heaven had quietly kissed the earth, so that the earth had to dream only of heaven in the glittering of the blossoms.

The breeze passed through the fields; the ears of grain rocked gently; the forests rustled softly; the night was so starry-bright.

And my soul spread out its wings wide, and flew through silent space as if it were flying home.

The composition date is uncertain, but is earlier than November 1853. The song was first published in 1854 by G. H. Wigand of Göttingen in a collection called *Albumblätter*, which also included seven songs by seven other composers. Later it was published separately by C. Luckhardt (Berlin and Leipzig), by Raabe and Plothow (Berlin), and finally by Simrock in Berlin.

The earliest known performance was given by Clara Heinemeyer on 31 October 1872 in Leipzig.

Varied strophic.

The text may be found among the "Geistliche Gedichte" in Eichendorff's collected *Werke* (Stuttgart, 1957–58, I, 306); the earliest self-contained collection of the poems was printed in 1837.

The same poem is also the text of one of Schumann's most beloved songs. Like Schumann, Brahms set verses 1 and 2 to the same music and verse 3 to a developmental variant that quotes from the principal strophe. Also like Schumann, Brahms changed Eichendorff's "nun" to "nur" in the last line of verse 1. Brahms alone, however, changed "stillen Lande" to "stillen Räume" in the last verse; Max Friedländer assumed that this was a mistake—a slip of the pen or a printer's error—and "corrected" it in his edition for C. F. Peters, but the Breitkopf & Härtel complete edition retains Brahms's "Räume."

The introduction comprises two statements of a "yearning" motive whose melodic contour and harmonies anticipate those of the strophe's closing pair of phrases. The dreamy chordal texture gives way in m. 7 to the even dreamier rocking sixteenth notes that predominate throughout the accompaniment. The piano plays a gentle duet with the serene melody and supplies the missing fourth measures of the vocal phrases by echoing the voice's third measure in phrases 1 and 3, and by anticipating the next vocal pitch in phrase 2. The expansion to five measures of phrases 4 and 5 and their borrowing of harmonies from the minor mode (especially the submediant) evoke the sense of wonder inherent in the lines "von ihm nur träumen müßt" and "so sternklar war die Nacht."

The piano begins the third strophe by recalling, with increasing animation, the principal strophe's first two phrases. The vocal line starts quietly, doubling the accompaniment's inner pedal, but an expressive appoggiatura at "Seele" signals its burgeoning excitement. The vocal phrase structure is altered to permit the joining of "spannte" with "weit" from the next line. At the climactic *forte* repetition of the two words, marked both *sforzando* and *sostenuto*, there is an expansive turn to the subdominant, in which ardent key both voice and piano complete the phrase by alluding to the strophe's beginning. Quietening, an enharmonic shift leads on to the Neapolitan, where an entranced "flog durch die stillen Räume" again refers to the strophe's opening phrase. Symbolically, a plagal cadence in the home key accompanies the first "nach Haus," and a tonic pedal underlies the remainder of the song. Another little emotional surge lifts the vocal line to the song's highest pitch at the repetition of "nach Haus"; during an expanded, coda-like repetition of the entire last line, shifting harmonies gradually wane, elaborating the plagal cadence and bringing the song to a peaceful, ethereal close.

Regenlied, WoO posth. 23 (Rain Song)

Text by Klaus Groth (1819–1899)

Regentropfen aus den Bäumen
Fallen in das grüne Gras,
Tränen meiner trüben Augen
Machen mir die Wange naß.

Scheint die Sonne wieder helle,
Wird der Rasen doppelt grün:
Doppelt wird auf meinen Wangen
Mir die heiße Träne glühn.

Raindrops are falling from the trees into the green grass. Tears from my dulled eyes are moistening my cheeks.

When the sun shines brightly again, the lawn becomes twice as green: my hot tears will burn twice as fiercely on my cheeks.

The composition date is uncertain, but it is earlier than summer 1872—perhaps as early as 1866. For unknown reasons, Brahms chose not to publish this song, though he sent a manuscript copy to Groth. The song was first published in 1908 by the Deutsche Brahms-Gesellschaft in Berlin; publication number 6.

Strophic, slightly modified.

The text differs only in its fifth line from that of "Nachklang," Op. 59/4. Groth's notation on the autograph of this song, that Brahms got a copy of the unpublished poem from Albert Dietrich in Oldenberg, may explain the discrepancy.

As in other Brahms "rain" songs, detached chords and a persistent pattering rhythm portray the falling rain. The downward spiral of the opening vocal line suggests droplets descending branch to branch, from treetops to lawn. When the text makes its transition from raindrops to tears, the accompaniment figure shifts to legato sixteenth notes. An expressive tenor countermelody underlines "Tränen meiner trüben Augen," and the harmonies digress toward the dominant minor and supertonic minor before reestablishing the home key for the characteristic broadened last phrase and repetition of closing text.

In the second strophe the reemerging sun is reflected in major harmonies—the melody is altered to conform—and the detached-chord figure is entirely lacking. Over the piano's burgeoning cadence on the dominant, the end of the first vocal phrase soars to the upper tonic to emphasize "doppelt." The crescendo continues to a climactic *forte* as the piano's melodic bridge to the next vocal phrase climbs yet another step higher. The vocal line then continues exactly as in the first strophe. But the concluding text repetition this time involves six syllables rather than four; accordingly, an additional measure is inserted, affording both heightened stress on "heiße" and a greater sense of final broadening.

The postlude begins by recalling the detached eighths evocative of rainfall, but they give way to a legato phrase reminiscent of the first strophe's "Tränen meiner trüben Augen"—a reminder that the real subject of the song is not rain but tears.

POETS AND TRANSLATORS

ALEXIS, WILLIBALD (pseudonym for Georg Wilhelm Häring; b. Breslau, 1798; d. Arnstadt [Thuringia], 1871). Edited the *Berliner Konversations-blatt*, contributed essays and reviews to literary journals, wrote travel books, and experimented continually with methods of presentation in the historical novels for which he was best known.
Op. 97/3: Entführung

ALLMERS, HERMANN (b. Rechenfleth, 1821; d. Rechenfleth, 1902). An essayist, novelist, and poet particularly interested in legendary lore and nature. His best-known works were *Marschenbuch* (1858) and *Rö-mische Schlendertage* (1859). He disapproved of Brahms's setting of "Feldeinsamkeit," finding it pretentious.
Op. 86/2: Feldeinsamkeit

BODENSTEDT, FRIEDRICH MARTIN VON (b. Peine/Hannover, 1819; d. Wiesbaden, 1892). Belonged to the Munich circle of literary figures that gathered around Emanuel Geibel in the early 1850s, sponsored by the Bavarian king Maximilian II and with the aim of preserving traditional poetic themes and forms. Bodenstedt's pseudo-Oriental *Lieder des Mirza Schaffy* went through 200 printings before its popularity waned.
Op. 3/4: Lied aus *Ivan*

BRENTANO, CLEMENS VON (b. Ehrenbreitstein, 1778; d. Aschaffenburg, 1842). Published the famous collection of folk poetry *Des Knaben Wunderhorn* (1805–1808) in collaboration with LUDWIG ACHIM VON ARNIM (b. Berlin, 1781; d. Wiepersdorf, 1831). His cultivation of the poetry of the Rhineland and of the medieval and student milieus was important in the history of German Romanticism. His works are marked by fantastic imagery and by abrupt, bizarre methods of expression.
Op. 72/3: O kühler Wald

CANDIDUS, KARL (b. Bischweiler [Alsace], 1817; d. Feodosie [Crimea], 1872). A cleric, theologian, philosopher, and poet. He worked as a clergyman in Nancy and later in Odessa, but despite his travels, he remained an ardent German patriot.
Op. 58/5: Schwermut
Op. 69/5: Tambourliedchen
Op. 70/2: Lerchengesang
Op. 71/3: Geheimnis

Op. 72/1: Alte Liebe

Op. 72/2: Sommerfäden

CONRAT, HUGO. A cultured Viennese businessman and a contributing correspondent for the *Neue Musikzeitung*. Charged with the translation
into German of a group of Hungarian love songs, he brought the resulting texts to Brahms's attention. Brahms subsequently came to be
a frequent guest in his home. Conrat's daughter Ilse sculpted the
marble monument at Brahms's grave site in Vienna.

Op. 103: *Zigeunerlieder* (trans.)

    1. He, Zigeuner, greife in die Saiten ein

    2. Hochgetürmte Rimaflut

    3. Wißt ihr, wann mein Kindchen

    4. Lieber Gott, du weißt

    5. Brauner Bursche führt zum Tanze

    6. Röslein dreie in der Reihe

    7. Kommt dir manchmal in den Sinn

    8. Rote Abendwolken ziehn am Firmament

DAUMER, GEORG FRIEDRICH (b. Nuremberg, 1800; d. Würzburg, 1875). A
teacher and homeopathic doctor by profession. Brahms set more
works of his than of any other poet. He was an expert on the history of
religions, and he himself discarded Christianity and Mohammedanism
before finally embracing Rosicrucianism. He was the first to undertake the guidance of Kaspar Hauser, the "wild boy," who surfaced in
Nuremberg in 1828. He was a particularly gifted translator; his *Polydora* collects poems of Classical Greece and Rome, China, Turkey,
Persia, India, and many other nations in an envisioned "world literature." Brahms visited him once, in 1872, only to learn that Daumer, for
whose fame Brahms was mainly responsible, had never heard of him.

Op. 32/2: Nicht mehr zu dir zu gehen (trans.)

Op. 32/7: Bitteres zu sagen denkst du (trans.)

Op. 32/8: So steh'n wir, ich und meine Weide (trans.)

Op. 32/9: Wie bist du, meine Königin (trans.)

Op. 46/1: Die Kränze (trans.)

Op. 46/2: Magyarisch (trans.)

Op. 47/1: Botschaft (trans.)

Op. 47/2: Liebesglut (trans.)

Op. 57/1: Von waldbekränzter Höhe

Op. 57/2: Wenn du nur zuweilen lächelst (trans.)

Op. 57/3: Es träumte mir (trans.)

Op. 57/4: Ach, wende diesen Blick

Op. 57/5: In meiner Nächte Sehnen

Op. 57/6: Strahlt zuweilen auch ein mildes Licht

Op. 57/7: Die Schnur, die Perl' an Perle (trans.)

Op. 57/8: Unbewegte laue Luft
Op. 59/6: Eine gute, gute Nacht (trans.)
Op. 95/7: Schön war, das ich dir weihte (trans.)
Op. 96/2: Wir wandelten, wir zwei zusammen (trans.)

EICHENDORFF, JOSEPH, FREIHERR VON (b. Lubowitz [Upper Silesia], 1788; d. Neiße, 1857). Poet and novelist, ranks among the greatest German Romantic lyricists. His poetry, particularly those works expressing his sensitivity to nature, achieved the popularity of folk song, and his *Aus dem Leben eines Taugenichts* (1826), which combines the dreamlike with the realistic, is a highpoint of Romantic fiction.
Op. 3/5: In der Fremde
Op. 3/6: Lied
Op. 7/2: Parole
Op. 7/3: Anklänge
Op. 69/6: Vom Strande
WoO 21: Mondnacht

FERRAND, EDUARD (pseudonym for Eduard Schulz; b. Landsberg, 1813; d. Berlin, 1842). Educated in Berlin, where he helped to organize a union of young poets. He turned to writing after a brief and unrewarding stint in the field of economics, published his first poem in the *Freimüthiger* in 1831, and (as "Tybald") was a frequent contributor to *Figaro*.
Op. 7/1: Treue Liebe

FLEM[M]ING, PAUL (b. Hartenstein, 1609; d. Hamburg, 1640). Outstanding lyric poet of seventeenth-century Germany. Brought a new immediacy and sincerity to the innovations of meter and stanza introduced by his teacher Martin Opitz. Flemming's love lyrics were unique for their time in their freshness and depth of feeling, and his religious hymns were distinguished by their fervor and dignity. He excelled in the sonnet form, which he was the first German to use effectively.
Op. 47/4: O liebliche Wangen
Op. 107/1: An die Stolze

FREY, ADOLF (b. Aarau, 1855; d. Zürich, 1920). A leading Swiss novelist and poet, and a professor of literary history at the University of Zürich. His most lasting achievements are his biographies of Swiss writers and his Swiss-German dialect poems, rooted in the style of folk song.
Op. 106/4: Meine Lieder

GEIBEL, (FRANZ) EMANUEL (AUGUST) VON (b. Lübeck, 1815; d. Lübeck, 1884). Leader of the Munich circle of writers. His *Gedichte* (1840) ran to 100 editions in his lifetime and earned him a lifelong pension from the king of Prussia. His lyrics are classical, idealistic, and nontopical, reflecting the taste of the time. In collaboration with PAUL VON HEYSE, he also

made excellent translations of Spanish poetry (*Spanisches Lieder-buch*, 1852) and ancient poetry (*Klassisches Liederbuch*, 1875).
Op. 85/5: Frühlingslied
Op. 91/2: Geistliches Wiegenlied (trans.)
Op. 94/3: Mein Herz ist schwer

GOETHE, JOHANN WOLFANG VON (b. Frankfurt, 1749; d. Weimar, 1832). The greatest intellectual figure of the German Romantic movement, retaining a lifelong passion for science, philosophy, and politics as well as literature. The sheer bulk of his writings was remarkable, running to 133 volumes in the Weimar edition. His formative years coincided with the *Sturm und Drang* movement; his later aesthetic theories were sharpened through his association with Schiller.
Op. 47/5: Die Liebende schreibt
Op. 48/5: Trost in Tränen
Op. 59/1: Dämm'rung senkte sich von oben
Op. 70/3: Serenade
Op. 72/5: Unüberwindlich

GROHE, MELCHIOR (b. Mannheim, 1829; d. Naples, 1906). Studied philology in Heidelberg, Göttingen, and Berlin. He lived for a time as a beggar in Vienna and traveled in the Orient; in Egypt, where he converted to Islam; and in Italy, where he died. Among his works are a tragedy, *Bernhard von Weimar* (1853), and many volumes of poetry, including *Reime und Reisen* (Mannheim, 1861) and *Sonettenkranz* (Baden-Baden, 1870).
Op. 58/4: O komme, holde Sommernacht

GROTH, KLAUS (b. Heide, 1819; d. Kiel, 1899). A regional poet (Brahms's father was also born in Heide) whose book *Quickborn* (1853) first revealed the poetic possibilities of Plattdeutsch (Low German). He taught literature at Kiel University. Brahms and he met in Düsseldorf in 1856, and they remained close friends.
Op. 59/3: Regenlied
Op. 59/4: Nachklang
Op. 59/7: Mein wundes Herz
Op. 59/8: Dein blaues Auge
Op. 63/7: Heimweh I
Op. 63/8: Heimweh II
Op. 63/9: Heimweh III
Op. 97/5: Komm bald
Op. 105/1: Wie Melodien zieht es mir
Op. 106/3: Es hing der Reif
WoO posth. 23: Regenlied

GRUPPE, OTTO FRIEDRICH (b. Danzig, 1804; d. Berlin, 1876). A disciple of Hegel, interested in natural science and philology as well as philosophy and literature. His major work was the three-volume *Leben und Werke deutscher Dichter* (Leipzig, 1872). Brahms owned his *Gedichte* (Berlin, 1835) and *Lyrisches Schatzkästlein der Deutschen* (Berlin, 1836).

Op. 107/3: Das Mädchen spricht

HAFIZ, MOHAMMAD SHAMS OD-DĪN (b. Shīrāz [Iran], c.1326; d. Shīrāz, c.1390). One of the finest lyric poets of Persia. His principal verse form was the ghazel, to which he gave a new freshness and subtlety. His poetry is characterized by love of humanity, contempt for hypocrisy or mediocrity, and the ability to relate the events of everyday life to the universal search for union with God.

Op. 32/7: Bitteres zu sagen denkst du
Op. 32/8: So steh'n wir, ich und meine Weide
Op. 32/9: Wie bist du, meine Königin
Op. 47/1: Botschaft
Op. 47/2: Liebesglut
Op. 57/2: Wenn du nur zuweilen lächelst

HALM, FRIEDRICH (pseudonym for Eligius Friedrich Johann von Münch-Bellinghausen; b. Cracow, 1806; d. Vienna, 1871). A dramatist whose poetry is theatrical rather than lyrical, and often sentimental. He held several official appointments in Vienna, among them Custodian of the Court Library and General Manager of the Opera and the Burgtheater.

Op. 94/2: Steig' auf, geliebter Schatten
Op. 94/5: Kein Haus, keine Heimat
Op. 95/2: Bei dir sind meine Gedanken
Op. 95/3: Beim Abschied
Op. 95/4: Der Jäger

HEBBEL, (CHRISTIAN) FRIEDRICH (b. Wesselburen/Dithmarschen, 1813; d. Vienna, 1863). A poet and dramatist who added a new psychological dimension to German drama. He was concerned not so much with the historical aspects of his characters and events as with the process of change as it led to new moral values, and with the conflict between the state's interests and the individual's rights.

Op. 58/6: In der Gasse
Op. 58/7: Vorüber

HEINE, HEINRICH (b. Düsseldorf, 1797; d. Paris, 1856). After Goethe, perhaps the strongest figure in German literature. Heine's works are lyrical, but frequently ironic or bitter. For many decades his reputation was stronger abroad than in Germany, where his aggressive satires and radical positions caused many to regard him as unpatriotic and subversive, an attitude exacerbated by the growth of anti-Semitism.

Op. 71/1: Es liebt sich so lieblich im Lenze!
Op. 85/1: Sommerabend

360   Poets and Translators

Op. 85/2: Mondenschein
Op. 96/1: Der Tod, das ist die kühle Nacht
Op. 96/3: Es schauen die Blumen
Op. 96/4: Meerfahrt

HERDER, JOHANN GOTTFRIED VON (b. Mohrungen [East Prussia], 1744; d. Weimar, 1803). Critic, theologian, and philosopher. The leading figure of the *Sturm und Drang* literary movement and an innovator in the philosophy of history and culture. He considered poetry to be a natural reaction to the feelings aroused by events. His influence made him a harbinger of the Romantic movement. His *Volkslieder* (1778–79) was one of the important early collections of folk-song texts.
Op. 14/3: Murrays Ermordung (trans.)
Op. 14/4: Ein Sonett (trans.)

HEYSE, PAUL (b. Berlin, 1830; d. Munich, 1914). A specialist in Classical and Romance languages and literature, and a prominent member of the Munich circle of writers. He became a master of the carefully constructed short story; he also published novels and many unsuccessful plays. Among his best works are his translations of Italian poetry. He received the 1910 Nobel Prize in literature.
Op. 6/1: Spanisches Lied (trans.)
Op. 49/1: Am Sonntag Morgen (trans.)
Op. 95/6: Mädchenlied (Am jüngsten Tag) (trans.)
Op. 107/5: Mädchenlied (Auf die Nacht in der Spinnstub'n)

HOFFMANN VON FALLERSLEBEN, AUGUST HEINRICH (b. Fallersleben/Brunswick, 1798; d. Corvey/Weser, 1874). A patriotic poet, philologist, and literary historian. His "Deutschland, Deutschland über Alles" was adopted as the German national anthem after World War I. His uncomplicated verses have the qualities of genuine folk literature, and those expressing his love of country and of humanity were of great significance to the German student movement. Their political overtones, however, caused him to lose his university post at Breslau from 1842 until after the Revolution of 1848. In the field of ancient Germanic literature, Hoffmann ranks among the most important and cultivated of German scholars.
Op. 3/2: Liebe und Frühling I
Op. 3/3: Liebe und Frühling II
Op. 6/5: Wie die Wolke nach der Sonne
Op. 6/6: Nachtigallen schwingen
Op. 43/1: Von ewiger Liebe (after Haupt, from the Wendish)

HÖLTY, LUDWIG CHRISTOPH HEINRICH (b. Mariensee/Hannover, 1748; d. Hannover, 1776). The most gifted lyric poet of the Göttinger Hain, a group of young poets whose work drew inspiration from folk song and ballad.

Hölty was equally adept in the ode, the elegy, the ballad, the song, and the adaptation of older forms such as the Minnelied. His mood of gentle melancholy, tempered by sincere religious faith, was appealing to Brahms.

Op. 19/1: Der Kuß
Op. 43/2: Die Mainacht
Op. 46/3: Die Schale der Vergessenheit
Op. 46/4: An die Nachtigall
Op. 49/2: An ein Veilchen (after Zappi)
Op. 71/5: Minnelied

KALBECK, MAX (b. Breslau, 1850; d. Vienna, 1921). Though Austrian, he was a member of the Munich circle of writers. He first met Brahms in 1874 in Breslau, and after settling in Vienna in 1880, became one of his most frequent companions. Kalbeck's greatest achievement, a four-volume biography of Brahms (1904–11), is still the basis of all Brahms research; he also edited several volumes of Brahms's correspondence.

Op. 86/3: Nachtwandler

KAPPER, SIEGFRIED (b. Schmichow/Prague, 1821; d. Pisa, 1879). A physician and writer who spent many years traveling in the Balkan states; he became distinguished as a collector and translator into German of Slavonic poetry.

Op. 69/9: Mädchenfluch (trans.)
Op. 85/3: Mädchenlied (Ach, und du) (trans.)
Op. 85/4: Ade! (trans.)
Op. 95/1: Das Mädchen (trans.)
Op. 95/5: Vorschneller Schwur (trans.)

KELLER, GOTTFRIED (b. Zürich, 1819; d. Zürich, 1890). The greatest German-Swiss writer of the Realistic school and a notable lyric poet. He lived for a time as an independent writer in Zürich and was clerk to the canton 1861–76. Despite his extensive duties as a civil servant, he continued to produce influential poetry, novels, and short stories; his collected works appeared in two volumes in 1889. Brahms first met him in Switzerland in 1866, and they remained mutually admiring friends—Keller was among the poets with whom Brahms tentatively discussed collaboration on an opera.

Op. 69/8: Salome
Op. 70/4: Abendregen
Op. 86/1: Therese

KOPISCH, AUGUST (b. Breslau, 1799; d. Berlin, 1853). A painter and poet who, inspired by folk material, wrote poetry based on legends and fairy tales, with a simplicity that gave it wide popularity. He lived for a time

in Italy and Sicily, whose poetry he translated into German and where he gained fame as a co-discoverer of the Blue Grotto at Capri.
Op. 58/1: Blinde Kuh (trans.)
Op. 58/2: Während des Regens
Op. 58/3: Die Spröde (trans.)

KUGLER, FRANZ THEODOR (b. Stettin, 1808; d. Berlin, 1858). An art historian and a biographer of Frederick the Great. Brahms was a family friend.
Op. 106/1: Ständchen

LEMCKE, KARL (b. Schwerin, 1831; d. Munich, 1913). Lectured on the history and philosophy of literature and art at Heidelberg, Munich, Stuttgart, and Amsterdam. He published novels, poetry, and works on aesthetics.
Op. 69/7: Über die See
Op. 70/1: Im Garten am Seegestade
Op. 71/4: Willst du, daß ich geh?
Op. 72/4: Verzagen
Op. 85/6: In Waldeseinsamkeit
Op. 105/5: Verrat
Op. 107/2: Salamander

LILIENCRON, (FRIEDRICH ADOLF AXEL) DETLEV, FREIHERR VON (b. Kiel, 1844; d. Alt-Rahlstedt/Hamburg, 1909). Began his career as a military man. Later he went to America (his mother was American), where he taught painting, music, and languages, trained horses, and played the piano in beer halls. Upon his return to Germany, he became a civil servant and turned to writing. His fresh and unconventional verse challenged the Romantic tradition and prepared the Realistic movement. His poems are characterized by vividness of impression, and they portray nature with a new realism.
Op. 105/4: Auf dem Kirchhofe
Op. 107/4: Maienkätzchen

LINGG, HERMANN (b. Lindau, 1820; d. Munich, 1905). A physician by profession, he was a member of the Munich circle of writers. His lyrics are more successful than his prose works.
Op. 105/2: Immer leiser wird mein Schlummer

MEISSNER, ALFRED VON (b. Teplitz, 1822; d. Bregenz, 1885). Studied medicine in Prague, but after brief service as a hospital physician, he gave it up to devote himself entirely to literature. He traveled extensively before settling in Bregenz in 1869. His writing was versatile and of a liberal stamp; his plays, criticism, poetry, novels, and travel books were widely praised at the time.
Op. 6/3: Nachwirkung

MÖRIKE, EDUARD FRIEDRICH (b. Ludwigsburg, 1804; d. Stuttgart, 1875). Lyrically the most gifted member of the Swabian school. His poems are graceful, original, and often humorous; their language is simple and natural, and they reveal a profound feeling for nature and for human psychology. Among his novels, *Maler Nolten* (1832) enjoyed great popularity.

Op. 19/5: An eine Äolsharfe

Op. 59/5: Agnes

PLATEN(-HALLERMÜNDE), AUGUST, GRAF VON (b. Ansbach, 1796; d. Syracuse, 1835). Almost alone among his contemporaries in rejecting the Romantic tradition in which he had been schooled, opposing its flamboyance and aiming instead at Classical purity of style. After 1826 he lived in Italy. His odes and sonnets and his *Polenlieder* (1831) are considered among the best classical poems of their time.

Op. 32/1: Wie rafft' ich mich auf in der Nacht

Op. 32/3: Ich schleich' umher betrübt und stumm

Op. 32/4: Der Strom, der neben mir verrauschte

Op. 32/5: Wehe, so willst du mich wieder

Op. 32/6: Du sprichst, daß ich mich täuschte

REINHOLD, CHRISTIAN (pseudonym for Christian Reinhold Köstlin; b. Tübingen, 1813; d. Tübingen, 1856). A lecturer in law at the university at Tübingen. He was the father of Maria Fellinger, who was a close friend of Brahms in his last years and who made the many photographs of him that survive from the mid-1890s.

Op. 97/1: Nachtigall

Op. 97/2: Auf dem Schiffe

Op. 106/2: Auf dem See

Op. 106/5: Ein Wanderer

REINICK, ROBERT (b. Danzig, 1805; d. Dresden, 1852). Both a painter and a poet, who specialized in poetry and stories for children.

Op. 3/1: Liebestreu

Op. 6/4: Juchhe

ROUSSEAU, JOHANN BAPTIST (b. Bonn, 1802; d. Cologne, 1867). Studied philosophy, philology, and history in Bonn and held various editorial posts in Hamm, Aachen, Frankfurt am Main, and (1845–54) Vienna. He was active as a writer, poet, and dramatist; his *Gesammelte Dichtungen* was published in 1845.

Op. 6/2: Der Frühling

RÜCKERT, FRIEDRICH (b. Schweinfurt, 1788; d. Coburg, 1866). A prolific poet, known for his facility with many different verse forms. He taught Oriental philology at Erlangen and Berlin universities before moving in 1848 to Neuses to devote his life to scholarship and writing. He published translations from Oriental sources, epic poems, and historical plays, but his greatest success came from his lyric verse.

Op. 91/1: Gestillte Sehnsucht
Op. 94/1: Mit vierzig Jahren

SCHACK, ADOLF FRIEDRICH VON (Brüsewitz/Schwerin, 1815; d. Munich, 1894).
Better known as an art critic and historian than as a poet. In 1855 he
settled in Munich, where he became active in the Munich circle of writers and collected a splendid gallery of paintings, of which he compiled
the catalogue and history. When Brahms and Billroth were planning a
trip to Spain (which never came about), Brahms sent his friend a copy
of Schack's three-volume study of Spanish literature and art.
Op. 48/7: Herbstgefühl
Op. 49/5: Abenddämmerung
Op. 58/8: Serenade

SCHENKENDORF, MAX VON (b. Tilsit, 1783; d. Koblenz, 1817). Primarily a writer
of patriotic poetry. He dreamed of reviving the pre-Napoleonic
German empire. His interest in the Middle Ages aligned him philo-
sophically with the early Romantics.
Op. 63/1: Frühlingstrost
Op. 63/2: Erinnerung
Op. 63/3: An ein Bild
Op. 63/4: An die Tauben
Op. 86/6: Todessehnen

SCHERER, GEORG (b. Dennenlohe/Ansbach, 1828; d. Munich, 1909). Trained
as a teacher, then studied philosophy and philology in Munich and
Tübingen. Interspersed with extensive travel, he held posts in
Stuttgart as lecturer, then professor, at the Polytechnical Institute,
and later as a government official and librarian at the Royal School of
the Arts. After 1881 he lived in Munich as an independent writer until
mental illness confined him to a sanatorium, where he died. He wrote
mainly children's literature, but also published an important collection of *Deutsche Volkslieder* (1851).
Op. 49/4: Wiegenlied (2)

SCHMIDT, HANS (b. Fellin [Livonia], 1856; d. Riga, ?). Was employed as a tutor
in the home of Brahms's lifelong friend the violinist Joseph Joachim.
Op. 84/1: Sommerabend
Op. 84/2: Der Kranz
Op. 84/3: In den Beeren
Op. 94/4: Sapphische Ode

SCHUMANN, FELIX (b. Düsseldorf, 1854; d. Frankfurt am Main, 1879).
The youngest child of Robert and Clara Schumann and Brahms's
godson, he died of tuberculosis at the age of 24. His poems were
not published, but Clara sent them in manuscript to Brahms for his
criticism.

Op. 63/5: Junge Lieder I
Op. 63/6: Junge Lieder II
Op. 86/5: Versunken

SIMROCK, KARL JOSEPH (b. Bonn, 1802; d. Bonn, 1876). Preserved and made accessible much early German literature, either by translation into modern German, by paraphrasing, or by editing. He studied law and literary theory. Because of a poem he had written in praise of the July Revolution, he was removed from his judicial post in 1830. He then retired to Bonn to devote himself to literature. In 1850 he was made an honorary professor at Bonn.
Op. 59/2: Auf dem See
Op. 71/2: An den Mond

STORM, (HANS) THEODOR WOLDSEN (b. Husum, 1817; d. Hademarschen, 1888). A master of the novella and an outstanding exponent of German poetic Realism, which aimed at portraying the positive values of everyday life. His models were the late Romantics, and his gentle, nature-oriented lyrics are characterized by their simplicity and formal beauty.
Op. 86/4: Über die Heide

THIBAU[L]T IV (b. Troyes [France], 1201; d. Pampeluna [Spain], 1253). Count of Champagne, king of Navarre. He was a royal chansonnier and was praised by Dante. He wrote courtly lyrics and gracious music, conventional and charming. Modern linguists assign great importance to his chansons, regarding them as a medieval milestone in the typically Gallic joining of clarity of thought with lightness of tone.
Op. 14/4: Ein Sonett

TIECK, (JOHANN) LUDWIG (b. Berlin, 1773; d. Berlin, 1853). A prolific writer and critic of the early Romantic movement. As adviser to the Dresden theater, and later at the Berlin court, he became, after Goethe, the greatest literary authority in Germany. A born storyteller, he gave his best work a fairy-tale quality that appeals to the emotions rather than to the intellect.
Op. 33: *Romanzen aus "Magelone"*
1. Keinen hat es noch gereut
2. Traun! Bogen und Pfeil
3. Sind es Schmerzen
4. Liebe kam aus fernen Landen
5. So willst du des Armen
6. Wie soll ich die Freude
7. War es dir
8. Wir müssen uns trennen
9. Ruhe, Süßliebchen
10. Verzweiflung

    11. Wie schnell verschwindet
    12. Muß es eine Trennung
    13. Sulima
    14. Wie froh und frisch
    15. Treue Liebe dauert lange

UHLAND, (JOHANN) LUDWIG (b. Tübingen, 1787; d. Tübingen, 1862). A Romantic poet and political figure, important in the development of German medieval and folklore studies. His poetry utilized the Classical forms developed by Goethe and Schiller, but his naive, precise, and graceful language is uniquely his own.
Op. 7/6: Heimkehr
Op. 19/2: Scheiden und Meiden
Op. 19/3: In der Ferne
Op. 19/4: Der Schmied

VEGA (CARPIO), LOPE FELIX DE (b. Madrid, 1562; d. Madrid, 1635). The outstanding dramatist of the Spanish Golden Age. Unbelievably prolific, he wrote as many as 1,800 plays, of which 431 are extant, as well as numerous nondramatic works in verse and prose, impressive in variety.
Op. 91/2: Geistliches Wiegenlied

WENZIG, JOSEPH (b. Prague, 1807; d. Turnau [Bohemia], 1876). A Czech patriot, one of the founders of the Bohemian national movement. Brahms's library included two volumes of his translations of folk poetry.
Op. 48/1: Der Gang zum Liebsten (trans.)
Op. 48/4: Gold überwiegt die Liebe (trans.)
Op. 49/3: Sehnsucht (trans.)
Op. 69/1: Klage I (Ach mir fehlt) (trans.)
Op. 69/2: Klage II (O Felsen, lieber Felsen) (trans.)
Op. 69/3: Abschied (trans.)
Op. 69/4: Des Liebsten Schwur (trans.)

ZUCCALMAGLIO, ANTON WILHELM FLORENTIN VON (b. Waldbroel, 1803; d. Nachrodt, 1869). The son of a lawyer of Italian descent, he also studied law, but he made his living teaching, first in Russia, later in Germany. He was a poet, translator, and folklorist, whose principal work (with ANDREAS KRETZSCHMER [1775–1839]), the collection *Deutsche Volkslieder mit ihren Original-Weisen* (Berlin, 1838–40), was much favored by Brahms, though it subsequently became evident that Zuccalmaglio's tampering had made highly suspect the authenticity of much of its contents.
Op. 84/4: Vergebliches Ständchen (?)
Op. 84/5: Spannung (?)
Op. 97/4: Dort in den Weiden
Op. 105/3: Klage (?)

SETTINGS OF FOLK SONG TEXTS

SELECTED BIBLIOGRAPHY

Bell, A. Craig. *The Lieder of Brahms*. Darley: The Grain-Aig Press, 1979.

Boyer, Margaret Gene. "A Study of Brahms's Setting of the Poems from Tieck's 'Liebesgeschichte der schönen Magelone und des Grafen Peter von Provence.'" Ph.D. diss., Washington University, 1980.

Bozarth, George S. "The Lieder of Johannes Brahms, 1868–72." Ph.D. diss., Princeton University, 1978.

———. *Three Lieder on Poems by Adolf Friedrich von Schack. A Facsimile with Commentary*. Washington, D.C: The Library of Congress, 1983.

Braus, Ira. "Brahms's *Liebe und Frühling II*, Op. 3, No. 3: A New Path to the Artwork of the Future." *19th-Century Music* 10 (1986–7):135–56.

Evans, Edwin. *Handbook to the Vocal Works of Johannes Brahms*. New York: Lenox Hill (Burt Franklin), 1970. (Reprint of 1912 edition.)

Fellinger, Imogen. "Cyclic Tendencies in Brahms's Song Collections." In *Brahms Studies: Analytical and Historical Perspectives*. Edited by George S. Bozarth. Oxford [England]: Clarendon Press; New York: Oxford University Press, 1990.

Finscher, Ludwig. "Brahms's Early Songs: Poetry versus Music." In *Brahms Studies: Analytical and Historical Perspectives*. Edited by George S. Bozarth. Oxford: Clarendon Press; New York: Oxford University Press, 1990.

Fox Strangways, Arthur. "Brahms and Tieck's 'Magelone.'" *Music and Letters*, 1940: 211–229.

Friedlaender [Friedländer], Max. *Brahms's Lieder*. Translated by C. Leonard Leese. New York: AMS Press, Inc., 1976. (Reprint of the London 1928 edition.)

Fuller-Maitland, J. A. *Brahms*. London: Methuen and Co., Ltd., 1911.

Geiringer, Karl. *Brahms: His Life and Work*. 3d ed. New York: Da Capo Press, 1982.

Harrison, Max. *The Lieder of Brahms*. New York and Washington: Praeger Publishers, 1972.

Jacobsen, Christiane. *Das Verhältnis von Sprache und Musik in Liedern von Johannes Brahms*. Hamburg: Verlag der Musikalienhandlung Karl Dieter Wagner, 1975.

Jacobson, Bernard. *The Music of Johannes Brahms*. London: Tantivy Press, 1977.

James, Burnett. *Brahms: A Critical Study*. New York: Praeger Publications, 1972.

Kalbeck, Max. *Johannes Brahms*. 4 vols. Tutzing: Schneider, 1974. (Reprint of the Berlin 1904–14 edition.)

———. ed. *The Herzogenberg Correspondence*. Translated by Hannah Bryant. New York: Vienna House, 1971.

Keys, Ivor. *Johannes Brahms*. Portland: Amadeus Press, 1989.

Litzmann, Berthold, ed. *Letters of Clara Schumann and Johannes Brahms 1863–1896*. New York: Vienna House, 1973. (Reprint of the 1927 London edition.)

McCorkle, Margit L. and Donald M. *Johannes Brahms Thematisches-Bibliographisches Werkverzeichnis*. Munich: G. Henle Verlag, 1984.

MacDonald, Malcolm. *Brahms*. New York: Schirmer Books, 1990.

Musgrave, Michael. *The Music of Brahms*. London and Boston: Routledge and Kegan Paul, 1985.

Pascall, Robert, ed. *Brahms: Documentary and Analytical Studies*. Cambridge: Cambridge University Press, 1983.

Platt, Heather. "Text-Music Relationship in the Lieder of Johannes Brahms." Ph.D. diss., City University of New York, 1992.

Sams, Eric. *Brahms Songs*. Seattle: University of Washington Press, 1972. (First published by the British Broadcasting Corporation, 1972.)

Schoenberg, Arnold. "Brahms the Progressive." In *Style and Idea*. New York: Philosophical Library, 1950.

Stein, Jack. *Poem and Music in the German Lied from Gluck to Hugo Wolf*. Cambridge: Harvard University Press, 1971.

Stohrer, Sister Mary Baptist. "The Selection and Setting of Poetry in the Solo Songs of Johannes Brahms." Ph.D. diss., University of Wisconsin, 1974.

INDEX OF TITLES AND FIRST LINES

LUCIEN STARK, Professor Emeritus of piano at the University of Kentucky, maintains a full schedule of coaching and performing. He is a widely recognized expert on the music of Brahms.